WERNER HOFMANN

Art in the Nineteenth Century

→

DAUMIER

Don Quixote

Munich

WERNER HOFMANN

Art in the
Nineteenth Century

Translated by
Brian Battershaw

FABER AND FABER

24 Russell Square

London

First published in England in mcmlxi
by Faber and Faber Limited
24 Russell Square London W.C.I.
Printed in Germany
All rights reserved

Contents

Text page

Translator's Note 10
I The Artist's Studio 11
II Nature and History 35
III Art without Certainty 50
IV The Inner Compulsion 89
V Pictures of Humanity 132
VI Mankind on Show 165
VII The Great Man 199
VIII The Earthly Hell 254
IX Still Life 288
X Woman as Myth 319
XI The Earthly Paradise 363
XII The Divided Century 403
Postscript 413
Notes 415
Acknowledgments 420
Index of Artists and Illustrations . . 421
Index of Names 435

Colour plates

I Daumier: Don Quixote 3
II C. D. Friedrich: Chalk cliffs at Rügen . 37
III Turner: Rain, Steam and Speed . . 53
IV Dillis: View of the roofs of Rome . . 75
V Goya: Carnival 93
VI Corot: L'atelier du peintre . . . 113
VII Delacroix: The Chios Massacres . . 133
VIII Monet: Etang aux Nymphéas . . . 197
IX Toulouse-Lautrec: May Belfort . . 229
X Ensor: The skate 253
XI Courbet: Les cribleuses de blé . . . 301
XII Cézanne: La Montagne Sainte Victoire 333
XIII Manet: Le balcon (detail) 349
XIV Renoir: Le déjeuner 369
XV Marées: The Orange Grove . . . 385
XVI Gauguin: Contes barbares 407

Groups of black and white plates opposite page

The artist's studio 12
The cult of the new martyrs and saints 24
Heroic solitude 40
Ideals of feminine beauty in 1800 . . 56
Idealized pictures of the past . . . 64
Random views – the birth of modern
    painting 78
The Dream of Reason 96
The portrait of the artist 116
The eye-witness account as an
    indictment of the age 136
The dramatic presentation of the past . 152
'Art itself is religion' 168
'The cosmopolitan carnival of gods,
    men, and artists' 184
The birth of Venus 200
Venus as temptress 212
The impact of the orient 232
The bondage of love 240
Still life 256
Nomads and outcasts 264
Gigantomania 276
Heroism in modern life 288
Work and workers 304
Youth and friendship 320
'The right to idleness' 336
The theatre 352
Light-worship 372
The Golden Age 388

To my wife

Translator's Note

The German approach to the problem of communication is somewhat different from our own. The appeal of the German writer tends to be addressed to the ear and through the ear directly to the heart. He is in fact far more frequently a lyricist, and sometimes his arguments do not have the tautness and precision of arrangement that the English reader is liable to expect.

Dr. Hofmann's book has presented me with certain difficulties of this kind, and I have therefore asked him to permit a certain amount of constructive editing. That permission has most graciously and generously been given. I have made use of it as discreetly as I have been able; and if the reader fails to detect the occasional intrusion of a second hand into the text, I shall feel that, in regard to that part of my work at any rate, I have been entirely successful.

A word of explanation is necessary on three points of translation. First, the author has very skilfully developed a certain idea of Nietzsche's – his antithesis between 'Historie und Leben'. Now it was obvious that I could not render a key-phrase such as this by a paraphrase. I had to find some phrase corresponding to it in English, and the only possible one was 'History and Life'. But Nietzsche had deliberately refrained from using the normal German word for 'history' which is 'Geschichte' and used the slightly precious and pedantic word 'Historie' because it conveyed a somewhat wider penumbra of meaning. The English word 'history' is, therefore, really not quite adequate, in so far as 'Historie' connotes not so much a science as a state of mind.

In his *Vom Nutzen und Nachteil der Historie für das Leben* Nietzsche uses the term to express his protest against the over-valuation of mere book-learning and the cerebral function in general at the expense of charm, grace, and imagination, and, above all, of really being alive at all.

Dr. Hofmann's use of the concept admittedly lacks Nietzsche's gargantuan spleen, and it is slightly less pejorative; but the definition I have given will suffice to make what he wishes to convey by it intelligible. And this is much to be desired, for the idea plays an important part in his argument.

Second, the word 'Historismus', which Dr. Hofmann uses mainly in the sense in which Meinecke used it, does not appear to have any satisfactory equivalent in English – to use 'historicism' on all occasions might be misleading – and so I have usually paraphrased it.

The other matter concerns the use of the word 'Form' which has, I think, a rather wider significance in German as a term relating to works of art than it does in English. There was, however, no other word to use, and Dr. Hofmann's meaning is quite apparent in his writing.

Finally, I should mention that the author himself has made a number of additions to the text of the book for incorporation in the English edition.

Brian Battershaw

I The Artist's Studio

COURBET's 'L'atelier' (The studio) (plates 1–3) was misunderstood by his contemporaries. Somewhat alarmed by the catchword of realism, they let their gaze travel uncertainly over the picture's more obvious features, spelled out the mere physical facts and reacted to the challenge of a painter who already had a reputation for political radicalism with a pleasurable shudder.[1]

When the first Paris exhibition was held in 1855, the Salon jury proved true representatives of their time. They rejected Courbet's work which was hung – an offering to a great city's itch for the outrageous – in a wooden pavilion, a pavilion over the entrance to which Courbet set the words 'Le Réalisme', his chosen slogan.

Yet there were some who themselves were adept with the brush and were ready enough to acknowledge the merit of this vast canvas and of its pictorial density. One of these was Delacroix, who expressed his admiration in his diary. Almost without exception, however, people were conscious of something provocative in the picture's vaguely suggestive and even slightly puzzling title. Foremost in complaint were the realists themselves, though the symbolists were not far behind. The realists felt the allegorical implications to be superfluous, the symbolists thought them out of keeping with the very robustness of the style. Nobody could make anything of the concept of an *allégorie réelle* – which the subtitle called it – while the painter's explanatory comment that the work was concerned with his own life over a particular period of time, that it was in fact a kind of pictorial autobiography, left the difficulties unresolved. Allegory and reality are mutually exclusive – such was the verdict that Courbet had to endure from Proudhon and Champfleury who were actually his friends. Like their fellows, the two realists could see no need for any hidden message and considered it reactionary to use ordinary popular human types as conveyors of some cryptic meaning. In the opposite camp there was equal incomprehension. For the symbolists art was a sublimation of reality. They could make nothing of the picture, and so naturally proceeded to find fault with it. Huysmans spoke of it as 'terrifying foolery', while Peladan maintained that it possessed neither perspective nor composition.

Yet Courbet's picture, which his age so signally failed to understand, is one of the nineteenth century's strangest and most widely illuminating documents. It is a *tableau clef*. In it the century's artistic development is for an instant arrested and a balance struck; the whole first half of the century is gathered together in it in concentrated form, while the second half is already foreshadowed. The themes which this picture unites within itself are nothing other than the great guiding visions of an epoch which, so our present complacent age supposes, jettisoned the real content of life and art for the sake of *la bonne peinture*. There is no contradiction in the explanatory subtitle; rather it represents the reduction to a formula of the central problem of a whole epoch; and that is why its analysis rightly stands at the beginning of this book.

Courbet declared, as we have seen, that this picture referred to seven years of his creative life, and this remark brought about a certain narrowing down in the interpretation of the work. Indeed, it encouraged a tendency to do no more than trace out certain biographical connections. Now 'L'atelier' is undoubtedly a pictorial account of the painter's life. It brings together the people whom he had encountered, it gives an account of the milieu in which his art had its home. It is both a self-portrait and a portrait of friendship. Yet linked with these layers of content, there are others which may truly be called allegorical but which only disclose themselves on a somewhat closer study.

'L'atelier' is among other things a picture of the ages of man. His existence begins with the mother – who in the picture sits in the shadow of the easel and is giving suck to her child. Her very poverty bears witness to a kind of basic humanity that knows no distinctions of class or rank. The next stage is that of childhood, which is here represented by the two boys. They are at the beginning of their earthly pilgrimage and their gaze is questioning and thoughtful. As man awakens to full manhood he both expresses and disguises himself by outward show. He presents himself to the world as an individual. Clothes, gestures and bearing spell the differences between one individual and another. The lovers, marvellously self-forgetful – it had been Courbet's intention to depict free love – are a prelude to the married couple. From the gentle image of young love that is insensible to the conventions, we pass to conventional things, to social smoothness and impeccable correctness of attitude.

The middle years follow, and in the left of the picture we see the descending steps of age; the grave-digger and the skull sound the solemn closing chord. And so the circle of life is rounded off at the point where it began – close to the symbolic figure of motherhood.

'L'atelier' is a cross-section of human society and in it its creator confesses to being a man of his time. In a letter to Champfleury he declares that his purpose is to bring together representatives of society's lower, middle and upper strata. On the right we see his own friends and the lovers of the arts; on the left is the ordinary world; there we see the common folk, we see poverty and wretchedness, and wealth, and we see the exploiters and the exploited. The dissonances which lie hidden within the structure of this world are made plain by the composition.

This was the element in its content, already deeply revelatory of the painter's mind, on which the critics concentrated and which they discussed in greatest detail. Yet here again we fail to do justice to the work if we place all the emphasis on one aspect of the whole – in this case on the implicit social indictment. That indictment undoubtedly has its place in the picture. Yet the types that enrich themselves out of the poverty of others – the merchant, the prostitute, the gravedigger and the priest – are placed in the midst of other figures who are either the products of the social system, like the unemployed worker, or, like the three hunters and the veteran of 1793, come from a world that is free of these particular conflicts.

What we must do if we are to understand the picture as a whole, a whole which is greater than the sum of its purely social components, is to place the different thematic layers one on top of another. Then we shall see that 'L'atelier' is one of the nineteenth century's truly great pictures of humanity. It is much more than a mere social cross-section; it plumbs great depths and poses the whole question of our human destiny. The picture makes visible the powers of growth and decay, the flowering and withering of life. The people in it are both bond and free, they have been banished from society or live in slavish dependence upon it, some live at its very edge, others at its shining heart. Courbet shows us the frailty of man and the vanity of our worldly existence. All stand there with empty hands. The artist alone has control over a palpable reality – his canvas. He alone enjoys true possession. In all other parts of the picture the dominant mood is indifference and resignation (the lovers stand like

1–3 COURBET *L'atelier du peintre*; 1855.

strangers in the midst of a world that seems unaware of them). Each of these parts has its individual symbolic note. Yet, held together and dominated by the central apotheosis of the artist and his craft, they interpenetrate. That is why the indictment lacks aggressive feeling or any sharp satiric point. Instead we have something that recalls Rembrandt, something that is the expression of a compassionate humanity.

2

It is idle to pretend that 'L'atelier' reveals its various meanings without any effort on the part of the observer. It does not meet his gaze, as does Ingres' 'Apotheosis of Homer' (plate 79), with a simple clarity of arrangement and design that the eye can take in at a glance. It does not force its message on the mind. Instead of continuity and homogeneity one even seems to detect interrupted starts and recurrent uncertainties, and one's first impression is one of disconnected juxtapositions. The great background with its suggestion of incompleteness, and of hangings or back-cloths imperfectly arranged, is too unsubstantial to hold anything together. It gives the whole the air of a shadowy stage picture that puts across a variety of meanings and fades away at its edges. There are uncertainties of depth and the eye is left to shift and determine the limits of the scene at will. We are confronted by painted curtains, veils and soiled pieces of stage-scenery. These last seem – particularly in the left half of the picture – to be part of a huge wall-painting which has itself remained a fragment and here and there deepens out into a third dimension. Plane surfaces border on sections that suggest space and depth; the world without and the world within seem somehow to be floating into each other. No realist ever painted in this fashion. Only he who dreams and knows the tired twilight of the eye in which night and day melt into a sad intermediate world, can venture to set that world down upon canvas.

What imparts such coherence as it possesses to the background against which the picture is set – and it is a coherence essentially loose and casual – is really the combination of pieces of stage-scenery. Between grey strips we get a glimpse of something that looks like a landscape. There is a round medallion that looks like the pale face of the moon. Yet nowhere do such islands of landscape become sufficiently defined for us to feel that we are confronting a palpable reality. They remain the visions of a dream which hide and disclose themselves without our bidding. Peladan, who made his criticisms from the symbolist angle, was not entirely wrong. The pictorial space is governed by no law of perspective and has no focal point; here we have a natural scene that floats and flows and has about it a quality of infinity.

It is the very air of unreality about the background of the picture proper that enhances the reality of the picture on the easel. Compared with the inconclusive hints that mark the depths of the painting, this picture within a picture is much more immediately real. What lurks in the depths of the picture proper is a world of shadows, a world made heavy with the stuff of dreams. Upon the easel this becomes tangible reality. The landscape upon the easel attracts the observer's attention and opens his eyes. It is the window that looks out on the unambiguous world of real things.

3

What is true of spatial relationships applies with equal force to the relationships between the people in the picture. They are vague and susceptible of varying interpretations. It has been said that the true determining element in the build-up of the picture's spatial content is the picture on the easel, placed as it is diagonally across it. It can be understood in two ways: if we treat this piece of canvas simply as a rectangular plane, it has the effect of pushing back the rest of the picture and dividing the foreground from the background; if we treat it as a painting, then we see in it the depiction of a slice of nature ablaze with daylight, with nothing dim, vague or dreamlike about it at all.

Just as the picture on the easel contrasts with the stage-scenery of the background, so the painter stands out against the other figures that people the world of stage-sets which is his studio. This is due to something more than the fact that the composition places him in the middle of the painting. What really distinguishes him from the others is that he alone stands in an active relationship to reality. The others are, each in his own way, undecided people possessing no clear immediate purpose; he alone pursues a goal; he paints, and, because he is performing an action, he is more immediately real than those who stand or sit around him. Of these only one, the reading Baudelaire, is in comparable measure master of his inward self. Yet the poet has entered into the reflected world of his book, while the painter is mastering the material world by recreating it and giving it form.

It is the same with the people in the picture as with the insubstantial background against which they are set. One has the feeling that unseen partitions have slid between their bodies. These men and women have nothing in common that truly binds them to one another. As with the background so with these juxtaposed groups; there are gaps of which the eye is not immediately aware, there is an element of the haphazard about their organisation, a lack of discernible relationship. In only a few cases does the mere physical act of standing, sitting, or squatting suggest communication, does it suggest an unspoken dialogue with a complementary figure. In the case of the mother that figure is the child at her breast; while with Baudelaire and the prone boy the figure is replaced by the book in the one case and in the other by the sheet of paper on which the youngster is trying his hand. With the two lovers the relationship has developed into complete equality of give and take between the pair, and there is full reciprocal interchange between one human being and another. Yet all this is most in evidence in the central group – in the painter whose 'dialogue' is with his work, in the little boy who stares at it all with marvelling attention, in the naked woman ('Truth'), whose sympathetic and understanding gaze contrasts with that of the others whose eyes for the most part seem to lack direction, and who appear to be looking at nothing in particular. In comparison with 'Truth' what superficiality do we not discern in the look of that woman in the expensive cloak as she turns her head slightly to the left? As to her escort, his fashionable side-whiskers tell us pretty well all that is worth knowing about him; we do not, and need not, see his face. Our imagination can fill that in – he is clearly the well-groomed type that is much the same all the world over. It is usual to refer to this couple as the fashionable lovers, and indeed they are the very embodiment of the fashionable world and all its flighty curiosity. We see the essential coldness of the human type that is for ever gyrating round the edge of things, that always remains an onlooker, that is always a member of the public. Here indeed is the Vanity Fair of civilization. People like these could at any time be seen wandering aimlessly round museums and 'salons', they pullulated in the grounds of World Exhibitions, those stamping grounds for creatures driven by the great collective desire for novelty.

The figures in the right-hand half of the picture – they are for the most part friends of Courbet – remain in distinguished isolation. The group on the left seems at first sight to be more strongly knit together, yet even here it is clear that every man exists for himself, is concerned with his own affairs, and has sunk into a kind of waiting mood that has no real end and no beginning. Mass-man, frozen into a dull collectivity, contrasts with the other half of the picture, though even here the figures are no less isolated from each other. The painter, however, belongs to both realms. It is therefore no mere chance that he occupies the centre of the picture. The powers that his very isolation sets free he transmutes by his creative act into binding elements.

The picture is a triptych, whose centre of spiritual interest is in the middle section. If we confine ourselves to this section, however, then the picture deals with nothing more than is expressed in the title; it is the picture of a studio which shows the artist at work. Yet it is much more than this; it is a glorification of the creative act through which the world knows its own meaning. 'L'atelier' is a pendant to 'The Apotheosis of Homer' (plate 79). In the latter we see a collection of men of genius in hierarchic grouping, one rank above the other, a pictorial expression of the narrowly exclusive tastes of a painter wholly governed by the ideals of classical antiquity.

To this Courbet prefers the loosely grouped gathering of friends who have little interest in anything outside their circle; hard by he puts the common people, who no longer have the power even to recognize themselves in a work of art. In Ingres we have an eclectic lengthwise view of history that covers a considerable period of time, a view that only takes account of the topmost reaches of human genius. Courbet on the other hand concentrates entirely on the world of his own day which the classicist's far-reaching gaze onto the summits of past history treats as virtually non-existent. In the company that surrounds the antique poet there is unanimity, harmony and the proud self-consciousness of distinguished men. In contrast to this, Courbet's cross-section of the society of his day is ready to accept disparity, high and low being placed alongside one another. Here is a painter whose faith in man is not concentrated on the past as Ingres' is, but fixed upon the future, though when he contemplates the present his gaze is sceptical and without illusion. There is nothing of adoration in this picture. There is devotion of a kind in the middle group. It is a discreet devotion, but it contrasts with what is shown at either side of the picture – mere indifferent physical presence. Depicted reality develops allegorical dimensions in which there is a hint of the relation of the artist to the world around him.

Rembrandt, whom Courbet discovered in Amsterdam in 1847, is not only the pictorial but also the spiritual godfather of this work. Five years before it was painted, a treatise had appeared by Alfred Dumesnil on the subject of Rembrandt's religious faith.[2] In it there was among other things an attempt to interpret the etching commonly known as the 'hundred florin' etching, a hundred florins being the price – an unusually high one to be paid in those days during a painter's lifetime – which Rembrandt actually received for the work. In this picture, as Dumesnil pointed out, the Pharisees and the philanthropists are shown on one side – all busily discussing poverty – while on the other are the people of Christ; and it is possible that Courbet was concerned with a similar contrast. It is possible that his aim was to show on the one side the writers, poets and critics, the men, that is to say, who stand apart from life, separating themselves from it by that very process of reflection through which they endow it with order, and to place over against them the common people who live their lives directly, and whose existence achieves fulfilment by the mere fact of its occurrence. What separates the two groups is much more than a physical distance of a few yards; there lies between them a no-man's-land which it is impossible to cross. On one side are the masses with their brooding and clumsily moving minds who know no word that can free them from their necessities, sitting and standing as though they were in chains; on the other are those for whom all this provides the very justification of the work they do. They describe that which anonymous humanity lives through before them – the 'heroism of modern life'.

The painter who wields his brush with such a gesture of assurance knows all about the resultant tensions. Does he intervene as a helper, like Christ in the 'hundred florin' etching – binding disparate elements into a unity? He works in isolation. People are all around him, and yet he is strangely cut off from them, from the very source in fact from which his vision of reality is derived. They are for him a background, an image in his memory, out of which, whenever he is in need of this, his artistry can bring profound experiences to the surface of his mind. When we think of the artist as thus cut off from men, we realize his tragic loneliness. Even when as a man he feels himself ready to give active help – and there is much evidence of Courbet's humanitarian inclinations – he only finds that this very trait tends to drive him back to his work, the work which enables him to give visible form to the vision within him. In the last resort it is not political convictions that count but mastery of the canvas. All that he has seen, all that he has willed or experienced, enters the service of this work of his and drives him forward towards its completion. Courbet, the realist, was always being reproached for an inability to free himself from drab reality. Yet what he sets down in paint in this picture is nothing less than a justification of imaginative power and the creative function of memory. He transforms his social environment into a vision of humanity, he shows that what the eye has observed can by the sovereign artist be intensified into a spiritual experience and recalled at will, so that a landscape can be painted even in the studio. Perhaps it is this very landscape that enables us to understand the 'message' of this picture. It is the only place in the picture which is wholly free from anything that can be called oppressive or burdensome. It is intended to be something through which we look outwards. In the picture of nature a man can recognize the affirmation of a purer and wholly durable world, a world with which he can feel a bond of affinity, a world where he can purge his spirit and be master of his soul. In it there is embodied – if something approximating to a religious concept is permissible – one of modern man's certitudes of salvation. Thus the painter's gesture becomes a prophetic intimation, while the two people at his side become endowed with a measure of faith such as can only accompany religious devotion.

The artist, the woman and the child – it is these who still see in the world the aboriginal freshness of the first day of creation. They stand to that world in a relation that is comprehensive and total.[3] Their capacity for experience is wholly uninhibited and is directed towards life as a whole. With these three figures there is indeed a community in the quality of their experience that sets them quite apart from the groups on each side of the picture. They embody the world of the simple and the true. Their relation with the real world is not severed by the process of reflection nor is it burdened by the weight and weariness of mundane trivialities. In contrast to themselves, their surroundings represent something entirely different – the complex world of civilization with its disguises and masquerades. In these three figures, however, there is real spontaneity and real freshness of vision and feeling. It is there in the child whose feelings are unregulated by any convention. It is there in the woman whose real self is unconcealed by any artifice, who reveals the truth of nature and the essential honesty of all that is truly natural. It is there in the artist himself who sees the processes of nature in terms of an incarnation of female fruitfulness which he is engaged in transforming into a work of art. This female figure must be understood neither as a model, nor as a muse, nor as a mere studio companion – she is the natural measure of things, she is herself the rounded fullness of life. 'The perfect woman of all ages', says Nietzsche in his *Vermischte Meinungen und Sprüche*, 'is the creator's recreation on every seventh day of his civilizing task, the resting of the artist in his work.' There is a similar quality in the artist's relation to the child, though here he is drawn to nature in bud rather than to nature in maturity. The artist of the nineteenth century who was simplifying his means of expression by a reversion to the styles of archaic and primitive epochs, was also finding in the child a source from which he could discover new spontaneous and unconventional forms – a naïveté which was expressed not in some remote domain of history but here in the present and before his very eyes.

In the first of his lectures on *Heroes and Hero-worship* Carlyle speaks of the poet as a kind of survival from the early days of the human race when the world which is now divine only to the gifted, was divine to whosoever would turn his eye upon it. Carlyle's primitive man is of the stuff of which poets and prophets were to be made; this type of mind still accepts the world as a whole; undisturbed by mere criteria of good taste it makes no distinction between beauty and ugliness, or between the commonplace and the sublime. That which moves the men who are possessed of it is simply the intensity of their apprehension, the degree to which they are truly alive; and with such men as these the champion of the realist creed has always enjoyed some measure of affinity. The realist rejects whatever may be the prevailing rules of the aesthetic game, and, in doing so, he also rejects – in theory at least – the discriminatory dissection of reality in obedience to what is in essence a condemnatory moral judgment. Where there is no order of precedence between ideal beauty and forms of beauty that fall short of it, all things are beautiful and worthy of being set down by the artist. All that is alive is right. That was the view of the Romantics. The artist combines all that his eye perceives in the unbroken texture of his experience and his world is therefore wholly coherent. This kind of realism has nothing to do with that later rather precious and circumscribed view that was formulated by Trübner in the words 'Every subject is interesting, even the least important offers enough to interest the artist. Indeed, the simpler the object, the more interesting I can make it by painting, colour and design' (malerisch und koloristisch).⁴ Courbet's relation to reality is on a deeper level; it roots, like his art, in an act of faith, and consists of more than a mere exercise in the ingenious use of colour.

5

'L'atelier' delves into some of the nineteenth century's most central complexes of motive. It proclaims the spiritual dignity with which in all the different classes of painting it contrived to endow the landscape painter's art. A deep longing for what is open to the skies, unfettered and natural finds its expression here. The landscape is a piece of the world that belongs to everyone. Because men feel they have been cut off from their first original spontaneity, they seek a second one and seek it consciously. In landscape an ageing civilization gains a new lease of youth and, freed from its historico-mythological ballast, turns its gaze towards the timeless and enduring in which history has no place.

Furthermore, Courbet's painting is one of the pictures of friendship in which intellectual élites erect a monument to themselves. It stands halfway between, on the one hand, the studio groups of the Impressionists which aim at little more than suggesting a sort of general atmosphere, and, on the other, those gatherings of men of genius characteristic of the idealist painters who so favoured the theme of human greatness but habitually projected it into the past. In the long series of self-portraitures in which the artistic world of the nineteenth century indulged, 'L'atelier' occupies a middle place between the mere factual account of life and the transfiguring apotheosis. In fine, regarded as a portrayal of humanity, this *allégorie réelle* belongs to one of the most remarkable and, from the point of view of the development of ideas, one of the most illuminating categories of painting that the nineteenth century produced.

Here are the great themes whose development demands a symphonic breadth of treatment. Embedded in between them and entrusted with walking-on parts are the symbolic figures of the new vision of humanity: the worker, motherhood, the outlawed and the rejected. Courbet shows us the relation of the individual to society, he shows us the problem of the isolated man and that which arises from his integration in the mass. There is a connection between the group on the left side of the picture and the mad-house scenes of the Romantics, for there is here already a suggestion of something that became more explicit in the second half of the century when wild unreason broke through the barriers of the asylum and became part of the stuff of ordinary life. We see it in Daumier's 'Un wagon de troisième classe' (plate 160), in Degas' 'L'absinthe (dans un café)' (plate 161), and in the metropolitan scenes of Toulouse-Lautrec.

21

Another of the century's dominant themes – the metamorphosis of womanhood – is distributed over various parts of the picture. We have the mother, and not far from her the harlot still dressed in her plain country clothes (to the right behind the grave-digger's top-hat); and we have the central figure of 'Truth'. In addition to these Courbet had originally painted in the elemental female figure, the animal-like *femme fatale*, giving her the features of Jeanne Duval, the mistress of Baudelaire. Originally she had been discernible next to the poet's head. Later, at the latter's request, Courbet removed the portrait. In the worldly couple and the pair of lovers we can recognize the various problems raised by the sex-relationship, the tension between *eros* bond and *eros* free.

6

All this would suffice to earn for this picture an exemplary place in the history of nineteenth century art. Yet its essential significance is of a deeper kind than has as yet been suggested. For it touches a conflict which went on throughout the century and caused the polarization of its creative powers, a conflict which men sought again and again to resolve. It was the conflict between allegory and reality, the conflict between the claims of higher truth and fidelity to objective fact, between life as we imagine it and life as we discover it to be. Once we have grasped this, its cardinal problem, we will understand the century in a way that has nothing to do with its isms, trends and the rest, for we will understand it in its artistic totality.

At quite an early stage the problem was recognized and explicitly proclaimed. This first happened at a time when it still lay hidden beneath the surface of the processes of art and only a sharp eye that could see far into the future was capable of apprehending it. On the 14th September 1797 Schiller wrote to Goethe as follows: 'Here too is an aberration on the part of the contemporary practitioners of the plastic arts which I can explain in terms of our ideas on realistic and idealist poetry, and which indeed affords a new proof of the validity of those ideas. I look upon the matter thus. There are two things necessary for the artist and the poet; he must rise above reality and yet he must remain standing firmly within the world of sense. Where these two things are combined, there you have truly aesthetic art. Yet within the world of nature that is formless and unfriendly, it is all too easy for him to let go at one and the same time both of reality and of the world of sense, and to become idealistic and, if he is endowed with a powerful mind, lose himself in mere fantasy. Alternatively, if, under pressure from his own nature, he desires or is actually driven to remain within the world of sense, he will come to a halt before reaching the truly real and will become a realist only in the restricted sense of the word – and if he lacks a sufficiency of imagination, in a sense that is mean and servile. In either case he will fail to be aesthetic. The difficult operation is the reduction of empirical forms to aesthetic ones, and the tendency will be either for the body to be lacking or for there to be a deficiency of spirit, truth or freedom. The old models, both poetic and plastic, seem to me in this matter to serve a most excellent purpose, for they can all show us an empirical nature which has already been reduced to an aesthetic one, and if we will but study them briefly they can give us hints concerning the whole business of such a reduction.

'Despairing of ever being able to reduce the empirical nature with which he is surrounded to an aesthetic one, your artist of today, if endowed with a lively mind and imagination, seeks help from fantasy against empiric truth, against reality; he inserts a poetic content into his work which would otherwise be poor and empty, because it lacks that which has to be drawn out of the depths of the object itself.'

Here is yet another voice that deals with the same complex of questions. Inspired by Goethe, Karl Philipp Moritz wrote in his treatise *Über die Bildende Nachahmung des Schönen* (Concerning the Creative Imitation of the Beautiful) that the artist's power must focus all the relationships within the entire whole and within that whole the highest form of beauty, catching as it were the rays of that beauty at their uttermost ends, and as with a burning glass bring them within the compass of a single point. From this focal point a delicate but faithful picture of that highest beauty must be rounded off, the measure of it being the scope of the eye, a picture which within its restricted compass comprehends the most perfect relationships in the great whole of nature as truly and as rightly as does nature herself. A little later he wrote 'Every individual thing of beauty that we find scattered far and wide through nature is onlyb eautiful in so far as the sum of all relationships in the great whole is to a greater or lesser extent revealed in it'.[5]

The Romantic generation, wearying of the classic formula of beauty, would no longer have anything to do with any 'sum of relationships'. They gave up all hope of a synthesis that would bridge a world of things that seemed to be perpetually flying asunder from each other. In France the choice of subjects now alternates between the present and the past. In Germany poetry endeavours to determine the relations between the general and the particular. There is a desire to call startling contrasts into being, to create 'a witty mingling of things, to couple the subjective and the objective' – 'Disparates' is the title which Goya gives to one of his series of etchings * – and to shock by endowing the unsisterly with a sisterly proximity. 'Poems', says Novalis, 'should be like fragments from a vast variety of things.'[6] One thing can signify everything and every individual thing is part of a vast interconnection between all things in which reality, imagination and abstraction merge into one another.

The poet of *Hymnen an die Nacht* (Hymns to the Night) in a much quoted saying presents us with the key to the problem. 'In our spirit all this is bound up together in a manner that is wholly unique, pleasing and lively. Things which are wholly alien to each other are brought together by a place, a moment of time, by some strange similarity, through an error or by means of some peculiar change. In this way there come into being the strangest entities and the oddest combinations, and one thing recalls all things and becomes the symbol of much else besides itself, and is itself called to mind by many other things and becomes the symbol of those things.'[7]

From the sober mid-century there comes the judgment of one of the leading historians of the Romantic movement and it is a judgment that is penetrating and far from friendly. 'Continually swaying between these two extremes, those of an arbitrary mood and an abstract universality, the ego is restlessly driven hither and thither. The unceasing task is to achieve a unity between realism and idealism by means of our own creative power. The mind throws itself empirically onto what is objectively real and seeks in doing so to illuminate the universe, the totality of all things, until at last it becomes alive to the fact that the kind of beauty that is universally valid can only be found where it happens to be found, in one particular thing, that is to say, and not in another, and that the soil upon which beauty can grow must first be found.'[8]

A little later when realism had almost begun to work according to a conscious and deliberate programme and the scales were visibly sinking in its favour, the critics, their nostrils aquiver at such doctrinaire predisposition, came out as champions of the imagination and of the artist's privilege to transform reality and set upon it a subjective imprint. They charged the realists with short-sightedness and with living in a narrowly positivistic world, a world of photographers who mechanically reproduced what they saw. 'I will set down things as they are, or rather as they would be if I were not there at all.' These were the words put by Baudelaire into the mouths of a supposititious realist.[9] It was because this kind of painting repudiates the temperament and personality of the artist, so they argued, that it lacks all unifying power, that it lacks the inner bond, the closed completeness of good composition. Even Fiedler was later to criticize Marées for seeing things after the manner of a detached and isolated individual, and of never being able to rise superior to that vision.[10] He designates

* This series is sometimes called Los Proverbios.

23

as a realist the painter who only knows of nature that which his eye can perceive in an instant of time. This judgment is admittedly that of yet another extremist, for Fiedler numbered himself among the 'aesthetics', so it was natural enough that he should condemn the equally extreme empiricism of the Impressionists, standing as he did at the opposite pole to them.

The realists themselves were conscious of the burden of empiricism. They believed, though they viewed the matter rather differently from their critics, that reality and allegory could be reconciled with one another, that valid symbol-figures could be found that would dominate both of the two opposing poles. Does not Flaubert in *The Temptation of St Anthony* let the Sphinx and the Chimaera seek redemption in mutual embrace? In this allegory the hope for mutual fructification between poetry and science lies in the reconciliation of faith and knowledge.

Let us listen to two more voices from the closing decades of the century which plainly show the secular importance of this problem. They are the voices of Nietzsche and Huysmans, the one sceptical, the other prepared to compromise. The philosopher's tone is resigned and his thoughts on the subject of 'What all art attempts but fails to achieve' are determined and even limited by that mood, and indeed the very title is an assertion of impotence. The reflections that follow recommend the abandonment of the empiric form. 'The ultimate and most difficult task that faces the artist is the representation of all that is permanent, at rest within itself, simple yet exalted, and wholly independent of any purely individual charm' (vom Einzelreiz weit absehendem).[11]

In France the insistence on the need for keeping close to reality had struck deep. It resulted in a cult of the proximate and disconnected, of the isolated and variegated, of the shifting kaleidoscope of purely physical facts. There was only one thing that had a chance of prevailing against that cult – a readiness to let symbol and reality co-exist and combine with one another.

In his novel *A Rebours* Huysmans describes in some detail the nature of this mongrel phenomenon to which he gives the name of spiritualistic naturalism. 'Our task should be to preserve the utmost sincerity and exactitude in our documentation of truth, scrupulously observing every detail and never for a moment abandoning the full, rich yet sensitive language of the realist; and yet we should also be as men who dig down to the living springs of the soul and do not seek to explain all of its secrets in terms of some disability of the senses. The novel should fall into two parts which nevertheless preserve the connection which in real life unites them with each other. One part should deal with the body, the other with the soul. The novel should show us the interreactions between the two, their battles with one another and their reconciliations. We should follow Zola's great road and yet construct a parallel path in the air above it, a way that would lead us beyond our present life into the world to come. In a word, what we must create is a spiritualistic naturalism.'[12]

7

The century ended as it began, deeply conscious of the rift in its soul. It was this awareness that made men at one and the same time aggressive and uncertain of themselves, for it involved all artistic creation in a clear and deliberate act of choice and confronted the individual with the need for decisions that were weighty indeed. The man whose age no longer has the power to grasp both reality and its sublimation in a single comprehensive grip, is faced with an ineluctable choice. He must either make himself master step by step of the empiric world around him, of the world of sense, or he must declare that this world has defeated him and seek his security in some refuge estranged from mundane actuality. If he fixes his gaze upon the world around him, he can no longer take in that world's ideal horizon. If his eyes are set fixedly into the realm that lies above mundane reality, then that of common experience will escape his vision. His eye is condemned to operate with two

4 DAVID The Death of Marat; 1793.

8–9 BOULLÉE Design for a cenotaph for Newton; 1784.

7 BLAKE Newton; 1795.

5 INGRES Jupiter and Thetis; 1811.

6
INGRES
Napoleon in his Coronation robes
1806

11 BARDOU Kant; 1798.

Painted from Nature by John Russell R.A.

10 RUSSELL The Face of the Moon; c. 1790.

12 RUDE Napoleon waking to immortality; 1847.

alternating sets of adjustments which can never be united upon a single focal point. The vision directed towards the bold outlines of distant things must sacrifice the detailed view of what is close at hand; it can only perceive the ideal formula. As against this the more near-sighted view tends to lose itself in the sheer multiplicity of material things. It becomes confused, it wearies and comes to a halt in the mere process of enumeration.

At this point our problem, which is essentially the problem of the century, discloses itself as that of interpreting experience in depth, for there is a contradiction between the old idealizing formulae and the very stuff of modern life. 'What chance has Vulcan against Roberts and Co', says Marx in one of his essays, 'or Jupiter against the lightning conductor? What chance has Hermes against the Crédit Mobilier? Can we conceive of Achilles in the age of powder and shot? Or of the Iliad itself when there is printer's ink and the printing press? Does not all song and saga, nay the Muse herself, disappear with the press-jack? Have not the inescapable conditions for epic poetry disappeared?'[13] One does not need to be an economist or a left-winger in order to see that the old symbol-bearers and the traditional allegorical types no longer have validity. Even as great a conservative as Jacob Burckhardt realized the inapplicability of the classic system of symbols when he proposed that the figures of boom and slump – to say nothing of the evil spirit of bankruptcy – should be placed over a stock exchange building.[14] (Actually this idea found anticipatory satiric expression in Daumier's stock exchange caricatures.)

The diagnoses of these two critics of the age lead us to the decisive question which the century was called upon to answer. Was it capable of finding new symbol-figures in terms of which – now that the old ones had proved no more than empty shells – the content of modern experience could find expression? Or did the things which most deeply moved the men of this time defy anything in the nature of a generalizing representational form? We may pose the same question in slightly different terms by enquiring whether the content of modern life is such that it is capable of sustaining a system of symbols at all. If we put the question in this form we must ask whether the artist who draws his themes out of the world around him is condemned to confine himself to the physical and material, to mere foreground matter in fact, and forbidden to read into the world of his experience certain specific contents of meaning. We can ask much the same question of the idealist who turns his back on the real world of his time and seeks to discover the true nature of his relation to the world around him. If he cares nothing for the life of his day, does that mean that he is in no way its bondsman? Is not the truth of the matter that he is willy nilly under direction from his own time, despite his claim to timelessness? Is there not then a common bond between men of a particular age, though some of them may have committed themselves to the world of experience while others linger perpetually in that of the imagination?

Such a bond most certainly exists and this book is devoted to the proof of its existence. It will seek to show that Delacroix's 'Dante and Vergil' (plate 81) and Daumier's 'Un wagon de troisième classe' (plate 160), Géricault's 'The raft of the Medusa' (plate 70) and Friedrich's 'The wreck of the Hope' (plate 14), can be traced back to a common development of ideas. It suggests a reinterpretation of the nineteenth century, for which the methods of mere form analysis and mere critical appreciation of style do not suffice, for these are only concerned with the specialized technical processes of the artist's craft. If we analyse the century according to the various horizons of its imaginative vision, a vision whose irradiating power is as evident in works that are wholly original as in those where there has been sympathetic yielding to alien influence, it will at once become obvious that its teeming riches, divergent as are often their actual forms, are built up around a comparatively small number of experiential constants. It is these that give to the epoch between Goya and Cézanne its character of a clearly defined entity.

33

The method adopted in the writing of this book is in certain respects that of the artist, since in order to build its bridges it falls back at certain critical junctures on intuition, and it is by that method that it seeks to make plain certain connections between the content of one picture and that of another in the development of ideas. It is by that method too that it seeks to disclose elements in such content that would perhaps normally have escaped observation. From the fullness of the available material I have endeavoured to trace out a certain basic pattern of pictorial content which, together with certain wish-images, will bring us nearer than anything else can to the essential character of the century, and this both from the point of view of the art historian and from that of the chronicler of the development of ideas. It was my intention to undertake an examination which, though by no means exhaustive, would nevertheless be a penetrating one. Yet to take my basic theme and then proceed to expound it to death was a prospect that held few attractions for me. I have therefore, though mindful of its limitations, assumed the privilege which, if he is to be more than a mere chronicler, the scholar shares with the artist. I have exercised the right to select. 'History selects its history in history' (L'histoire choisit son histoire dans l'histoire). These pregnant words of Gaston Bachelard would seem to justify my decision.[15]

II   Nature and History

I

THE central portion of 'L'atelier' depicts the 'rapport' between man and woman. The creative power of the man is guided by the anxious and sympathetic understanding of the woman who watches him. There is no meeting of eyes, no interlocking of arms as with the pair of lovers, there is no dialogue – there is nothing but the proximity of the two bodies and an imperceptible emotional current that flows between them and gives them a sense of being at rest. In the inward attunement between the sexes we discern the fundamental axes around which we build our image of man – that of the male and that of the female.

The type of thinking that professes to be enlightened, factual, and exact sets little store by these two power potentials; it is suspicious of all that harks back to the aboriginal and spontaneous in man, it identifies sex with barbarism, instinct and feeling with confusion and chaos. It arranges the world according to rigid, sharply outlined concepts, all of them deriving from the chimaera of progress, the bright sun of reason being sovereign over all. The active energy of the male is the very essence of this self-glorifying world. The only things that stir its heart are the poetry of action, and continual confirmation of its intellectual capacities. Man measures himself by the yardstick of mere intellect. By and large he would have us accept him as one seeking to attain a definite goal by clear and logical means. No shadow of uncertainty must dim this image, and he who projects it sets himself on the apex of the whole created world and makes use of what is in it according to his pleasure. Blake's 'Newton' (plate 7) is a symbol of that coldly calculating rationality.

This process of continual dissection by the conscious mind sets man at a distance from nature and makes of him a historically conscious being.[1] Man alone can stretch himself out into the past and into the future; he alone possesses memory and so has history. Animals and plants lack this time-dimension, theirs is the eternal present of the moment. Man, however, is only man within the framework of the changes wrought by time; these are essential to his development, for it is in and through his encounter with the unknown that he attains his full stature, carrying forward what he has won into the future. Danger and daring are of the essence of his being, for man, the creature that lives on the level of history, is exposed and unprotected, and is alone with himself and all his works. But his historical consciousness is surety for his supremacy. Since, moreover, history is made by the personal responses of men to a variety of situations, it is the basis for his most cherished conviction, for his belief that every human being is a unique and unrepeatable individual.

Man, then, thrown back wholly upon himself, treats all creation as subservient to his own ends, making of it no more than the setting of the great drama of humanity. In history the freely ranging mind continually proclaims its victories over unconscious nature but in it, as we have seen, there is also manifested the *principium individuationis*. Yet there is more to it than that. The formative forces in history are election, favour, predestination,[2] all of them things which further differentiate between one personality and another, selecting this man and elevating that. The end-product of this process, and its visible monument, is the Great Man, the price of whose greatness must necessarily be loneliness. But in him is concentrated – however the tides of progress and decay may rise and fall – all that makes the race of man worthy of its high vocation; in him there is found the capacity to face and deal with fate.

Thus it is in the fact of being an agent in history that man in his essentially masculine view of the world finds himself justified. It is this that imparts to him his dignity as the ruler of the world, it is in this that he proves himself a personality. And yet this essential process of self-realization, of rising to the greatness without which he is nothing, entails, in the final analysis, the payment of a price – and that price can be formidable.

Let us glance again at man as he faces nature and its powers, and seeks to master them. Let us consider him as he replaces nature with artefact, as he sets planning in the place of organic growth. The works of man push their way in front of the creations of nature, and since nature is for man only a means for the creation of the desired image of himself, the raw material which must bend to his will, it is clear that he will be deaf to nature when she speaks out of his inner self. The conscious jettisons the unconscious, the forces of reason reject those of instinct, the abstract arrogantly claims precedence over the physical and concrete – over nature, in fact – and with this usurpation there is a drying up of those springs from which man receives the first certitudes, the certitudes concerning the riddle of creation and his own existence; for these come to him as revelations, they are not rational acts of cognition.

Man's efforts in the sphere of history seem deliberately designed to achieve the end which they undoubtedly effect: this end being to fetter man with the shackles of deductive thought and hurl him onto the Procrustean bed of universal reason. All that is imprecise, uncertain, and mysterious is thus kept out of his way, every direct and spontaneous gesture is tamed, every instinctive action is disciplined and curtailed. All that is vital is devitalized by convention, all that is primal and aboriginal is civilized away, and man is caught in the coils of his own intellect which in his pride he mistakes for the trappings of authority. His image loses its complex and irrational features, it shrinks to a mere arrangement of inter-related parts where the proportion between one and the next is measurable and exact, and where anything unpredictable has been eliminated. The world reflects his own image back to him. All its joints and crevices lie bare and self-explanatory in the cold daylight of his boasted enlightenment.

Hegel's philosophy of history provides a kind of culminating point to this self-assertion of the intellect; yet a form of thought that thus identifies reality with reason can lead nowhere save to fossilized self-admiration. For the intellect which in the Hegelian scheme rules over history as world-mind or world-intellect, nature can have no positive or independent significance: the progress of the intellect towards freedom must inevitably separate it from the dark mindless bondage of nature herself. This whole conception of the world, and of the nature of the historic process operating within it, is essentially a masculine creation.

2

During the very period when Courbet was identifying the feminine principle in life with the powers of nature, Bachofen in Basle was exploring the inter-relationship of nature, mind, and history. The traditional thinking of the historian had tended to be rigid and restricted in its concepts. Bachofen was searching for a way to admit new forms of historical apprehension, forms which would enable him to penetrate into the experience of the earliest men. There, awaiting discovery and inaccessible to any sounding by pure abstract reason, lay the dark depths of human nature. There the conscious awareness of history had not yet freed itself from domination by the forces of nature. There it was

still the law of matter, and not the free-ranging rule of the mind, that determined the fate of peoples. In this matriarchally ordered world Bachofen saw 'the subordination of the mind to physical laws, the dependence of human development on cosmic powers'.[3]

In 1862, one year after the publication of his *Das Mutterrecht* (Matriarchy), there appeared Flaubert's *Salammbô*. It was just at this time that Bachofen began, while in Rome and other parts of Italy, to embark on oriental studies, the result being *Die Sage von Tanaquil* (The Saga of Tanaquil) which appeared in 1870. In this work what may be called the 'oriental-sensual' principle of life is boldly and deliberately contrasted with the history-conscious patriarchal spirit of the West. In those royal mistresses of Asia Bachofen discerned the essential type of the *femme fatale* of the ancient world, and he did so at the very moment of time when the imagination of poets and painters was beginning to be captivated by the figures of the great courtesans, by Cleopatra and Messalina, for instance; nor can it be denied that by his thought, aided as this was by keen intuitive sense, he played a significant part in that 'return to matriarchy' which was becoming evident in the century's art and literature. He thus confirmed what he, himself a product of the humanistic tradition, designated as a 'melancholy truth' – the fact that at the end of its development the outlook and modes of feeling and belief prevailing at the earliest stages of a people's life force themselves again towards the surface. 'The cycle of life brings the end back to the beginning again'.[4] The moment had arrived in the development of Western ideas when life, 'that dark, driving, insatiable, self-desiring force', was passing its judgment upon history.

This interpretation of life, this conception of it as a dark and mysterious force, is also to be found in the second set of Nietzsche's *Unzeitgemäße Betrachtungen* (Unseasonable Observations) which deals with the 'advantages and disadvantages of history for life'. Nietzsche sees the opening of a yawning gulf, he sees the development of a deep and dangerous estrangement between history and life, between vested cultural interests and spontaneous creative power, between the past and the present. His analysis traced one of the many fissures by which the nineteenth century was divided. Man no longer possessed the courage to forget, the courage to act spontaneously; his instincts had begun to weaken. The charade of historical objectivity, in which living features are replaced by masks, was paralysing his vital powers; he spoke with a hundred voices, and could look dispassionately at the world from the viewpoint of any creed you pleased. Everlastingly he 'let historical artists prepare for him the festival of a World Exhibition'. Yet he no longer had even a vocabulary that belonged to himself, he had no creed that was wholly his own, he had no consciousness of self that did not glance obliquely at the past.

History and life, intellect and nature, male and female – these are the contrasting modes of experience that activate nineteenth century art. The split of which Nietzsche made men aware is discernible in all the phases of that art. Sensitive to the prevailing tensions, the artist treated the past's authority now as an inhibiting and now as a stimulating force, and spontaneity of gesture was at continual cross-purposes with the restraining influence of traditional forms. Art was always at a cross-roads; instinct and inner certainty pointed in one direction, while reflective cerebration and scholarly erudition pointed in another. There stand opposed to one another on the one hand the new forms in which the untrammelled upsurge of the spirit sought unprecedented expression, and on the other the approved stylistic gestures that lay ready to hand; the licence of the unconscious warred with the unyielding disciplines of reason. The whole history of nineteenth century art is really one of uninterrupted encounter and friction between these two forces, each of which served continually to bring about an accentuation of the peculiarities of the other. To suppose that we are concerned here with nothing more than a new chapter in the familiar quarrel between *anciens* and *modernes* is to oversimplify the historical picture out of all recognition.

The whole thing is much more complex; the battle-fronts shift and interpenetrate. To hearken to the rallying call of the present does not imply a protest against the past – let alone an unconditional identification with the contemporary world. The male and female principles interpenetrate. The mythopoeic enthusiasm for the Great Man, for instance, moves along the paths of irrational experience, yet is, for all that, something unmistakably masculine. We must therefore distinguish it from what belongs unreservedly to the feminine principle of the unconscious and its related myths. Often historical implications are embedded in the present. Often the past is discernible – simply by reason of the formal qualities of the picture concerned – behind an open assertion of unconventionality that is essentially in the modern mood. One has only to think of Manet's 'Le déjeuner sur l'herbe' (plate 123) and the recollection of Raphael which has managed to work its way into that painting.[5] Of course, when both sides elevated their views to the dignity of an absolute principle, when one side was determined to ascribe all great and genuine art to the past, while the other, outraged by any such flight from the present, not only insisted on the exclusive validity of newer forms but would have it that only the 'here and now' was worthy of the creative artist's attention, then the fact of their being in opposite camps became too obvious for either quibble or misapprehension. Yet it is precisely in the work of the most outstanding artists that the attraction of these two poles can time and again be discerned, though their influence is often disguised.

There is a saying of Nietzsche's that both the historical and the unhistorical are necessary for the health of an individual, a people, and a culture. If this idea is valid, then in applying it to the art of the nineteenth century we might formulate it as follows: without the double voice of history and life, without the dialogue between the historical consciousness on the one hand and the forces of life and nature on the other, the nineteenth century would be something of which it would be easier to take a comprehensive and summary view, it would be something easier to analyse; yet it would also be essentially a poorer thing, in flatter relief and more uniform in its accents. If we are to understand it, we must keep both of these two formative powers in view and subject them both to examination, we must recognize the desire to submit the whole sphere of history to a wide and searching review[6] as one of the great authentic needs of the century. We must, however, also understand how irritating – nay, humiliating – to the men of that time was this imputation of sovereign and unattainable excellence to the past; for it is only then that we will be able to gauge how intensely men longed for a new vitality and a new driving power in artistic creation.

Yet none of this should lead us to suppose that the two partners always had equal shares in the store of forces that moulded the century. These were in fact quite unequally divided. At first it was those who experienced the world historically, whose imaginative and creative power weighed more heavily in the scales. Gradually, however, reason, analytical and essentially masculine, lost the start that it had gained. Then the wider horizons opened up by the direct experience of the living world and the dynamic and ever-changing forces of nature, began to provide a more powerful set of symbols for the interpretation of life than anything that history could supply. The factual and cerebral approach of the historian was too pedestrian. The artist sought a return to the elements. Dreams, instinct, and revelation claimed him for their own.

There seem to be some grounds for regarding these changes in the whole manner of approach to life as part of a larger process which affects not merely the quality of individual experience but the entire relationship between the individual and society. There is an illuminating sentence in the preface of *Das Mutterrecht* which has considerable bearing on this matter. 'Everywhere', writes Bachofen, 'the increasing sensualization of existence (Fortschritt der Versinnlichung des Daseins) coincides with the dissolution of political organization and the decay of civic life. In place of an elaborate articulation'(of the political organism) 'the law of democracy, of the undifferentiated mass, asserts itself together with that freedom and equality which distinguish the natural life, the life that belongs to the physical and material side of human nature, from that which is politically ordered'. One might almost think that these words, which actually come from a passage on ancient aphroditism, were being addressed to the nineteenth century, for at the very time when Bachofen was examining the cults and ways of life of antiquity, an aristocratic society was giving place in Europe to a democratic one and, thanks to the liberal ethic of laissez-faire, the old rigid order was in dissolution.

We can illustrate this point by another example. No less a man than Burckhardt, himself a fugitive from the present who had sought asylum in the past, attributes the weakening of the Greek *polis* to the fact that the individual had become wholly independent of the state. This development went hand in hand with the emergence of an apolitical human type who simply avoided anything related to public life or in any way connected with politics, and lived his life wholly as a private person. In so far as such a type represents a kind of return to nature, we may see here a further confirmation of the principle in question. This trend too will become apparent in the art of the second half of the century.

3

If we select works of art that belong to different formal traditions and group them together according to what Schopenhauer calls 'internal significance' (innere Bedeutsamkeit) they will often quite readily reveal a common spiritual experience. We would not be wholly off the mark in saying, for instance, that it is in its formal language that the art of Courbet differs from that of Böcklin and the art of Daumier from that of Meissonier, and not in its essential content.

This point was, of course, made earlier and it is one of some importance to my argument. I have however to examine my subject from yet another point of view, and in order to make my analysis as clear as possible, I propose to classify the century's two distinctive modes of perception as male and female. As we study the history of the epoch we will necessarily become aware of a shift of emphasis in this respect. It passes from the historical world of the male to the organic world of womanhood. And though it is not my intention that this book should attempt anything in the nature of a strict chronological scheme of development, it seemed for all that desirable that I should take note of this aspect of the matter. Here then are the types of question that will be dealt with in the following pages.

First of all something must clearly be said about the effect on the arts of the new outlook on history which had its beginnings in the eighteenth century and owed so much to Goethe and Herder. This new outlook, to which German scholars have in more or less recent times given the name of 'Historismus', synchronizes with the emergence of a wholly new kind of artistic consciousness, and it is at this point of time that we must place the great divide. Henceforward works of art came to repose, both in regard to their form and to the thought by which they were informed, upon an entirely new basis. The whole nineteenth century, and not merely that part of it that looks backward, has its origins in this trend.

The recapitulation of the past reaches its culminating point in the picturing of man in the different phases of his cultural history, and a special chapter will deal with this matter. Another of the century's dominant ideas is that of the Great Man, and in this figure history's aristocratic principle of selection is concentrated in visible and significant form. Painters and sculptors place themselves at the service of hero-worship. The higher the Great Man is raised by his fame, the more loosely is he bound to his surroundings. In the end no society is capable of carrying him and loneliness becomes one of his essential marks. The nineteenth century inwardly experienced all the pathos of this lone-

13 C. D. FRIEDRICH Monk on the seashore; 1809–10.

17 MARTIN The Last Man; 1849.

18
FUSELI
The Bard; 1796.

16

MOREAU

Prometheus; 1868.

14. C. D. FRIEDRICH The wreck of the "Hope"; 1821.

15 CONSTABLE Stonehenge; 1835.

FEUERBACH
Iphigenia; 1871.

19 Victor Hugo on the "Exile's Rock", Guernsey (photograph.)

20 VICTOR HUGO *Ma destinée*.

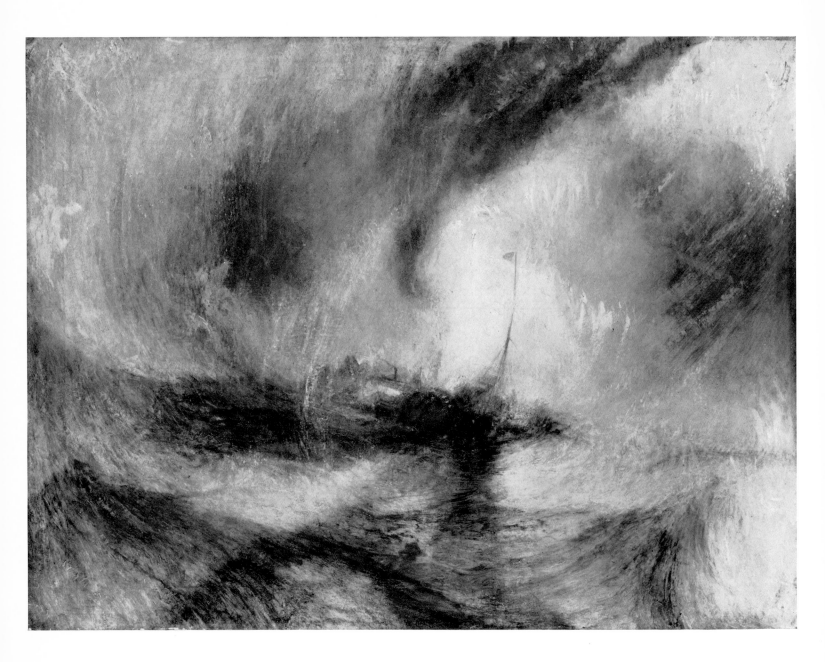

22 TURNER Snowstorm; 1842.

liness. Indeed this pathos had for the century all the arresting power of a stigma – and its art found adequate symbols for the expression of this fact. Yet this is not only the century of the isolated genius, it is also the century of the 'lonely crowd'. One conditions the other.

The artist sometimes stands on the level of the demi-god and sometimes on that of the name-less beggar. He is priest, prophet and hero, but he is also an outcast, homeless, a 'wanderer' (Zug-mensch), as Novalis calls him, and the shamed and abased are his brothers. Never before was he so preoccupied as in this century with his own special myth, and nothing is more revelatory of the artist's feelings about himself during this period than the symbolic figures – if we will but examine them – with which the epoch surrounded itself.

The essentially male and world-transforming ideas of the century sought to impose a com-munal religion in the gospel of work; and this organized world of artifice attained its triumph in what was perhaps the most remarkable of all its creations – the World Exhibition. This last was a reconstruction of all the pasts that ever were, a museum of mankind that stretched forward into the present. It was a manufactured golden age, an apotheosis of man's mastery of the universe.

Behind this institutional world, with its tragic conflicts in the zones of feeling, dream and in-stinct, there waited that all-embracing, unifying force, woman – the force that gives the whole world coherence and leads man back to the powers of nature. First I must seek to show after what fashion it was that those artists conceived of nature who knew themselves to be in tune with the organic and instinctive. We will find here a predominance of the dynamic, the vital, the unstable and the changeable. For men with this kind of vision there were to be no abstract rules; improvisation was to be all. The delight in elemental things was to bring the artist into conversation with the ele-ments and his brushwork was once more to repeat the creation of the world.

Applied to human relationships this delight in the elemental occasioned a search for the un-conventional, for uninhibited spontaneity. The animal became a symbol in which man recognized his own unfettered appetites. Orientalism and exoticism, failing to exhaust themselves within the framework of the ethnologist's apparatus, set off a search for symbols of our primaeval nature which were felt to have survived into the present day, and the changes wrought by this, the artist's pact with instinct, were richly in evidence. Conventional *eros*, draped with the gracious charms of mythology, was wholly done away with. In its place we have an elemental thing to which man sur-renders in utter self-abandonment. All these varied streams of experience flow together in the central figure symbolic of the 'natural' world – in woman, who appears as a mother, both kind and terrible, a guardian and a threat.

This world, too, has its vision of a golden age. It is eloquent of that feminine propensity for natural companionship in which freedom and equality reign supreme. At length these peregrina-tions through the realms of the 'natural' had to come to a halt before the question: 'Where do we come from? What are we? Whither are we going?' Here was the eternal question of the origin and significance of man. This time, however, it was not posed by the ranging curiosity of the historian. Rather was it the expression of an artistic trend that was feeling its way back to mythical origins.

III   Art without Certainty

I HAVE said earlier that the breakdown of religious certitudes had effects extending far beyond the confines of institutional religion and that outside those confines the artist was probably more profoundly affected than anybody else. The compact three-storey arrangement of the world, in which heaven, earth and hell were conveniently inter-connected by invisible staircases, would no longer serve as an intellectual or any other kind of assumption, and the disappearance of this unspoken postulate produced fundamental changes in the artist's approach to his task.

One of the most significant of these changes – though a variety of causes were no doubt at work in producing it – was the severance, so far as the artist's manner of experiencing them was concerned, between past and present. In retrospect we can see that such a development was almost bound to have occurred; for if past and present can no longer be seen as parts of a coherent unifying super-natural plan, they tend to be particularized and fall apart. But the results of the breakdown of the supra-sensual framework of life were reflected, even if only indirectly, on a much wider scale. Every-where a kind of disruptive duel broke out between the universal and the particular, between the symbolic and the real. Landscape, portraiture, indeed every category of art was affected. There was a loss of meaning, of significance, and nowhere does the artist appear to have been more poignantly aware of this than in his portrayal of man himself, whom he now tended to see as an orphaned being, a creature lost, rudderless, and cut adrift in a universe grown suddenly hostile.

I

In 1793 David painted a picture of Marat murdered in his bath (plate 4). This is not a historical painting in the accepted sense of the word. It is the work of a painter who held the dead man in honour but whose ambition it was to paint him as though he had been personally present at the event in question – to give, in a word, the authentic account of an eye-witness. He approaches the human to within arm's length, so close in fact that the corpse, shrunken as it is, becomes the only human fact in a yawning bottomless void. Undoubtedly David has rearranged reality – by stretch-ing it on the framework of two linear axes which run sharply into one another. He has nevertheless done nothing to embellish it, his only purpose being to enhance the stark directness of the painting's impact. He has emended, but only to free the naked truth from any adventitious adornment, so that the pitiful weakness of the human creature may show itself undisguised. Where so much is so sharply and so brutally revealed, where there is such utter mercilessness of form, can we speak of composition at all? Not, surely, of composition as David himself had practised it in his early days as a pupil of Boucher, not of composition in the sense of those felicitous rhythmic consonances, of those brilliant formal combinations which round off the content of a picture and resolve it into a fluid arabesque! The whole finality of the death, so sudden and so unprepared for, is expressed in the slackly dangling arm (a relic, this, from antiquity[1]) that seems almost to be hanging out of the picture. So near is this death to the observer that its very nearness is in some eerie way converted into distance, for there is nothing that leads into the picture from the background. To look at it is to be confronted directly with brutality unrelieved. The terse geometry of the objects corresponds exactly with the vertical and horizontal lines of the frame. Hence the breath-taking nearness, which yet in some magic fashion withdraws from our approach and touch; hence the great remote and inaccessible emptiness of the background from which nothing stretches forward into the centre of the picture to relieve mind and eye.

This method of presentation intensifies the impression of loneliness. There are no liberating or, in either sense of the word, 'engaging' lines to connect up the two halves into which the picture is horizontally divided. The antithesis of body and void is scored in such a fashion that a single word might be coined to express the painting's real significance: 'cut-offness'. Cut off has been the life of this man and cut off his body from the world that surrounds it: the unrelieved smoothness of the background seems almost to fall on him, cutting as it falls like the axe of a guillotine. The narrow bathtub is a coffin.

A cutting off! The picture itself is a cutting off in the sense that it is a 'cutting-out' – a symbol of fragmentation, a symbol of temporality unrelieved by grace. The almost embittered opposition of upright and horizontal draws a despairing line of severance, it severs this world from the world beyond.

All this results from a sobering-up process that was part of the classicizing spirit. In the old ordering of a picture which still prevailed in the Rococo, the concrete and material was always given a kind of liberating echo in the background. All that had substance was present in two dimensions and yet radiated into space. It was part of a world that was almost tangibly one. The organic, the geometrical, and the ornamental combined to make an inextricably connected whole.

All this was now a thing of the past. Already in an earlier painting, in David's 'Oath of the Horatii' (1785), the background is broken up into layers of relief and the geometrical discipline of the figures is strictly separate from the background's bodiless stage-scenery. The continuous interpenetration of body, background and surface is interrupted. In the present picture the severance of the figure of Marat from the background is complete. Its plastic actuality is in complete contrast with the offsetting flat and empty background.

David's 'Death of Marat' is part of a development that stretches back to the very beginnings of the eighteenth century. Scholars are quite right in speaking of a revolution in historical painting;[2] the increased urge for explicitness of expression and a new sense of the unique and significant – all were crying out for strict historical fidelity. This demand implied a radical breach with custom. Till then portrayers of court and state occasions had been satisfied with a lofty approximation in which a vague sartorial modelling on antiquity alternated with the light-hearted modernization of the past.[3] The actual event portrayed was given a symbolical-allegorical dress. A monumental example of this practice is the Medici cycle of Rubens. Even Velasquez's 'Surrender of Breda', a picture that broke with all precedent in depicting so recent an event, exalts the whole scene onto a symbolic and allegorical level – even though it is accurate in its portrayal of the actual happenings.

Generally speaking, Renaissance and Baroque artists were more concerned with the glorification of their subject than with accuracy about details of time and place. Their pictures, essentially unhistorical in spirit, fail to convey the special pathos of remoteness and since they do not really attempt it, they can merrily 'mix seventeenth century wigs, stars and orders with Roman tunics and the Greek cothurnus'.[4] They display a powerful and unimpaired self-assurance, which however has not yet really learned to focus fully onto its own time and can – in part for that very reason – still afford to dispense with the documentary exactitudes of the conscientious chronicler. In every event portrayed there is, over and above the actual facts with which it is concerned, a moral and supra-temporal content. History is not yet a field for scholarly research nor is it limited by such considerations. When there is a battle, higher, mythical powers guide its fortunes. Genii determine victory and defeat, Gods protect the hero. Man in action is not yet thrown back upon himself, he is the executor of a historical plan which has its roots in the Christian conception of the world.

Around 1720 Thornhill, the English historical painter, was commissioned to paint a picture of the landing of George I[5] and had to ask himself whether he was to indulge in a pictorial glorification of that event or depict it as it actually was. He gave some thought to the problem, weighing the one alternative against the other – much as, a century later, his countryman Soane was to do when, availing himself of the romantic's freedom, he designed a church in three different styles. Thornhill noted down the pros and cons of the matter. 'There was', he observes, 'a great crowd, which to represent would be ugly and not to represent would be false'. In the end he decided against a purely factual representation of this unique event and in favour of a glorified version.

Yet half a century later the opposite view was to establish itself. English historical painting had made its decision, set its face against the glorifying tradition and rejected the rule of the 'universal human'. It was now all for local colour and exactitude of period detail. West's 'Death of General Wolfe' (1771) and Copley's 'A boy attacked by a shark' (1778) are important documents illustrating this trend, though at that stage an adequate expressive form for such a purely 'temporal' conception of representation had not yet been evolved. It was left to David to hit on this – in his 'Marat'.

2

Devotees of historical accuracy could not do anything but utterly reject the marginal embellishments of allegory; they had outgrown their childish innocence. Now, cool and precise, they set themselves to recapture every unique feature of period and place that appertained to a person or an event. A coronation ceremony of which every detail tells us when and how it proceeded – one thinks of David and Menzel – is an objectively informative document from which we can learn a great deal more than from, say, the representation of an act of homage supervised by the allegorical figures of Pax and Justitia; and since a real awareness of history engenders distrust of all symbolic sublimations of hard fact or its distillation by this means into anything in the nature of universality, there was a tendency to sacrifice symbolic content to factual fidelity.

There is a clear breach here. An artist who is determined to represent every event strictly in the colouring of its time, sees both past and present happenings as transient things, as things that have happened once and will never happen in precisely that way again. David, whether he is depicting the dead Marat or the battle of Thermopylae, always supposes himself to be producing a pictorial document which accurately records the facts of the event concerned. Along with this breach, which imposed on the subject this limiting temporal particularity, there went yet another division, that between past and present, between what has been documented from historical sources and what has been directly experienced, in a word between history and life.

If a painter gives visible form to the self-awareness of his own time, then he is really choosing the role of an eye-witness. He must in these circumstances reject the help of the older models. The living form and that on which tradition has placed its stamp become two different things. For all that, if his subject is some past event, then his actual sense of history forces him to some extent to conjure up the spirit of the relevant period by adapting his own method of representation to whatever may be that period's most characteristic style. In such cases this borrowed tradition-stamped form may well supplant the living one. It was in such a borrowed form, one deriving ultimately from the

antique, that David clothed his 'Rape of the Sabine Women'. He felt that it somehow confirmed its historical accuracy.

This stylistic drag of the past was, as we have seen, bound up with the awakening sense of history. We may therefore say that it was the sense of history which, by sharply dividing the present from the past, gave birth to the ultimate crisis of style. Up till well into the eighteenth century European painting had been capable of containing the tension between history and life, and of resolving it within the framework of its own style – much as it succeeded in finding a common denominator for real and ideal. In the nineteenth century the strictness of artistic scruples caused all such accommodation to fall under suspicion of compromise, and what till now had been something in the nature of a peaceful co-existence degenerated into a conflict between two distinct modes of consciousness.

With all the sophisticate's appetite for problems, the century wavered in exquisite uncertainty between the attractions of rival altars. Past or present? At which of these shrines should it worship? And – the cognate dilemma was equally agonizing – was it external reality or some higher significance that was the true essence of the artist's theme? Nietzsche's words on the disadvantages of history for life show the extent to which men were thinking in terms of two quite separate things and not of an organically connected whole. History and life were in fact already conceived as two mutually exclusive entities. Life was finding itself able to dispense with history, while the labyrinth of the past held the wanderer prisoner and permitted no escape into the present.

Thus a living connection was broken, the partnership between the impulses of tradition and innovation was dissolved. For what is style but the integration of an antiphony, the resolving chord of the eternal counterpoint between tradition and the urge for novelty of form? What indeed is style but the mysteriously successful attempt to derive from the substance of history a new procreative power and to preserve that substance as a living, and therefore a changeable, thing? Style therefore is always a kind of bargain, an understanding between yesterday and today – in the best sense of the word, an accommodation. It is an organic thing, the formal product of a yesterday made real in the present, and a today whose self-awareness is not yet under the tutelage of memory.

Since the second half of the eighteenth century the assocation between these two things had become insecure, style now being a matter that only the expert was qualified to assess. It could no longer be taken for granted. It was something that had to be thought about and was for that very reason evanescent. Its presence resulted from a deliberate *fiat*. It was a thing premeditated and deliberate, an aesthetic recipe.

Yet to indulge in such stylistic purism, to make style the goal of conscious striving, is to sign style's death warrant. It is to make of it a creature of the retort, something that can only be preserved within an artificial container.[6] Style that is planned and calculated withdraws from life. Life in its turn rebels against constraint, against tradition and against rules. Life is only truly life in so far as it renounces convention. Here is the secret of the challenging quality in the nineteenth century's 'living' form. It lies in its freedom from the restrictive grip that style can exercise.

Both of the spheres of imaginative vision, that of the real and the ideal, and that of history and life, were originally contained in one and the same act of artistic perception, even though they did not always exactly coincide. A glance at their origin and an examination of their radicalization will help us to grasp the character of the artistic conflict by which the nineteenth century was torn.

The reality that forces itself directly upon the senses was not the nineteenth century's discovery any more than was the transfiguration of the data of experience according to the canons of an ideal world. Since the Renaissance, painting has tended now towards sublimation, now towards the mere imitation of that which presented itself as reality to the artist's eye. Yet these two methods of portrayal continued to lack the polarizing 'either ... or', and they could still claim a common ground-style. Something very similar is pointed out by Theodor Hetzer,[7] who shows how in the old masters earnestness and mirth, nature and ornament, truth and beauty were not mutually exclusive opposites.

Till recently the ideal form had derived from historic knowledge and yet had not been irreconcilable with the living one which needed nothing upon which to model itself since it contained within itself the living spirit. Never had the painter's eye so lost itself in its own direct experience that it had become the latter's slave. Conversely when art had employed a formal language that was exalted and objectivized – we can disregard the inbreeding of vested academic interests – it had not cut itself off from its vital and vivifying source: the universal type of absolute beauty did not deny that it originated in the line and colour perceived by the physical eye.

Only a closed conception of the world could have permitted such a continuing see-saw of emphasis and thus, within the compass of a single coherent field of vision, have found place for both ideal and reality; and though the pedantic niceties of dogmatizing classicizers may sometimes have set up an interminable desire for puristical abstractions, the fact remains that a common stream of life flowed through all the categories of pictorial art. An English portrait, a Dutch landscape, a mythological Italian painting – all possess a kind of common substratum that lies at the heart of the picture, there is a common message which the mere concept of style is inadequate to describe, there is a pictorial rhythm in which the geometric mingles with the organic in a single community of function. Surface and background melt into one another to form a single bodily whole.[8]

Schiller's reference to the old models and his recommendation of their use is notable, for it questions by implication the artistic validity of such a combination of elements. The fact is that abstract thought was now beginning to extract the 'style' from the living complex of form and make of it a model, a thing hallowed by class-room usage, and demonstrable by calculation. The fluid combination of elements which had been acceptable in pictures since the Renaissance, congealed into a formula which in its turn became the subject of argument; flexibility gave place to a fixed and unyielding pattern, and such forces of life as still remained broke out into opposition. The artistic representation of the real and the ideal, of the living and the exalted, assumed radical forms. Boundaries were disputed and defined. Dissatisfied with mere appearance, men would, when dealing with the real, have nothing less than the complete reality; they desired to savour reality in that crass, unadorned and literally style-less state in which it presented itself directly to the eye – without compositional embellishment, without any kind of polish to enhance its attraction, without any tangle of ornament. As to the ideal, it must, they felt, be freed from the merest after-taste of the material, it must be groomed in fact for idealism without suspicion of compromise.

A new type of artist began to emerge – we will deal with him at length in a subsequent chapter – a stranger to all quietness of mind whose consciously reformist activity set a barrier between himself and the past. To get down to the roots – that was the aim he set himself – to win through to the ultimate certitudes concerning the nature of the real and the ideal, to attain scientific precision in the assessment of history's legacy of form. It was not mere irresponsible virtuosity that brought about the disappearance of what had been one of the most characteristic traits of European painting – its treatment of all the constituent parts of a picture as pertaining to a single homogeneous whole; rather was it the essentially moral integrity of just those artists who rebelled against Rococo frivolity and the meretricious pathos of the Baroque.[9] What these men desired was to strip away all that was empty and conventional, to renew the language of form and deepen its content. They were beginning to find that the traditional pictorial forms were no longer adequate, and to discover in the course of their self-examination that the agreeable dialogue between ideal and reality had come to an end,

55

that past and present were becoming incompatible with one another. All subsequent attempts to re-establish the previous happy relations between the two derive from the knowledge of this fact. The day was over when such relationships could be taken for granted.

3

The eighteenth century saw the end not only of 'style' and the old pictorial forms which had been valid since the Renaissance, but also of a certain uncomplicated quality in man's relation to the world, to near and distant nature, to the realm both of sense and of the supra-sensual, to the present and the past.

Till that time two things had been accounted as axiomatic. First, that ideal form, conforming to classical laws, held a higher rank than form which approximated to sensible reality and derived its life from the concrete thing which it portrayed, in a word that the historical world of the religious or mythological picture made the content of any such picture superior to that of other categories of painting – to the *genre* picture, to landscape, portrait or still life.

Such a hierarchy in art is peculiar to the aristocratic conception of the world; it embodies its striving for a hierarchical ordering of things, and in so far as it rates the products of imagination higher than those of empirical experience, it contrasts with the bourgeois-democratic hunger for facts, which is so well exemplified by a saying of Dr. Johnson's, 'I had rather see the portrait of a dog than all the allegories you can show me.'[10] The bourgeois wants to know what it's all about. One might further remark that this aforesaid appetite for hierarchy found an ally in a purely artistic consideration. It was felt that the painting of an 'Assumption of the Blessed Virgin' entailed more actual artistry than the simple reproduction on canvas of a kitchen still life. In a word, the ennobled form and the exalted nature of the subject matter counted for more than individual power of expression when that power happened to be directed towards a subject that belonged to the everyday order of things and lacked any higher symbolic significance.

In the nineteenth century all these nicely balanced relationships fell victims to one thing, the purely subjective lust after expression. Till now there had obtained a tacitly acknowledged connection between the humble and the exalted, between reality and the ideal, and this had prevented the artist from flying off at a tangent. Both at the nether and the upper end of the scale a measure of moderation had been observed. The artist had avoided the purely abstract and schematic formula of beauty but had been equally cautious of the more crass forms of realism. Within the universal there was always the particular; and it is here that we have the common denominator of all art between the Renaissance and the Rococo. The Christian heaven and the heathen Olympus each had enough sensual warmth for men to experience them as something close to life, while the humdrum realities of this world were endowed with at least that minimum of charm which the aristocratic taste of the time required. Although some distance lies between them, the goddesses of Tiepolo and the kitchen maids of Chardin belong to the same world.

So long as this firm ordering of things held the pretensions of artists in check and satisfied the demands of the public, it prevented any usurpation by the one sphere of the territory of the other. At the end of the eighteenth century, however, the frontiers became indistinct. The material and formal hierarchy could no longer assert itself. Every pictorial category began disputing its place with its rival. The ideally beautiful found itself on the defensive against what were essentially subjective expressions of character. No supreme category was any longer acknowledged nor was there now a firm belief in absolute beauty or a style in which contradictories could be reconciled. There was only a multiplicity of historical 'models'. Artists now felt that they were called upon to put their true selves onto the

23 PROUDHON Joséphine Beauharnais; 1805.

24 SCHICK Frau von Cotta; 1802.

25 INGRES Mademoiselle Rivière; 1805.

26 CANOVA Pauline Bonaparte; 1808.

canvas and seized upon whatever subject – or object – they felt to be most nearly akin to their inner ego. They were, one might add, quite as arbitrary in the selection of their formal medium. This is as true of the classicists as of the realists, and of the pseudo-Gothic-mongers as of the Pre-Raphaelites.

I must underline this fact once more. It was the determination of the artist, a determination with deep moral roots, that provided the driving power which effected the breach between the ideal and the real and led to the divorce between history and life – and indeed when each of the two ways of seeing things began to proclaim its autonomy that divorce was inevitable. The artist's urge to be a law unto himself had a twofold effect. In some cases it led him to be as faithful as he could to his momentary empirical experience of the real world and to any genuinely spontaneous inspiration; in others it impelled him to claim for his own the legacy of the past, its stylistic media and subject-matter. All that happened during the century can be explained in terms of these two divergent aims. The artist – so the realists and Impressionists claimed – must speak the language of his time. The idealists prescribed exactly the opposite. The artist, they alleged, should take his vocabulary from the past, for true art is dependent on guidance from historical models. Both sides professed with equal vehemence to be in search of the original and spontaneous springs of art.

Theodor Hetzer, when writing on Goya, spoke of the crisis in art in about 1800. There can be no doubt that at about the turn of the century a note of polemical acrimony entered into purely artistic judgements which communicated itself to innovators and critical reactionaries alike. Portrait, land-scape and historical painting all got involved in this conflict of views. Bourgeois positivism insisted on closeness to nature, on direct contact with the subject, and on an awareness of the world before the artist's eyes; it insisted on the artist becoming subjectively involved with his subject. Those of the opposite view appealed to the authority of the ancients who had set up standards valid for all time, within the limits of which the artist should do his work.

In the famous debate between Goethe and Schadow on the threshold of the new century, this conflict assumed the concrete form of thesis and antithesis.[11] The mature poet, now firmly established on the Olympus of classicism, forgot that he himself had once insisted on the artist's freedom to look upon 'the face of his beloved, his boots, or the world of antiquity'.[12] He now complained that the old models were being disregarded, and demanded unconditional subjection to absolute beauty. The angry remonstrance he directed towards the artists in Berlin leaves no doubt of his displeasure or of his serene contempt for the contemporary trend as a whole. In Berlin, he alleged, the 'prosaic spirit of the age' was most clearly manifested; there poetry was extruded by history, the portrait was taking the place of character and the ideal, and mere patriotism was usurping that of the human and universal.

To this Schadow replied that whoever 'correctly and faithfully imitates' is on the right road to beauty, that a perfection which is only dreamed of and assumed, can do nothing but lead us astray, that art is essentially a national thing, and that the artist must follow his inner voice. 'I prefer Hogarth to Fuseli', says Schadow, 'because he expresses the national spirit.' The controversy between the poet and the sculptor is of outstanding significance in so far as it summarizes the artist's problems in about 1800. Certainly it is quite as eloquent of the general state of affairs as are the pictures painted about this time in the different countries of Europe.

4

The new passion for facts spelt the end of the belief in the miraculous. In the nineteenth century the supernatural is no more than a product of subjective fantasy. 'The time is no more', said the father of Heinrich von Ofterdingen, 'when divine visions are a part of our dreams, and we are and shall always be unable to understand just what were the feelings of those chosen men of whom the Bible tells. In those days there must have been something very different about dreams, as indeed there was about human affairs in general. In this our present age there is no longer any direct communication with heaven. Today the ancient tales and writings are the only sources from which a knowledge of the supernatural world – in so far as we need it – can be obtained. Now, instead of any such explicit revelations, the Holy Ghost speaks to us through the understanding of wise and well-disposed men, and through the lives and destinies of the pious. Our modern pictures of the miraculous have never greatly edified me nor have I ever believed in the mighty deeds which the clergy have related. Even so, if anyone else is edified, I would not seek to prevent him from being, nor would I ever seek to disturb any man in his faith.'

Such a picture of the miraculous by a wise and well-disposed man is Ingres' 'Louis XIII's vow' (1824), (plate 94). The visionary spirit is lacking. The earthly confronts the heavenly, and there is no connecting element between them. Before the king – and before the observer – there appears, not the mother of God, but an image reflected by the memory of revered prototypes and enlivened by quotations from Raphael. The petty virtuosity of detail leaves one with the embarrassed feeling that one is looking at an altar picture which in some way has suddenly acquired a third dimension – a masterpiece of illusion no doubt, a pictorial tour de force. But there is no miracle here to overwhelm the soul. Surely Venturi was right when he spoke of this painting as a *genre* picture.

We know that Ingres was not too happy about this commission which had been given him by his native city of Montauban. He recognized that he had to unite two different subjects, and his imagination, disciplined as it was by the Aristotelian doctrine of the unities, sought for some means of combining two historically disparate events – the vow of the king and the Assumption of the Blessed Virgin. Some donated pictures of the Italian School which might perhaps have provided a measure of guidance, seemed to him to be useless for his purpose by reason of their anachronisms. He complained that the dress of the seventeenth century lacked pictorial beauty. He was in Italy when the commission reached him, and not the least of his worries was the difficulty he experienced in finding in that country the historical documentation he required.[13]

Thanks to his sense of history he found himself beset by problems, as indeed is all too evident from the picture. The vision of the Divine falls apart into two disparate historic events. Idea and reality no longer coincide. Knowledge extrudes faith. The 'direct intercourse with heaven' has come to an end.

The weight of earthly things had become too great, and now doubt together with a mixture of uncertainty and good will had caused a chasm to open up between this world and the next. It is clear that empirical knowledge had caused the certitudes of salvation in the Christian scheme to be called in question. They became a territory in which man had lost his way. The complex and variegated nature of the material world no longer squared with Holy Scripture. The 'old models' that fitted the Christian world plan well enough, that acted as a kind of summary of all it stood for and so played their part in giving a specific meaning to history, had lost their compulsive power – man was in fact discovering how completely his life and history were of this present world. A new dimension entered into man's image of himself and the knowledge grew upon him that it was the material world from which he had come and over which his past was deployed; and now he began to realize how active a part he had played in the shaping of that past, how positive in word and deed had been his reaction to events, and how vast were the records of his activities that he had left behind. A historical, empirical, and essentially secular view of the world was from now on to replace the dogmatic pattern fashioned by religion.

The new mood received a powerful stimulus from the world of letters.[14] At the time when historical accuracy was being raised to the critical touch-stone of painting, Voltaire broke down the barriers which the Christian dogmatic scheme had till then imposed, and which till then had separated sacred history from secular. All things, as Meinecke says, were now on a dead level, all things were equally interesting and potentially subject to the same criticism. It was this spirit that was now infecting the arts; the secularization of history had assisted the development there of an analogous trend, causing the arts to reject the allegorical and supra-temporal stage directions to which it had hitherto been subject.

Voltaire's work is also significant in another particular, for it was he who brought all manner of details, especially those relating to manners and morals, within the purview of the historian and so endowed the past with a liveliness that was wholly new. This tendency too is found in the art of the period and it was to produce an important consequence, for the more individualized the past became, and the more distinctively the characteristics of any period were portrayed, the more sharply the present stood out in relief. The new mode of experiencing history called into being a more concrete awareness of the contemporary world.

There was yet another contributory factor that helped to produce this fundamental change of outlook – the French Revolution, which served as a kind of mark or datum-line dividing present and past. Löwith has put the matter with admirable succinctness. 'It was', he writes, 'the French Revolution that, by reason of its destruction of tradition, first had this peculiar historicizing effect: it caused its own age, in contrast to all that had gone before, to feel that it was part of the contemporary world and to conceive of itself as looking forward to the future.'[15] Whether one declared oneself to be a man of this 'today' or execrated it, is of course neither here nor there. The essential thing is that past and present were divided.

Yet, as I have pointed out, the very fact that they excluded one another with ever greater violence, caused the distinctive character of each to stand out in sharper relief; and their very antagonism showed how vividly that character was appreciated. The man who flies from the present proves that he has a sharply outlined conception of the nature of that present, and he who casts himself for the part of a contemporary painter takes up an unmistakably polemic attitude and sets his face unequivocally against the past.

All this caused both past and present to become 'historicized', and marked with the stamp of their time. If the older painters knew nothing of the scruples of conscience which this process imposed upon the artist, this merely shows how naïve was their attitude, an attitude that left them undisturbed by any nagging appetite for archaeological exactitude where historical painting was concerned. In that world of fair appearances, still gently breathed on by the winds of myth, it was not historical fidelity but mere inspired guesswork that reigned supreme.

It was left to the eighteenth century finally to make an end of all this. It fetched the actors of the drama of history down from the stage, and brought them into the glaring light of day where they could be seen acting their piece in the midst of a known and recognizable world and in a particular and recognizable period of time, and where all ambiguity or imprecision about these things had been out-lawed. And immediately the older school of historical painting with its makeshifts and compromises seemed to acquire a kind of opera-house unreality and to be cursed with a total lack of objective veri-similitude. Now the artist, if he hoped to survive the critics, was compelled to load himself down with documented details of manners and costume, and it is symptomatic of the whole process that David should confess in a note on his 'Rape of the Sabine Women' to having set himself the aim of reproduc-ing the antique way of life with such meticulous care that if Greeks or Romans were to stand before his pictures, they would recognize in them the work of one thoroughly familiar with their usages.[16]

Thus the artist's endeavour was to look even on the past with the unerring gaze of an eye-witness: yet the more faithful he remained to the colouring of a particular period, the thinner the symbolic content of his picture became. David's huge Coronation picture and Ingres' 'Napoleon in his Coronation robes' (plate 6) never get beyond a vast display of costume; in fact they do not attempt to reach that symbolic sphere to which the imperial office belongs. Where there is such absorption in documentary detail, symbolism must needs disappear and retire to an antipodean position where it can seek complete imaginative freedom. Idea and reality fall asunder.

Yet symbolism refused to lie down without a struggle – indeed it was still very far from being dead. While West and Copley sought to make an actual historial event come alive before our eyes, James Barry filled his 'Death of General Wolfe' with classical gestures.[17] He was fully aware, however, of the dilemma in which he had got involved – a dilemma which drove him to some curious expedients. He first painted his figures in the nude and then clothed them in the uniformes of the time in order to demonstrate – at least so it was said – that there were here two irreconcilables which it was impossible to combine. Barry's 'spiritual portraiture' was further developed by Blake. Freed from the costume and all other features that belonged to a particular period of history, the divine nature of the Great Man was to stand forth unveiled and unconcealed (plate 7). Canova's statue of the nude Napoleon is another example of the trend in art. The majesty of a ruler of men seemed something that pertained to the ideal and was therefore irreconcilable with the dress of any particular time.[18]

Actually the conflict between the human-universal and the historical-particular had already brought the whole question of the representation of the nude human body into the argument. Once again idea and reality were ranged on opposite sides. Naked man is man eternal, man who belongs to all time; clothed man belongs to a specific period of history, and his clothing is the clothing of his age. The one represents all humanity, the other represents but his own time. Both modes of representation found their defenders. For those who admired the antique ideal, it was inconceivable that it should have a frock-coat or a pair of knee-breeches superimposed upon it. Their opponents regarded any such exaltation of undraped physical prowess as utterly outmoded.[19]

The classical form being inappropriate to that day and age, it automatically acquired the remoteness of a museum-piece; and it seemed as though anyone who believed that the Greeks had for all time established an exclusive claim to absolute beauty, would be compelled, if he was to remain possessed of that beauty, to banish himself from the contemporary world. Ultimately such well-nigh religious veneration for the canons of the antique could only breed a sense of helplessness and confusion. Those affected by it no longer had confidence in their own time or even in their own more recent history, and, if they held the 'naturalness' of the ancients in special honour, could only view their own age as a costumed masquerade, a thing made stiff by a riot of conventions and pretences which stifled all that was original in man. 'What are we now to fashion?' asked Herder in 1778. 'Plants, trees, scorpions? The compliments we pay each other? Our clothes? Nature has gone from amongst us and has hidden herself. Art and rank, mechanism and patchwork are there. Yet it seems to me that these can be fashioned in neither wax nor clay. Let a man go into our market-places, into our churches and halls of justice, into our drawing-rooms and houses with a desire to model or carve. Carve what? Chairs or men? Crinolines? Gloves? A bunch of feathers on somebody's head? Ceremonies?'[20] Herder's words exemplify a strong though negative awareness of the present; they suggest that the thought of his own time inspired the speaker with distaste amounting to positive embarrassment. The antique norm would have nothing to do with the pedestrian affairs of our artificial world, it turned aside to a higher and essentially poetical reality.

The converse of course was equally true. The humdrum of the here and now insulated itself against all surreptitious penetration by the classical ideal. One of the chapters of Stendhal's *History of Painting in Italy* seeks to establish the thesis 'That Beauty in the antique mode is incompatible with modern passions'. The two things acted upon each other. The man who was guided by the ancient models could no longer leave his mark on the contemporary scene, while he who sought to make a

27 C. D. FRIEDRICH Monastery burial-ground under snow; 1810.

28 KLENZE Valhalla.

9 TURNER The opening of Valhalla; 1843.

30 BLECHEN Ruined Gothic church; c. 1835.

31 MOLLER Design for the rebuilding of Cologne Cathedral; 1813.

32 SCHINKEL Medieval town on a river; 1815.

reality of the 'modern ideal' was forced to abjure the classic forms. 'There was once a time', says Stendhal, 'when beauty communicated itself to the mind in strong living forms; today it chooses to express itself in elegance, in the witty mobility of the mind, in the despair of loneliness (which the ancients never knew), and in restlessness of the passions. In antiquity all was achieved through the man, our modern taste lets the woman triumph. Today we have more admiration for strength of the soul than for power of the body.'

In view of all this, it is easy to understand why in the nineteenth century the propriety of the nude ceased to be taken for granted and why nakedness began to be felt to be provocative. People stood before it embarrassed and unfree. When Stendhal observes that the people of his time felt shocked by the nude, he is not expressing some Nazarene conception of chastity, rather he is giving utterance to his belief that the 'modern ideal' is irreconcilable with antiquity's undraped picture of psychically undifferentiated manhood. The artificial civilization of the nineteenth century was no longer sufficiently ingenuous to see in the nobility of the naked body the signature of the divine and the symbol of nature unspoiled. Naked man, whether or no he be true to the classical ideal, had become nothing more than man undressed. The undraped was no longer something that could be taken for granted. Its mythical and magic powers had disappeared. 'On the one side the bloodless, smooth and frozen beauty of the classical age, on the other the life of the undraped, the drastic, and the ugly.'[21]

Nudity raised to high significance, and nudity which is nothing more than the nudity of the undressed – both kinds made men ill at ease, both kinds created a stir, a sensation. Napoleon, who knew well enough what kind of a public figure a Caesar should cut, was disturbed in just such a fashion when Canova convinced him that his statue in Milan would have to follow the classical example and dispense with any clothing whatsoever.[22] His sister Pauline probably experienced fewer scruples about posing in the nude and may well have enjoyed the stir she caused by doing so (plate 26). Wherever nudity could not come to terms with anaemic propriety of manners, it acted as an irritant and a challenge. This is as true of Goya's 'Recumbent nude' (plate 119) as it is of Ingres' 'Turkish bath', of the model in Courbet's 'L'atelier' as of the seated figure in 'Le déjeuner sur l'herbe' (plate 123); it is even true of Makart's 'Charles V's entry into Antwerp' (plate 88).

5

The conflict unleashed by the divorce between the universal and the particular extended to landscape, and here too the great debate and the more searching process of self-questioning and self-examination was continued with unabated force.

A year after his 'Marat', David was imprisoned in the Palais du Luxembourg. He seized the opportunity to paint what he could and his 'View of the Luxembourg Gardens' was the result (plate 33). Here the painter looks behind the façade, he refuses to paint cultivated nature, nature composed by man; instead he paints something at the edge of things, something the landscape-gardener has forgotten. Like his 'Marat', this too is a kind of 'cut-out'. Like the picture of the dead politician, it dispenses with rhetorical gestures, with the niceties of decorative balance. In both instances we have a pictorial indiscretion, a peep through a keyhole – admittedly only a pretended peep – in one case at a man who has been murdered, in the other at a back yard, at a segment of 'undressed' nature. As to composition, even from the point of view of highlighting and emphasis there is less of it in the landscape than in 'Marat'.

The usual circumstances in which it was painted may have helped bring this about, yet that a painter should have given in to those circumstances, that he should have neglected every compositional embellishment, that he should have stressed in his picture the tensionless horizontal strips that shut out the view – all this is significant enough. There is no unfolding of the background. There is no movement from its depths towards the edges of the picture – it is all 'just there' and reproduced as it was. An indifferent piece of nature that makes no pretensions at being decorative and is wholly lacking in any kind of charm, a bare piece of earth in the foreground, stiffly contained by a fence, a few strips of vegetable garden, the trees irregularly disposed – the emphasis is on what there is in it of the cut-out, on the fortuitous and the irregular.

I have already said that the great schism did not spare the landscape painter's art; here too, then, as can well be imagined when we reflect on such work as that just described, the eye-witness found himself in conflict with the stage-manager. Men driven by the urge to set down a reality which they had personally experienced, could see nothing but clichés in the traditional forms of painting, in pictures whose gay façades concealed for some a complete lack of content: 'What an overloading with objects', Friedrich once remarked, 'and yet how empty and dead is the whole. The picture is like a huckster's stall with things lying heaped up and higgledy-piggledy. Nothing has any proper relation to anything else.'[23] Just as the arbiters of Weimar swore by 'the ideal portrait of character' (das Charakter-Idealporträt), while their opponents insisted that a portrait should show 'the limited and personal qualities of the individual concerned' (das Beschränkte und Persönliche des Individuums) – and even made this the 'foundation and touchstone of the historical painting'[24] – so in the painting of landscapes the emphasis was now on what was near at hand, clearly defined, and of unmistakable identity rather than on the poetical 'nowhere in particular' of the idealist school.

The idealist landscape painters, however, were not content with a mere 'limitation of nature'; they strove to sublimate and purify her, to extract from the real world's mass of fleeting data what was lasting and permanent. There is admittedly no such thing as an ideal of a beautiful tree, but this type of artist could always fall back on some idealized and poetic composition of natural scenes. This was precisely what the 'naturalists' set their faces against. 'There is no such thing as universal tree', said Lavater, 'there are only particular trees'; while Constable said that 'art is to be found under every hedge, and in every lane' (*Letters to C. R. Leslie, R. A., 1826 - 1837*, London, 1931).

In the end this deepened sense of landscape brought about the development of two schools or trends. The first of these devoted itself to the examination of reality. It opted for 'pure seeing' and declared that 'painting is a science, and should be pursued as an inquiry into the laws of nature' (Leslie: *Memoirs*). Constable, the author of this argument, gave a warning against overloading nature with extraneous conceits after the manner of, say, Ruysdael who treated a landscape as an allegory on human life and expected the beholder to treat rocks, ruins and water as fraught with symbolic meaning. 'How are we to discover this?' asks the worthy 'naturalist'.[25] Yet did he not paint an essentially mythical landscape himself that was demonstrably on the borders of the symbolic? (plate 15).

The other school was bent on seeking out the mysterious correspondences which sometimes exist between certain states of mind and certain of nature's moods. Even men of this persuasion, however, could not dispense with all fidelity to nature. Even they were compelled, in the words used by Carus[26] about Friedrich, to dip their hands 'into the tangled mess of the stale, prosaic and humdrum' (in den Wust des Alltäglichen, Prosaischen und Abgestandenen); yet behind the actual image on the canvas there existed for them – if only subjectively – a meaning which gave the whole its raison d'être, which justified it at least to themselves as a work of art. The landscape thus became a mirror of the inner mind. The life of the spirit and the life of nature were things related. Runge insisted that landscape as a pictorial category had begun to replace historical painting, and saw in the former one of the 'pinnacles' of the art to come.[27] Amiel was later to coin the famous phrase in which he referred to landscape as 'a spiritual state' (an 'état de l'âme'). In landscape painting the subjective impression and the painter's ideal conception of nature can come together.

From their first beginnings in the early days of the century, both parties – those who regarded landscape as an 'impression' and those who regarded it as a symbol – discarded traditional pictorial forms. Like David in his garden picture, Constable, Bonington and Friedrich all refrain from using the customary props to support the general design. The whole area of the picture tends to grow more empty. They appeal through the suggestion of more elemental things.

This process of simplification imposed the strictest discipline of form in the work of Friedrich, and the commentary of Heinrich von Kleist on Friedrich's 'Monk on the seashore' (plate 13) has become famous. 'The picture with its two or three mysterious objects lies before us like an apocalypse. It is as though it had Young's 'Night-Thoughts', and since with all its monotony and sense of infinite distance there is nothing in the forefront of the painting but the frame, the effect on the observer is that he feels as though his eyelids had been cut away. It must be admitted that the artist has blazed a new trail in his art.'

These remarks contain no more than the truth. Certainly a new road was opened here. The vast area of space in the background is no longer coterminous with the edges of the picture and appears to be of infinite extension. The picture is not 'composed' at all. The limits of the actual painting, the lines of the frame, are in no way identical with those of the artist's imaginative field of vision. One feels that this bare strip of beach continues without end, that it is in front of us, next to us, and behind us. Thus Friedrich too is painting a 'cut-out', but he is monumentalizing it into something that, maintaining a continuous uniformity, surrounds the observer like a wall. It is this element of endless uniformity that is the new pictorial medium, and it is this that imparts its peculiar solemnity to the work. The emphasis on the horizontal helps to drive home this note of monotony. The background, divided into sections though it is, gives a sense of limitless depth, yet there is no penetration into depth on the part of any human being. The depth shown in this picture is something wholly remote from man, something against which he cannot measure himself. It does not arch over him as the backgrounds of pictures once did, backgrounds that may on occasion have been as limitless as this one but still somehow remained within the bounds of perspective. Here, however, there is an endlessness that is a threat to man, it is something to which he is exposed and cannot adapt himself. The narrow bit of ground on which he is placed contracts to nothing, if compared with the devouring immensity of the sky. By means of the very vastness he allows the latter to assume, the painter withdraws it from man and exalts it into something wholly alien to him. No pathway of perspective leads into the picture, there are no pieces of scenery to act as mediators with the observer. The monk whose figure is here the measure of the magnitudes conveyed to the mind, seems distant to the point of inaccessibility. So distant is he from us that it would seem impossible even to approach him. When we look at him, our gaze seems to cross an invisible chasm. There is about this picture something that suggests a monologue, a monologue that none but the speaker is there to hear; it is a symbol of the isolation of the creature that can no longer assert itself against nature, that no longer has any part in what happens in the natural world but stands as a mere observer at the edge of it. This picture is indeed an apocalypse.

'Chalk cliffs at Rügen' (colour plate II), also by Friedrich, at first creates the impression that the artist had thought better of it and returned to the conventional principles of composition. Yet it is precisely in this picture that the sense of space – which seems to assault the mind with all its form-destroying power – is more strongly felt than in many another painting in which the quality of monotony is quite undisguised. The three human figures take up the forefront of the picture and are placed at the very edge of the precipice. Then in the middle distance, without any kind of link or transition, the chalk cliffs tower upward. Their bizarre formations have a flat and thin appearance; they have no bodily quality. Behind them, again without any kind of transition or connecting element, lies the sea. No horizontal line defines the limit of its extent. Once again man is cut off from nature and is a mere spectator at its edge. The sky seems to rush downwards, and there is nothing to check or arrest it as it falls. In the zone of the rocks it seems positively to crash into them. It is as though a force irrupting out of space were actually shaping their outlines. It is not the rocks that thrust their jagged points and reefs upwards by the strength of some power residing within themselves. It is the sky that possesses the initiative. It is the sky that both moulds and destroys the forms. So great is the power of this boundless sky that its very emptiness has substance in it. The sky seems actually to be a bodily thing.

If the picture is placed upside down, its negative form resembles a set of mountain peaks. It is well known that some of the painter's contemporaries did accidentally reverse his pictures in this fashion, and Goethe in one of his severer moods sharply criticized Friedrich's 'Verkehrtheit'[28] – a word with an unfortunate double meaning, since it conveys the idea of what may be called 'wrong-way-roundness', and also that of perversity, or even absurdity. But there is no 'Verkehrtheit' about this picture which superbly expresses the sense of the remoteness of the universe from man, the utter detachment of the vast space portrayed in it from the world of the observer's experience. It is a mood that we shall encounter again and again.

6

It was in the works of Goya that art-historians pinpointed the characteristic features of art at the turn of the century. They were the disintegration of spatial continuity as established by perspective, and the transformation of the background into something like a void. Let us select as an example his 'Lunatic asylum' (1800) (plate 50). What reminds us of 'Marat' here is that the human figures are all contained in the lower half of the picture. This relegation stresses all that is inarticulate and sombre in these lives that are so hopelessly out of adjustment with the world around them. The people in the picture are either gesticulating, solely for the benefit of themselves, or, alternatively, have degenerated into inert clods. Those of the latter type are helplessly crowded together on a narrow stage which completely lacks any organic connection with the background. At the point where the floor should have joined the walls, there is a yawning void. To the right the background seems to dissolve into limitless distance. Its few curves and arches are arranged in parallel. They are aligned bluntly one next the other. There is no application of the rules of normal perspective, no foreshortening. The background simply sinks away – one might almost say that it oozes away – in between walls of stage-scenery. This background represents something that to man is alien and unfamiliar. It repels him or draws him into the labyrinth of its pits and recesses. There is discord between that background and man – there is enmity. It is precisely this last that, radically emphasizing as it does the exclusive reality of the temporal world, distinguishes the 'Lunatic asylum' from the older models.

Goya's painting shows how utterly beyond the reach of salvation or any kind of redeeming grace are the people he portrays. Their gestures are made in emptiness. They connect with nothing. Here are no echoing forms that respond to one another with a rhythmic answer. All connection with the surrounding world has been destroyed. While man sinks down under his own physical weight and seems to be fettered to the ground, the third dimension assumes the threatening form of infinity. These great arches are endless, yet they provide no way of escape.

Here we touch on the feature that, more than any other, stamps its peculiar character on this world. There is no escape from it and no escape from the isolation it imposes. The forms no longer converse with one another, the human beings in it have fallen back into monologue. Nothing now connects the individual with his surroundings or with his neighbour. How admirably the note which Goya attached to the sixth of his Caprichos fits the 'Lunatic asylum': 'El mundo es una máscara; el rostro, el trage y la voz, todo es fingido. Todos quieren aparentar lo que no son, todos engañan y nadie

se conoce.'²⁹ (The world is a masquerade. Face, clothing, voice – all is a lie; everyone seeks to appear what he is not, all deceive one another, and no one knows himself.) We have reached the point where the old pictorial forms have utterly ceased to serve the artist's purpose, for these were still concerned with a type of man for whom the world was a familiar place where he could pass his days in confidence, and in which he could find his way. In Goya this present world is all confusion and is cut off entirely from the world beyond.

More forcibly than anyone else, the great Spaniard expressed the new element that became discernible in art at this critical point of time; and with lifelong perseverance he carried the logic of the matter to its ultimate conclusions. The new trail blazed by Friedrich confined itself to the creation of new forms of landscape painting, while David was soon to barter his tremendous revolutionary drive for the methods of an official eclectic routineer and so exchange 'life' for 'history' – for history is the place of exile for those who seek to create a pictorial cloak for the loneliness of man, a cloak which will hide his bondage to the temporal world. In contrast to that of such men as these, Goya's all-embracing genius found expression in every category of painting. He invented landscapes that were nothing less than symbols of the emptiness of the real world. He painted still-lifes in which the object portrayed was represented as crudely material, as a thing with no relevance outside its own material confines.

Above all, he revolutionized the whole conception of design and composition. With Goya there disappeared something whose presence had assured historical continuity in European painting from the Renaissance down to Fragonard – who died in 1804, incidentally. With Goya there disappeared the arabesque, the draughtsman's calligraphy, the rounded flowing harmony which unites men with objects, objects with landscape, and the lifeless with the living. It was with Goya that every constituent element in a picture began to exist wholly by itself. Moreover, his draughtsmanship, to quote Malraux, 'finally destroyed something which had permitted whole centuries to make an ornament of the most ill-graced object and turn it into a symbol of harmony.'³⁰ It broke with the Baroque's flow of line and with the curling and coquettish ornamentation of the eighteenth century. It discarded all that smacked of formulas, it avoided all the nicely corresponding formal grooves, and won a new stratum of experience for the artist to master and mould – the creature's isolation and decay, an isolation which was nonetheless filled to the brim with life.

Goya represents a summit but he was not an exception to the rule. We have only to glance at David and Friedrich to realize that. On the other hand, we must not suppose that the breach between this world and the next, between the near and the distant, between sensible experience and imagination, was something with which only those artists were concerned who consciously set themselves against the old pictorial forms. Even while painters still believed themselves to be adhering to these, one could already detect a dissonant element in the pattern and composition of pictures. There was a loss of the old relationship which once combined figures, human and other, plane surfaces, and background into a single unity. Actually this trend was already discernible – in the last quarter of the preceding century – in Fuseli's drawings.³¹ Later it was to become apparent in Blake.

Fuseli makes use of the classical heritage of form, and yet he makes use of it in a fashion that is peculiarly his own. The figures no longer seem to tread a solid common ground. There is a breaking up of the picture's spatial continuity. The distances portrayed are vague, imprecise, and no longer susceptible of measurement. The relative magnitudes of the different figures are governed by no clear principle. They are, as it were, torn out of their proper spatial *loci*, and drawn onto the front of the stage. The picture itself still permits us to have the normal experience of space, but the actors in it have forfeited their places in the three-dimensional setting, a setting which itself is still taken for granted. As a legatee of the heritage of the linear arabesque, Fuseli naturally reacted to his pictorial problem in a different way from Goya. He lets the figures that have been torn out of their spatial setting weave about, as it were, in the flat, or joins them together in a kind of curving garland.

7

Those who employ the accepted distinctions of style-analysis tend to rely in this matter on the elasticity of their terminology, and, seizing on certain isolated characteristics of classicism, regard the paintings of David, Goya, and Friedrich as coming under that head. In such cases they point to the different layers of relief in the background and to the isolation of all three-dimensional bodies. It is quite wrong, however, to apply the term 'classicism' – which must of necessity imply an effort to recapture bygone forms – to works of art which deliberately seek to break with the past, to works of art the whole weight of whose essential significance lies in the fact that they point towards the future. Such a procedure argues an over-narrow point of view and is peculiar to men under a perpetual compulsion to look over their shoulders at a bygone age. What such critics fail to grasp is that the pictures here under review were begotten of a deep disturbance of the artistic consciousness of the time. The faith in the old models had disappeared. Man suddenly knew that he was alone in the world, he knew that he was thrown back upon himself. He had come to experience the terrifying burden of the knowledge that he was part of this present world of matter and that no one could save him from his captivity. All inter-course with other worlds had been broken off. If man was now to find his bearings in this one, he could only attempt to do so by seizing on fragments, on such disconnected parts of it as chanced to make their impact upon him (plates 33–43).

The marks of this process of orientation show themselves in the feeling that both the observer and such parts of the world as he observes, are things cut off and isolated, that there is no longer in this disorder a clear path leading to any discernible goal. Man is alone with himself in a world in which he stands orphaned and unprotected and has no firm hold on anything at all. Because he lacks such a hold on anything, he has no hold upon himself, and it is precisely this that is so evident in the pain-ting of Goya, David, and Friedrich. The root cause of it all is to be found in the sense of insecurity and danger that is bound up with this new way of experiencing the world, and it is this that drives the artist into that radical form of expression which his work now assumes. Never before had the crude fact of a man's being dead been made to hit the observer between the eyes as it did in David's painting of the murdered Marat. Never before had a piece of landscape been reproduced that was so palpably a fragment torn arbitrarily out of the living world, as was that corner of the Luxembourg garden. Never till then had any picture shown man so solitary, so helplessly exposed to the universe as was that monk by the sea. Around his isolated figure is 'the cold iron mask of formless eternity' (Jean Paul).[32] There is no longer a clothing for created things, and the human creature stands shivering at the edge of an infinity which opens up beyond him, alien to all that pertains to man. Man walks alone or – as in the 'Lunatic asylum' – is sucked up into a collectivity and banished into a hell that belongs wholly to the temporal world.

The poet whose visions most nearly reproduce this sense of a dreadful abyss in which man has been utterly forsaken by God, is Jean Paul. The poem in question is his *Rede des toten Christus vom Weltgebäude herab daß kein Gott sei* (Declaration of the dead Christ from the top of the World Edifice that there is no God) – a dream which, after letting him experience all the agonies of one driven into separation from God, enables the dreamer on awakening to find his way back to the haven of the Faith. 'We are all orphans – you as much as I. We have no father.' So Christ calls out to the dead children. 'How lonely is each one of us in the great sepulchre of the universe.' It is this feeling that man is utterly alone and that there is no redemption from his loneliness, that marks the birth of the nineteenth century. It was from this zero mark that it had to set forth in its effort gradually to come to terms with the world, to learn to treat it as a friend and sublimate its material crudeness.

In this situation art was forced into an unrestrained self-assertion. Sheer despair compelled it to centre its whole faith upon itself. It no longer possessed a hold in any other world, and for that very reason it had nothing save itself to stake, or believe in. If it was to survive, it had to expend the whole of its power in the attempt. It was the beginning of a century of mighty striving, striving which often made greater demands on the individual than he could bear. 'Art, when it becomes free and is released from both the compulsion and the prop of religion, must from that moment depend upon itself.' So writes Fernow in his monograph on his friend Carstens.[33] This goes to the heart of the matter. The bondage has been rejected and the prop along with it. In its enhanced self-awareness and self-confidence art could no longer endure the status of pupilage. It had now to make its own decisions.

53 DAVID View of the Luxembourg Gardens at Paris; 1794.

34
NIEPCE
View from his window; 1826
(the first photograph in the world)

35
STIFTER
View of the Beatrixgasse at Vienna; 1839.

36 CÉZANNE *Les toits* (view of Paris); c. 1880.

37 MENZEL View of an outlying quarter of Berlin; c. 1847.

38 COROT *Le pont de Mantes*; 1868–70.

39 CÉZANNE *Les marronniers du Jas de Bouffan*; 1885–87.

40 VAN GOGH *Jardin de la maison de santé à Arles*; 1889.

41 MANET *Les paveurs de la rue de Berne* (The Roadmenders); 1878.

42 MONET Pont de l'Europe; 1877.

43 SEURAT *Port en Bessin*; 1888.

IV   The Inner Compulsion

VERY early in the period here under review we can trace the beginnings of the quarrel which, among all the century's disputes in the matter of art, is easily the most important, and which even today remains unresolved. It is a quarrel of decisive importance, for it concerns nothing less than the nature and function of art itself and the difference between true art and false. It is the purpose of the pages that follow to describe the occasion out of which it arose and also to undertake, however tentatively, some kind of enquiry as to which side was in possession of the truth.

I

Art that has nothing to hold on to, nothing to direct or restrain it, must by that circumstance be both a gainer and a loser. Possessing, as it does, no firm tie with things, lacking a specific commission, having no sovereign but itself and no advocate but itself to confirm its rightness, it can only seek security and support within its own domain. Art thus becomes to itself a problem, a responsibility, and a theme.

Now this is precisely what had begun to happen in European art during the period in question, with the result that new strains, ever increasing in intensity, were placed on the artist's creative power. New impulses of a predominantly revolutionary kind were also admittedly released, the personal factor being called into more active life – indeed it was the personal element that now as often as not attained a decisive voice. Yet at times the effect was just the opposite. The artistic impulse was sometimes stifled, and the artist's sensibility weighed down so that he was actually deprived of his freedom. Art, which is for ever searching for itself and seeks to find in that process the justification of its own existence, is in perpetual peril of moving in a circle, it is profoundly restless and must forever be changing position. Yet in this very unrest lies its greatness, for this wide-ranging mobility calls for explorer's courage.

Even so, something more was entailed here. As Fernow had already observed before the eighteenth century had closed, art had now 'to strike root in its own soil',[1] it had henceforth to set its house in order in such manner as, in its own free judgment, it decided to be best. It had incurred a new responsibility. Its newly won right involved a positive duty – a duty of critical thought, of enhanced self-analysis and self-awareness.

While the artist sought to accustom himself to the idea of his own creative autonomy, while he was endeavouring to view this new freedom in its historical context, art came to find itself within the sphere of relevance of what were strictly scientific fields of enquiry. Aesthetics sought to hold fast the phenomenon of beauty within a framework of fixed conceptual terms and the art-historian became concerned to lay bare a clear sequence of historical development. Both of these last were aids to art which the eighteenth century had supplied, aids to an art that had been freed from the bonds by which it was once held captive, and could now orient itself along new lines.

If one is to attain a true understanding of oneself, a conscious effort is required. This is a truth that we should bear in mind when considering Hegel's diagnosis of the position of art in his day.[2]

As his *Aesthetics* show, Hegel had realized – and the discovery came none too soon – that art had won its freedom and he had ceased to be interested in any work of art that was limited by its subservience to any specific purpose; he was only interested in 'art which is free both in its ends and in its means.' Now it is perhaps remarkable that man should have discovered the freedom of art at that very moment when he began to subject it to the concepts of analytical thought; yet that is what happened, and art's new-won autonomy was thus converted into a new form of subservience – to a rule quite as arbitrary as any that had gone before. Autonomous art is of necessity an art that puts questions to itself, and so subjects itself to a new type of constraint.

Hegel was well aware of the new approach that all this involved. He contended that 'thought and the purely analytical function of the mind' (der Gedanke und die Reflexion) had overshadowed art. He also says, 'What is today stimulated by the contemplation of a work of art – apart from the sheer delight which it inspires – is our faculty of judgment, in so far as we submit to our considered scrutiny its content, the artistic means which it employs, and the appropriateness or otherwise of both to one another.' In view of art's own attitude towards itself this kind of thing was only to be expected. If the product of an art that has gained its autonomy steps into the witness-box to give evidence concerning itself, it becomes in a very special sense of the word 'questionable', for it is only proper that we should ask it questions.

It was in the midst of this highly critical development that art-history was born. It was the inescapable corollary of a development in art that was compelling men to concern themselves with artistic theory, and rousing them to an interest in the past. The art of the nineteenth century became aware of itself as a link in a historical chain. Even its most daring innovators, men deeply sensitive to the character of their time, tended to search the past for spiritual kinsmen and brethren in the faith. Art-history furnished these searchers of their own souls with the necessary documentation. The museums, themselves phenomena that are logically related to the basic trend, provided that documentation in visible form. Even realists and Impressionists, men who would occasionally be quite ready to set fire to the Louvre,[3] began going to school with the old Dutch and Spanish masters. In the galleries the painter encountered the historian and sometimes both stood before the same picture. Autonomous art could not dispense with these imaginary discussions with its ancestors, for these had now to replace the authority to which the artist had once been subject.

2

Aware that it had a history behind it, European art at the close of the eighteenth century found two different ways of presenting itself. Each of these led to one of the two Nietzschean polarities, 'Historie' – a word that can here only be rendered as history though this misses some of its overtones – and life. As he viewed the process which art-history described, the artist, like a good many others, was made conscious of past and present as two different fields of experience, and oddly enough this differentiation originated in the general outlook of historians themselves, as we shall see in a moment.

Along with the dogmas of religion, all other value-concepts which had once been held to have universal application lost their status of absolutes. Their validity became dependent on time and place. A special mode of life was now regarded as proper to every stage of culture; every form of polity, whatever its limitations, began to be accepted as being proper to its own special circumstances; every law of taste was looked on as an expression of its own age and of the conditions prevailing therein. The yardsticks of beauty, goodness and nobility became relative things. 'What was truth at one time represents error at another', writes Montesquieu.[4]

Art itself could not remain exempt from the general process of relativization. Yet despite this, the dynamism of its new essentially evolutionary and relativist concept of history was in actual fact continually being negated and checked. For the truth is that the very minds that were preparing the way for an organic and evolutionary interpretation of history were somehow inhibited where the realm of art was concerned from carrying their ideas to a logical conclusion, and took refuge in the dogmas of classicism; Montesquieu himself postulated a normative ideal of beauty. Winckelmann, the discoverer of the historical sequence of styles, did the same. Herder did so too, though he went so far as to admit that no two painters ever saw the same object in quite the same way.[5]

Now if everyone sees – and is allowed to see – things differently from everyone else, then art is an ever-varying but uninterrupted act of creation which must be carried out afresh with every work of art that comes into being. Man's course, as Carlyle says, 'can be the facsimile of no prior one, but is by its nature original'. Yet it was the chief characteristic of the historical approach that it shut its eyes to this fact. In order to give art some supra-personal and objective hold or reference point, it proclaimed new dogmas, dogmas which, as we shall see in a moment, were really full of a certain kind of wishful thinking. It sought to get at the formative principle behind every phase of history and culture, yet could not refrain from assessing what it scrutinized by the measure of some purely ideal conception. It thus involved itself in continual and hopeless contradictions.

The explanation of this curious phenomenon is however not difficult to find, for the truth is that the historical approach was largely rooted in a rejection of its own time and like every such movement was compelled to offer some positive substitute for the thing rejected. The more it denied the more vehemently it was driven to affirm. Meinecke stated the whole position with great clarity when he said that the very origin of *Historismus* was bound up with 'a malaise, a tendency to criticise the contemporary world and the spirit which informs it, all this being mingled with certain ideals concerned with a better kind of humanity and a better social order ...'

As with social theory, so it was with art, which in this particular was a peculiarly sensitive field. In both cases, however, one had a proliferation of perfectionist dogmatizing – with much the same results. 'The ideal,' to quote Meinecke again, 'which was once a source of power for the new *Historismus* was necessarily and from the very start a restraining influence on its development. It reintroduced a static element into the new dynamic treatment of history, since it threatened to make – and to a large extent really did make – past order, real or imagined, into the yardstick by which both past and present were assessed. Again and again, at the time when *Historismus* was beginning, the idea of a golden age acted both as a positive and as a restraining force upon pure and objective historical thought.'[6] These words might well be applied to art and its relation both to the bygone and the contemporary. This golden age could be identified with antiquity, the Renaissance or the Middle Ages. Those who truly believed in the present, however – and this for art was the decisive factor – would always identify it with their own time.

To recapitulate, the perspective of the historian tended to view things in two ways. He would endow a period of history with an organic unity of form, work out 'a point of view for every phase' and 'judge the individual in the light of what has preceded him and the character of his age.'[7] On other occasions, moving in a quite contrary direction and reversing the whole conception of an inner logic dominating each period, he would elevate a certain canon into a dogma of universal validity.

This divergence is already apparent in the eighteenth century. That century was admittedly seeking to discover the essence of every historical phase, for it assumed every such phase to have a unique organic life of its own. It did so in a manner that reminds us of a telling phrase in Ranke's

Politische Gespräche (Political Conversations). 'All life carried within itself its own ideal,'[8] an observation echoed by Wagner's, 'das Leben ist sich selbst ein Gesetz' – life is its own law. And yet it seemed inclined to contradict itself and impose quite arbitrarily an ideal of its own choosing upon every manifestation of life. Till the revolution that ideal lay in the past. As to the present it was treated as being in a state of rightless pupilage and it was to the past that it was sent to school. Here among the problems in which historicism involved itself is to be sought the origin of that discord which sprang up in the nineteenth century between history and life, between the present and the past.

3

Art, as we have seen, was profoundly affected by this fundamental schism. According as the artist identified himself with history or with life, with tradition or with the unproven and untried, he found that germ of primitive spontaneity which he sought, either in the ancient models, which allegedly bore the stamp of a beauty that can never vary, or in a process of organic unfolding which has nothing to do with history at all. For the first group art lay ready to hand; its final perfection had long since been attained. For the others the story of art was a story that had no ending: every individual could add to the sum of artistic creation some form or feature as yet unexpressed and undiscovered. Such new elements could neither be foreseen nor deduced, for the law that shaped them lay hidden in him that brought them forth. Whereas one type of artist surrendered himself to a dogma, the other refused to bow before an ideal, before something that claimed to have said the last word for all eternity.

In the former case, what Burckhardt calls the 'historische Generalrevision', the evaluation of history, took the initiative out of the individual's hands. He decided on a particular style from the past and obediently followed it: he slipped beneath this mantle of style that was held ready for him, and with the mobility of an eclectic made his appearance in this disguise. The outward guise thus assumed not only made any contact with the real world unnecessary but it even relieved him of the task of setting his own imagination to work. Ingres had no true vision of the Mother of God but merely a memory of the madonna types of Raphael. Nature herself was seen according to the manner in which a pre-existing work of art had prepared and arranged her. 'Vous apprendrez des antiques à voir la nature, parce qu'ils sont eux-mêmes la nature' – you will learn to see nature from the ancients, for they themselves are nature. Thus runs a saying of Ingres. When he declared that he was no innovator but merely sought to conserve and pass on the ancient teaching, he was uttering the *credo* of all artists who were thus fascinated by the past. Such men claimed to perform no more than mediatory functions, though they claimed a priestly dignity in their execution. Their claim to be artists rested on the punctilious service of the gods of their choice. 'After Phidias and Raphael nothing essential in art has yet to be discovered; none the less, there is still a task for their successors: the preservation of the cult of truth, the perpetuation of the tradition of beauty.'[9]

Thus on the one hand we have a cult, a dogma and an essentially religious veneration, and on the other an exaltation of the sure touch of original genius together with a complete rejection of all institutional thinking and all regimentation. To the latter way of thinking art was self-realization and not a form of divine worship, and yet although men of this persuasion would have nothing to do with the masking function of a historical style, they were for all that by no means blind to history. They merely refused to conserve the past as a lifeless dogma. What they desired was not to copy a ready-made formula but to make their own the glowing inspiration that lay concealed in an apparently formal gesture, and to appropriate for themselves the seemingly inexhaustible power that lay behind it. When a man like Gauguin can say of Raphael that we can observe the same feeling in his land-

scapes as we do in his portraits,[10] then what he refers to is simply Raphael's power of meaningful and coherent formal creation, a power that is indivisible, in the sense of being incapable of analysis, a power which must be felt as a natural growth that is all of one piece. Such a power cannot be reproduced by a mere humble borrowing of styles.

Obviously there was nothing like a hunger for history involved when Gauguin cast a backward glance at an old master. There was no concern here with any mere formula that could, so to speak, be peeled off from, or lifted out of, the work. What he sought to do was to absorb into himself the very pulse-beat of the living formal whole.

This conception of form is essentially organic in so far as it is not concerned with combinations of ready-made patterns but feels every act of creation as something unprecedented and unique. For there is nothing ready-made about form. It is not a thing that can be codified. Form is procreation and it develops according to its own inherent law, but it is not a thing bound by any fixed pattern. Form is like some growth of nature in that, as with the leaves of a tree, it never repeats itself like a mass-produced article, mechanically and without any kind of variation. Every form is unique. There is an echo of this truth in a saying of Friedrich's, 'The artist's feeling is his law. No single artist can be a yardstick for all, he can only be a yardstick for himself and for such spirits as have some kind of kinship with him.'[11] Baudelaire, quoting Lavater as his authority, declares, 'Every individual is a harmonious entity; therefore every individual has his ideal.'[12] It is not hard to understand why those who hold this essentially fluid conception of form could have no faith in a ready-made style or in any arbitrarily chosen model. Rather, they felt, must we search for criteria which will enable us to judge whether a particular form is right or not, and whether it is full or empty of meaning, in the unique individuality of the work of art concerned.

It is the mark of such an approach that it discerns and expresses a universal and dynamic relationship between things – and this is as good a reason as any for applying to it the term 'organic' to distinguish it as sharply as possible from all that pertains to *Historismus*. Form is now seen as an impulse that streams onward past the limits of any particular object and is compelled to exercise a mixing and melting influence. We see this in the work of Fuseli and Blake, as also in that of Delacroix. Ingres declares that the artist must even 'draw smoke', i.e., give it a clear separating outline. Everything must be translated into the graphic finality of the descriptive line. With the other kind of artist his vision and vital energy combine and even transform what he sees into new shapes and new relationships. Thus Delacroix observed that sand which the waves on the sea shore had formed into stripes resembled the markings on a tiger skin.[13] A twig, seen by itself, was like a tree; a piece of coal had the same formal characteristics as a mighty rock. The great is contained within the small. All things are related to one another.

4

Let me go backward a little and trace this fundamental schism to origins that lie buried even more deeply in the past.

With Ingres, as we have seen, the line separates, it distinguishes and defines. With Delacroix it combines, invents and romances. In the one case colour is applied with meticulous exactitude within the areas which the lines have surrounded and is smoothed down until all marks of the brush have been completely effaced. In the other, the texture of the paint is left exactly as it was when the paint was put on; the vibrating rhythm of the brush strokes is an actual part of the linear framework. Drawing and colour cannot be separated from each other here.

If we want a vivid illustration of the contrast between these two types of approach, we have but to read Goethe's rejoinder to Diderot's *Essay on Painting*. Diderot describes a painter before his easel, excited to the point of positive intoxication by the very sight of the untouched canvas. 'If a painter has a really lively feeling for colour, you will see him fix his eyes upon the bare cloth, snorting and with his mouth half open, while his palette is a picture of chaos. Into this chaos he dips his brush and draws forth from it the product of his creative power – as he sits down again you will see that which was in nature come alive upon the canvas.' Only he who can show a sort of spontaneous facility in the mastery of his colours can claim to be an artist at all, in Diderot's view. 'If after, say, a quarter of an hour's work, such order as there was (upon the palette) has not been brushed into complete confusion, then you may be sure that the artist is cold and that he will produce nothing of importance.'

Goethe may not be wholly off the mark when he speaks of the tomfoolery that often goes with a touch of genius ('fratzenhafte Genialität'), yet, for all that, he shows a strange lack of understanding. Claiming to speak for 'deutsche Gesetztheit', the balanced German view, he remarks, 'We ourselves have already declared it to be the artist's task to change, by a process of skilful and expert mixing, the character of the actual colours of the pigments while they are still separate, and to individualize and organize them in accordance with the character of the object to be represented; but whether it is necessary to do this in quite so wild and tumultuous a manner is a matter on which a thoughtful German may legitimately express his doubts.' This is the same person speaking as the man who in his *Sammler und die Seinigen* (The Collector and His Own) could grow enthusiastic about bold spontaneous brushwork, wildly applied, and with a touch of violence about it – 'das Kühne, Hingestrichene, wild Ausgetuschte, Gewaltsame'.

We should be on the wrong road, however, if we sought to discern in the differences between Goethe and Diderot an instance of some quarrel between the draughtsmen and the colourists. The tumultuous gesture is not something of which the brush alone is capable, there is also a draughtsman's *furioso* which needs no palette to communicate its excitement. But just as the pencil can communicate the artist's creative excitement, so can the brush on occasion betray a complete absence of it. There is a certain unmistakable smoothness of paint with no sign about it of anything like a flowing movement. The real contrast is not between pencil and brush but between two methods of formal expression, of which one has the effect of something open, variable and improvised, while the other seems concerned to achieve the last word in perfect execution and an impeccable structure of formal language.

Now perhaps we can see why the dynamic feeling of a Delacroix never got itself trapped in the stylistic vocabulary of the past – say of the Baroque – while the perfectionism of Ingres lapsed again and again into quotation, into the lifeless reproduction of past styles. It is also easy to recognize the gap that opened between the conscientiously recording naturalist and those painters who let their own act of creation remain visible in the picture. Even when the painter has laid down his brush, these 'open' pictures have about them an air of having just been begun which is curiously exciting; while in the case of the others there is a certain relevance in Whistler's epigram that though they were finished, they had never really been begun at all. What may be called the definitive form devotes itself either to the detailed imitation of nature or to the historical style (in Ingres and the Pre-Raphaelites we can find instances of both) while the variable form addresses its challenge to the artist's – and also the observer's – imagination.

As a result of this tension, two divergent forces had been operative since the end of the Middle Ages – one giving to art the shape that it was in general to assume for some time, the other, a disrupting and dissolving one, tending to stress the individual character of the artist concerned. The tension resulted from a difference – which dated from the Renaissance – in the means of formal expression. From the moment that the painting of pictures began to involve the making of preliminary sketches, studies and 'roughs', this practice was bound to affect certain phases of artistic development. The form taken by what was at first no more than a tentative essay, and the impress of the artist's personality that it inevitably carried, gradually came to be ends in themselves – the final goals of artistic achievement.

Till well into the eighteenth century, in fact as long as style – which still held all artists in its grip – acted as a mediating influence between opposing schools of thought, and as long as artistic creation aimed at a specific standard of perfection, and the clear finished articulate form was accorded a higher place than the product of a transient inspiration, however felicitous, for just so long the sketchlike mode of representation continued to be a mere preliminary to the final form that a painting was to assume. It was only when the concept of absolute beauty was compelled to abandon its sovereign and co-ordinating position, and the living quality of a work together with its unmistakable personal character became the supreme criterion, and when the objective standards of formal perfection, which till then had been taken as impersonal and absolute, became subject to attack by men whom an inner compulsion drove to assert their purely subjective certitudes – it was only then that artists began to pin their faith on one side or the other. The perfectionist now began to reject categorically what he regarded as an unfinished thing, while the other frowned at the articulately finished product which he regarded as being empty of life. The two things of which one had once followed, tandem fashion, after the other, were now harnessed as a pair and ran side by side. The conservative forces clung to the idea of the detailed, that is to say fully finished and perfected work, that articulates word for word, while their opponents favoured suggestion, approximation and summarizing abbreviation. They discovered that an idea committed in a flash to paper or canvas bore the artist's signature, the inimitable stamp of his personality, in a more durable and unmistakable form than the rigid fidelity in the reproductions of forms or formulae that was common to recording naturalist and style-bound idealist alike. Inspired evocation stood ranged against the definitive and explicit, suggestion against mere describing narrative.

Two camps were in process of formation. In the one were men concerned with increasing fluidity of form, in the other were men preparing for a retreat to fortified positions to defend an ever growing precision of form and meaning. Both sides were reconciled to what they would have to endure; in the one case it was a charge of chaotic lack of form – this was the fate of Turner, Delacroix, and the Impressionists[14] – in the other, the indictment that there was no spark of life in their creations. This dialogue was to reverberate throughout the whole of the nineteenth century.

5

That new and tumultuous forces were stirring was evident at the century's beginning, and this became increasingly clear as the years went by. Writing on the exhibition of pictures in 1833, Heine had the following to say:

'The new age will bring forth a new art, an art which will be in enthusiastic harmony with the age itself. It will not be an art which has borrowed its system of symbols from a faded past. It will be an art which will of necessity bring forth a new technique that is quite different from that prevailing up till now. Till then we will have to permit the prevailing of self-intoxicated subjectivity in colour and sound, of a cult of the individual that the world no longer holds in check, and of personality that has freed itself from God with all such a personality's native *joie de vivre* – all of which is to be preferred to the old art where all is mere surface appearance.' Here the logical conclusions have been drawn from Diderot's idea of creative chaos.

44 GOYA "The Dream of Reason brings forth Monsters".

45 GÉRICAULT Anatomical study.

46
GOYA
Saturn; c. 1817

47 FUSELI The Nightmare; 1783.

48 GÉRICAULT The Death of Hippolytus; c. 1815.

49 GÉRICAULT *La folle*; c. 1821–24.

50 GOYA Lunatic asylum (detail); 1800.

51 ENSOR "L'entrée du Christ à Bruxelles en 1889"; 1888.

52 DAUMIER The strong man.

53 DAUMIER *Ecce homo*; c. 1850.

54 GOYA Pilgrimage to San Isidro; c. 1817.

Here is a clear recognition of the fact that life in its open dynamic form has a recognizable mode of expression, has its own peculiar symbols. The sheer ability to bring forth something that is alive, a kind of creative intoxication, a devouring appetite for life, these are the marks — they constitute a kind of symbolic code of behaviour — by which we can recognize that subjective spontaneity which the artist is eternally seeking within himself, and whose presence he will always be ready to detect in others wherever he encounters the unfinished, the unconstrained and the unconventional. The work of Delacroix could be compared by his contemporaries to children's drawings[15] – a thing that could certainly never be said of Ingres – for here there was a spontaneity, not derived at second hand but native to the artist himself.

Actually we see at work here the same two forces that we identified earlier. There is the rationalizing masculine outlook that saw things historically and at a distance, and there is also that different way of seeing things – intuitive, organic, natural, and dominated by impulses that are essentially feminine. We saw before that a rigidly historical interpretation of life tended to subject the understanding to certain strains. Man when viewed in this fashion is only truly man in so far as he frees himself from nature and attains mastery over it. Those who took this 'masculine' view applied a corresponding test to the artist, his function being seen as an instance of this kind of mastery. 'Theoretically', says Hegel, 'even an indifferent idea that happens to spring up in a man's mind is superior to any mere product of nature, inasmuch as in the former there is an activity of the spirit working in freedom' (in solchem Falle ist immer die Geistigkeit und Freiheit präsent).[16] The true artist, Hegel claims, must not allow himself to be dominated by an arbitrary reality. He must prove himself master of 'the chaos of the fortuitous' and not be subject to the 'direct impact of things upon his senses' (der Unmittelbarkeit des Sinnlichen) if he is to attain to a higher reality born of the spirit, for 'true reality lies beyond what is directly experienced or perceived and lies beyond the objects in the world outside us' (jenseits der Unmittelbarkeit des Empfindens und der äußerlichen Gegenstände). Such is the established principle behind classicism's derivative picture of the world, and these words really express the historical viewpoint to which the classicist doctrine properly belongs, for it is, as already indicated, the mark of classicism that it rates the forms that lie ready to hand in the art of the past more highly than the spontaneous act of form creation. It lets artistic creation proceed by way of a detour over borrowed forms and finds it impossible to dispense with the advocacy of a past style.

It was only with difficulty that the historical argument concealed its bankruptcy in the face of all aesthetic problems behind its contempt for empirical forms. The more it appropriated from the past, the more difficult it became to make any clear and decisive assertion; for the vessels, within which the effects of such 'direct impact upon the senses' were expected to subside into clarity and tranquillity, were simply those normative models which conscious thought had borrowed from the arsenal of the past. The ballast of traditional forms which the past placed at his disposal prevented the artist from ever finding himself. Instead of achieving renewal he could only clothe himself in a variety of fancy dress and don the masks of ever varying styles. The inspired moment, the vital creative element regimented into conformity with the rigid subdivisions of stylistic history and there held prisoner, hid itself away.

6

I have here to note an interesting and extremely important development. It is nothing less than a kind of identification on the part of many artists of their technique with their subject matter; for what I have to discuss is the emergent artist's attitude towards nature, which became for him not so much a theme as a mirror to reflect his own striving. Let me examine very briefly the course of this strange and immensely significant phenomenon.

History said 'the past is right'. In doing so it had only a particular phase of the past in mind which it proceeded to raise to the level of an ideal. It ended however by giving its approval to every phase without exception and endeavoured to see even the strange and horrible ones in what it felt to be the right perspective. All that mattered was that these things belonged to the past.

Classicism's opponents were equally sweeping in their assertions. They cared nothing for the canonical validity of the past, they put their trust in the forces described by Heine, 'the sheer ability to bring forth a living thing, a kind of creative intoxication, a devouring appetite for life'. They sought to command spontaneity through the powers of intuition and not through those of the reason. The stylistic bonds which were part of the historical reinsurance process, were thrown off and spontaneity was exalted over derivative forms. Aesthetic dogma gave place to the direct encounter with reality experienced without distorting prepossession, borrowed gestures yielded to those directly expressive of the mind, even though the former may have been the more perfect. 'There are everyday, vulgar touches which often impart a sense of life', wrote Delacroix in his diary in 1824. The artist who sought his creative imperative not in the beautiful and exalted but in life itself, accepted the challenge even of the arbitrary and fortuitous. The work of art, it was felt, must now come into being not in some region far beyond the 'direct impact upon the senses' but at that impact's very centre; nor should it ever congeal into frozen finality, but it should always remain close to life, mobile, with power streaming through it, and variable. And yet this longing for spontaneity could on occasion be far from naïve, since time after time conscious deliberation had to be called into play; for some kind of control could thus be put on the creative act which might otherwise have died from sheer self-sufficiency and lack of contact with the world outside. The diaries of Delacroix bear continual testimony to this effort. The conflict arising from an obsession with the unfinished and the need to translate it into a finished work of art, is one of the main subjects discussed in that great dialogue which throughout his life the painter carried on with himself.[17]

Despite this it was held that feeling and instinct would provide the creative act with a broader basis and enable it to draw upon a deeper-lying source, upon the unconscious and the irrational, upon that very fullness of life that intensifies our perceptions of things and vitalizes our feelings. The artist, it was held, seeks to encounter the world without memory or knowledge, and that is why he experiences something like kinship with the child, for the child too is carefree and has this same directness of feeling and expression.

History and its stylistic masks could give the artist no guidance and so he took refuge with nature. He pondered the question of the origin of form, of the means of expression that should be valid and full of life, and the finished models of the past gave him no answer. To provide that answer it was to nature that he turned. Nature would set before his eyes an example of a power that acts without reasoning, a power that as it were takes its own activities for granted, that is alive and inexhaustible in its unfolding, that without any questioning brings forth its products in growing profusion. That is the reason why, in nineteenth century painting, all creative energies seem to concentrate on 'natural' themes – landscapes, still-life, the female figure. That is why it is in this sphere that we find the artist more active than in any other. For the painter himself now wanted to become a part of nature. He wanted her freedom to help him win his own, he wanted her uninhibited quality to be communicated to himself. He wanted to be done with all speculative and deductive thinking, all theorizing about morals and aesthetics. He wanted, in a word, to subject himself to life and be heir to all its astonishing riches.

When we speak of this turning towards nature, we are apt to have the high noon of the Impressionists chiefly in mind. But there was much more to it than that; it was more than a mere appetite for empirical reality, which, the classicist maintained, had no intrinsic value of its own. What men were groping after were those states of intoxication when everything is seen to be in dissolution and flux; they were seeking to penetrate those zones of experience that are under the domination of purely animal urges. So they sought for the rounded organic form, but would take discords in their stride so long as they made them feel that they bore within themselves a true element of life. They did not shrink from the ugliness of primal chaos so long as they could also record its passion. They claimed for their own the realm of the dream, but also, and with equal insistence, that of the destructive forces of the real world. What is truly alive often has barbaric traits and seeks its nourishment among outlandish peoples. It violates the conventions of civilization when these become a hindrance. Thus nature, conceived as the original and inexhaustible source of all being, became something much more tremendous than a mere experience of the eye. Men were overwhelmed by this wide and variegated vision of the natural and elemental, and the creative urge, fleeing from all that smacked of the rational, found its roots in the very forces of nature herself and in her powers of growth. The artist pressed on towards the chaos of the first hour of creation, yet he also let himself be carried along by the maelstrom of cosmic dissolution (plates 20 and 22). He sought the life-spring for his creative act in the dream, in intoxication, in the spontaneous expressions of pure instinct. 'The excitement', says Van Gogh, 'the earnestness of this feeling for nature, which are the things that guide us – these are sometimes so powerful that one does not feel one is working at all ... I only feel I am alive when I am thrusting forth work quite wildly.'

7

Now, from the frenzies of inspired creation to the milder climate of reflective thought – and here let me begin with a truism.

Every stylistic aid or prop that an artist makes his own, is at one and the same time a hindrance and a help. It helps him to walk, but confines such borrowed powers of movement to a narrow and sharply circumscribed area.

Now this was already realized in the early part of the nineteenth century, and what is particularly noteworthy is that it was soon realized by certain professional philosophers and theorists – as well as by artists with a turn for theorizing. In both cases there was a clear grasp of the fact that art could never be a purely cerebral affair, let alone something that could be learned by rule of thumb. Stress was laid on instinct, on feeling and on forces rising out of the unconscious depths of the personality.

There is a draft of a letter of Runge's from the year 1808 which puts this point of view with considerable force and even with a certain stridency. The study of the old masters, he writes, useful as this may be in itself, cannot help the artist 'unless he reaches or is brought to the point where he can grasp and contemplate the present moment of his existence with all its joys and sorrows, where nothing that he encounters is other than a personal contact with the most far off things and at the same time with the very core of his own being, with the remotest past and the most glorious future'.[18] What makes Runge's words especially interesting, however, is that they echo certain ideas of Schelling's – it was to Schelling, by the way, that the letter was to have been sent – ideas which the philosopher had developed in a speech in the previous year.

Schelling categorically rejected all deliberate archaizing, and he insisted with some vehemence that art must return to its true fountainhead, a fountainhead which could only lie within its creator, the artist himself, and which could not now be found in any pre-existent masterpiece, primitive or other, whatever might be its excellence. 'The insistence', he says, 'that art, like all living things, must proceed from its primal origins and ever return to them afresh if it is to renew its life, may seem a harsh doctrine in an age that has so often been told that it can abstract the most perfect beauty (which it will find all ready and waiting) from existing works of art and so attain its ultimate goal in a single stride. Do we not already possess supreme excellence and perfection? How could it be then that we should be expected to return to the point of our first untutored and unformed beginnings? Had the great originators of new art had such thoughts as these we should never have beheld their miracles. These too had before them the works of antiquity, figures sculptured in the round and work in bas relief which could easily have been translated into paintings. Yet such appropriation of something which they had not won by their own efforts, and which for that very reason was informed by a beauty they could not fully understand, could not satisfy an artistic urge wholly bent on producing original work, an urge bent on its own free begetting of beauty with a native vigour of its own (ein Kunsttrieb – der durchaus auf das Ursprüngliche ging, und aus dem das Schöne frei und urkräftig sich wieder erzeugen sollte). Such men were not afraid of appearing simple, crude and even barren when compared with the lofty standards of antique art. They were content to spend much time in modestly fostering their art in the bud until the time for its glorious blossoming should come. How comes it that even today we gaze upon these works of the older masters, from Giotto to the teacher of Raphael, with veneration, often indeed preferring them to any others? Surely it is because our respect and admiration is compelled by the sincerity of their effort, the great earnestness that is evident in the very limits which they voluntarily imposed upon themselves. Now our present generation stands to these men in the same relation as they once stood to the ancients. There is no living tradition that unites our age with theirs. No bond of progressive organic growth binds one to the other. We must recreate art even as these men recreated it, but with a native power of our own, if we are to rise to their level. That Indian summer of art in the sixteenth century and the beginning of the seventeenth could still show a few blossoms on the ancient stem, but it produced no seed-buds capable of bearing fruit, still less did it plant a fresh stem that could produce a new growth. Yet to consign the mature works of European art to an inferior place and to pick on its simple unassuming beginnings and set about imitating them, as some have sought to do, would only imply a further and even more serious misunderstanding of the matter. The primitives themselves did not seek to go back to some primal beginning. Had they done so their very simplicity would be no more than a mannerism and a hypocritical pretence.'[19]

A few pages later Schelling comes to his real point: 'Like anyone whose work lies in the sphere of the mind or spirit (jeder geistig Wirkende), the artist can only follow the law which God and nature have written upon his heart; he can follow no other. Nobody can help him, he can only help himself. Nor can he borrow from the outside world, for what he did not bring forth for its own sake would, by reason of that very fact, be worthless. That is why no man can give him directions or prescribe the way that he should go.'[19] There is resignation in these words. Schelling had recognized, as we have just seen, that the bond of the living tradition had snapped. Some decades later Baudelaire was to say the same – 'the grand tradition has disappeared';[20] the artist must depend upon himself, he must follow his inner law and can hope for neither guidance nor applause. Rarely indeed has the position of the modern artist been more succinctly described. Schelling's words are not a prophecy but a commentary on the crisis of art around 1800. The conclusions arrived at by him are illustrated by the pictures of David, Goya, and Friedrich. The monk by the sea symbolizes the artist whom nobody can help and for whom nobody can point the way.

Schelling has no ready-made solutions to hand, but he formulates the principle to which every attempt at creation must be subject: it is the principle of the form that has grown organically and

112

is answerable to nothing but itself. If a form is forced on something from without, as happens in the case of the eclectics, then it does violence to that thing's nature, but this does not happen if it flows forth from the nature of the thing itself. If the artist follows the idea that is at work creatively within himself, then he forms the individual and particular into 'a world in itself, a species, an eternal archetype' (einer Welt für sich, einer Gattung, einem ewigen Urbild). It would, however, be wrong for him to rely exclusively on his powers of reason to grasp the 'eternal concept' to which all things are subordinate. With the activity of the conscious mind there must be combined 'an unconscious power'. It is only then that works of art of the highest rank can come into being. In nature there is disclosed to man the spontaneous but as yet unconscious poetry of the spirit. Even so, Schelling admits, art cannot begin at so deep a level as nature. That is why art tends to seize on what is highest and most developed, the human form.

In taking this view Schelling fails to foresee that the new element in the art of the nineteenth century was to culminate in the attempt to make a start at a level which was quite as low as that at which nature had her beginnings – that of the formless, the pre-morphous – and in doing so to embed man in nature, to allow him to be resolved into the cosmic. Yet there were those who seem not to have been unaware of the direction in which things were actually moving.

In another letter, Runge draws attention to the renewed interest in landscape painting and shows remarkable insight in discerning what lay behind it. 'All our energies seem to be concentrating on the landscape' (Es drängt sich alles zur Landschaft), he writes, 'seeking something definite in its very lack of definition, and yet not knowing how to set about finding it.'

Schelling thus had a clear grasp of the artistic problem of his day, though the course things were actually to take was somewhat different from what he supposed at the time, for it was the devotees of the clearly defined, and of final detailed execution, who favoured the human body, because this was compact and intimately articulated throughout, and so conformed to what they were seeking. The variable, arbitrary mode of expression on the other hand – itself a thing without a beginning or an end – was felt to be best served by the landscape and it was in that field that it achieved its most abundant development.

Thus the nineteenth century returned from the highest and most fully developed to what is most primal; it returned from the abstract to the organic, from man to Nature. There thus occurred a change in the part played by man. Instead of dominating Nature, he had entered into her.

'They mistakenly turn back to history and so confuse themselves. In this new art – in the landscape cult (der Landschafterei) if you like to call it that – is there not a new summit to be attained – a summit that may well be fairer than the previous ones?' It is no mere chance that this letter of Runge's closes with the thought that we must once more become children if we are to achieve the best. For the child is the first seed of the mature human form, it is the symbol of a state of beginning in which there is an awakening out of the unconscious, and where life still proceeds according to the pulse-beat of the powers of Nature. That is why for Runge it is the symbol of the first gentle unfolding of the world.

8

Schelling replaced the essentially rational idea of perfection which derived its guiding principles from the old models, with an organic one – which, as a matter of fact, was not without an ancestry. The eighteenth century had already conceived the idea that the existence of any creature was justified by its power truly to be itself, by the creative life within it. This conception of 'wholeness' or 'completeness' admitted of no distinction between good and evil or even between beauty and ugliness in the accepted sense of those terms, even though the concept of beauty was allowed to enter into the discussion. All that was alive was right, even when it was opposed to man and failed to fit into his categories of morality. 'Good is an entirely relative conception and there is nothing that is good in itself, yet everything in Nature is beautiful in itself if it is what its kind and purpose meant it to be. A lion is beautiful even though he may not be useful to man.' Thus Heinse, the 'aesthetic immoralist'.[21]

From the principle that self-realization is the end of every creature it was not too difficult to deduce an analogous theory relating to art. On such a view the work of art conforms to no external necessity but to the inward compulsion of its creator. The measure applied from without was replaced by something growing from within. This conviction – a somewhat irrational one perhaps – ultimately gave birth to the belief that a work of art must develop by means of a principle of organic growth. 'As the tree can be traced back to the root, so must we be able to derive the development and flowering of an art from its source of origin. That source contains within itself the whole nature of its final product just as a whole plant and all its parts lie hidden in a single seed.'[22] This idea of Herder's is not unrelated to that of Goethe's 'Urpflanze' or primal plant – and this is yet another reminder that in the beginnings of the historical argument the vision of organic wholeness was already alive. Yet the very awareness of the inner logic that had shaped every stylistic gesture of the past must, as I have already pointed out, sooner or later have made that gesture's uniqueness plain, and what is unique cannot be achieved all over again a second time. All its completeness and essential rightness degenerate into mere deadness if we stand outside it and try to feel its real quality from without. What was for the past inevitable is for the present a matter of free choice – one among several stylistic crutches – and the historical attitude uses up its energies in this process of mere choosing.

As soon, however, as the fact was grasped that an epoch must not be assessed by any standard claiming permanent validity but by the principle of its own inner growth and the measure of the resources that are native to itself – here we are already touching on the idea of Riegl's 'Kunstwollen' or 'will to art' – as soon as it was understood that a Gothic cathedral cannot be explained or understood in terms of a Greek temple,[23] there came into being a wholly new approach to the understanding of the organism which is a work of art. This could now be understood in terms of its own inner compulsion. This compulsion had its roots deep in the individual himself, so that – I stress this point again – every creative act produced a pattern that was unrepeatable and unique.

Here we have a wholly novel way of looking at things and one which was consistently to play its part in the shaping of the century's outlook. If critical judgment could no longer fall back on any universal norms, if it had to confine itself to the uniqueness and consistency of any particular work, then it was compelled to face a very weighty decision, in so far as it had to draw a dividing line between art which was genuine and art which was not. Art which is genuine has roots in an inner compulsion, art which is not may be satisfied with a borrowed formula, an effort to recapture the spirit of a style by means of an attempted empathy that comes wholly from the outside; whether it does so or not, it lacks the seal of a consistent inward compulsion. Here lay the test.

A new scale of measurement was thus established. Subjective sincerity, springing from the certitudes which the individual carries within himself, now took primacy of place over the ideal representation of some allegedly universal truth. Of course when all objective criteria are abandoned and the only touchstone is the purely subjective quality of a state of mind – real or supposed – there ceases to be any absolutely reliable safeguard against the imposture of the inspired charlatan and it is surely this that was at the bottom of Schadow's rather startling observation that Rembrandt, for aught we know to the contrary, may have been 'the greatest liar that ever appeared in art, but one who never contradicted himself, always maintained a high degree of consistency and took care to ensure perfect agreement between one statement and another' (höchst übereinstimmend und konsequent).[24] For all that, the test that since the eighteenth century has tended to decide the rank and significance of a work of art has been the compulsive necessity that has brought it into being and its consistency with itself.

Now such a wholly subjective standard of measurement was new. As long as the impersonal carrying power of a prevailing style took some weight off the artist's shoulders and made it easier for him to master content and form, there was no plainly discernible line of distinction between the genuine and the fictitious. It was merely a question of the degree to which the artist had been permeated by his personal inspiration under the protecting edifice of the dominant style. It was only when artistic form became an object of free choice, when the connection with the living tradition had been broken and the artist had to decide between pupilage to a directing past and the law within his own heart, only when style was no longer self-evident and taken for granted, that the old naïveté disappeared and a new factor entered into the artist's activity. From now on a quality of essentially ethical conscientiousness was demanded of the creative act; it was put to the test and asked to bear witness to the reputability of its author. Was that same author dealing in wares that were not strictly his at all? Or was he bringing to market that which was truly his own? Was he perhaps sedulously or even complacently keeping to the all too well trodden paths of the past? Or was he with quiet determination following the road which the law within him and his own age prescribed?

The art of the nineteenth century is essentially an artist's art.[25] It is free from tradition and therefore has no hold in anything outside itself which could act as a restraining influence. Since they are judged by their inward consistency, its creations must submit to a very strict differentiating analysis – an analysis of uncompromising harshness, that rejects the idea of a moderately good performance, which so long as style existed provided style with a kind of testing ground. The line dividing weak art from strong, the line between dead formula and living expression, between patchwork that is empty of life and true creation of form, was now drawn in with a ruthlessness that was wholly new.

9

Our own age – and this is particularly true of its assessment of the nineteenth century – feels unresponsive to form that has been refined down to mere style. It prefers the loose to the disciplined gesture. The Impressionists and their circle are at the very centre of popular esteem. All that is fluid, changeable, and unfinished can be certain of the public's favour. There is a certain perception of truth behind such trends of popular taste, since forces that are really driving towards renewal, prefer to express themselves in 'life' rather than in 'history'. Vital and pregnant art forms have in the nineteenth century almost always something daring and revolutionary about them. The process begins as early as Goya. Here already the artist was deliberately committing himself to a venture, to something that was the very opposite of the formulae of the eclectics and to the hesitancy of the conservatives, and the mere fact of this opposition enhanced the force of the impetus behind him. We may indeed say that the whole history of nineteenth century art is one continuous act of self-liberation, though the process takes place at various levels – that it is one continuous effort to endow the means of artistic expression with an increasing spontaneity. It is continually passing from the detailed to the summarizing vision and turns its back with increasing determination on those minutiae of execution that are irrelevant to its purpose.

Despite all this, however, a historical survey that concentrated all its sympathies on the trends described above would stand in need of considerable revision. I should call such a view of the matter

55 INGRES Self-portrait; 1804.

56 GÉRICAULT Portrait of an artist.

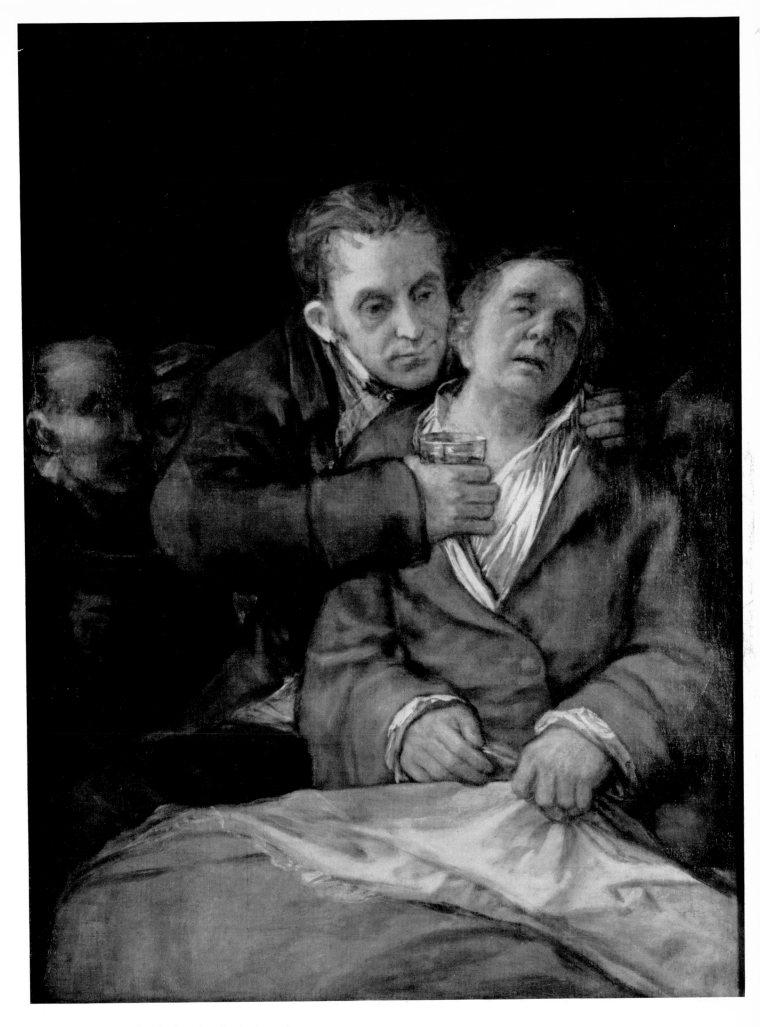

57 GOYA The artist with his physician, Dr. Arrieta; 1820.

58 DELACROIX Michelangelo in his studio; 1850.

59 DAUMIER The artist sitting before his work; 1863–66.

60 BÖCKLIN The artist with Death playing the violin; 1872.

61 MARÉES The artist with another painter called Lenbach; 1863.

62 DEGAS The artist with his friend de Valernes; 1868.

63 RENOIR Richard Wagner; 1893.

64 CÉZANNE Self-portrait; 1885–87.

65 VAN GOGH Self-portrait; 1889.

66 GAUGUIN Self-portrait; 1889.

false, one-sided and misleading, for it really does justice to nobody. It exiles from the century those painters of ideas with historical and philosophical pre-occupations who, like 'heavy unhelpful men of learning' (Diderot), lost themselves in meditation on their subjects, and it equates devotees of *la bonne peinture* with the kind of artist to whom – to quote the deliberately barbed phrase of Leibl[26] – it is a matter of indifference whether he paints a landscape, a man, or an animal. Such simplifications make it impossible to present a coherent historical picture of the century. For if one party merely paints for the sake of painting and the others seek refuge with Phidias and Raphael from the monstrosities of the present – where must we look for an expression of the century's real needs and of its real essence? Is it really true that there is no common ground between Courbet and the Böcklin of the 'Isle of the Dead' or between Daumier and the Pre-Raphaelites?

If we assume that the masters of improvisation and of the 'free handwriting' were the essential artists of the nineteenth century, then we shall have gathered together an impressive elite yet we shall hardly have thrown much light on all the different artistic strata which were part of the make-up of the age. If the 'painters' – the accent is here on their aptitude as colourists and improvisers – prove to be not only the best but also the most representative artists the century produced – then we are faced with another and even more pertinent question – namely for what those others stand who cannot be ranged under *la bonne peinture*.

I am anxious not to be misunderstood. 'Life' is superior to 'history', the living form to the derivative or merely costumed, inventiveness means more than a talent for quotation and what is subjectively right carries more conviction than objective beauty at second hand. Realism has more vitality within itself than all the good will of the Nazarenes and Pre-Raphaelites and it may well be that Impressionism, that most felicitous development of the loose and open form, really does provide the nineteenth century with something like a substitute for absolute beauty. I have no wish to dispute the fact that the open form possesses a higher potential of energy and inventiveness, that it conduces to an autonomy of artistic means. I hold nevertheless that the quality of the nineteenth century cannot be understood in its entirety, if we confine ourselves exclusively to the masters of the 'free handwriting' and of the unalloyed application of colour. Whoever denies this makes things too easy for himself, nor will such a man ever be able to visualize the true shape of this epoch, marked as it was by this deep and significant division. It is not enough to concentrate exclusively on those trends which we view today as the revolutionary element of the age. Rather must we set the dynamic forces side by side with those that resisted change and so strike a balance. Only thus will we get the century's true character into perspective.

Yet it is equally insufficient to point to common features in the themes of Daumier and Meissonier – as in 'The barricade' and the 'Visit to the artist's studio' – for that merely serves to recall what our superficial view of the matter tends to overlook, namely that the nineteenth century provided its artists with a homogeneous background of spiritual experience, a fact that held good whether those artists were men of genius or epigoni, whether they were spirits bereft of freedom or men confident in their powers, men obsessed with problems or men who handled their brush without a care in the world. In this particular matter the century was as consistent in its character as any that preceded it. It was divided in its choice of artistic means and as to the domains where it sought the subject matter which it used as a vehicle for the conveying of its experience. One need only compare Ingres' 'Golden Age' (plate 207) with the paradisial transfiguration in the pictures of Renoir, whose conception of an earthly paradise was stated in terms of sunlight and lightness of heart. In the one case we have antiquity, in the other the present; in the one case classic linear harmony, in the other the open rhythms of colour. In both cases an essential ideological aspect of the nineteenth century finds expression.

129

It is of course true enough that not every strictness of form represents the essential bondage of the eclectic, not every detailed piece of representation is to be equated with the deadness of a photograph; conversely not every slick dab of the brush should lightly be assessed as an expression of an inner compulsion. The fact that painters tended more and more to paint in a direct, personal manner, and the equally incontrovertible fact that the whole trend of painting was making for a sensual loosening of forms – a victory this for the female principle over the male – should never make us forget that there were in this century great and vital personalities who remained unaffected by this trend.

10

In the search for its true self the art of the nineteenth century explored two domains in which it hoped to find the longed-for treasure of primal artistic spontaneity. These were the domains of the approved historic styles and of the art form which had been achieved by the unaided endeavour of the contemporary artist, the art form that was wholly free from any suspicion of the historical – in brief, the two domains of history and life. This polarity is also inherent in the tension between the masculinity of the disciplined line and the essentially feminine riot of colour. It also finds expression with quite remarkable consistency in the themes chosen to satisfy the artist's need for self-interpretation. For those who look back to the past, the history of art itself becomes the subject chosen for treatment, the others focus on the processes of artistic creation.

Thus there came into being a new and extensive chapter of secular pictorial historiography – a pictorial history of artists and of art. Here too is proof that art had itself become a theme for art. The painter was paying homage to the masters on whom he depended. Cornelius decorated the twenty-five loggias of the Pinakothek with episodes from the history of German and Italian art up to the beginning of the sixteenth century and completed the series with a 'modest addition of later French art'.[27] Overbeck painted an art-historical altar picture, 'The Triumph of Religion' (plate 90). In the Antwerp Museum de Keyzer depicted various events in the history of Flemish art, while in the Vienna Kunsthistorisches Museum Makart painted variations on the theme of artist and model in the recesses beside the stairway. Nor did the sculptors remain idle. They provided the museums with busts and statues of the great artists of the past, they embellished these surrogates for churches, dedicated as they were to the historic cult of genius, with the saints which churches obviously required.

Such a coupling of historical review with self-portraiture did no more than touch the surface of things. 'Art', says Schlegel, 'rests upon knowledge, and art's body of knowledge is its history.' Unfortunately the historical painters turned their knowledge of the history of art into a kind of 'story of art told in pictures', something savouring of a certain kind of illustration that arrests the mind for a moment but has no real depth of meaning. Earlier centuries had made allegories about art. It was left to the nineteenth to historicize it. The underlining of significant attributes gave place to the sentimental anecdote. Fundamentally these were *genre* pictures.

The case of those artists, however, who had truly developed their own art-forms is a very different one. They resisted the dogmatizings of history, they freed the creative act from the coercive rules of the past. By experimenting with them they assisted the formal means of their craft towards the attainment of an autonomy of their own. The organic form here was also a means by which the artist portrayed himself, but it sought to do this in the very act of creation. A sketch of Delacroix or Daumier gives a deeper insight into the mysteries of artistic creation than any picture of the discovery by Cimabue of the shepherd boy Giotto while the latter was drawing sheep in the sand.

In the process of creation, the nature of which is not obscured for us by any claim to finality, a picture discloses its true origins. We can see the formal elements as they come into being, as they multiply and melt into one another. This explains why the 'organic' type of artist feels himself inwardly so strongly drawn to all forms of open, variable experience – to the effects of water, of cloud and atmosphere and to the landscape in general. What is natural no longer has need, as it had with some German Romantics, of quotations recollected from the history of art. In Corot's vibrant applications of colour, in Turner's ecstatic *brio*, the elemental forces of nature free themselves and become directly perceptible to the eye. In the camp of the 'finished' art form, men were afraid of the feminine and seductive quality of colour[28] which was held to be responsible for the ruin of the painter's craft, even as Eve was responsible for original sin.

The process of painting calls the world into being. Reaching back into primal chaos, it offers us the colourful spectacle of the birth of the universe. The 'painter' withdraws his creative means and his experience of life and the world back into the domain of the element, and there finds a home where they come to life anew. The primal and aboriginal, once redistilled out of the stylistic peculiarities of the past, is brought forth by him out of the unfinished and pregnant form. The Impressionist's brush not only recapitulates and makes manifest the coloured glory of the world's creation. It also makes glorious the very process by which a work of art comes into being, and with it the creative function of the artist who brings beauty out of chaos itself.

V Pictures of Humanity

I

WHEN God hides His face, man becomes the available candidate for the cosmic presidency. In this instance he was never much more than a candidate, since in the nineteenth century it is, to say the least, doubtful whether he ever attained to the actual divine office, though on one or two occasions he came so near to doing so that the difference hardly seems to matter. The point is, however, that, like any other presidential candidate, he was now subjected to intense and searching scrutiny, and sometimes that scrutiny produced real admiration. Rather more often, however, it produced a deep and often anguished pity and that sense of outrage evoked by the sight of one who has been cheated out of his inheritance – but of that I speak elsewhere.

With this new scrutiny of man, there went an enhanced sense of his essential unity. A number of factors contributed to this result, of which the growing disappearance of distance through improved communication was not the least. Michelet, among others, was alive to this new feeling and in his *Bible de l'Humanité* (1864) praises the good fortune of his age. 'What a fortunate age ours is,' he cries, 'when contact through electricity gives the whole world as it were a unified soul, a present in which all can share. When the historic link and the possibility of harmonizing our various time-pieces not only make us aware of a past in which all men were brothers but also of a joint spiritual inheritance.'[1] About a decade earlier Thoré-Bürger was writing in the *Revue Universelle des Arts:* 'We have now reached a standpoint from which we may gaze back into the past and see the unbreakable chain of universal tradition. Throughout the ages humanity has been aware of itself and has, in a sense, achieved its own immortality ... it now remains for humankind to become aware of its role in the tangible universe, to see the whole round world as clearly as it has seen daylight through the thickets of history; to realize its world-unity, to accept finally its place in a unified globe and a shared role in time and eternity.'[2]

Here we already have the programme of the World Exhibition, discussed in a later chapter, in which the nineteenth century gave shape to this idea of mankind as a single entity which was to be viewed both laterally and in depth. How did this way of looking at things affect the artist?

In the year 1855 in which Gérome painted his 'Age of Augustus', Chenavard exhibited his 'Cycle of Man', originally intended for the Pantheon, at the Paris World Exhibition, and the rejected Courbet put his 'L'atelier' on view. It may seem odd to lump these three things together. Can we indeed compare a picture that shows a jumble of labourers and idlers, and of artists, women and representatives of the bourgeoisie, with one that calls to mind the peaks of human history?

Courbet was satisfied with the mere gathering together of men and women belongin tog different age groups and different strata of society; Gérome painted the apotheosis of an age, deeply conscious of its moral import; Chenavard welded together the slow unfolding of cultural and religious history into an austere symphonic structure. Do not the differences between these three far outweigh their similarities? Perhaps they do, but they are differences between things that exercise an influence on each other, and which together form a unity and give us a vision of the single great

whole of humanity as it exists spread all over the world and stretches back throughout the ages. Indeed, taken in conjunction with one another they begin to form just such a whole as Michelet and Thoré-Burger believed their age should envisage.

Once more we can see the tension between history and life. Courbet, the realist, remained within the confines of his own age. He painted human variations on an autobiographical theme, while Chenavard's erudition explored all the paths of world history. Even so, behind the formal and thematic contrast, there lurks a common conviction which the two painters shared. It is this same belief in the unity of mankind. It is a belief that, as I have already said, the great World Exhibitions were designed to sustain.

To express the idea of man by means of historical illustration does not necessarily help towards a better understanding of it than to express it in a contemporary setting showing the commonplace events of ordinary life. Long before realism broke up the accepted hierarchical ordering of subjects and set itself the definite task of portraying man as he actually is – the historical painters till then having painted nothing but dolls in fancy dress – Schopenhauer had realized, as we can see in his third book of *The World as Will and Idea*, that a certain idea can be visually rendered on different levels. Man can be revealed in the lowly or in the sublime. This is a fundamental truth and provides a key to the iconographic disguises of the nineteenth century, disguises which made it possible for a painter to transfer the judgment of Paris to an ordinary place of entertainment (plate 129) and for a poet to discover the greatness of a Dido, a Juliet, or a Medea in a humble serving girl.[3]

There are in fact two ways of telling the story of man. One can present him in historical perspective, or one can present some basic human situation that has an implication of universality. Schopenhauer puts the matter thus:

'There is no individual and no action that wholly lacks wider significance; the idea of humanity is progressively unfolded in all and through all. That is why nothing whatsover that enters into human life should be excluded from the painter's view.' We do the Dutch wrong if we rate the representation of biblical events or of the happenings of world history more highly than we rate the work of such painters as these, and hold that only the former subjects are of any account. The external significance of an action is independent of its inner significance. The first is concerned with the action's consequences in the real world, the inner significance depends on how deeply the idea of humanity is understood. The first is of account, therefore, in history, the second in art. 'An action that is of great historical importance may from the point of view of its inner significance be a very ordinary and even a very mean one. Conversely a scene taken from everyday life may be of deep inner significance, when a bright and clear light is shed on human individuals and human actions and desires so that even the most imperceptible little cranny is brightly illuminated.' That is why Courbet's 'L'atelier' is as much a picture of humanity as Chenavard's wide-stretched panorama of history.

2

That sensitive and at the same time detached empathy that seeks, as it were, to get right inside the very body of the past and to study all available facts with complete freedom from prepossession, that trend in historiography to which German scholars have – almost within our own time – given the name of *Historismus* was already forming men's minds at this time, and its effect was to put the distinctive stamp of a particular time on both past and present. It caused yesterday to be contrasted with today, it consigned history and life to two separate areas of imaginative vision.

In both cases there was an acceptance of a certain relativism of values, and indeed from the very beginning of this period a certain relativism was in the air. The same minds that, during the French

Revolution, inspired the proclamation of human rights for the political individual, were ready, when looking back at the past, to accord equal value and equal dignity to all religions, all cultures, and all forms of polity. All these were manifestations of the phenomenon 'Man'. Perhaps, after all, the co-existence of these ideas is not so remarkable since the ending of all differential evaluation in the sphere of history – 'all that is history is right' was the keynote of the historical approach – had a certain vague relationship with the general demand for freedom, equality and brotherhood, which is after all just another way of correcting another kind of differential evaluation.

However this may be, man was the norm – and the resulting conception of human solidarity which marked the eighteenth century led to two closely related ways of apprehending this phenomenon of the species man, each being pursued with something like the conviction of a religious faith. They were two ways whose difference is implicit in what I have already said. One consisted of a progressive searching through the past in order to build up thus a unified and coherent picture of man's essential nature; the other, with the same purpose in view, subjected the present to scrutiny. Both were concerned to obtain a comprehensive picture of mankind.

The method and spirit of the two modes of procedure was in some respects very similar; nor is this surprising. The idea of the human norm and of the essential 'rightness' of man necessarily leads to a sympathetic and detached examination of causes wherever man appears, at least on super-ficial examination, to have been rather conspicuously 'wrong'. That is the approach of the method we have come to know as historical, and the parallel with the new exact and studious approach to the contemporary scene is not hard to see. The historical outlook is admirably summed up in a passage of Burckhardt which has already been quoted in part, and there can be no doubt that much of it can be applied to the new study of the social scene. The tendency of history to explain – and even approve – all things by referring them to the context of prevailing circumstances has its counterpart in the equally wide social sympathies of the contemporary world. 'We have a point of view', writes Burckhardt, 'for every phase and seek to do justice even to facts which may to us appear strange and terrifying. Earlier ages had but one point of view, or at best a very small variety of such points of view; at times a purely national one predominated, on other occasions one that was wholly religious was paramount. Islam had regard only to itself, while for a thousand years the Middle Ages looked on antiquity as wholly delivered over to the Devil. Today, however, our historical judgment is engaged in a wholesale revision of all famous individuals and causes, and we judge the individual in the light of what has preceded him and of the character of his age. Through this false claims to greatness have in many cases been rejected and true greatness acclaimed.'[4] To the historian every epoch of history is of interest; wherever man manifests himself, there the true student follows his traces. The student of the contemporary scene is engaged in a similar process of cautious revision and so above all is the artist who aspires to be an eye-witness of his time; in the different ranks and classes about him he sees the reflection of all mankind.

During the same period when the nineteenth century was engaged in the study of cross-sections of history, it made a number of surveys of its own time. These tended to reveal man, particularly in his sociological aspects, under a wide variety of types. In the year 1840 there appeared in Paris the first instalments of the illustrated serial publication, *Les français peints par eux-mêmes*. While the historian was seeking to gain knowledge of mankind in the past, this social encyclopaedia endeavoured to hold fast the transient moment and to preserve it for future historians to study. 'What is said and done today', says the preface, 'will one day be history', a statement which again shows us that our sense of the present and our sense of the past are interdependent. Every year, the editor remarks, has practices peculiar to itself, and mankind changes its follies and its vices every twenty-four hours. Would it not therefore be better for the historian to confine himself to such realities as these instead of losing

135

himself among the wars and battlefields of the past? Similar advice was being addressed by the painters of the contemporary scene to their more retrospective colleagues.

In the nine volumes of the above-mentioned publication hundreds of human types were described – and described with systematic thoroughness. Every profession, every kind of person that was in any way out of the ordinary, every class had its say in this great lexicon of the world stage. In it the whole human comedy – principals and supers alike – was subjected to analysis. The commercial traveller, the deputy, the poet, the misunderstood soul, the grave-digger, the rentier, the beggar, the blue-stocking, the provincial, the labourer, the adulteress – all are there. Yet this kind of review encountered the same difficulty as the historical panorama. The more comprehensive its plan, the harder it was to summarize, the harder it was to see its subject as a whole. The net result was a sum of isolated factors, a sedulous juxtaposition of individuals, professions, and social classes. The intensive analysis of each tended to set it apart from the rest and made a unified view less and less possible to attain.

In the decade that followed, while Gustav Freytag was writing his *Bilder aus der deutschen Vergangenheit* (Pictures of the German Past) there appeared another monumental documentary analysis of the present, for it was during this period that Henry Mayhew made the first attempt to publish the history of a people as obtained from the lips of the people themselves.[5] Based on a wide range of historical material, this work is a mixture of first-hand description, statistics, and interviews. In it the conditions of life and work of the London proletariat are analysed in a wholly scientific and objective spirit, and the conversations which the author had with beggars, labourers and prostitutes are reproduced without the slightest attempt at embellishment.

For the artist it was quite impossible to shut himself off from this kind of encyclopaedic interest in man. He too sought for a 'point of view for everything'. According as he opted for history or for life, he sought to do justice to the great hero of history or to the anonymous member of modern society. Nineteenth century art drew two lines through mankind. One of these cut through it lengthwise, opening up a long perspective into the past and bringing into view a wide panorama of slow historical growth, the other formed a cross-section through man's condition in the present. We thus have two distinct ways of looking at mankind. Courbet was associated with the latter, and Chenavard with the former.

3

The new cult of man conquered all manner of new territories. We shall see throughout this book how the cult of the artist tended to replace that of the saint. In much the same manner world history replaced the story of man's salvation. 'Is not Man's History, and Men's History, a perpetual Evangel?' asks Carlyle in *Sartor Resartus*. It is thus surely no mere chance that historical pictures of humanity should have made their way into sacred edifices and should have begun to usurp the places where once had stood the altars and the pictures of the older cult. Chenavard's idea of turning the Church of Ste Geneviève into a 'Sanctuaire de toutes les intelligences'[6] was by no means unique. It was merely the radical expression of a trend that had begun to dominate European thought since the end of the eighteenth century.

In the nineteenth century churches, monuments and museums began to get curiously mixed up with one another, strange mongrel creatures being the result. There ensued a sort of comedy of mistaken institutional identities with all the traditional complications. For Goethe the museum was a shrine, Hölderlin called it an 'aesthetic church'.[7] The temple of Art, now pronounced a holy place, produced as its inevitable counterpart the 'museumized' church.

On the site of the battle of Leipzig there was planned a kind of Gothic cathedral which was also to serve as a national monument and a sanctuary of the arts. The entrance hall, so Görres tells us,[8]

67–78
*The eye-witness
account
as an indictment
of the age*

→

67 GOYA Murat's troops executing inhabitants of Madrid on 3rd May, 1808; 1814.

68 GROS Napoleon visiting people stricken by the plague at Jaffa (detail).

69 DELACROIX The Chios Massacres; 1824.

70 GÉRICAULT The raft of the "Medusa"; 1819.

71 DELACROIX *La barque de Don Juan*; 1840.

72 DELACROIX *Liberté guidant le peuple*; 1830.

74 COURBET *L'homme blessé*; 1844.

75 DAUMIER The uprising; c. 1860.

76 MENZEL Public funeral of victims of the March Revolution; 1848.

77 ROMAKO Tegetthoff during the Battle of Lissa; c. 1880.

78 MANET Execution of the Emperor Maximilian; 1867.

was to be decorated with paintings of German myths and history, and dedicated to 'the great dead of our country'. This monument of victory would give the arts what at the time they lacked, 'a great sanctuary and an institution to which their powers and their hearts could devote themselves, and where the art of the century could blossom forth as a single flower. As the cities of the Middle Ages gathered themselves around a church, so a school of German art would form around this monument'. Thus the church was thought of as the potential rallying point for a 'school of art', and thus art itself was elevated to the rank of a religious cult. Again one recalls Wagner's, 'Das Kunstwerk ist die lebendig dargestellte Religion' (The work of art is the living representation of religion – from *Das Kunstwerk der Zukunft*).

The political efforts of the Romantics to transform the church into a temple of national heroes lasted until the middle of the century. Even the Vienna Volkskirche was to be turned into an Austrian Hall of Fame after the fashion of Westminster Abbey. During the same period the monuments of 'Great Men' were elevated almost to the point of sanctification.[9] Boullée's Newton Cenotaph (plates 8 and 9) and Gilly's memorial edifice in honour of Frederick the Great – neither got beyond the drawing board – are essentially productions devoted to a religious cult in which mankind was to venerate the lonely godlike man of genius. The mausoleums of artists were also touched by this atmosphere of sanctity. The Thorwaldsen Museum in Copenhagen and the Canova House in Possagno are lay churches. Those who enter them do so not as 'the public' but as pilgrims.

The spirit of these symbolic structures found concentrated expression in the great buildings which in their various ways paid tribute to national greatness and to the greatness of leading figures of the nation concerned – the Valhalla of Regensburg (plates 28–29), the London Houses of Parliament whose 1200 recesses, plinths and pillars tell the story of the British Empire, the Albert Memorial which shows the Prince Consort surrounded by 169 artists of all ages, the Paris Acropolis planned by Préault but never actually built, the Austrian 'Heldenberg' at Kleinwetzdorf, and the Paris Pantheon.

At a time when church, monument, and museum were each imparting to one another something of their own significance – so that in the end all attained complete equality of rank – the erection of 'sacred' edifices became something more than just another task for the architect. Such buildings became models illustrating the history of styles which for their full appreciation needed something in the nature of the historian's eye. Since all such creations – including museums and monuments – partook of the nature of a church, little was left that could truly be called a house of God.

4

The cult of man – and particularly of man in his historical perspective – having penetrated the churches, it is not surprising that it exercised a deep influence upon the arts, or, indeed, that they should in their turn have tended to endow such a theme with a discernibly sacred character. The museums, those sanctuaries of the history-conscious soul, were of course particularly suitable places for illustrating the history of human culture and of man in general throughout the ages, and already in the closing decades of the eighteenth century we find James Barry carrying out six murals depicting 'The Progress of Human Culture' for the rooms of the London Society of Arts. This however is but one example of a wider trend. The nineteenth saw the fostering – particularly in Germany – of a kind of pictorial philosophy of history. This phenomenon could already be observed in 1818 when, on the occasion of a farewell feast for the Crown Prince of Bavaria, the German artists of Rome designed a cycle of pictures whose pseudo-religious content was quite remarkable. In the central picture – on the 'altar wall' – the various arts sit enthroned under a German oak, while buildings in rural surroundings suggest by their character both Germany and Greece. In the Predella, Samson overcomes the Philistines, and on the side-walls we see the princely protectors of the arts and the four great law-givers – Moses, Solon, Numa Pompilius and Charlemagne.[10]

In Munich, whither he was later called, Cornelius, the spiritual father of the project mentioned above, distinguished himself by conceptions of an even more elaborate character. He adorned the Glyptothek with scenes showing the more reputable activities of the Greek Pantheon, and the Pina-kothek with a compendium of the history of German and Italian art. An excursus into eschatology, his 'Last Judgment', was appropriately reserved for the Ludwigskirche.

Nor did Berlin lag far behind Munich. Schinkel's 'Development of Life on Earth' in the Altes Museum, a work exceptionally rich in the variety of its figures, was followed by Kaulbach's six periods of world history that decorate the staircase of the Neues Museum. Among works of this kind we should also take note of Overbeck's 'The Triumph of Religion' (plate 90). It is worth recalling that this explicitly 'sacred' picture was painted specially for a training institution for the arts, the Städelsches Institut in Frankfurt, its avowed purpose being 'to make the pliable spirit of art's alumni receptive to pure and exalted ideals' (den bildsamen Geist der Kunstzöglinge für reine hohe Ideale empfänglich zu machen).[11] The ideals of art and religion having become identical, the places once reserved for the saints, at the feet of the Blessed Virgin, are taken by artists.

Now Cornelius' biographer commends the absence from his work of any denominational colour-ing, and one must admit that the facts are as stated. Indeed, though he did not disdain the themes of revealed religion, we look in vain for any kind of personal conviction that is worthy to be called a faith. Behind all the sedulous erudition there is no sign of any warm and sympathetic feeling for life. Such detached catholicity of taste and interest recalls a saying of Burckhardt's about the New Testament: 'There is a world here that is quite different from that of antique art and we are rich in this respect – that we can enjoy both and do justice to both.'[12]

Whatever may be said of Cornelius, however, those who entertained this encyclopaedic view of history were profoundly aware of the 'sacred' character of their task; and it was precisely here that a difficulty arose, for they also understood the essential uniqueness of any historic event. They thus found themselves faced with the problem of coming to terms with the contradiction between the general and the particular. Cornelius, devoted as he was to a nobility of form that was really no longer of this world, would have nothing to do with the positivist's demand for strict historical accuracy. His unbending idealism rejected all such considerations as correctness of circumstantial detail and of general historical atmosphere. Yet at the opposite pole of historical painting where the past was spied on through a keyhole, it was just the peculiarities of time and place that were emphasized to such a degree that all universal significance tended to disappear. With Cornelius we have – and this must certainly be admitted – depth of meaning reflecting a real depth of thought; with the masters of the historic genre we have an episode, the recounting in paint of some arresting incident. 'Seni and the corpse of Wallenstein' is a good example (plate 86).

The fact is that the painter of 'sacred' pictures in a history-conscious age had a double task to perform. He had to raise the historical event he was portraying to a symbolic level; and at the same time he had to give a true rendering of the event itself. He had, in a word, to create at one and the same time both a symbol and an illustration. Here, as we have seen, there lurked a contradiction. It was thought that it could be resolved by simply endowing a purely factual subject with a certain tran-scendental symbolic power. Indeed, it was thought that a purely factual subject, factually treated, could actually convey a universal message more effectively than the language of symbolism proper. 'Who is it that gives a worthier representation of the Holy Ghost, he who paints him as a dove super-imposed over a bundle of rays, or he who sets before me some great and noble man, such as a Luther or a Huss afire with divine enthusiasm?' So Vischer put the matter in his *Kritische Gänge*. We must compare this utterance with the passage in Schopenhauer where he deals with the crisis in Christian art, the passage to which reference has already been made. Every historical event, it was there stated, has both a nominal and a factual significance. The former is 'the external significance and consists of something added by conceptual thought, the latter is a reflection of the idea of mankind which the picture reveals. We can take as an instance of the former the finding of Moses by the Egyptian Princess – a most important moment for the whole of history. The factual significance, however, the actual thing that we behold, is a foundling who is being saved by a woman of high rank from a floating cradle, an event which may actually have taken place'.[13]

Being concerned with nothing more than the bare facts that meet the eye, Schopenhauer only takes account of the factual significance of this event, even though it is of great historical importance, for only the initiate who knows something about period dress can add the nominal significance. Vischer, on the other hand, elevates the historical event which occurred once only and was therefore unique, into a manifestation of divinity. God's dwelling is everywhere and nowhere, His body is the whole world, His true presence is the human spirit, and where that spirit is truly great, there God is manifested. The temporal thus becomes a substitute for the divine, which itself is merely immanent. Let us remember that in the nineteenth century the museum could become a church and the church a museum. Here there is a similar exchange of symbols; once the 'Great Man', of whom more will be said in a subsequent chapter, could become the representative or deputy of the Holy Ghost, he began to claim for himself the mission of the Saviour and Redeemer. Since there could no longer be any intercourse with the next world, history was combed in a search for the Great Man, who was now the substitute god, and the divine was declared to be present everywhere.

This brings me to a consideration of the more explicitly religious phases of nineteenth century art. The humanizing of the divine, as Vischer describes it, implies nothing less than the sanctification of man, or even his elevation to divinity. Here, however, we are not so very far from another view of man, a view that sees human conduct – both in suffering and in triumph – as deriving its symbolic meaning from the acts of God and of His Son. The nineteenth century failed to impart any new features to the strictly traditional conception of Christ, but it would be wrong to infer all too hastily from this that the ancient faith no longer meant anything. In the new picture of the Son of God, in which His identity was so often a concealed one, His presence is essentially an immanent presence; the 'Roman shepherd' of Delacroix is Christ upon the Mount, Millet's 'Peasant family' is the flight into Egypt. Since Goya, however, it is the outlawed and the despairing who have been the symbolic representatives of Christ.

But the converse also holds good. If a human type could be made to suggest Christ, Christ could be made to suggest a human type. Daumier's 'Ecce homo' (plate 52) shows us not only the rejected Redeemer, it also shows us the nameless man who must daily endure the mockery of the world. Goya is again to some extent the turning point, for since Goya no attempts at depicting the strong and comforting Redeemer have succeeded in carrying conviction.

This 'actualizing' of Christ is a persistent theme, and very significant in its persistence. Its import is clear enough. If a defender of the realist school[14] hails as the true exponent of modernism an artist who dares to paint a Crucifixion taking place among soldiers, policemen, and men wearing modern business suits – Ensor's 'L'entrée du Christ à Bruxelles' (plate 53) is a case in point – it is not merely because such a conception 'actualizes' the biblical narrative, but because it enables us to see an analogy between the ordinary happenings of today and the events described in the Old and New Testaments.

This method of either putting Christ in a modern setting or letting him be symbolized by a contemporary situation is one of the two forms adopted by the religious picture in the nineteenth century;

Gauguin's 'Ia Orana Maria' (plate 98) and Segantini's 'Ave Maria' (plate 92) are examples of it. An event of ordinary life is given a symbolic dimension, human beings and even inanimate objects become things sanctified. The nameless woman becomes the Mother of God, a dove is taken for the appearance of the Holy Ghost (Flaubert: *Un Cœur Simple*). This is what leads Rilke to speak of the bottles in Cézanne's still life as saints. It is not the external but the inner significance that counts.

The other form of religious picture makes use of a rather similar method of substitution, but instead of using a scene of ordinary life which happens to be ready to hand, it uses some well known and well established work of art. A mingled sense of inadequacy and awe holds the artist back from any attempt at a 'direct intercourse with heaven', as Novalis calls it. He seeks for artistic mediators in whose work the divine takes clear and visible form. Ingres makes use of the mediation of Raphael (plate 94), Gauguin of anonymous Breton sculptures ('Le Christ jaune', 'Le Calvaire'), while Van Gogh copies Rembrandt's 'Resurrection of Lazarus' and Delacroix's 'The Good Samaritan'.

This latter process set in as part of the Romantic movement, at the time, that is to say, when people began to hold that the old stories and writings were, as Novalis says, the only sources 'from which we can obtain knowledge of the supernatural world' and where for the first time aesthetic speculation began to convince men that a work of art could stimulate religious faith. Friedrich's 'Tetschen altar' (plate 91) is the first and the most radical witness to this romantic religiosity that stands wholly apart from the Christian pictorial tradition to which for centuries art had conformed. The Crucifixion is shown not as something directly perceived by the eye of the artist himself but as a pre-existent work of art, while nature forms a kind of devotional setting and, like those 'aesthetic churches', the museums, which were the true sanctuaries of the Romantic movement, serves to call up a particular kind of mood. What Wackenroder's monk in his *Herzensergiessungen*, or pourings forth of the heart, experienced as two distinct worlds of God – the free landscape and the interior of the temple sanctified to God 'with the image of the Crucified One' – these two worlds Friedrich has endeavoured to melt into one, and he sought to do this by consecrating nature as God's house.

I would add yet one word. The road from the beginning of the century to Monet's variations on 'Rouen Cathedral' (plate 206) is shorter than might at first appear. Once again the artist's vision has recourse to a pre-existent work of art. The light-fantasies of the Impressionists transform hard reality into a non-material glory of colour. They are like those mystical apotheoses of sound which we owe to a composer of that time. I speak of Anton Bruckner, his symphonies and his organ music. But there is yet another and more direct relationship with the world of music. Debussy's *La Cathédrale Englou-tie*[15] suggests that Monet's churches should be viewed as the creations of a dream. They are indeed like that enchanted Cathedral of Ys which – so the legend tells – was once seen by a fisherman in the early morning as it rose out of a transparent sea. It is surely possible that Friedrich's visionary churches also derive from this legendary material which can be traced in every part of Europe.

5

The basis of Chenavard's decorations of the Pantheon is a kind of calendar, devised by the artist himself, which divides history into a number of clearly distinguishable periods.[16] History is arranged according to the different stages of human life. The youth of man is conceived as the period between Adam and the Babylonian separation of tongues. The human span between the seventeenth and forty-second year corresponds to the period that reaches its culminating point with Jesus Christ. Then follows the third stage in which a single religion is dominant, the sciences reach their peak, and the different tongues begin to mingle. If sculpture and architecture were most significant in the first age of man, the third is distinguished by painting and music. Eventually, mankind, having been delivered

79 INGRES The Apotheosis of Homer; 1827.

84 BOULANGER Flute-player rehearsing at Napoleon's Roman villa; 1861.

85 FEUERBACH The Symposium; 1873.

82 COUTURE Rome in her decline; 1847.

83 CHASSERIAU Tepidarium; 1853.

80 INGRES Ossian's Dream (detail).

DELACROIX Dante and Vergil crossing the lake that encircles the city of Dis, guided by Phlegyas; 1822.

88 MAKART Charles V's entry into Antwerp; 1878.

89 MENZEL The Battle of Hochkirch; 1856.

86 PILOTY Seni and the corpse of Wallenstein; 1855.

87 DEGAS War in the Middle Ages (entitled *Les malheurs de la ville d'Orléans*); 1865.

90 OVERBECK The Triumph of Religion; 1840.

over by Christianity to pain and sorrow, relapses into childhood. The rise of America marks the beginning of the fourth age. After this there begins a brotherhood of the different races, a single world language comes into being and the distinctions between the social classes disappear. About the year 2800 A.D. history ceases and about 3500 there is an end of all religions. The last 700 years see the death of the human race, which, according to the plan of its historical stage-manager, will attain an age corresponding to that of eighty-four in a human being.

For Chenavard all religions were of equal value. When he felt his plan was threatened by the veto of the Church, he made the following confession to Théophile Silvestre: 'I already saw myself as the High Priest of a new cult. I wanted to make a dogma of reason and a god of man. The moment I showed that one religion ranked as high as another and that they have all been devouring each other since the beginning of the world, people were no longer able to lull themselves into illusion. The Roman Pantheon was the temple of all the deities. I should like to make the Paris Pantheon a temple of all Great Men.'

The story of man was to be told in forty-two murals. It was to begin with the flood and end with representations of the four great emperors, Alexander, Caesar, Charlemagne and Napoleon. It is significant that there were to be only three references to the life of Christ. These narrative pictures were to be followed by a frieze showing the Great Men of all ages from antiquity down to Saint-Simon. The arches spanning the four columns supporting the dome were dedicated to the four ages of man: religion, art, philosophy and science. The figures symbolizing the latter, Moses, Homer, Aristotle and Galileo, stand in front of these pillars. In place of a high altar Chenavard designed a composite structure consisting of a ship, the symbol of Egypt, an ark, the symbol of Israel, and a crowning chalice, the symbol of Christianity. By way of summarizing all his ideas, the artist conceived a huge circular painting divided horizontally into three sections. In the uppermost one were allegorical figures representing the world religions, while the middle one was occupied by the heroes of history of all ages and the lowest contained a representation of the chaos into which all things must ultimately fall to be born anew out of fire. The whole composition was dominated by the figure of one who was apparently rising from the dead. Théophile Gautier saw in the latter the embodiment of the Logos, the symbol of the divine spark in man. If the Pantheon was conceived as the temple of the world's greatest men – and Chenavard's own words prove that it was – then it seems clear that this particular figure symbolizes the Superman (plate 104).

The Pantheon cycle marks a turning point. It marks the fullest and most essentially epic development of history's encyclopaedic representation of man. Its great breadth of vision was also characteristic of something else, a device which was very typical of the rather special pictorial appetites of the age – the panorama. This admittedly depends for its effect on a mere capacity for illusion, a quality that hardly ranks very high in the scale of artistic attainment, whereas Chenavard's work in the last resort depends on the scope and suggestiveness of his ideas. Yet in either case the enormous volume of detail causes the spectator to be preoccupied with sheer enumeration.

The idea of a historical museum of man as conceived by this artist-philosopher was in line with the practice, indulged in by the great World Exhibitions, of setting on view documented accounts of cultural and religious history; and it is worth noting that in the Paris Exhibition of 1855 was shown a part of Chenavard's Pantheon designs. In these pieces of what was really consecrated ground – they were of course consecrated to Progress – a new cult was being instituted. A series of exhibits would be set up illustrating the story of man, together with shrines of the various religions, which really served the purpose of museums, and the feast of human brotherhood would thus be duly proclaimed. Nor was the painting of religious history behindhand in following this fashion of world-wide mutual embrace – as we can see from Hans Canon's picture showing the different creeds and religions uniting in homage to Christ. It is significant that this picture of a triumphant world religion was not painted for a church but was exhibited at the Vienna World Exhibition of 1875.

According to Chenavard's prophecy the death of mankind will be preceded by an age in which sience and industry move forward to their greatest discoveries. The human race will then intone the Hymn of Brotherhood in a universal language. This hope must be reckoned among the many pleasing Utopias produced in France at the middle of the century. It was a hope entertained not only by men like Ballanche and Quinet whose minds moved along more or less historical lines but by faithful demo- crats like Thoré-Bürger, Castagnary, Hugo, and Courbet. Both parties – that of history as well as that of life – had the same passionate devotion to the ideal of human brotherhood, both sought equally to turn their art into an instrument for its service.

6

Whereas with Chenavard, whose artist's imagination could only find its bearings in the past, these aspirations could do no more than produce empty and insubstantial prophecies, those other artists who sought to find the true image of man as part of their direct perception of the present, did succeed in evoking a vision of this ideal of theirs which they could translate into pictorial terms; for instead of gathering together the symbols of all ages and all peoples, they confined themselves – to use the words of Schopenhauer – to 'what was directly presented to their vision'. The rest of the passage is well worth quoting since it is as good an assessment as any of what these men were consciously or unconsciously endeavouring to do. 'To hold fast and make permanent within a painting the fleeting world which is for ever changing its face, to hold fast a single phase thereof which nevertheless bespeaks the whole – this is an achievement of the painter's art which seems to bring time itself to a standstill – in so far as the particular is elevated to the idea of its genus.'[17]

The task, as envisaged by Schopenhauer, was not an easy one. The danger of being involved in too wide a spread of subject matter was one that threatened both the devotees of the historical approach and those exclusively concerned with the present. It continually tempted men to dissolve the human essence in a process of mere enumeration and so reduce it to a series of isolated events, each of which was a kind of law unto itself; it tempted them to lose themselves in a multiplicity of aspects, in the fortuitous, in a maze of episodic fragments, in short to succumb to what was transient and temporary and so become oblivious of what in man is permanent and universal. Impressionism is the history of this temptation and of the overcoming of it by the artist.

Chenavard's cycle brings to an end the historical interpretation of man. Courbet's 'L'atelier' is the first picture in which the painter, though concentrating wholly on the present, contrives never- theless to depict man's essential and omnipresent features. It is a picture of life that follows man from the cradle to the grave. It is a picture expressing the democratic faith in what is common to all men. This matter was discussed earlier in some detail; there are, however, two further aspects of it that remain to be dealt with, for they serve to explain more fully the nature of the essential relationship between the work of Courbet and the great pictures of humanity of the second half of the cen- tury.

'L'atelier' is what we might term a collective picture. Let us disregard for the moment the element of self-portraiture. Then we shall see that it is not the individual that is important in the painting but the group, and, ultimately, the whole species of 'man', which here speaks to us with so many different voices. There is nothing here – as there is in historical paintings – in the nature of an interconnecting nexus of action. The figures are just there – in essentially passive attitudes. They simply are as they are, and that is all the picture has to say about them. It is not men who are in any sense agents in history, that we see. We see men that are outside history and simply exist, and it is they who are here 'elevated to the idea of a species'.

Admittedly, the idea of humanity is not exhausted by this passive state of being thus anonymously 'there'; the artist also shows us the central feature of our modern experience of the world which is the omnipresent existence of the mass. Collectivity in the nineteenth century is the essential mode of human experience, the vessel in which essential human experience is contained. It manifests this character in two ways: on the one hand when men are drawn together by the despair that results from being utterly deserted, when their existence becomes an inferno from which there is no escape; and on the other hand when in some happy hour of relative security men are able to have a sense of community, when they feel that a bridge has been built between 'I' and 'Thou'. In the one case we have the earthly hell, in the other the earthly paradise.

Both of these strata of experience are symbolically present in Courbet's picture. In the left half of the painting, life sinks to the sombre level of brooding despair; but in the young pair of lovers, in the artist, in 'Truth', and in the two boys it frees itself and rises to a restrained but very positive approval of its own existence. It is this intermingling of happiness and resignation that provides the picture with what are almost a series of lyrics, all expressive of different moods. Seen in the context of the history of art, 'L'atelier' has its ancestry in two kinds of imaginative vision. One of these reaches back to the rather sombre and earnest manner of portraying the ordinary facts of human existence that was so typical of the brothers Nain, who for the first time – at the beginning of the seventeenth century – painted the face of sober and dignified poverty. For them life is no riotous feast, as it was for the Dutch, but something which excited a certain deep but controlled emotion. The human type that they so especially favoured, a type that reminds one somehow of a still-life, was seen by Courbet in a new light. The other line of connection with the past – this time a more recent one – combines 'L'atelier' (I speak particularly of the left half of the picture) with those madhouse pictures in which the European Romantic movement sought to express – and so master – the trapped quality of human life, those pictures in which 'Every man thinks himself that which he is not', as Goya says, 'every man enacts a masquerade for everybody else' (plate 50). The madman has now become the man who is rejected and outlawed. From the human heap of the insane it is but a step to the human heap exposed to wind and weather in Delacroix's 'La barque de Don Juan' (plate 71). In the realism of the mid-century which avoids all pathos, the romantic gesture of madness had lost its force. What remained was the terrible estrangement between man and man. Closely related to madness, too, is that collective sense of abandonment which is one of the symptoms of that state of having no hold on anything in life and so no hold upon oneself, which marked and formed the man of the nineteenth century quite as much as it did his art. To express the matter rather differently, madness was for the artist nothing other than an exaggerated expression of a perfectly real human condition, the extreme form in which it became visible to the eye. The group in the left half of Courbet's picture is raised in Daumier's 'Un wagon de troisième classe' (plate 160) to the level of a monumental symbol of mankind's utter bankruptcy of spiritual comfort, a bankruptcy from which there is no escape.

One may well say that the two great collective themes of the nineteenth century – the earthly hell and the earthly paradise – grew and branched forth from Courbet's painting. Let it be noted, however, that I speak not so much of an actual influence as of a spiritual connection. I merely say that that more richly and elaborately conceived picture of mankind in which man's sorrow intermingles with his transfiguration, is in 'L'atelier' already superbly prefigured. From Courbet right down to Toulouse-Lautrec the broad stream of an art that was intensely aware of the present, defended its practice of almost arbitrarily selecting its repertoire from the cross-section of humanity which sociological investigation was presenting to its view, with the result that the real encyclopaedic theme behind *Les français peints par eux-mêmes* – a work which was essentially a caricature of contemporary life – attained a more human profundity, and was permeated and so ennobled by genuine art. The second half of the century sought time and again to make a symbolic whole out of the variegated and disjointed visions of the empiricist, and to weld them together into an *allégorie réelle*. The analytical representation of individual social types – the labourer, the peasant, the drunkard, the washerwoman, the prostitute – was transformed in the great rounded conceptions of the epoch into mighty symbols of life (plates 163, 166, 168, 170, 173).

The living thing, so much more telling pictorially than mere historically circumscribed recapitulation, ultimately achieved its victory over history. Man became spellbound by the changes and everlasting repetitions of life, he reckoned now with the partnership of nature, whose organic fullness recalled him from the essential particularity of the historical consciousness. The mode of historical experience is heterogeneous and discontinuous, it is concerned with the unique and unrepeatable – natural development is a steady transition, an uninterrupted movement around one centre, a fluid unfolding. Once the great hero, explained invariably in tragic terms, had ceased to be the main point of attraction, the artist's imagination sought to find a meaning in other subjects which he could actually see before him and got to know by direct experience rather than through historical erudition. He turned to the different ages of man – perhaps, by the way, these do vaguely correspond to the different periods of history with which historical painting was concerned – to motherhood, to the child (plates 209–218), to the relations between man and woman. It was 'L'atelier', with its two lateral groups and symbolic easel landscape, that introduced this change, though in its central section it still shows an interest in the apotheosis of the Great Man. Among its spiritual progeny are Manet's 'Old musician' (1862), Marées' Neapolitan fresco, Seurat's 'Un dimanche d'été à la Grande Jatte' (1884–86) (plate 190) and the last great picture of humanity that the nineteenth century produced, Gauguin's 'D'où venons-nous? Que sommes-nous? Où allons-nous?' (1897), (plate 217). The interpretation of these pictures will be left to a later chapter.

VI   Mankind on Show

It is only when we pass beyond the direct impact of sense and feeling
and that of external objects, that we come upon genuine reality

Hegel

THE religion of humanity had some strange excrescences. This was essentially the age of an accelerated dialectic. Everything was at any moment liable to turn, if not into its opposite, then into its caricature, and this process was responsible for one of the most important and also one of the most puzzling manifestations that the century produced.

The World Exhibitions are the nineteenth century's official visiting cards.[1] The conception behind them, first realized in London in 1851, emphasized the triumph of a world made by man, a world of which man was the central reference point. They proclaimed the victory of an essentially masculine mastery over nature – the victory of the force that allegedly changes the world.

Yet these apotheoses of Progress were also demonstrations of historical consciousness, and they looked both to the future and to the past. Every such World Exhibition was also a kind of global fashion-show – did not Nietzsche say 'We are the most studious age in point of costume'? – the costumes in question being 'the moral tenets, articles of faith, artistic tastes and religions.'[2] The many parts played by the nineteenth century, the many historical costumes in which it decked itself in these exhibitions – which were a mixture of panorama, museum and shrine – all served the purposes of a very striking piece of mass stage-management. It was here that the century dramatized itself and the world became its theatre (plates 99–110).

The whole paraphernalia of modern civilization's sophisticated complexity was exhibited side by side with some odd find from the distant tropics, while giant Canadian firs could be seen next to Sèvres porcelain; all that was touched by, or related to, the activities of man, qualified for exhibition in these super-museums – in a word the entire world was here on show. Geography and ethnology, industry and art were translated into visual terms in this vast sample collection from all peoples and continents, and were jumbled together in these cosmic laboratories. Real objects, abstracted out of the world of actual profane reality, divorced from their living and conditioning surroundings, were duly groomed for exhibition to the gaze of a bemused public. Only a fragmented and purely eclectic sense of reality could ever have hit on such a thought!

To trace the origin of these World Exhibitions back to the old fairs of the traditional type is as mistaken as it would be to connect them with the collective itch for simply staring at shop windows, or with the festivals of the Baroque. To adopt any such view would be to confine oneself to the mere external aspects of the affair, to treat it as just another phase of ordinary business life – a phase admittedly relieved by jester's pranks – and to ignore its marked ideological implications.

Undoubtedly the World Exhibitions took over the functions of the traditional fairs, yet they were distinguished by an implicit but systematized quasi-philosophical dogmatism that was peculiar to themselves. Fundamentally they were less concerned with what they sold than with what they represented. Between producer and customer there stood not – as of old – the simple and serviceable huckster's table but the spectacle of a theatrical performance. The article on view was arrayed in stage costume; it was wrapped about with solemnity. The exhibitor's stall did more than merely display the merchandise, it provided it with a synthetic sanctuary. In a blaze of self-satisfaction, such merchandise was placed on a pedestal where it received quasi-religious honours. It thus assumed a higher reality, not the reality of a work of art, nor that of an article of common use nor even that of a sacred object, but the reality of a fetish.

To be placed thus publicly on view is indispensable for the fetish, for it means that the largest number of people can have a part in it. Not everyone can make it his own, but all may stare at it. The fetish character which Marx ascribed to merchandise is too narrowly conceived, for it is confined to its economic content and derives from the nexus of production. In fact, however, the fetish is a structural characteristic of the entire nineteenth century and the World Exhibitions are the places where its character is most fully revealed. In order to possess themselves of some recognizable measure of reality, which they professed to represent, they brought into being an artificial fenced-in world, a higher reality that lay beyond and apart from ordinary profane reality, and although the visitor was himself moving through a solid factual three-dimensional world, he was confronted by what was essentially a painted illusion. This popular encyclopaedia of man could only achieve something arranged and composed, and in the end the grand comprehensive view that men had hoped for, the uplifting synopsis of all races and peoples and all fields of human activity failed to materialize; it disintegrated, and proved to be a thing that lacked any cohesion between its constituent parts. Actually these distilled essences of reality did no more than call into being a surrogate puppet-world which, by impersonating and at the same time veiling the real one, sought to nullify its demands.

What can one say of the mind of an epoch that seeks refuge from reality in a distilled world of appearances? We have here projects that might deservedly be called far-sighted. Why were they placed with exhibitionist complacency in the shop window – instead of simply being realized without further ado? We have all manner of machines and apparatus designed to produce goods or to achieve some other useful purpose – why did they remain strangers to the factory and the workshop, why did they continue thus remote from life as mere immaculate abstractions? In no other century would such a thing have been conceivable. Yet men conceived it now, though in the end only two things were made manifest – failure and fear of reality.

In the Paris Exhibition of 1855 a model of a workman's dwelling was on view, but it was no more than the feeble alibi of a ruler who did indeed manage to get some kind of order into the layout of his capital, but who never contrived to touch the slums behind those rigid rectangular facades. What was this but a propagandist surrogate intended to compensate men for a real world that was, and is in fact still, unsubdued? Thanks to these World Exhibition, the unrealists of every persuasion – utopian social reformers, starry-eyed apostles of world-brotherhood, masters of ceremonies of the masked balls of architectural styles – enjoyed a jester's licence and were permitted to do as they pleased. In these hole and corner refuges they could erect a fleeting world of stage scenery; released as they were from the bedrock of hard fact and from any reality experienced at first hand, they could dream their dreams of art and a new society undisturbed.

Even the halls where machinery was exhibited served only to push reality into the background. A machine when treated as a mere exhibit is a presumption and a pretence. Delacroix seems to have been uneasily aware of something of the kind when on the 5th of August 1855 he wrote in his diary: 'I am deeply saddened when I look at all these machines. I have no liking for these pieces of matter which, standing there alone and with nothing but their own resources, seem to be laying claim to admiration for their achievements.' Divorced from its function, a machine is no more than an idol, smooth and precise. It is no more than a pretentious symbol, something that is worlds apart from what we see in Menzel's 'The rolling-mill' (plate 169). The difference between the two is that between mere stylization and the descriptive epic.

What here accepted the credit of being a representative cross-section of humanity was a world of mere appearances that had borrowed from art, in so far as it made some pretence at composition, while borrowing a tangible three-dimensional quality from the real world. The aim was to create an *allégorie réelle* of civilization, to give all continents, races, and cultures a forum where they could appear and show themselves. Yet it all ended with a mere piling up of heterogeneous objects which in the moment that they entered this arena and put themselves on view, were transformed into fetishes. They were surrounded by illusion and seemed to be trying to cast a magic spell by which men could be persuaded to regard them as ends in themselves. Yet they soon congealed into a kind of mummified state in which, like mummies, they were never truly alive nor – so it seemed – truly dead. As to the machines, they lost what little semblance of life they had and became mere cult objects.

Meanwhile vast salons were reserved for the plastic arts, but here a similar process of make-believe was in operation, since the products of such art were – like the products of industry – no more than merchandise, for in this world all things were merchandise – and in the end man himself.

2

The great mystical swindle was not without its compulsive power. It could sweep the paltry impediment of logic aside, synthesize opposites and bring contradictories to a glorious reconciliation.

Here was a 'canned' reality which was also temporary and transient and liable at any time to be countermanded, cancelled, and sent to oblivion, a temple of civilization which was nevertheless no more than its purely provisional home which was at one and the same time a museum and an experiment – and there lay the contradiction in the whole ideological concept. *Homo faber's* self-assurance demanded for him a place in the Hall of Fame; his belief in Progress, a belief which would not accept anything as final, drew life from the very fact that the world is subject to change. When he thought with favour of the museum, it was because he was glancing backward and searching for a comprehensive representation of human history. Yet in his experimental mood he called in question all that was past. Both these moods had to find expression and this is why in the World Exhibitions an agglomeration of historical styles stood side by side with the creations of an advanced architecture in glass and steel.

Yet the conflict between these two leading ideas was forgotten when the people got down to the business of proclaiming the basic tenets of the fashionable philosophy. Then the past became the herald of the present and the future the culminating point in the triptych of a proud humanity.

Such a spirit of harmony between past and future was infectious. Vows were now taken that were to ensure the reconciliation of all peoples, and the triumph of the spirit of unity over the conflicts of interest and class seemed just around the corner. These sociable inclinations have an almost spectral effect in an age which more than any other condemned man to loneliness.

It was in the World Exhibitions that civilization sought to enact the ceremonies of its religious cult. Their halls evoked the lovely dream of mass-beatification, and in their Temples of Fame homage was paid to Progress and all the good things that were to go along with it. How intense was the enthusiasm for this spectacle, how deeply religious was the colouring of the emotion it aroused, is proved by contemporary utterances. Prince Napoleon in his inaugural address at the Exhibition of 1855 spoke of a temple of harmony and happiness. A new world religion, that of humanitarianism, was proclaimed. Even the greatest were not immune to the seductions of the new gospel. Victor Hugo, exiled by the empire, sent a message of greeting in 1867 to the Paris Exhibition of that year, in which he enjoined on the people of France their own dissolution as a nation. 'Thou shalt be France no longer', apostrophized the seer, 'thou shalt become Humanity; effulgent, radiating outwards, it is thy destiny to dissolve completely, and just as Rome became Christianity, thou, o France, shalt become The World.' It was, to say the least, a not inconsiderable summons, but this idea is eloquent of the whole wild syncretism that was part of the World Exhibition philosophy.

In these show-places there was no longer any hierarchy of values – still less any logical arrangement. An attempt was indeed made – in London in 1851 and in Paris in 1867 – to arrange the different exhibits according to their kind. Unfortunately there had also to be a division according to nationality and in the case of the different national sections nationalist exhibitionism was quite ready to accept a heterogeneous jumble as long as its own peculiar appetite was satisfied. The mighty circular halls – that of Paris in 1867 and the Vienna Rotunda of 1875 – depended for their effect on the same optical trick that ultimately led to the invention of the panorama. Both habituated people to look at things in a circle, and so conveyed the impression of endlessness, of the negation of the finite and particular and so of order itself.

Some looked upon these temples as the creations of a dream, others as the railway stations of civilization, filled with luggage that was only meant to be looked at and with cheapjack wares. Out of doors there was a proliferation of picturesque pavilions, distributed apparently without any kind of plan. Everything was supposed to be connected with everything else – though the effect produced was that nothing was connected with anything. Nothing existed for its own sake. Every juxtaposition whether fortuitous or deliberate was an expression of boundless universality and tolerance. The Turkish mosque stood next to the lighthouse. Trade, by which nations were united, was confronted with the nationalism that divides them, the Red Cross Pavilion was neighbour to the crowning achievements of the arms industry. In this labyrinth every road was the best road, for all were interconnected. All things were at a common level.

3

When admirers of these World Exhibitions sought for comparisons, they spoke of 'temples of Harmony' or of 'Louvres of the future.' Adolphe Guéroult distinguished three elements that were working for the creation of a new cult: the Church, the Opera and the Palais de l'Industrie at the exhibition of 1855. Of these the exhibition was the most modern and the one best designed to be an embodiment of the nineteenth century.[3] Wagner's concept of a 'collective work of art' had a sudden new relevance, and certainly this mass offering of artistic and mechanical effects-ranging from the fireworks to the monster concert – was as much a centre of pilgrimage as was the Festspielhaus in Bayreuth. Both were substitutes for churches.

For all that, the powers of this new syncretist religion were insufficient either to liquidate the old cult or to lay a firm foundation for a new one. The old gods were still allowed to count in so far as they were put on view as exhibits illustrating cultural history. An Egyptian temple was reconstructed, as were Mexican holy places. Buddhist deities were put on view, and a Turkish mosque was set up quite close to the pavilion of the Papal State. Past forms of religion were neutralized by being reduced to the level of museum curiosities. What remained was, as we see from the speculations of Chenavard, the façade of abstraction called religious history. It was quite logical that this process should extend to Christianity and its cults and reduce this too to a mere museum piece.

In view of all that has been said, it is hardly surprising that when a Catholic chapel was erected in 1867, it was not dedicated to the celebration of the Mass or to prayer, but to the exhibition of cult objects of the most recent design. What happened, what indeed had been bound to happen, was that once again an age which accorded the museum the sanctity of a shrine, turned the church into a museum. Actually, both aspects of this process were widely in evidence, and what applied to

91 C.D. FRIEDRICH The Tetschen altar; 1808.

95 SCHNORR VON CAROLSFELD The Annunciation; 1820.

94 INGRES Louis XIII's vow; 1824.

92 SEGANTINI *Ave Maria*; 1886.

93 LEIBL Three women at church; 1882.

97 PUVIS DE CHAVANNES The Prodigal Son; 1879.

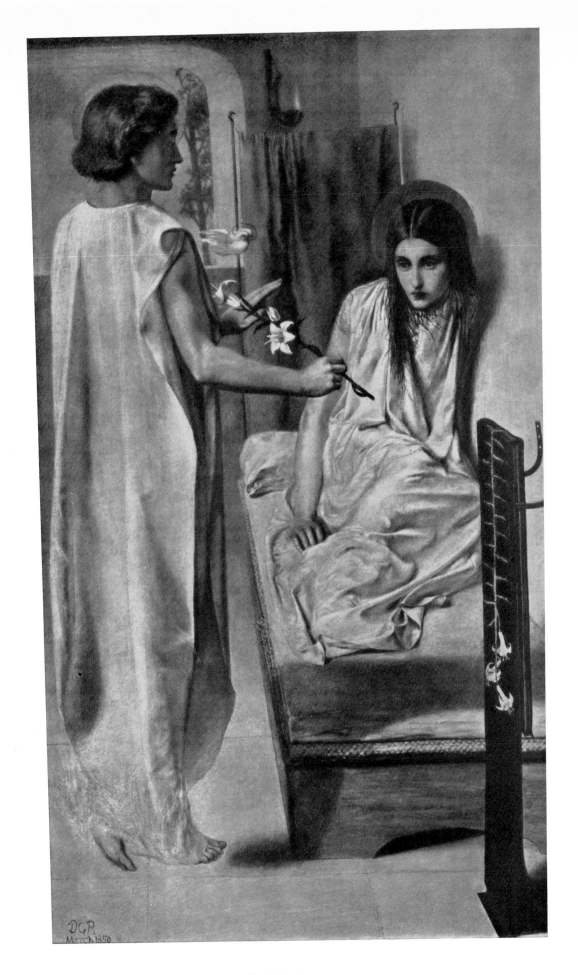

96 ROSSETTI *Ecce Ancilla Domini* (Annunciation); 1850.

IA ORANA MARIA

98 GAUGUIN *Ia Orana Maria*; 1891.

the museum applied with equal force to all related institutions – particularly when an association of ideas could be evoked by symbolic decoration or suggestive architecture (the merest whiff of the Gothic could do wonders in this respect). In 1851 Pugin designed a mediaeval court for the London Exhibition which was adorned with sculptures and works of decorative art.[4] The visitor's feelings were, according to a contemporary observer, similar to those of one visiting a shrine.

In a world of surrogates a church had become something between inverted commas. It was no longer the gathering place of a community but a place of transit for a curious public. It had become as empty of real significance as the holy places of non-European peoples – with whom it now shared the physical juxtaposition of mere unrelated co-existence.

This sterile and museum-like quality did not wholly escape the people of that time. They saw that this substitution of a mere façade for reality had about it something artificial and remote from life. Renan, sceptical, and even disgusted by this hullabaloo about civilization, contrasted the World Exhibition with the festivals of the Greeks and the pilgrimages of the Middle Ages. Seen in the light of this comparison, the present seemed to him sterile and hectic; it appeared to him to be squandering its powers on superfluities and to be obsessed by the style-destroying ideal of mere comfort which it had imported from England.

It is plain enough that the new form of divine service never quite came off. Admittedly, this peep-show of Progress brought pilgrims from all over the world who were eager enough to gape at what was set before them, but the transformation of the merely curious and credulous into a community did not materialize. The individual remained no more than an onlooker, the multitude mingled to form a mere public.

This quality of being shut off from anything resembling true spiritual participation is well illustrated by an event which took place at the closing of the London Exhibition in 1851. A concluding banquet was arranged at which the Prince Consort and the members of the committee were present, a banquet that was served upon a raised platform (plate 103). At the feet of this distinguished company, and in the surrounding galleries, was a thick crowd of all those who simply wanted to say they had been there – as though the thing had been a play, a ceremony of consecration, or a coronation. The saying that the exhibition conditions the onlooker is true in reverse and the Great Ones of the century knew what they owed to the masses. They had indeed put on an act, and much as the shop-window travestied a piece of merchandise into a fetish, so here the great show effected a sublimation into the extraordinary. The banquet became a ritual, the onlookers did indeed transform it into a pseudo-sacred act, like something enacted on an operatic stage – though performed in this case by that other surrogate church of the nineteenth century – but there was no true collective devotional participation.

The masses, then, formed no organized body; they did not become a community in the sense of becoming a congregation, they remained amorphous, they vacillated and were unstable, they went through the collective motions of enthusiasm but remained inwardly unsatisfied. Once the hoped-for act of faith failed somehow to come off, the miracles that were to have been enacted were recognized for what they were – stage effects now seen in the tawdry and unconvincing illumination of the footlights. What was allegedly gigantic and colossal was seen to be a matter of mere quantitative power and so became subject – at least in capacity to evoke emotion – to the law of diminishing returns, and so the whole sorry business developed the characteristics of a second-rate side-show with the latter's complete inability to transport people out of the world in which they lived.

In these museums of civilization all was possible and all that was possible allowed. The past was reconstructed with the meticulous diligence of the scrupulous archivist while, with a happy abandon to the law of trial and error, the future was made the subject of imaginative guesswork.

A long row of tableaux suitably enlivened with wax figures showed the History of Labour, while an open air exhibition described the development of human dwelling places – from the pile structures and caves of a more primitive age up to the present day – by means of a series of painstakingly accurate reconstructions.

With such delving into the past there went the itch for the annihilation of mere physical distance, which could fortunately be satisfied without the imaginative strain of an excursion through time. The enterprising visitor could encounter Laplanders' tents cheek by jowl with Russian country houses, could see Chinese gardeners at work, could undergo the mildly hazardous experience of being shaved by an Arabian barber, and end by standing himself an American drink in an American bar. And so the supply of quaint and novel experiences passed imperceptibly out of the past into the present until at last even the commonplaces of contemporary life, the things which to the European were known and familiar, became strange and exotic through mere proximity to the unusual; at length the citizen of the nineteenth century stood as awe-struck before the products of his own civilization as before the offerings of the remotest continents. Yet all this was but another manifestation of the enormous hunger for illusion which in one way or another these World Exhibitions succeeded in satisfying. No other institution was in this respect their equal. Their bright stylized world of shams enabled the visitor for hours on end to forget the commonplace realities with which he was daily surrounded.

Although, as we have seen, they failed to produce a genuine act of faith, these World Exhibitions with their general air of innovation and experiment did contrive to propagate a new quasi-religious ideal. They seemed to bring home the fact that the world was constantly changing and that to change was to be in tune with it. The Exhibitions were indeed themselves visible demonstrations proving that there could be no finality in human affairs. Their very existence could hardly be justified on any other basis. The organizational and technical efforts needed to bring any one of them into being were enormous. Competitions in town planning and architecture had first to be arranged and, when all was ready, the final product was put to use for a few brief months. After that it was torn down and only a handful of particularly ambitious buildings were allowed to remain for use on future occasions. This process was of the very essence of a world dedicated to technology. Change was its permanent condition as it moved towards a visionary perfection.

4

These transient model cities were realizations of a town-dweller's fantasy that had a long history behind it. They were creations embodying an idea of international co-existence in which two Biblical archetypes – the Tower of Babel and the New Jerusalem – enjoyed secular rebirth. Their spiritual and even their architectural prototypes were manifold.

Actually, the art of architecture had long been positively bristling with edifying – not to say utopian – implications. The age in which princely, and for a time even sacred, edifices were commissioned, came to an end with the French Revolution, and the architects, now seeking new fields for their talents to conquer, enlisted under the banner of human beatification. Claude-Nicholas Ledoux is one of the most interesting representatives of this transitional phase, which derived its grandeur of gesture from the aristocratic age and its engaging idealism from a society that was flirting with the democratic idea.

Ledoux anticipated the revolutionary upheaval and as early as 1774 presented his King with plans for an ideal city. Joseph II of Austria and Paul I of Russia were to be counted among his admirers, and he published the whole of his work in a magnificent volume in 1804 – two years before his death – giving it the imposing title *L'Architecture considérée sous le rapport de l'Art, des Mœurs et de la Législation*. Though the actual dedication on the title page was to Czar Alexander I, it was to humanity that it was really addressed.

This architect's ideas have a clear connection with the World Exhibitions of the second half of the nineteenth century by reason of their humanitarian symbolism. The regeneration of man is usually considered to lie somewhat outside the normal duties of an architect, let alone of a building contractor, but Ledoux aimed at nothing less. Through bricks and mortar, he was determined to create a framework of harmony within which the working population could live together. In his ideal city, unity of hearts was to be the bond which bound men together, every inhabitant being under the obligation to contribute to the pleasure of the whole. God's Temple still towered above all other buildings, but it was no longer to be the sole gathering-place of the faithful. Hard by it there rose the sanctuaries of Philosophy, of Morals and of Brotherhood – places of thanksgiving and of communal recollection and meditation.

Like the idea of the World Exhibitions, this sanguine attempt at mass organization assumed the cessation – immediate, or at least impending – of all clashes of interest. Work and pleasure, which with growing industrialization were more and more to undergo a forcible separation and were ultimately to develop into mutually hostile and mutually exclusive opposites, were in this idealized picture to be reconciled and live in neighbourly amity. Work was the backbone of social order, and that is why the halls of industry stood in the very centre of the plan. Around them lay a circle of dwellings, parks, and gardens in which everyone was to find pleasure and recreation. The sober daily round was to have a paradisial setting.

The great exhibitions were equally concerned to achieve a harmonious combination of work and pleasure, though it was often pleasure qualified by a determined effort on the part of the authorities to edify the mind; the latter aim was attained by a discreet mixture of instruction and symbolism – as exemplified by a 'Tower of Humanity' or a 'Great Heavenly Globe'. Here were the centres where the drifting crowd was to tarry and worship. There is surely something here of the spirit of Ledoux. The difference, however, between Ledoux and his spiritual progeny is clear enough, for Ledoux's plans were designed to fit a concrete reality. His ideal city of Chaux was not to be set up just anywhere but in a particular area of the Franche-Comté in a real world where man was to be an active and responsible being and a joint creator of the whole. The efforts of the World Exhibitions on the other hand, though inspired by related ideas, were confined to a world of stage scenery. That is certainly one of the reasons why they were bound to fail.

The transformation of the art of architecture whose basic function had always been the service of some useful human purpose, and whose task now appeared to have been debased into the creation of objects purely designed for show – this transformation, so glaringly in evidence at the World Exhibitions, expressed a trend that was one of the nineteenth century's characteristic features, a trend in which optical charm became the supreme consideration. All was here façade and a pullulation of decorative irrelevance. The century had a restless desire for adornment and sought to endow its architecture with a tortured vivacity that had to startle the eye with unexpected effects – like the tricks of the parlour magician. It was undeterred by mere solidity; indeed, the more sober and lapidary the building, the more room there was for decorative embellishment. Even the earnest Ledoux had been unable to gainsay this appetite for costume, though in his case it satisfied itself within the framework of a poet's fancy.

But all this too was in the spirit of the time. That a building should be satisfying some normal human or administrative need was never enough. It had in some form or other to play a part in a masquerade – or at least in a symbolic ritual. In his *Harmonie de la Nature*[5] Bernardin de Saint-Pierre suggested that the customs houses of Paris – customs houses were among the few buildings that Ledoux was actually permitted to erect – should be transformed into memorials to the country's heroes. Purely utilitarian buildings were thus to become museums and national sanctuaries. On patriotic festivals they were to be adorned with flowers and garlands and illuminated at night. Food and drink were to be dispensed there to the people and the weary traveller was to find shelter within their walls. So these buildings were to surround Paris like a crown of fame and fortune.

But the poet's imagination went further. Mere utility was not enough – even when thus embellished. There was also to be interest and amusement. Bernardin de Saint-Pierre expressed surprise that no one had yet conceived the notion of putting gutters to artistic use. It should be possible, he averred, to let jets of water shoot forth from them and so add a touch of liveliness to the roofs of houses and temples. It should also be possible to furnish chimneys with some kind of crater-like disguise and achieve pleasing effects with the smoke that issued from them. These suggestions may strike us as a little ludicrous; yet the connection with the World Exhibitions is unmistakable, for there was implicit in Saint-Pierre's ideas the childish pleasure in startling effects which was later to develop into the wild and lavish fantasies of the Saint-Simonists and finally produce the light and water spectacles of the great exhibitions.

5

François Fourier's architectural ideas[6] have their roots in the utopian socialism of the first third of the century. Formally they represent nothing new and their message of felicity was that which Ledoux had continued to deliver. Fourier's 'Palais sociétaire' was expressly dedicated to the collective service of man, and it is not its architectural values that make the building interesting but the multiplicity of functions it was designed to perform. There were dwellings to house two thousand people, schools, workshops, and shops. The great halls of the central section were intended for use as a stock exchange, for receptions, balls, and concerts. Everything was accessible to everybody. One could pass from the workshops into the dwellings and from these into the halls used for artistic functions. Work was to live cheek by jowl with pleasure. The whole population was to take part in this. The voices of thousands were to be united in choirs and their bodies brought into rhythmic unity in mass dances. Here we have the general conception behind the great musical events of the World Exhibitions, events such as that, for instance, of 1855, when Berlioz conducted a school concert in which nine hundred singers and instrumentalists took part.

In Germany, too, the Romantic school of architecture concerned itself with plans for buildings that would similarly further a harmonious communal and public life (plates 28–32). In Schinkel's Gothic architectural fantasies there is the same dream of a communal world order, though here it is hierarchically organized. It is the order described in Novalis' tract *Die Christenheit oder Europa* (Christendom or Europe). It is this emotional impetus that imparts to the Gothic revival at the beginning of the century the fire of its enthusiasm, without which it would have been little more than a matter of archaeological pendantry. It was an enthusiasm which would hardly have existed had it not been felt that the borrowed style was instinct with a very specific way of life. It was a desire for a certain syle and quality in the life of a particular period, and not merely a concern for architectural form, that added the names of Ruskin and Morris to those who pleaded for a Gothic rebirth. The Middle Ages were transfigured into a period in which the ideal became reality and its architectural witnesses were felt to be monuments and symbolic productions of a builder's art that sought to furnish all mankind with a home. The rebuilding of Cologne Cathedral was not motivated by a mere wish for the completion of a residual fragment; it was rooted in the feeling that the cathedral church would be both a national monument and a museum of the past.

Whereas in France the active practice of art in some form or other was to be the business of everyman – or so at least Fourier saw the matter – in Germany the accent was on the mere improving experience of contemplating art's – and in particular the architect's – productions. This rather special kind of 'communal' architecture was, as it were, crystallized (and in a very characteristic fashion) in the Prince's Palace, though it should be added that these designs never got beyond the drawing board. While Passavant[7] was expressing the hope during the first decades of the post-Napoleonic era – essentially an age of restoration – that a full 'folkish' communal life would soon come into being 'so that something truly great and worthy should result for the public life of the country', it was Schinkel's declared ambition in his design for the 'Crimean' castle, Orianda, to create something that would have 'a beneficent and salutary effect' (wohltätig und gedeihlich) on people as a whole.

Schinkel's plan for a princely residence is even more explicitly intended to serve the cause of popular edification. The creator of this complex structure was moved to corresponding complexity of language in his description of its manifold purposes. Roughly those purposes were as follows: It was to be situated conveniently near a great city and was to have all the amenities that go with a highly cultured princely life and at the same time tend to facilitate the performance of princely duties. It was to have grounds where popular festivals could be held, and buildings where the distinguished persons of the land could be honoured in monuments, where the sciences and fine arts could be both pursued and enjoyed, and in which the common people could share in these agreeable activities. It was to have yet other buildings for such festivals as were customary at the time and yet more where the prince could perform such judicial functions as pertained to his governmental duties. Finally, it should contain the prince's own residential quarters. The whole should express both externally and internally the full dignity of the high purpose envisaged.[8] These elaborate formulations are in line with the complexities of purpose the building was designed to serve – all this being a typical feature of the Romantic imagination. If we dissect this palace into its variegated constituent parts, we already have a foretaste of the 'public' architecture of the World Exhibitions which granted equal rank to every building and to every exhibit.

Schinkel's plan for a royal residence on the Acropolis once more coupled the architecture of utility with that simply designed for exhibition and show. It thus coupled reality with the museum. Decades later, Semper designed the Vienna 'Kaiserforum', in which the two Court museums balance the two wings of the Hofburg, all of the buildings holding equal rank among themselves both in form and spiritual significance (plate 105). The ruler's residence pairs with the centres of culture. It is surely no mere chance that out of the whole great project only the two museums actually succeeded in getting built. This is not difficult to understand. To the nineteenth century the building of a temple of art represented a more genuine task than the building of an imperial palace.

6

The great exhibition had yet another ancestor. That ancestor was Nature, but Nature domesticated into a pleasure garden. The skilfully composed landscapes of rocks and grottoes, with their aquaria, artificial lakes, and beds of exotic flowers were praised as a 'triumph of artificial nature'.[9] (It was just about this time that Baudelaire wrote *Les Paradis Artificiels*.) They were arrangements of nature constructed for the townsman's eye which was avid for this particular kind of enchantment, and were marked by that planned and purposive clarity of design that invariably distinguishes a piece of stage scenery.

Once again we have a mongrel product. We see Nature, but it is Nature rearranged, Nature with make-up on, and it is precisely in this that the great exhibition, though essentially a symbol of the active and formative masculine principle, is also in touch with the world of imaginative vision in which the organic and feminine principle is at work.

Some decades before the beginning of these World Exhibitions Blechen portrayed in a spirited picture the scenery of such an earthly paradise that knows neither change nor ageing (plate 100). The palm-house which Schinkel had built on the Pfaueninsel was by Blechen enlivened by a group of Indian women, who, in the words of a reviewer, transported the observer into the world of a fairy tale. In so far as this mixture of winter garden and harem tended to become a meeting place for fashionable society, it took on the character of a multipurpose building and so approached close to the general concept of the exhibition hall. Nor was Schinkel's creation wholly unique. An enormous glass house, equipped as a winter garden, was erected in Paris in 1847 – four years before the first World Exhibition in London – and served as another fashionable place of recreation and agreeable idleness. With its ballrooms and cafés, its reading-rooms and art-exhibitions, it offered a veritable feast of diversions.

These 'jardins délicieux', as Boullée calls them, were surrogate worlds of escape, in which people endeavoured to find an aesthetic screen against any reality that might be experienced at first hand. Tropical vegetation, and, in the case of Schinkel's edifice, a depth of waters, conjured up a labyrinth of forgetfulness for those whom the world they lived in had failed to satisfy. Makart's studio (plate 109) is also such a substitute for reality – the hot-house of an imagination in constant need of artificial stimulants.

One could cite further cases such as that of Ludwig II of Bavaria, for instance, who in the sixties built a winter garden in which he satisfied his hyper-sensitive urge for self-withdrawal and found a distinctly exotic seclusion. Hard by the king's apartments was a hall nearly a hundred metres in length containing a world of wonders brought together at no small expense – tents and summer houses, a lake, a waterfall, and behind them all a painted vision of the Himalayas.[10]

7

So far we have spoken of sociological predispositions and of the spiritual appetites prevailing at a particular time, we have spoken of the dreams of architects and of architectural whimsies; and we have shown how certain tendencies in all these things anticipated what were later to become features of the great World Exhibitions. It seems to be time, therefore, to speak of a movement which undeniably forms a bridge between the humane projects of the architects and social reformers on the one hand and the new miracle cities of the great World Exhibitions on the other. That movement was Saint-Simonism.

The Exposition Universelle of 1855 was a Saint-Simonist apotheosis.[11] When its patron, Prince Napoleon, promised 'more creature comforts for the benefit of as many as possible', his prophetic utterance was couched in terms of the Saint-Simonist vocabulary. A brother of a prominent member of this reformist movement was Alexis Barrault (who incidentally planned a canal from the Nile to the Red Sea), and it was he who was responsible for the Palais de l'Industrie. There was a certain aptness about this, for the mystical enthusiasm for Progress which inspired the World Exhibitions was only a continuation of the Saint-Simonists' well-nigh religious veneration for the attainments and potentialities of modern civilization. Industry was acclaimed as the only effective instrument for the spread of the Western way of life, and the veneration for it took on the character of a kind of 'cult of the eternal'.

The reconciliation of the exact sciences with the new gospel of salvation was to produce everlasting peace, prosperity and harmony. Man applying his active energies to the world and so transforming it, gave a pseudo-religious justification to his appetite for a steadily expanding empire over matter. He set himself the task – very flattering to his self-esteem – of turning the Kingdom of God upon earth into a reality. The New Jerusalem was to come into being.

The Saint-Simonist Trinity consisted of Science, Industry, and Religion. The Saint-Simonists divided history into organic – that is to say religious – and critical periods. Since they held their own age to be organic, they were faced by the necessity of providing it with a religion. Their method may well be described as that of world sanctification. It professed to achieve a sublimation and ennoblement of this world's values. In reality, it merely contrived to reduce all things to a dead level. 'Modern France', so wrote a contemporary critic of Saint-Simonism, 'transforms all things into god, and merely succeeds in having no god whatever, for where all men are kings, no man is king at all. It transforms all the crafts and activities of man into a cult, so that it may dispense with the one cult that is true and real. A religious view of life is being introduced which is actually on the same level as pure irreligion.'[12]

In a sense the peculiar defects of the World Exhibitions were analogous to this, the peculiar Saint-Simonist weakness. As the Saint-Simonists, by making a god of everything, ended up by having no god at all, so the World Exhibitions by exhibiting everything, ended by really exhibiting nothing whatever. One cannot stress this peculiar feature too often. The vast quantity of objects failed to make a whole nor was there any logical connection between the whole and its constituent parts. There was only a heterogeneous accumulation which, since everything within it was evaluated equally, was nothing more than an accumulation of fragments. Articles of common use, works of art, cultic objects, and machines, all without exception enjoyed the hallowed state accorded to the exhibits in a museum, all constituted in equal measure the paraphernalia of a religious cult. And precisely because in this world all things were considered worthy of exhibition, and because the dignity with which they were thus endowed was expressly designed to make men forget any original function or utility they may have possessed, the whole underlying conception was reduced to absurdity.

The same thing, one might add, occurred at a different level, with love, which the Saint-Simonists conceived as a divine feast whose splendour was enhanced by the number of the participants. Such polygamous love for everybody could only put an end to marital love, to the love of parents and the love of children. Indeed, such wishful dreaming of a dissipated love – dissipated in both senses of the word – recalls the advice of Victor Hugo, to whose general thinking on this matter allusion has already been made, when he appealed to France to burst her national frontiers and mingle with the world. It should be noted that this urge towards the boundless, this devouring appetite for the collective act of love was the correlative of a mental attitude by which the nineteenth century was very strongly marked. Oddly enough, it was one that drove people in a diametrically opposite direction – towards an ascetical urge for solitude.

The World Exhibitions were the shrines of this emotional collectivism and of that rooted belief in the great human harmony at whose birth the technician was to enact the part of *accoucheur*.

The Saint-Simonists, preoccupied as they were with a whole complex of problems, had dedicated themselves with equal enthusiasm to the question of emancipation and to the project of a Suez Canal. It is, in these circumstances, hardly surprising that their visionary zeal should, among other things, have concentrated on architecture, a subject on which their views were nothing if not original. In 1832 Enfantin[13] criticized the architecture of his time because of its alleged lack of 'movement'. He insisted that 'durability, stability, and movement' were the three factors determining the quality of a building, and seems at times to have anticipated dynamic open-skeleton architecture. Such a bald statement, however, hardly suffices to give a picture of his soaring imagination, and it would be best to let Enfantin speak for himself: 'The structure of a building should resemble the molecular structure of bodies. There must be solid areas allied with empty spaces. There must be flexibility, scope for movement. The various structural elements should be arranged as the molecules of a body are arranged'. Iron, incidentally, is given the leading part in bringing into being the 'architecture sacerdotale' of the future, which is quite remarkable in its way, since the use of iron in building had not at the time got beyond its modest beginnings. From construction in iron Enfantin expected to see wholly new 'musical and optical' effects. Iron tubes were to serve both as supports and as organ pipes. 'The whole temple could become a sonorous orchestra, a gigantic thermometer. The association of different metals, and the activities at the heart of things comprising the ceremonial, might lead to the most stupendous galvanic, chemical, and mechanical effects in a sanctuary having, by means of a lightning-conductor belfry, direct contact with the storm raging outside.'

This vision of a musical-architectural composite work of art—already dimly conceived by Runge[14] and afterwards followed up by Gaudi's Sagrada Familia[15] – passes the limits of any normal man's imagination. It dreams of a temple of the electric generator, of a temple made of gigantic magnets, of a temple of melody and harmony, of a sanctuary through whose lens-like apertures there pour streams of light and warmth. Various performances are to epitomize life here on earth, while electricity and magnetism testify to the existence of hidden and mysterious powers. Metals and costly fabrics meanwhile embody the qualities of splendour and display – and all this is placed in a setting of wonderful cascades and luxuriant vegetation, this last being visible behind the temple's windows. Life in the sun is symbolized by light and warmth. To represent human life is, of course, the task of the arts, and so music, painting, and sculpture appear in a gay procession, one next to another. Panoramas and dioramas are to bring all places and all ages into unison at a single point. 'What an immense communion! What colossal enhancement of the moral status of a whole people! What a glorification of God, and his Messiah, and all humanity!'

Here, incidentally, there is already an anticipation of one aspect of the entertainment industry: the transformation of scientific experiments into feats of occult magic, so that Progress becomes an indispensable ingredient of mass bemusement. My main point, however, is that Enfantin's architectural dreams give a foretaste of what was so marked a feature of the World Exhibitions, namely the inherent theatricality that inevitably accompanies the elevation of applied science to divine status and the attempt to stir massed humanity by the wildest conjunction of optical and acoustic effects. The various stage-trappings of a popular museum of humanity – all are there as is, amongst other things, the spell cast over the public's imagination by the panorama, that mongrel got by fiction out of reality. Last but not least we have the stupefying but spectacular illusion that space and time have been abolished and that all things that are, or ever were, are gathered together here and now.

Even the most gigantic of the stunts that in the nineteenth century became a solid reality, seemed at times less portentous than these wild and feverish fantasies, but what in that century became fact was fantastic enough. One thinks of the monster concert of 1855 and the awesome fuss inside Galeron's Celestial Globe (plate 106). The outside of this construction was embellished with painted stars while inside was a floating ball, representing the earth, on which approximately a hundred people could be seated and which was surrounded by a painted starry heaven. From here the spectators could witness the circling of the planets. 'All around us,' apostrophized the press, 'there stretches endless space, disturbing and mysterious!' In order to heighten the sacred tone of the whole performance, a giant organ played fantasias of Saint-Saëns while admirers murmured of a French Bayreuth.

The cult of cosmic infinity thus provided art, science, organ music, and the coursing of the

99 MANET *Dans la serre* (In the conservatory); 1879.

104 CHENAVARD *La Philosophie de l'Histoire*; 1855 International Exhibition, Paris.

105 R. VON ALT The Vienna Hofmuseum (after Gottfried Semper); 1878.

102 The Crystal Palace: the 1851 International Exhibition, London.

103 The closing ceremony of the 1851 International Exhibition, London.

100 BLECHEN The palm-house on the Pfaueninsel; 1834.

101 BÖCKLIN Pan among the reeds; 1857.

110 CARPEAUX *La danse*; 1869.

108 The Emperor's Pavilion; 1867 International Exhibition, Paris.

109 R. VON ALT Makart's studio; 1885.

106 The Celestial Globe; 1900 International Exhibition, Paris.

107 Panorama of 1867 International Exhibition, Paris.

planets with an opportunity to unite in a single vast piece of mystical showmanship. Among other progeny of the Saint-Simonists we must include electrically controlled fountain displays and the pyrotechnical phantasmagoria that took place upon the Eiffel Tower in 1889. This itself, by the way, is an emblematic descendant of Enfantin's electric generator, described above, and of his gigantic thermometer: it is really modelled on the steam-hammer,[16] a thing that only has real significance when it is in motion. The dynamic of the Eiffel Tower derives from the translation of actual into potential motion; it is vertical energy. This formal transformation caused the real thing which actually suggested the design to be forgotten, and enlarged the construction's symbolic content into universal significance. Thus a functioning piece of machinery was turned into a monument of labour.

8

The activities centring round the exhibition usurped the place of divine worship – which meant that the power once possessed by the older cult to bind people into a community and keep them so bound, was no longer effective, and that the leaderless masses, now lacking all counsel yet still full of longing, were searching for a new divinity. The World Exhibitions are documentary illustrations of the crisis in the faith of Europe.

In the days when the Church was still the secure centre around which all earthly life revolved, she was able to tolerate all the various fairs held at places of pilgrimage on feast days, for men knew the dividing line between sacred and profane and there was no danger of their forgetting it. Once the relationship between the two became imprecise and the boundary line began to waver, once the hierarchies of value ceased to be self-evident and clear, then surrogate religions were bound to occupy territory which the old cult was failing to hold.

The story of the relationship between the World Exhibitions and genuine artistic creation is really analogous. The borderline between art and artifice, between the work of art and the mere conjurer's trick, were deliberately blurred. True art indeed became discredited by a degraded travesty of itself, while yet another marginal misunderstanding, which was to have far-reaching consequences, served further to increase the confusion; this was the mixing together of art and industry. Galvano-plastics, for instance, began to deliver original works of art – which thus ceased to be anything of the kind – over to the processes of mass-production. They were now to belong to all. The principle of the greatest good for the greatest number succeeded at last in turning the work of art into a piece of mass-produced merchandise intended for mass use. It now seemed natural enough that Barye should set up as a 'Manufacturer of Art-Bronzes' and exhibit his products not in the art gallery but in the Palais de l'Industrie.

The exhibition, as we have seen, constituted a surrogate for the real world, and it is worth noting how it pushed its way between the opposing poles of art and experiential reality, squinting all the while in both directions at once. It out-trumped art with cheap illusions, and reality by the simple process of doubling it.

Whereas a work of art, be it painting or sculpture, is concerned to confront the world of experience with another – and, as Hegel would have it a 'higher' – reality, the tools of the artist's craft were now used for a quite different purpose. The panoramas and dioramas relaxed the tension between the real object and the picture, for they aimed not only at imitating reality but at replacing it. The 'mareorama' not only showed a picture of a stormy sea. It gave the supposititious 'passenger', standing on a swaying deck and surrounded on all sides by a horizon of stormy ocean, the assurance that this is just what happens in reality.

Such deliberate creation of artificial effects by means of a reconstructed reality was taking place on the widest scale. It could have been seen in the *tableaux vivants* in which the various phases of human civilization were illustrated, and in reconstructed historical and exotic buildings. The degree to which actual reality can be devalued and pushed into the background by its artificial mimetic surrogate, was made apparent in the reconstruction of 'Historic Paris' at the World Exhibition of 1900. Next to buildings which had long fallen victims to the demolishing pick, stood others which the visitor could himself have seen standing in their original form in that same city of Paris only a few kilometres away. And yet how pale, how profane the real Paris must have seemed beside that artificial one which presented the visitor with such a convenient synopsis, such a serviceable abridgement of space, and spared him all waste of his own time on the commonplace and irrelevant.

Here was the great kingdom of 'as if'. A mere work of art could no longer still the public's hunger for tangible and unmistakable reality. The panorama exploited this appetite. All its efforts centred in the attempt to abolish the difference between fiction and the real world. How flat and lifeless must have seemed the illusion offered by a mere picture, compared with that provided by the panorama which seemed to show something that could actually be touched, that had a real material existence, which indeed offered itself as an actual substitute for reality.

The panorama was indeed a substitute for reality; it was also a substitute for art. What was said above about surrogate religions applies here with equal force, for this 'substitution' began to occur at the moment when a crisis took place in the relation of the work of art to reality, when, in a word, the public experienced the awakening of an appetite for eye-witness accounts and when, as a result, the artist's conception of reality failed increasingly to communicate. An estrangement began to take place between the artist and his public. There was a coarsening of popular taste which now followed the line of least resistance and turned its back on any creative work which required that the observer's imagination should co-operate with that of the artist. The panorama made things more easy for it than anything else, and that is why this kind of popular taste, which is really a negation of taste, enjoyed these great exhibitions which with all their riot of spectacle were nothing but panoramas themselves.

9

The iconographic repertoire of the World Exhibitions, the central ideas, that is to say, which they endeavoured to translate into concrete terms, were in large part derived from the themes which the art of the nineteenth century had already made available. The four most important ones were the glorification of labour, the evocation of the earthly paradise, the flight into exotic worlds, and the reconstruction of human history.

There is some excuse for the World Exhibitions if their representations of the ever-repeated theme of labour were often stilted and inadequate, since sincere artists all too often failed to get at the real heart of their subject. This is curious, since the nineteenth century was the first to discover the deeper ethos of man the worker, and it was much stirred by the theme. Admittedly, realism inscribed the slogan of social consciousness upon its banner because it was in tune with its time, but it was really using a popular catchword to express something a great deal deeper. In a way, the artist considered the worker his counterpart – one is vaguely reminded of Carlyle's comparison between 'the toil-worn craftsman' and 'the inspired thinker'; but the real reason why the worker held the artist's imagination may perhaps be more succinctly expressed. It was because the worker stood in a genuine and active relation to reality. In his labour he had all the positive quality of a man taking possession of a *res nullius*, and there was as yet no estrangement between himself and the real world.

Ancient and biblical features, which were not lost on the age, were immanent in Courbet's 'The stonebreakers' (plate 168), Millet's 'Les glaneuses' (plate 167), Van Gogh's 'The sower' (plate 173), and in 'The youth of the Iron Age'. There is deep emotion in these heroic gestures, they have the dignity displayed by undivided and elemental human beings. This is as true, despite formal differences, of Daumier as it is of Puvis de Chavannes.

But this heroic interpretation in some measure evaded the actual facts. It overlooked that alienation from his true personality which marked the urban worker and which was the real basis of Marx's social criticism. From Courbet right up to Van Gogh the picture of the worker as a human type was conditioned by the earnest mood and the simplicity of what was essentially an agricultural or peasant background. Nothing in it suggests the whirr of machinery or the soul-destroying mechanism of the factory process, nothing the 'new-fangled man' of the industrial age whom Marx hailed in his writings. When these painters wished to look for the real infernos of our civilisation, they did not go to the factory worker at all, but sought out street-singers or entered railway carriages or places of nocturnal amusement. Menzel's 'Rolling-mill' alone reproduces the collision between man and the machine. But the painter fails to see the enslaving grip of these vast pieces of apparatus and transfers their fiery demonism to man himself. The monotonous uniformity of the work-shop recedes completely before the dramatic tensions of action.

How far then did even true art succeed in doing justice to this subject? There were, of course, artists who felt the need for a more abstract conception of work as a part of the universal human lot. To achieve this purpose, use was made of one of a number of formal settings. Walter Crane drew a 'Triumph of Labour' which shows 'the international solidarity of Labour' in allegorical form. Makart's 'Festival Procession' of 1879 brings the whole theme within the perspective of the World Exhibitions. The various professional and vocational groups, arranged according to rank and transported out of the age of Dürer into the present, really play the part of supers in a *tableau vivant* illustrating cultural history. The whole work is very like a circular painting. It seems to have no end. Criticism was enthusiastic in its praise for the work of this painter-turned-stage-manager, and greeted 'the attempt, made wholly in the spirit of our fathers, to let art with all its force and all its splendour re-enter once again the living daylight of the present.'[17] The critics overlooked the fact that art was not really entering the daylight, living or otherwise, at all. What was happening was that reality was being theatrically disguised. They also failed to note that Makart was working with anachronisms which plainly showed that, so far from letting art enter the present, he was himself actually running away from that present. The railway, for instance, characterized by the colours red and black, was transported into the closed stylistic painting of the sixteenth century. The living daylight of the present was in fact hiding behind a historic mask.

Rodin's project for a 'Tower of Labour', which was to be part monument and part sanctuary, would have had a perfect setting in an exhibition ground. Such a tower would have formed the sacred crown to that display of scenes designed to illustrate the development of labour which were on show in the exhibitions of 1867 and 1889. Proudly indeed could *homo faber* look back on the epic of his conquest of the world, his faith in Progress well satisfied by a continuous line of development ending up in the machinery halls of the present. They are the culminating point in this meandering history, and that is why they had to be accompanied by background vistas of the past. While painters like Courbet and Millet divorced labour from its normal setting and showed it in the form of unbroken elemental human types, the World Exhibitions were staging *genre* pictures of the advance of civilization. For they saw in labour an instrument by which civilization was furthered. For them man as nature made him was not an end but a starting point, and that is a view that not everyone will accept.

Another of the leading ideas behind these World Exhibitions was the earthly paradise, and here perhaps for once, the exhibitions came close to the vital art of the day and tried, stammering, to speak its language; for these exhibitions did sometimes really become a setting for sensual, seductive pleasure – there was actually a 'jardin des voluptés' in 1867 – a setting where harmony and the delight of sense were supreme and all cares had at least in theory been dispelled. In this great show every visitor was cast for a part, even if it was only the part of super, but his role was to be happy and gay. In point of fact, the people who wandered through these vast fair-grounds in their Sunday mood were actually playing the parts assigned to them by the Impressionists, they lived for the untroubled pleasures of the eye, for a moment they regarded pleasure as the only purpose of their lives and meandered aimlessly from one impression to the next. Transfigured by the playing of light and water and with nature providing a kind of great garment around them in the form of bright and colourful vegetation, these artificial paradises, though employing means that were far from artistic, spoke softly of a world that would be more beautiful, more poetic than the present one.

In the superb water-lily pictures – those paraphrases of the four seasons[18] – which Monet began to paint in 1915 for the Orangerie, there is a kind of sublimated echo of all this. The general plan of the pictures made use of the panoramic form. The observer was not conceived as standing before any one picture but in the centre of an oval ribbon of painting. He was to feel himself surrounded by the twilight of the submarine world. He was thought of as standing in some chapel of a nature religion, a chapel devoted to meditation.

10

In the end the history of the human race itself, that darling theme of the painter-philosophers, was subject at these World Exhibitions to a wide measure of re-interpretation. This first occurred in a series of exhibitions concerned mainly with the history of civilization, and dealing with the history of labour, the house, transport, and the theatre. The 'Tower of the World' (1900) deflected what had hitherto been a purely historical interest into the present. Now 'sample products' produced by the natives of all the participating countries were on view. But here again there was a discord, that strange process of alienation passed from lifeless objects to human beings. The 'native' became an object himself, an object to be exhibited in the shop windows of racial science.

It was much the same with the historic or exotic building now torn out of its original surroundings and transferred to the 'Street of the Nations', though here too the World Exhibitions were doing no more than dress up an old idea; actually the notion of such an architectural conglomeration can already be found in a study from the year 1834 by the young Nikolai Gogol, whose words are sufficiently interesting to bear repetition here – Carlyle's Herr Teufelsdröckh, incidentally, voices very similar views. 'A town,' says Gogol, 'must be able to show a great diversity of masses, if it is to give pleasure to the eye. The most varied kinds of taste should be married to one another within it. Let there be set up in a single street a dark Gothic building, a building in colourful oriental style, a colossal Egyptian structure, and a Greek edifice full of pleasant harmonies. Let there here be gathered together in harmony the lightly rounded milk-coloured cupola, the high church tower so full of the spirit of devotion, the oriental Mitra, the flat Italian roof, the Dutch roof, steep and richly decorated, the four-cornered pyramid and the angular obelisk. There should be a street which would at the same time be a chronicle of the world's architectural history. Such a street would in some measure represent a history of the world's taste.'[19]

Now this is exactly what these 'Streets of the Nations' were endeavouring to offer the visitor – and once again the World Exhibitions were simply following a fashion, for the notion of such an open air museum of architecture could be found elsewhere than on the exhibition grounds; the whole of the nineteenth century's stylized architecture was influenced by it. The Vienna Ringstrasse

is a kind of procession à la Makart of different architectural styles; it is the work of architects who with their buildings were seeking to set before us what Ferkel calls 'a petrified history of the world'. Furthermore, when the plan was put forward to create this 'museum quarter' and plant it in the very centre of a great modern city, a further suggestion was made which provides additional proof of the connection between our modern way of building cities and the World Exhibitions. It was recommended that the different nations of the dual monarchy should each have their own quarter within the metropolis – in a word the imperial city was conceived as an ethnographic museum.

In 1856, a year after the Paris Exhibition, an international agricultural exhibition was arranged in the Palais de l'Industrie, and on this Delacroix made the following entry in his journal: 'Let us leave to Hungary these oxen encumbered with horns they do not know how to use: of what use to us, in our level pastures, are these cows that have come down from Swiss Alpine heights? Poor, deluded people, there is no happiness to be derived from mere absence of toil. Take a look at these loafers condemned to bear the burdens of life today and unable to make any use of the time which in any case these machines are shortening for them in the long run. At one time travel was a distraction for them, rescuing them from the torpor of the daily round, showing them other climates, other customs, relieving the tedium which haunts and pursues them. But nowadays they are swept along at a speed which allows them to see nothing. They recognize the various stages of their journey only from the names of railway stations which all look alike. Even when they have been all over Europe they have a feeling that they have never gone far from these dull stations which seem to follow them wherever they go, like their idleness and their inability to enjoy anything. The way of life, the various local customs they went to the ends of the world to investigate? They will pretty soon find out that they are much the same everywhere.

The Ottoman Turk has already adopted the imprisoning garb of what he takes to be civilization. Instead of contemplating the smiling Bosphorus bathed in sunshine, in peace and quiet, they shut themselves up in stuffy little theatre boxes to stare at French music-hall turns. Music-halls, newspapers, all this ado about nothing ... you find it everywhere, all over the world, much like those everlasting stations with their Cyclops engines and their savage whistles. There's no longer any question of "seeing". One gets to a place for the sake of leaving it.'

It is no mere chance that these thoughts on travel should be set down in connection with a visit to an exhibition. Travel, in the perverted form which Delacroix here describes, is connected with the whole business of exhibition-mongering. For there attaches to these exhibitions something of the universality of the railway-station; they are indeed the eternal railway-stations of civilization in which space and time are suspended. They can be set up in any country you please and look the same in London as they do in Vienna or Paris. They set vast masses of people in motion. Bands of pilgrims from all over the world stream together into them. They serve the travel industry – but only to make an end of travel. Since the whole world is brought together at a single point, a visit to a World Exhibition saves us the trouble of voyaging round the world. The world of the laboratory retort, which can be enjoyed without effort, is substituted for reality.

VII The Great Man

I

THE nineteenth century saw two kinds of historical painting – the descriptive and the visionary. The painters of historical *genre* paintings did not really paint pictures at all; they merely created what the theatre, in its more unassuming days, called *tableaux* in which they showed us some dramatic – or supposedly dramatic – moments of conflict, terror, joy, surprise, despair or what have you. Moreover, even as those other painters who had cultivated an intense awareness of the present sought to be eye-witnesses of their time, believing as they did that this was the artist's true function, so these creators of the *Sittengeschichtsbild* – the phrase is Vischer's coinage[1] – sought to perform the same function with regard to the past.

Sittengeschichtsbild means a picture of the history of manners, and the practitioners of this form of art were only too eager to display their complete familiarity with the world they were setting on canvas. Unfortunately – being the prisoners of their vows to historical fidelity – they all too often relieved their consciences by the mere heaping up of piles of antiquarian documentation. Even so gifted an artist as Menzel tends to lose himself in the purely material, in meticulous pendantry as to the exact design of a military button.

I said earlier that the awareness of history – and its correlative, a heightened awareness of the present – was a means of focusing the artist's eye on a particular period, and even on a particular moment of time. In either case everything tended to be crowded together into the compass of a single instant. The artist either chased after the fleeting 'impression', or he pursued a kind of historical anecdote that had sufficient poignancy about it to produce a slight tingling of the nerves. The world never stands still but is in continual process of becoming, and this holds good whether we are concerned with the uninterrupted changes of nature or with the drama of history, which as an actual entity does not exist at all – even though the comprehensive cyclical representations of Chenavard seek to make us believe otherwise – but as it unrolls, consists merely of a sequence of scenes. If we were dealing with a film we should here speak of camera angles. (I would remark in passing that the revelation of changing nature as employed by the Impressionists, is something that can be very fruitful indeed, artistically speaking, and can go hand in hand with a genuine formal gain. In colour, moreover, it possesses a genuine equivalent of the draughtsman's craft – and this is precisely where it differs from the sentimental pictorial recounting of the historical episode, which is a matter of conscious stage-management.)

The keyhole perspective which was exploited in the opposite camp to catch the spontaneous and, as yet, unconventional gesture – one has but to think of the peeps behind the scenes and into dressing rooms of a Daumier, a Manet, a Degas, or a Toulouse-Lautrec – that same keyhole perspective was used by the painter of historical *genre* paintings, though not as means of finding new formal expression for his art but simply in order to produce a special kind of inquisitive excitement. It was designed to satisfy our curiosity and nothing more. It was a servant to an appetite for banalities on the part of the public, to its crude 'picture hunger'[2]. It was the slave of a particular situation that happened to possess anecdotal potentialities, and never sought expression in any new pictorial form or the use of radically new means.

The painter simply reconstructed history and presented the onlooker with what would in the humbler world of popular entertainment be called a *tableau* or 'living picture'. What fascinated the artist was the interesting and the sensational. His work was that of historical reporting. It was journalism pure and simple. He reproduced an important event with all the pride of the initiate whose privilege it was to have been present – as an eavesdropper, an onlooker, or even a spy – when Columbus discovered the American coast, when proud Thusnelda was led in the triumph of Germanicus, when Mary Queen of Scots heard the reading of her death sentence, and when Cromwell, standing at night by the open coffin of Charles I, reflected on 'the majesty of misfortune'[3]. The more conscientiously the event was surrounded by the circumstances of its own time, and the more authentic the background, the more it caugth the fleeting moment. It became an actual happening or – if it was conceived in a tragic spirit – a misfortune, as in the work of Piloty.

And yet in any deeper sense how uncommunicative these pictures are. Dozens of Great Men have their dying hours portrayed, but never once is there a portrayal of death itself, nor is there ever suggestion of death's elemental character or of its inevitability. Governed as they are by a spirit of almost exaggerated punctiliousness, these paintings offer a flawless historical reliability – but nothing more. They remain wholly on the level of the events they portray, and in portraying them the painter assures us that matters went thus and in no other fashion. The symbolic element in a ruler's death is wholly lost through the emphasis on externals – it remains an episode. Inferences from the particular to the general can only take place in the mind of the observer – the picture itself does not help him to draw them. And so historical painting continued to wrestle with its self-imposed problem of historical fidelity and with the fictional role it had chosen of being an eye-witness of events.

The other type of historical painting, the type that I have called visionary, sought to raise itself to a level where it was more than a display of impressive elaboration. It was to signify more than the physical eye would actually see upon the canvas. Now if a human action is to have symbolic force, it must be intelligible without consultation of the history book. For example, 'Napoleon visiting people stricken by the plague at Jaffa' (plate 68) gives the painter the opportunity of once again presenting the Great Man, but he presents him, symbolically, as a saviour, a *roi thaumaturge*, the mere touch of whose hand is sufficient to bring healing.[4] What was once done by the Son of God and the Saints, it is now the privilege of man to perform, the kind of man whom Hegel called a demi-god. The nineteenth century had a very intense feeling about this purely secular gesture of healing. In connection with some observations about the awakening of Lazarus, Rosenkranz in his *Aesthetics of Ugliness* speaks of this picture by Gros in eulogistic terms and adds the words: 'He, their very soul, appears among them unmoved by any sense of danger ... in the midst of these hideous figures he stands, erect and full of pity, a giant among men, and lays his hands upon the boil of one of the diseased.' One is reminded of Stendhal, who, moved by what the man in the street was saying in Milan, drew a parallel between the spirit of Napoleon and that of St Charles Borromeo.[5]

In the picture the Great Man almost pronounces his own canonization. Transfigured into the iconographic attitudes already known in religious art, Napoleon's visit to the sick is a revelation of the divine vouchsafed for the saving of men. (One could name yet other forms of indebtedness to certain types of Christian art. The 'Death of Marat' (plate 4), for instance, recalls the *pietà*, though in its total lack of consolation, it goes beyond any lamentation over Christ: no one is at hand to care for the dead.[6])

Another work representing the saints and martyrs of humanism is Delacroix's 'Liberté guidant le peuple' (plate 72). Here too a kind of divine pathos raises a mere episode to a symbolic level. The picture is a perfect example of the *allégorie réelle*. The woman carrying the flag is 'a mixture of Phryne, Poissarde and the goddess of freedom', and around her are people of the most varied origins. Heine makes typical journalist's fun of them, though even he was bound to confess later that 'a great idea has ennobled

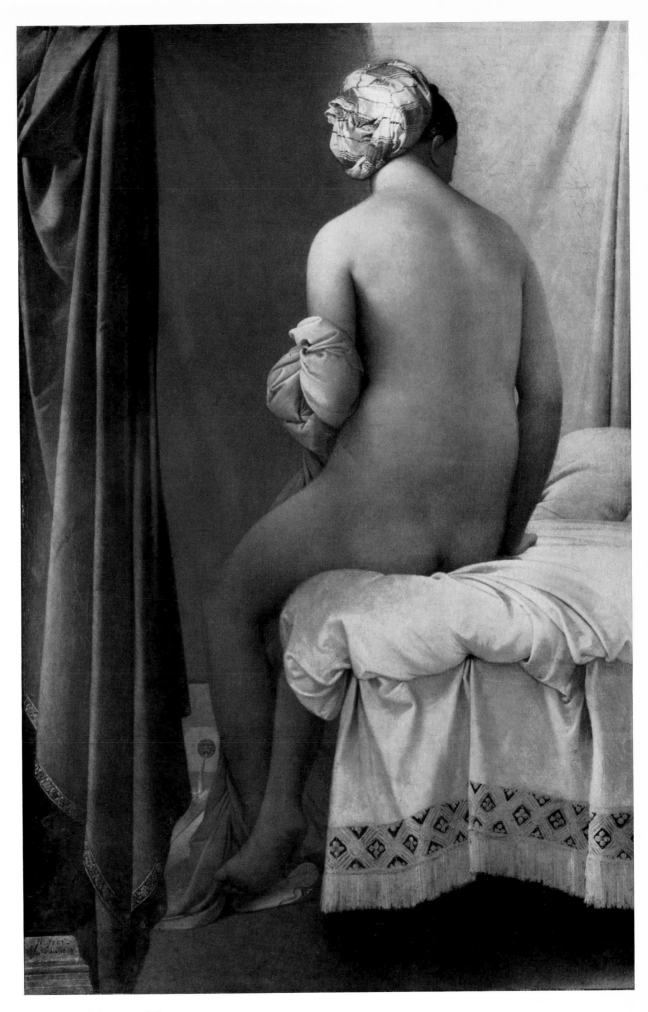

111 INGRES *Baigneuse*; 1808.

112 INGRES Venus Anadyomene; 1848.

113 REDON Birth of Venus; 1910.

114 COURBET *Femme à la vague*; 1868.

115 BÖCKLIN Triton and Nereid; 1875.

116 DEGAS *Le bain;* c. 1890.

117 RENOIR *Les grandes baigneuses*; 1885–87.

118 CÉZANNE *Les grandes baigneuses*; 1898–1905.

these common people, this *crapule*, has sanctified them and reawakened the slumbering dignity in their souls'.[7] The real theme of this picture, however, which is to be sought at a deeper level than that of the mere democratic manifesto, is not political freedom at all, but freedom *per se*, the loosening of all bonds, the breaking forth of the unfettered instincts. Delacroix expresses what a recent writer, referring to Baudelaire, has called 'the erotic power of the crowd', that 'intoxication of humanity in the sense of licentiousness' which Baudelaire called 'a challenging picture to be painted' for a painter. These people are intoxicated. Set aflame as they are by this figure of a woman, the cruelty of lust and of death find equal expression in their faces. They are seen at a moment when life is at its highest potential, when every inhibition has been cast aside. This herald of freedom is not merely the revolution come alive, a goddess in human form (in 1848 Wagner's fevered pen let itself be carried away by just such imagery[8]); it is the triumph of the instinctive, which like some secret and seductive sign, casts a spell under whose potency life and death, despair and sensuality, are all united. The companion piece to 'Liberté guidant le peuple' is the death orgy of Sardanapalus (plate 152).

This is one kind of sublimation of the historical event. In it, as we have seen, a single personality is raised to heroic and even quasi-divine status. The painter falls back on Christian iconography or on allegory. There is also another way of lifting a historical event from the narrow confines of a particular time or place. Instead of using some prominent historical personality, the painter uses the anonymous hero. In doing so, he banks on a factor in history that is new – what Gutzkow calls 'the rule of the mass-spirit'.[9] The tension between the great leader and the fascinated multitude (a tension accentuated with dramatic clarity by Gros and Delacroix) gives place to something different. We have the historical picture that is essentially pessimistic but that introduces a serious, artistic intention into the portrayal of 'catastrophe' – an expression used of Piloty, the salon painter.

There are no longer any heroes – least of all military ones – who rise in apparent security through the riot and confusion of a battlefield, there is no headlong charge fraught with the intoxication of certain victory. There are neither leaders nor led. War is execution – in the double sense of the word – a carrying out of orders even to the cold-blooded taking of human life. We can see the beginning of the trend in Goya's 'Murat's troops executing inhabitants of Madrid on 3rd May, 1808' (plate 67). Here there is no fighting, whether at a distance or hand to hand; there is simply a bloodbath. The gap between the two human groups does much more than separate men of two opposite camps. It destroys that very thing to which the traditional battle-piece had always clung – the chivalrous entente between victor and vanquished. Goya separates the two groups so sharply that all reconciliation is ruled out. On the left, in the warm colours of earth, sweat, and blood, are the men of the rebellion, a confused heap; we seem to see an agonized twitching, then utter collapse; there appears to be no other movement. On the right in the cold metallic colours of murder are Napoleon's men. The bodies of the condemned are torn open, their faces are uncovered or hidden as though in terror. The others stand wearing a kind of mask, and there seems to be a threat in the very way they are packed into their tightly laced uniforms, in their smooth swords, in the sharp line of their gun barrels, and in the huge shakoes that hide their faces. These are no warriors, they are executioners.

Once more Goya's method of expression succeeds in giving the impression of men in a trap. In the Delacroix, Freedom goes storming over corpses – and how picturesquely the scene of the battle seems to present itself at her feet. The central figure gives the whole picture a liberating diagonal movement. Gros' picture of a solemn event – a miraculous healing – is similarly dominated by a central figure. In the Goya, there is no active centre, no liberating pictorial rhythm. All the tension is packed into the actual figures, is concentrated almost to bursting point in those terribly expressive limbs and bodies; and it is a tension that not even the despairing gestures of the victims can help resolve. In the very centre of the picture are the guns. They seem actually to stick out of the soldiers' bodies, as though they were a part of them; they aim at the rebels who are now irretrievably delivered over to death. All the tensions between the two human groups seem to be passing through the narrow channels of these gun-barrels – the two groups are collectively under their spell and are held together in a grip that is closer and crueller than any clench in hand to hand fighting.

The impression of arbitrary force which the picture evokes is, in the final analysis, due to the following elements: the horizontal position of the gun-barrels which cut the picture horizontally into two sections; the monotonous repetition of the tightly packed bodies of the soldiers; the hillock which cuts off the background and seems somehow to weigh down the observer, though it does not actually continue its line of ascent; the men condemned to death, whom fear seems to be positively pressing into the ground. Here are the reasons for the enormous physical weight of the picture and the story it contains, and for its sharp note of dissonance. There is no fighting here, there is indeed no real action, merely a pitiless execution – and the execution of an order. And since the picture has no protagonist, no centre of action, no liberating expansion, all its emphasis falls on the automatism of collective killing. Since no energies are being discharged against other energies, there is over the whole a dreadful stiffness, a complete absence of motion. Never did the nineteenth century so ruthlessly hold fast to a fleeting moment and so forcibly endow it with permanence.

Manet's 'Execution of the Emperor Maximilian' (1867) (plate 78) depends for its effect on a somewhat similar emphasis. This is no mere question of form, though there is an echo of Goya's work in the hard horizontal parallels, but we can also see a spiritual kinship and here too Manet owes a clear debt to the type of historical painting which Goya had created. Since the French Revolution, war has been an event which touches all the different strata of a nation, and in which all have their energies roused and share in a single community of experience – perhaps of suffering. Bearing this in mind, we cannot but see that Manet provides Goya with an answer, for the shooting of the insurgents is an act of oppression which must sooner or later bring about the shooting of those responsible for it, or, failing that, of those who by reason of past acts or from the very nature of their rule could be regarded as the potential committers of similar crimes. But before such an action can have any moral force behind it, certain conditions must obtain, and the liquidation of a usurper – and as such the ill-advised Maximilian must have been regarded – could only have been considered a subject worthy of the artist's brush in an age when the 'spirit of the masses' was a ruling force.

Manet shows us a death sentence being carried out without ceremony and even without excitement. The agents of the execution have the imperturbability of men performing a routine act which it would never occur to them to call in question. The soldier loading his gun for the *coup de grâce* might have been standing on a shooting-range. Where is that 'pure chivalry' of which Adalbert Stifter spoke in his memorial address, where is the figure 'to which the poet and the artist look up so that its true nature may shine forth'?[10] The painter saw more clearly than the poet; his eyes were freer from illusion; he saw the real issue more plainly than that J.P. Laurens who painted in 1882 such a sentimental picture of the Emperor's last moments; he saw that there was nothing here but an official act carried out by human machines.

The three condemned men and the soldiers are all on the same level. Just as they are near to each other spatially, so there is no spiritual distance between them – and thus no possibility of raising one figure above the rest in the role of a supposedly Great Man. Above everything else, as in the gallery of a theatre, there is the crowd of onlookers, gaping and curious, for whom the performance which it has demanded is being enacted. These are the people whose will is being carried into effect. They are the new factor by which history is being determined.

There were other painters who were equally ready to portray the perverted appetite of the masses for this kind of show, though they took pains to transpose their portrayal of it into more distant times –

times when Christians were being persecuted and gladiatorial combats staged. Perhaps Manet was able to see this appetite of the masses in the world of his own day, and here we can see an 'inner significance' if we compare him with Goya. The people who were being shot in 1808 might well be the same people as those who were looking over the wall half a century later.

Goya conquered new territory in that he gave to historical painting the power of a certain direct impact and freed it from the empty phrase, dispensed with the peculiar pathos conferred by distance, ignored the accepted formulae of decorative composition and came physically close to the subject he was looking at in a manner that was entirely new. The learned historians of the brush chose the industrious but inartistic method of pretending to be eye-witnesses; Goya, the true artist, made his point by means of a radical reorganization of the formal pattern.

There is, however, a difference between the role of the mere eye-witness and actual participation; it is a sense of just such participation that is conveyed by Romako's 'Tegetthoff during the Battle of Lissa' (plate 77). To obtain his effects the painter uses the means that had enabled Goya to achieve his absolutely direct and shattering impact – an impact of the kind produced by something that is actually happening right in front of us, and is so near to us that we can almost feel it. Like Goya, he completely dispenses with any perspectival point of reference, and does not attempt to build up the background in depth. There is the same sudden and abrupt confrontation of the observer with the event depicted and the well-nigh total abolition of distance between him and the occurrence itself. The moment reproduced is that when the Austrian Admiral's ship is actually ramming her enemy, a manoeuvre that finally decides the battle. But the collision is not seen from some safe neutral vantage point; rather, the painter has placed himself directly in the bows of the attacker. The situation on the Austrian vessel, with the Admiral on the bridge and the sailors beneath him at the wheel, is presented to the painter's eye with utter immediacy, as though he had just caught it through a telescope. There is nothing to break the abruptness of its impact upon him, and the whole scene is built up in a flat, almost two-dimensional vertical plane. Decades later, this was to become the technique of the film-camera's eye.

I spoke of the symbolic quality of the event portrayed. By this I mean that the picture calls two things up in our minds: the reckless courage of a single man, determined on victory at any cost, and the purely technical and mechanical processes involved in the carrying out of his decision which reduce the human beings involved to mere inactive onlookers. Once the decisive order to ram has been given, then both combatants, the seen and the unseen, are delivered over unconditionally to the consequences of that order. The monstrous element in this battle episode, monstrous in that it is wholly beyond human control, is accentuated by Romako through this breath-taking two-dimensional flatness, this 'spacelessness' in the picture. The human beings stand like islands lost in the chaos. In the centre stands the Admiral, in the posture of the traditional Great Military Hero, who has on this occasion become the victim of his own determination and must abandon himself, like any of his sailors, to the consequences of his own action. His standing almost rigid in the very forefront of the picture has an ambivalent effect. It emphasizes the direct and inevitable quality of the issue now at stake, an issue which can no longer be evaded, and it turns the observer into a kind of opposite number confronting the Admiral himself. At the same time, there goes forth from the figure of this man as he stands there, immobile, a fatalistic resolve which exercises a peculiar, spellbinding fascination.

At this point I should like to refer to a picture which shows the Great Hero in a similarly divided role, though here the procedure is more cautious; it is Menzel's 'The Battle of Hochkirch' (1856) (plate 89). We see an army surprised; just stirred out of its sleep, it must now face the enemy that has taken it by surprise. A line of men is being hastily formed, officers are springing to their posts, and a crowd of grenadiers are climbing with some effort out of their trench to close the ring of defence. Here are no epic figures, no popular heroes, hurrying without much personal effort from one victory to another. Here we simply see human beings reaching for their arms while still drunk with sleep, so that they may save their skins. All is in confusion. The completeness of the surprise leaves room for nothing but improvisation. The qualities of uncertainty, indecision, and impermanence that mark the moment are actually imparted to the composition which itself seems to show a note of vacillation. It has no firm or disciplined rhythm, no inner control, no sharp accentuation; the picture is somehow open at all sides and capable of being indefinitely extended. In the midst of his soldiers, and yet in some strange fashion separated from them and surrounded by emptiness, appears the king. He is himself a victim of surprise like the rest and the situation has taken the reins out of his hands. Events have overcome him and all but made him superfluous. His presence remains unnoticed, his commands unuttered. There is no time for cautious strategic considerations. The moment demands the personal initiative of every man concerned. It will only admit of decisions suited to extreme peril. There are now neither leaders nor led.

This eighteenth century battle is seen through the eyes of the nineteenth century. Menzel's indiscreet gaze loves this sudden confusion, this impression of men being unexpectedly aroused, this element of surprise, this muddle from which there seems to be no escape. As early as 1846 an interior, 'The disturbance' (Die Störung), sounded this *Leitmotiv*; and the street and market scenes transposed it into the ordinary chaotic and busy life of a great city in which no man takes any notice of any other. In the case of 'Bonsoir, Messieurs' (1858) Menzel took this moment of surprise from the *genre* picture and transferred it to the historical picture, where he sharpened it into an episode. Frederick the Great enters a castle occupied by Austrian officers and they are so astonished at his appearance that none of them thinks of overpowering him. This act of bravado shows that there are situations which the Great Hero can in sovereign fashion master by his presence of mind. The 'Battle of Hochkirch' shows the limits of this power. The general has lost the commanding initiative, he is forced onto the defensive and robbed of all chance of direct action. By letting the King ride aimlessly and almost ghostlike through the confusion, his eyes fixed not on the enemy line but on the chaos among his own troops, Menzel turns the military commander into an anxious eye-witness of whom events no longer take account. He removes the King from personal involvement in the actual fortunes of the battle, and lets the very fact that he is now no longer able to play a part in determining them, endow his mere presence with a kind of radiant spiritual dignity. That the king has thus been removed from all direct participation, offers an opportunity of sublimating his loneliness and of making a kind of apotheosis of the whole without in any way abandoning the form of the historical painting.

The pictures discussed in this section show that some of the great artists of the nineteenth century were endeavouring to give an insight into history without that deliberate over-emphasis on detail and theatrical pose that was so characteristic of most of the painters of the day. Gros was still attempting to make us see the commanding dignity of the ruler in a sacred healing gesture, but Delacroix is already dimly aware that the people will be the determining factor in future history. In the case of Goya, however, this knowledge breaks through to the surface and in doing so begets a formal structure that is wholly new. The full import of historical events is indeed immanent in Goya's work, yet he is moved to a brutal and unvarnished directness. A new category of historical painting was developed during the nineteenth century by Goya's spiritual progeny that treated of the new factors in history, of mass action in which the authors of great events had perforce to remain anonymous, and of the new techniques of war which made those events impersonal. The Great Hero ceased to be the *spiritus rector* of all that happened in the world and become its executor – sometimes its prisoner.

119 GOYA Recumbent nude (*Maja desnuda*); 1797–98.

120 INGRES Odalisque; 1814.

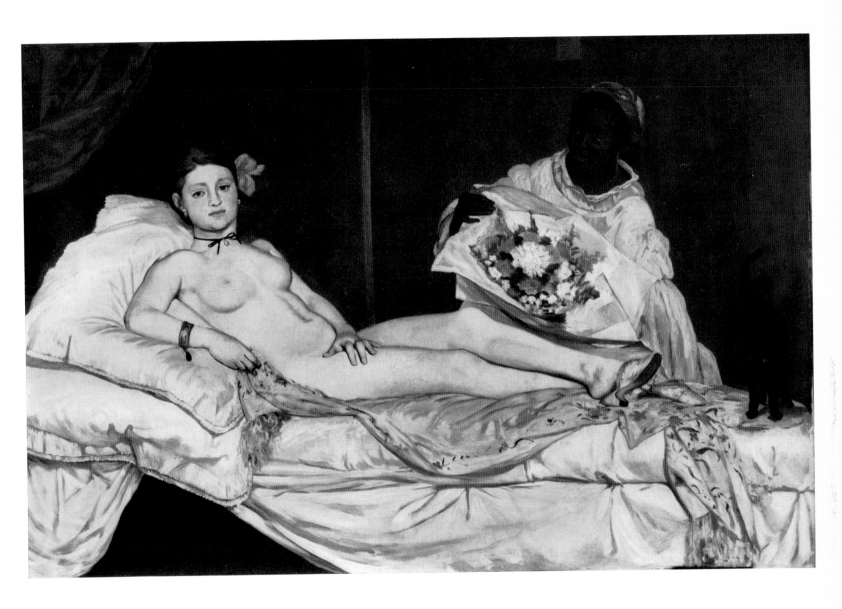

121 MANET Olympia; 1865.

122 COURBET *Les demoiselles au bord de la Seine*; 1857.

123 MANET *Le déjeuner sur l'herbe*; 1863.

124 CÉZANNE *Une moderne Olympia;* 1873.

125 RENOIR *L'esclave;* 1872.

126 DEGAS *Intérieur (le viol)*; 1874.

127 MANET Nana; 1877.

128 TOULOUSE-LAUTREC *Au salon de la rue des Moulins*; 1894.

129 TOULOUSE-LAUTREC *Maxime Dethomas au bal de l'Opéra*; 1896.

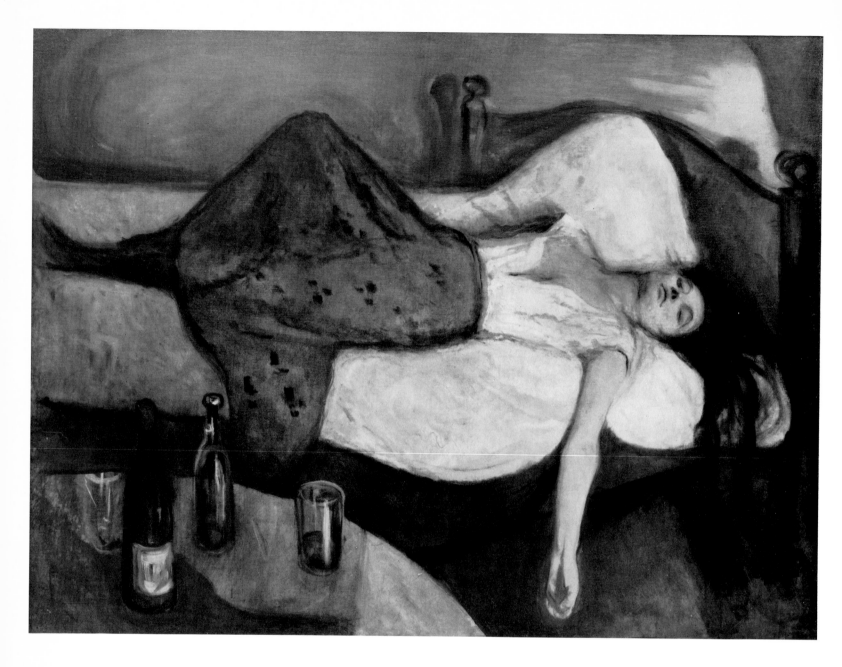

130 MUNCH The morning after; 1894–95.

Though it saw the end of the Great Man's role as moulder and controller of human affairs, it was the nineteenth century that not only broadened and deepened the cult of this figure, but through its art, provided it with its mythology and its symbolic types, and furnished it with an iconography that satisfied all its various requirements. In its reverent contemplation of this quality of human greatness – and more especially of greatness in the artist – nineteenth century art proceeded along two paths, both of which had already been indicated by current trends in historiography. The starting-point for the one was the realization that a historical event can only be understood in its context; it ended in the positivist diligence over detail that was the hall-mark of the *milieu* theory. The other path took its direction from the idea of that 'inner necessity' that is the characteristic of genius, and from a recognition of the fact that human greatness tends towards irrationality and the breaking of established rules – all this being part of the urge towards uninhibited self-realization.

There is implicit in this dual approach a question of great moment – and to some extent it reflects an even more fundamental debate. Was the man of genius merely an ordinary man with a few fortuitous superadditions of talent, themselves quite possibly developed as the result of a favourable environment? Or was he a being apart, working out, often with groanings of the spirit and without even a full comprehension of that which moved him, a unique and frequently tragic destiny that was peculiarly his own?

Here surely was a controversy in which the artist and the man of letters were peculiarly fitted to engage; and it is natural that the conflict should, in this particular territory, have been especially sharp.

Flaubert has something to say on the subject. In a preface to some poems by his friend Bouilhet, he comments as follows on contemporary positivist shortsightedness: 'The over-minute enquiry into the nature of the atmosphere that surrounds any particular writer often prevents us from appreciating the true features of his genius. In the days of Laharpe it was taken for granted that a masterpiece came into being as a result of certain rules, and was indebted to no man for its existence. Today, however, we seem to think that we have discovered the reasons for that masterpiece's existence when we have carried out a meticulous search into the circumstances surrounding it.'[11] The reference here is of course to Saint-Beuve, who said that he himself was incapable of judging a work without taking its creator into account. Even more unequivocal is the confession of Taine: 'Anyone who seeks to understand a work of art, an individual artist, or a group, must make himself familiar down to the last detail with the general spirit of the age to which these belonged, and with the way of life then obtaining. It is here that the ultimate explanation will be found, it is here that he will find the original cause that determined everything else.'[12] The matter could hardly be put in plainer terms. The artist is the product of his surroundings and the credit for his achievements must go to the age that brought him forth. Burckhardt really says much the same when he speaks of the 'precedences' or *Präzedenzien* which condition every individual.

For Taine and Saint-Beuve the artist was not only explained by the circumstances of the world around him, he was positively determined by them. He could not get away from them and his relationship with them was definitely causal. This method makes of him a 'social being'. Admittedly, the Great Man who is thus conditioned by his environment has 'decorative prominence', yet he lacks the hard contours of isolation. Fundamentally, he is much as other men are.

The other less rational conception of which I spoke, the conception of the genius driven by inner necessity, is less concerned with historical accuracy, and sets its sights directly on these high peaks and on little else besides. It assesses greatness by its very inexplicability, and gazes spellbound at the lonely man of genius, awestruck by his very remoteness from the rest of mankind.

Before we ascend this 'Mont Blanc' of the lonely – it was Schopenhauer who saw in this image a symbol of these 'highly gifted spirits' – it might be well to look at what the artist had to say, to examine, however cursorily, the views of those whose painting depended on historical research. What manner of man did they conceive the artist to be? One thing is significant. They seldom showed us a painter alone. We almost always see him having some kind of dealings with the people about him. Some kind of a dialogue seems to be indispensable; it brings painters, poets, and philosophers into sympathetic proximity with one other, it humanizes their dimensions, it turns them into important but no means inexplicable personalities. The Great Man is embedded in his surroundings, he is carried by the circumstances of his time and firmly fixed in them. He is not an outsider but simply a prominent member of human society. One could cite innumerable examples: 'Molière conversing with Louis XIV', 'Milton dictating *Paradise Lost*', 'Montaigne visiting Tasso', 'Diderot reading to his friends', 'Raphael and Michelangelo in the Vatican', 'The two van de Veldes in their studio', 'Boucher being presented to the Pompadour', 'Van Dyck learning to draw', 'Charles V picking up Titian's brush', 'Michelangelo nursing his servant', 'Filippo Lippi and a nun', 'The funeral of Titian', 'Poussin meditating among the ruins of Rome', 'Tintoretto painting his dead daughter', 'Leonardo dying in the arms of Francis I', 'The betrothal of Raphael'.[13]

Here I may perhaps be forgiven for a digression. Is it not something of a paradox that those very painters who sought, with such a palpable passion for exactitude, to show us the Great Man within the framework of time, lacked the power to wrestle with the facts of their own; that their own time held nothing which their art could grasp, and that they should thus have been compelled to seek a refuge in the past? Is it not strange that they had not the honesty to make a faithful portrayal of themselves and of their own mental and spiritual processes, let alone the capacity to endow their illustrations of history with any 'inner significance'?

These retailers of the entertaining historical anecdote failed utterly to establish that intimate relationship that should bind an artist to the world in which he lives. That was only achieved by those painters who deliberately and unhesitatingly let their personalities make contact with their own epoch and let themselves gain knowledge of it by direct experience – by the realists and the Impressionists.

And that brings me to the answer given by these same realists and Impressionists to the question here under review – and there is in that answer a certain faintly tragic irony. Deliberately following the democratic line, these men demythologized the image of the genius hovering in some timeless realm. The 'artist', with all the self-approbation that term implies, turned into a workman with both feet on the ground. This anti-romantic aspect of the artist's image of himself got rid of all motives for social conflict, and of the tension between the elect and the anonymous multitude. The artist now wanted to be a part of the age in which he lived. In the moment when he decided on such participation in the common lot and started to paint familiar, ordinary and unpretentious things – for there was nothing now that seemed unworthy of the painters' brush – he not only abolished the accepted hierarchy of subject matter, but descending from his pedestal, found his own existence as little beset by problems, and as free of any need for explanation, as that of the world about him. Both were as they were – and that was all that needed to be said. He lived and created – or at any rate wished to do so – in perfect accord with his surroundings.

Here I must speak once again of 'L'atelier', for it illustrates better than any other example the attitude of those artists who felt themselves to be bound up with humanity. 'All these people serve me and take part in my own activity', said Courbet to his friend Bruyas. And indeed, 'L'atelier' is a picture of friendships which are not exclusively confined to the community of artists but rather confront that community with a wider vision of mankind as a whole, though we should never lose sight of the fact that the artist conceived himself as a giver and not merely a receiver, and that in so far as he played this part, he felt he could justly claim the central place in the picture. Courbet's 'Portrait of his friend

226

Proudhon' – there is significance in the fact that it was interpreted by Courbet as a historical picture – is really the picture of an environment which shows the philosopher not in thoughtful isolation, but in his garden while at work, surrounded by his children.

The Impressionists increased the accord between the artist and the world around him and presented it in an even more unconstrained form. Manet's 'Musique aux Tuileries' (plate 186) contains, scattered about the crowd, portraits of Champfleury, Astruc and Gautier. Renoir painted his friends in the tap-room of la mère Anthony (plate 180), and in the 'Déjeuner des canotiers' he turned them into an excursion partly of ordinary townsfolk. In 'Le Moulin de la Galette' (plate 204) he lets them take part in a popular Sunday amusement. What have we here? A reporter telling of the real world? The notes of an eye-witness? No, quite as much as the 'Apotheosis of Homer', these pictures put on record a wish for harmony and true community. Yet, though his work may at times seem outwardly to have some kinship with the picture of Ingres, the impressionist painter refrained from arranging any gathering of men of genius, but fitted himself into the nameless crowd by whom – and here lies the irony of his position – he knew himself to be mocked and despised. Among these nameless people he sought to forget that he, who himself in his pictures transfigured such simple lives into the purest poetry, was for all that shut out from any experience which they could enjoy in common with him.

There are, however, other pictures of studios, pictures that are dark and tragic and give a far less optimistic and sensuous impression of the artist in the midst of a bourgeois world. And indeed, such works often come closer to the real mood of a century in which the misunderstood artist was the great artist, than do the scenes of the Impressionists, coloured as these so often were by wishes and dreams.

Again the rule applies that similar forms of experience can find an outlet either in the past or in the present, the determining factor in this choice being the artist's attitude toward history and life. To place on view what had happened in his own life Delacroix assumed the mask of Michelangelo, while Daumier simply painted a painter in his studio.

In 1830 at the age of 32, Delacroix published his essay on Michelangelo in the *Revue de Paris*.[14] His challenging Romantic pictures 'Vergil and Dante' (plate 81), 'The Chios Massacres' (plate 69 and colour plate VII) and 'The death of Sardanapalus' (plate 132), were at that time already done. The critics saw in him a subversive anarchist. Indeed, far from being enviable, his reputation verged on the scandalous. Already he knew that he was not understood – that he would never be understood. The character-sketch of the great Florentine served him as a means of self-revelation. For Michelangelo had also been the victim of perpetual misunderstanding and his 'wild genius' had been despised by the mediocre. Perhaps Delacroix felt that he was himself at the end of his own youthful powers when he stressed the fact that Michelangelo never touched brush or chisel between his twenty-fourth and thirtieth year. Perhaps the resignation discernible in the master whom he so much admired was already present in himself. There can be little doubt that Delacroix was thinking of himself when he asked the question so typical of the Romantics, whether genius was permitted to make mistakes; and then almost abruptly left the answering of it to the arbitrament of subjective passion. In the last part of the essay, his attempts to reach an understanding of this 'truly godlike man' crystallize into an idea for a picture that comes very close to being anecdotal. 'I seem to see Michelangelo late at night at the moment when, frightened by his own creations, he becomes the first man to experience that secret terror which he himself had sought to awaken in men's souls . . . Or I see him at that instant when, weary of painting, which would not vouchsafe him a truly exalted expression of his ideas, he summons poetry to his aid to succour his restless spirit.' This 'expression of deep melancholy' was to be reproduced in the picture which twenty years later was to originate from this idea. As a studio picture it should be grouped with those other biographical indiscretions of which mention has already been made; yet it is something more, it is a symbol of unrelieved loneliness. The figure of this man, lost deep in thought, takes on the burdened and tortured quality which Michelangelo's imagination was again to impart to the stone on which he worked. Alone with the work of his hands, the artist seems transformed into the world which he had created.

Daumier eschewed the Romantic's round-about method of first going back to the genius of the past. His painter at the easel is the symbol of that reflective imagination that frees itself from within. It needs no supporting environment, no external incentive. This painter, sitting as he does between two canvasses, is no Michelangelo, yet he is a figure worthy of a sculptor's chisel.

The popular theme of a studio visit is the subject of one of Daumier's works, though it is not clothed in the agreeable disguise of the Rococo, as Meissonier would have conceived it, but rather as a theme which makes plain the great gap between the artist and his public. Four visitors[15] are gazing at a canvas – well-meaning people ready to compliment and applaud, yet in all probability not quite convinced in their hearts by what they are about to say. Perhaps one of them is a potential buyer, another an influential critic. Behind them, upright and even domineering, stands the artist. There is uneasiness in his face, which is hardened with displeasure and shows a certain critical tension as though his patience were coming to an end. There is something self-righteous and uncompromising in his attitude; there is something in it of the mulishness of a Don Quixote, whose figure one is tempted to recognise in the picture of the rider that hangs on the studio wall immediately over the artist's head. 'Let me but prove myself in my saddle, stay behind in your huts and your tents...'; so, as he departs, we can imagine the lonely man crying out with Goethe to those who always stay behind.

3

In few particulars did the cult of man borrow more liberally from Christian iconography than in its representation of the fellowship of the saints. It may well be asked how it came about that if loneliness was, in the nineteenth century, one of the essential marks of the artist, he could have much to do with fellowship at all; but they are really only two aspects of the same thing. If a man has the feeling of being a member of a particular community, and is satisfied with the task that devolves upon him in that capacity, then he has no constant need for the society of men whose ideas are in some special way in accord with his own, he needs no sworn professions of faith, no atmosphere of religious self-dedication. Moreover, if he is an artist, he can, when a style has not as yet become imperative, disregard such strict formal laws as the English Pre-Raphaelites imposed upon themselves, and this too leaves him freer to pick his company, if any, where he pleases. Yet in a century where the artist was confronted with problems at every turn, he was bound to hope for strength and support from an association with like-minded people. We must, however, distinguish between two aspects of this phenomenon. On the one hand, we have the bond of friendship based on the experience of things felt in common; on the other, a gathering of men of genius united in a Pantheon of fame – in short, we have 'life' and 'history' again. Both, when presented in pictorial form, represent the secularizing of the tradition of the devotional picture.

It is true enough that not every picture of a studio or of a group of poets or artists has the disciplined strictness of a painted confession of faith, nor is every gathering of Great Men necessarily endowed with a sacramental character. There is little sign of the firm grasp of any unifying spiritual conception, or of formal concentration around any central idea in Alfred Stevens' great panorama '1789–1889, the Story of a Century' – surely one of the most comprehensive gatherings of men of genius ever painted – which was produced for the Paris Exhibition of 1889. The casual lining up of the six hundred and forty actors in this monster show, their ranks occasionally broken by the representation of important events, fails utterly to constitute a true community, nor is it committed to any common act of faith.

It is worth noting in passing that a similar plan for a painting of contemporary history was engaging the mind of an artist from whom such a project would hardly have been expected. In 1879 Manet wrote

to the municipal Prefect of Paris and put forward a suggestion for the decoration of the great assembly room of the new town-hall. Admittedly, Manet only proposed to throw in his great men more or less parenthetically. There were to be 'a number of designs which would contain – if I may use a current phrase that happens to express my ideas particularly well – representations of "the belly of Paris", of the great corporation, in their everyday surroundings, and of the public and social life of our time'.[16] Manet had in mind the following thematic groups – the Paris of the great markets, the railways and bridges, the subterranean town, the horse-races and the gardens. There was also, however, to be a gallery surrounding the ceiling (round which the public could walk) which was to be used for pictures of all men alive at the time who had rendered conspicuous service to the city. These pictorial schemes which combined the gathering together of men of genius and 'palingénésie sociale', were conceived by a painter of whom Zola had said that he cared neither for historical events nor for ideas! (It is perhaps worth recalling that in the same year as Manet addressed his proposals, which incidentally remained unanswered, to the municipal authorities of Paris, Makart in Vienna conceived his 'Festival Procession' – in which the different professions and ranks of society appear in historical disguise.)

However, this brings me rather far from my theme, since I am here only concerned with those works in which the cult of men of genius and, incidentally, of friendship rises to the level of a surrogate religion and deliberately makes use of the form of the devotional picture in order to give expression to an essentially religious feeling. The ritual representation of friendship and the *sacra conversazione* of Great Men both had their beginnings in the Romantic movement.[17] I spoke earlier of Overbeck's 'Triumph of Religion' (plate 90), but I should also mention the Madonna of Heinrich Olivier which has surrounding figures of painters and poets. A painting of Pforr's goes a step further. This was inspired by Wackenroder's art-loving monk who had a vision of the 'great and blessed saints of art'; they appear to him in a kind of nocturnal picture-gallery in which he meets Raphael and Dürer hand in hand.

In Pforr's picture the two painters kneel before a female figure representing 'Art'. The 'new altar in honour of God' which Wackenroder wanted to set up, and which Overbeck's 'Triumph of Religion' helps us to visualize, was turned by Pforr into an altar to art. Soon the matter goes further still and the artist himself takes the place of the allegorical figure of art. Such a painting, and one obviously designed to inspire an essentially religious devotion, was produced by Delaroche in 1841 for the Paris Ecole des Beaux Arts and was actually to be seen in one of the shrines of the new surrogate religion, namely in the hall where the prizes were distributed. In the centre of a semicircle made up of the great artists of all peoples and ages stands Apelles with Phidias at his right and Ictinus on his left. At the feet of this 'Trinity' sits a female figure, the Genius of the Arts. Ingres' 'Apotheosis of Homer' treats the same theme – the adoration of a Great Man by men of genius – again of all ages – who are that Great Man's spiritual kinsmen. If we decide to treat the figure seen apparently rising from the dead in Chenavard's 'La Philosophie de l'Histoire (Palingénésie sociale)' (plate 104) as the embodiment of the Superman, then the similarity of the whole conception of the painting to that of the devotional picture is remarkable. Incidentally, the theme of the Ascension or Resurrection is similarly secularized in Cézanne's 'Apotheosis of Delacroix'. The symptomatic character of the movement outlined here is immediately apparent. The older art furnished its devotional paintings with representations of the *civitas terrena* – as far as such paintings permitted this world to spread itself within them at all – and these rounded off the general content of the picture and were anchored in the temporal order. Now this procedure is reversed. The men of genius being gathered together choose their god from amongst themselves, and it is he who is the centre of their religious aspirations.

The cult with which the Romantic movement sanctified friendship, originated, as I have already indicated, in the circumstance that the artist was cut off from the world. The friends form a cell of understanding which provides them with something, however slight, on which they can hold to in a hostile world. They are thrown back upon one another. But there is also another element at work here. The friend is part of the masculine conception of the world in which man is cursed with eternal loneliness; in other words the friend is an essential compensation. He is a leader and a teacher who guides through the world's hazards those whom it is his task to protect. Even the groups in the kind of 'friendship picture' of which there are, as we have seen, so many examples, tend to take on the dignity of religious gatherings. There is a faint suggestion that we are witnessing a modern version, evoked largely through literary imagination, of great bygone relationships – of that between Hamlet and Horatio, that between Faust and Wagner, or that between Vergil and Dante – and the one conceit is quite as Romantic as the other. Alternatively, however, we seem at times to be witnessing some new pact between Faust and the Devil, the guardian angel having turned into the demonic seducer.[18]

The friend at the artist's side can on occasion assume a threatening aspect, and friendship thus portrayed seems sometimes to be instinct with the message that all is vanity, and to have – and here again we relapse into a popular form of religious art – the hidden meaning of the traditional dance of death. The companion waiting at the end of the road is the skeleton. A deep and far-reaching symbolism endows the latter with the features of the last friend who writes *finis* to it all.

Böcklin, in one of his pictures (plate 60), shows us a friendship of just such a kind, and we see the artist holding a questioning discourse with his companion, the whole somehow suggesting a scene in a popular ballad. A more discreet tone is struck by Géricault in his 'Portrait of an artist' (plate 56) with its compelling suggestion of the transience of all things. The tools of the painter's trade acquire symbolic value, while the skull with which he has daily intercourse speaks to the thoughtful man a warning *memento mori*.

Death as a physician! We might well chose that as the title for Goya's 'The artist with his physician, Dr. Arrieta' (plate 57), which is also related to paintings of this category. The picture has, admittedly, a number of layers: one of bitterness, one of despair, and one of comfort. Weariness of life is epitomized in the seemingly crippled figure. It is as though the diseased body were already reaching out into the next world and anticipating the agony of its last hours. The fact that the doctor is standing behind the sick man imparts what is almost a threatening note to his figure, yet at the same time his attitude recalls memories of the *pietà* and of the Throne of Grace.

Among these mysterious representations of transience we must count the double portrait of Marées and Lenbach (plate 61). It does not speak to us of death but of danger and insecurity. It shows us a twilight world, the faces expressing something half-way between second-sight and blindness; the eyes seek they known not what and seem full of questioning insistence.

Both the realists and the Impressionists – and this shows the spirit of sociability that informs their conception of the world – take all the aristocratic solemnity out of friendship, all that makes for distance between human beings. Friendship, like love, turns into what is essentially an open and easy companionship that manifests itself in many forms. Renoir's pictures of bucolic groups know no such thing as exclusiveness; the circle of friends loses itself in the crowd (plate 204).

How different are the Pre-Raphaelites. In Ford Madox Brown's 'Work' (plate 164), Carlyle and Maurice assume the roles of knowledgeable and distant onlookers – a new Dante and a new Vergil helping and leading mankind. No easy intimacy here.

Cézanne was the first to re-endow friendship with an independent and vital quality of its own, to make it once more a simple thing of the heart, unencumbered by ideas. He did this in 'Les joueurs de cartes' (plate 182). This great and lonely man was the first to re-emphasize the exclusive strictness of such a bond and show us the nature of a conversation that is silent because it needs no words. In the figures of these two men playing cards, the man who was so deeply wounded by the loss of the friendship of Zola, the companion of his youth, reveals his persistent devotion to the ideal of friendship that he still entertained,[19] and it is just this ideal that causes him to reveal his inward hurt in the handling of his subject; the force of this feeling endows the picture with its perfection and monumental greatness of form. It is thus that it contrasts with those representations of friendship which were founded on a mere similarity of minds – like the pictures of Zola and Alexis.

Friendship, as we have seen, was yet another form of surrogate religion for the Romantic movement. It made use of religious feeling to build a bridge between 'I' and 'Thou' and, conversely, it gave to the union between friends the solemnity of a religious creed. 'What,' asked Novalis' Heinrich von Ofterdingen, 'is religion but an eternal understanding and an eternal union between loving hearts?' Where such an understanding hallows the relations between one man and another, it is an intermediary that unites man with God. 'Where two or three are gathered together, there am I in the midst of them.' Runge's 'The artist with his wife and brother (We three)' (plate 175) endows this symbolic relationship with the firm purpose of a vow. Each of these three persons possesses the certainty that the 'eternal understanding' is making him or her partake in an act of faith. This gives the picture its reverent religious character.

Tieck referred to his friend Novalis as a new Christ for whom 'he would himself wish to be a stout Paul' (ein wackerer Paulus sein möchte),[20] while Novalis aspired to write 'a new Gospel' and to form with Tieck, Schlegel, and Schleiermacher a new company of four evangelists. We must think of these friendship fantasies that proliferated under the Romantics when we stand before those pictures of homage which were to be painted in honour of his great contemporaries half a century later by Fantin-Latour. Since they lack the exuberant display of cultural history which distinguishes the 'Homer' of Ingres, it is not immediately apparent that what they really do is to give their subjects divine status, and this fact tends in consequence to be overlooked. When Fantin-Latour first began to busy himself with the picture that was later to receive the title 'Le coin de table' (1872) (plate 179), he was thinking of a portrait of Baudelaire surrounded by decorative foliage. There were to be two groups, one on each side, offering their homage to the poet. In a letter he wrote: 'I shall paint Baudelaire after the portrait which I managed to fit into my "Delacroix". The twelve apostles seem to me to be a subject which will greatly excite public opinion'.[21] Later this general conception was abandoned in favour of a loose group of figures. The artist also dropped the plan for a portrait of Baudelaire. The original arrangement provided for a rigidly symmetrical distribution of the 'twelve disciples' similar to the dispositions in 'Hommage à Delacroix' of 1864 (plate 178). This very strict quality in the proposed composition may have been inspired by a painting of Philippe de Champaigne, 'Le Prévost des Marchands' (Louvre) in which the leaders of the merchants kneel before a crucifix. In place of the Cross, Fantin-Latour set the portrait of Delacroix, the artist-god.

At the end of the century the work of art was taking the place of its creator and to no man did this change of trend do greater justice than to Cézanne. The homage which Maurice Denis expressed in paint was not done to the man but to the power of Cézanne's art as expressed in his pictures, for it is these that contain the real content of his life, which has here taken visible form and can now never again be lost. The picture on the easel had become the ikon of the artist-religion.

4

Except for Delacroix's 'Michelangelo' and Daumier's studio pictures, we have so far confined our discussion to artists who felt entirely secure in their relation to the world around them. Such men were either members of some group of friends who had become associated on the empirical principle of simply being there for each other, or they belonged to some ideal circle of men of genius. They were either, like Courbet, men whose sympathies made them a real part of the life of their time and brothers of the whole

131
ROSSETTI
Astarte Syriaca; 1877

132 DELACROIX The death of Sardanapalus; 1827.

133 DELACROIX The death of Sardanapalus (detail); 1827.

134 MOREAU *L'apparition (Salomé)*; c. 1876.

human race, or members of a Nazarene-like religious community. In either case their life moved within a firm and recognizable framework and their work was bound up with a certain set of circumstances, real or imaginary.

This conception of the creative type is fundamentally untragic and at times even sanguine. There are indeed occasions when it is quite in accord with the official, and eminently satisfying, conception of the dignity of the artist. Over against these we must however set a number of highly self-revealing works which take a different view of the artist and subject his personality to a different interpretation.

Divorced from the empirical and historical circumstances that surround it, the figure of the artist becomes a symbol of an essentially negative relationship to the world, it becomes the symbol of genius, suffering and despised. There was indeed in this regard a special mythology of the Great Man, and it found valid expression in a number of forms. These by no means referred to the artist alone; they referred to the exceptional man of every sort and kind, to the man who sought his way outside the rules and conventions. 'Man can be great in only one of three ways – as a poet, as a priest, or as a soldier.' These words of Baudelaire's[22] are curiously applicable to the symbolic figures in which the nineteenth century discerned the Great Man's tragedy – Dante and Ahasuerus (the Wandering Jew), Napoleon and Prometheus, Mazeppa and Don Quixote. Michelangelo's saying, with which Delacroix prefaced his essay, holds good of them all. 'I go my lonely way on paths which no man has made for me.'

Men who went into the desert were well-known figures among religious contemplatives. They withdrew from the world into the *vita solitaria*, so that they might engage in dialogues with God. So long as it is sustained by faith, such solitude has something firm on which to lean. It is only doubt and loss of faith that force men into the new dimension of experience which is that of being utterly forsaken. The melancholy of Christianity, having sunk deep into such a man, could not do other – once faith had broken down – than produce this feeling of isolation. Let us recall von Fernow's remark – 'Art, when it becomes free and is released from both the compulsion and the prop of religion, must from that moment depend upon itself.' The price which it must pay for its freedom is loneliness. Constant wrote in *Adolphe*, 'Independence has isolation as its result.' Delacroix quoted this saying in his diary.[23]

The waste and the ocean of which Lautréamont sings, and on which Rimbaud's 'drunken ship' wanders, are the symbolic domains of the infinite and the immeasurable – the abiding place of one who has rejected all human ties and condemned himself to wandering and rootlessness. Flaubert feels urged to return to the desert and its Bedouins in order to preserve his dignity and his freedom.[24] 'The greatest passions are dependent upon loneliness,' says Chateaubriand, 'and he who carries them into the desert returns them to their kingdom.'

To the image of the sea and the desert we must add that of the steep cliff, the abyss, and the bottomless pit. On an island and on a mountain peak this feeling of awful separation from men becomes almost a physical thing, and yet man-the-artist's proud sense of mastery is strengthened here. 'My sorrow,' writes Kierkegaard, 'is my knight's castle. It rests like an eagle's nest upon the summit of a mountain and towers high above the clouds. None can storm it.'[25] The Abbé Galiani compares the philosopher to an eagle: 'To soar on high and possess talons, that is the destiny of the great geniuses.' Nietzsche brings this idea into his aphorisms, while Friedrich shows us man exposed and helpless in such surroundings. We see him upon the shore of the boundless empty sea, an island in that immensity and standing as though he had a kind of kinship with those rocks around him; or we see him at the edge of an abyss – and there can be no question but that all this mirrors a spiritual experience personal to the artist.

The search for symbols leads ultimately to the visualizing of the Great Man in the form of a figure of stone like a great rock. Schelling says of Winckelmann that 'in his time he stood majestic like a mountain peak in his loneliness'.[26] For Carlyle Great Men were living rocks, and the same idea is immanent in the words of one of Delacroix's contemporaries who wrote of him thus: 'Lonely upon a rock, high above all the noise of the universe, his is the egoism of the gods. Let none require of him that he should descend into the realms of men.'[27] It is in these high regions, inaccessible to man, that Nietzsche sets his Zarathustra, it is here that Rodin's 'Balzac' (plate 157) has its true place. When Gautier thinks of Goethe, he calls to his aid a picture of a god by Ingres. He visualizes that remote Olympian as Jupiter, with Bettina kneeling at his feet (plate 5).[28]

On the shores of the sea or on the peaks of mountains man learns what it means to encounter the elements; it is here that he tests his strength, but it is also here that he feels the seductive depth of the abyss. That is what Brentano means when he speaks of being utterly exposed and when he writes in a letter that he had spent all his life upon a mountain top.[29] Here we have the key to that strange capricious self-isolation of Friedrich, who, disregarding all danger, would remain for long periods by the side of the stormy sea. Coupled with this desire for solitude is the longing for nature, for nature strong and untamed, and not yet held in check by civilization. Both feelings can be traced back to Rousseau, who declared that man in solitude was man in his natural state.

Man sought to be alone with the elements. Byron, a second Leander, swam the Hellespont. Joseph Vernet was tied to the mast, so that he could draw the drama of the stormy sea. The longing to get back to the primal and aboriginal drove some men to search out the actual locations of mythological events, while others sought to satisfy it by the exploration of life in the present and so pointed the way to modern pictorial reporting.

The desire for solitude in all its different aspects was responsible for more than certain artistic themes. It actually determined the kind of place in which the artist chose to live. Victor Hugo had a glass-roofed look-out built on Guernsey from which he could feel himself directly confronted by the immensities of sea and sky. (In the towers built for tourists this sensation of being on a summit became a collective experience; and in the circular paintings which so often provided mass entertainment for the people of the nineteenth century the encounter with nature as it surrounded man became a tame thing and was translated into a clever optical illusion.) Another example of this is the building by Carmen Sylva of a pavilion on the Black Sea just above the surf so that it seemed to float in emptiness.

Richard Wagner's home in the Palazzo Giustiniani brought the remoteness of an island existence into the tired scenery of a town heavy with age. Herrenchiemsee, the home of his royal friend, was an island place of exile, a world of aristocratic escape. Here we no longer have the naked and unrestrained encounter with the elements as Friedrich contrived to recapture it at the beginning of the century; here people are seeking the kind of protective covering that one can feel in Böcklin's villas and in his islands of the dead — all of them things that are heavy with symbolic significance. Nor is it in the imagination alone that these islands and rocks are places of burial; men actually use them for this purpose. Rousseau's tomb is on an island in the park of Ermenonville with poplars all around it, while Chateaubriand rests on St Malo. Paganini's body was for some years buried on a remote island in the Mediterranean, after long wanderings from city to city. The most famous of all island tombs is that on St Helena.

Islands, sea, mountain, desert — these are the vehicles for the projection of a certain kind of feeling, symbols for the absence of all precise measure and form. They provide the surroundings in which the symbols of human greatness are placed; the mood which these things convey had always to be clearly suggested before the Great Man himself was described.

The Great Man is nowhere at home. A strange wanderer, Novalis calls him, who from time to time passes through the places where we ourselves have become established. He has no abiding place and is a stranger in the midst of our settled fenced-in way of life; he is Melmoth the wanderer, he is the flying Dutchman, the Prodigal Son, he is Byron's Manfred, Nietzsche's Zarathustra, he is Ahasuerus, the Wandering Jew, condemned for life; but he is also Schlemihl who, blameless himself, is hurled into misfortune.

In painting it was Friedrich who first succeeded in expressing the tragic greatness of the homeless man. His figures wander through a mighty alien nature, lacking all ties with any community of men or with the world surrounding them. And when they pause and give themselves over to the contemplation of the limitless distances of space, then they know that they are at nature's very edge but prevented by an invisible wall from surrendering their ego to the greater whole. These figures are surrounded by a glassy stillness and the utter precision of the picture's design; the complete absence of any irrelevant detail is the formal equivalent of that immovable and indestructible silence. The experience of loneliness can assume a rare degree of cleanness and purity and so produce a solemn and even numinous effect.

John Martin's 'The Last Man' (1849) (plate 17) comes straight out of the disturbed and fevered world of the English Romantic movement. At the edge of a yawning abyss there stands a dignified prophet-like figure, while in front of him there stretches a great hollow broken by chasms and cracks in the ground. Forlorn ruins are visible in the background, nature is withered and dead. It is the world's end presented in dramatic terms. There are dim movements across the sky; there is the strange and rather heavy solemnity of something happening everywhere and nowhere that was later to make Nietzsche uneasy about Wagner.

This great stretch of unfamiliar terrain that seems to vanish, almost to stream away, into the distance – it is all most typical of the late Romantics, and particularly of the English Romantics – turns the whole world into a petrified maelstrom. At the time when this English fantast was seeing his visions, the French realists were seeking to fit the figure of the wanderer – for which, incidentally, the earlier Romantics had failed to find any strong formal equivalent – into the framework of normal human relationships. Courbet turned the world-wanderer into a modern Ahasuerus – not one that must carry about with him the judgement of God but an earthly bringer of good fortune. Courbet's apostle, Jean Journet, a Fourierist missionary, went not into the desert but into the world to preach universal harmony. Courbet who in his own way was also a preacher and tried to bring happiness to others, took up the wanderer's staff; but he remained among the people of his own world whom we see offering him their greeting: 'Bonjour, Monsieur Courbet' (plate 176). Somehow the unprotected and exposed role of the wanderer did not suit the taste of the century's middle period. Only the *peintres maudits* ('accursed painters') who followed after the Impressionists and were the contemporaries of Rimbaud, the disappearing commercial traveller, found in the wanderer a reflection of themselves.

Gauguin is an instance of this, as can be seen from his picture 'Bonjour, Monsieur Gauguin' (1889) – an ironic reference to Courbet's title. The picture shows the artist against a stormy landscape, walking towards a garden gate near which stands a peasant woman. Van Gogh sees life rather differently. He has a stronger feeling for the rootlessness of existence, a stronger awareness of being everlastingly driven from one place to another. He shows himself to us upon the highway, and seems to possess all the determination of a true pilgrim whose faith is burning within him. We are reminded of some words, spoken by an artist at the beginning of the century, which are as true today as when they were uttered. 'The road of the artist has no goal. He must move forward without respite or rest. Once he stands still, then, alas, he goes backward; he can see how what is behind him sinks away in a blue mist. Yet for all that there is no ending to his road. So he hurries onward till death overtakes him' (Franz Pforr).[30]

The pilgrim, the monk, the prophet are all figures that give concentrated expression to the artist's loneliness. On the nature of the actual psychological process involved Nietzsche has a pregnant observation: 'This turning inward (Verinnerlichung) comes about when certain powerful urges which, thanks to the arrangements of peaceful society, are prevented from discharging themselves externally, seek, while working together with the imagination, to keep themselves inwardly harmless. The need for enmity, cruelty, revenge and violence turns back on itself, it "withdraws".'

Yet, all this while, the figure of the wanderer with his strange and lyrically attuned restlessness was being confronted by a different image, that of the hunted man furiously rejecting all constraint and always ready to give explosive outward expression to the tumult within. Two irreconcilable moods subsist alongside one another – on the one hand inward recollection, a longing for lost human ties; on the other, an abandonment to the all-too-powerful tyranny of instinct… Mazeppa, the Cossack Hetman of whom Byron sang, is the symbol of the artist overcome by such animal urges. Mazeppa had dared to approach a noble Polish lady and as a punishment was tied naked to a wild horse which we see carrying him away. As the horse gallops madly on with nothing but its own exhaustion to check it, the helpless man is attacked by birds in the wilderness – exactly like Prometheus, that great symbol of rebellious daring.

Mazeppa is not only the man who is defeated by the dark powers of animalism, he is also the out-lawed and rightless man whom society rejects and mercilessly delivers over to ruin. He is, to quote a catchword, 'Man in revolt'. All this made him, among the French Romantics, one of the dominant themes in artists' spiritual self-portraiture. The pictures of Boulanger, Vernet (plate 135), Géricault and Delacroix provide ample evidence of its popularity.[31] Both symbolically and as a fact of history, the fate of this outlawed man was in keeping with the age. The intoxicating Dionysiac urge for expression found in it a dynamic inspiration, indeed it found its hero in this figure, for Mazeppa is the violent man who suffers violence, he is the hunted hunter Dionysus, the one who tears others to pieces and is him-self so torn.[32]

One of the greatest figures in all the literature of the world, and wonderfully eloquent of that experience of loneliness which the Great Man must undergo, is Don Quixote. He is the solitary man who stands outside and beyond all established institutions, condemned everlastingly to be different, the man who is a stranger within the framework of society, and whom society takes for a fool, the rider in the desert who deliberately refuses obedience to the conventions. Turgenev gave a lecture in 1860[33] in which he compared the trusting knight to that other great questioner, Hamlet. Cervantes' great charac-ter here became a tragic searcher after truth, one who believed in something eternal and immovable. The Russian now conceived the idea of a historical *genre* picture, 'a picture worthy of the brush of a master with a profound and searching mind – 'Shakespeare reading Don Quixote'.

Three years later Doré's illustrations appeared. They are a riot of mingled anecdote, horror, and grotesque humour but do not penetrate to the real depths of their subject. The Don Quixote whom Turgenev had in mind was nothing less than the creation of an artist who in his own time was himself an example of a great spirit kept beyond the pale, and who was recreating his own self-portrait in the figure of the wandering knight. Daumier's 'Don Quixote' is something entirely peculiar to Daumier – it is neither a *genre* picture nor an illustration (colour plate I). Would Turgenev have recognized in it his own interpretation?

Daumier seized on the feature that lay at the very root of Don Quixote's precarious existence – his loneliness, the consequence of his estrangement from the world; he could no longer find his way in the world around him.[34] This loss of hold on reality exiled him from the 'normal' system of human and social relationships and confined him to a private conception of the world, one that belonged to him alone. He thus becomes a symbol of the artist to whom the world of empirical reality can offer no rest-ing place, and who finds a stronger and more essential reality in his dreams. Nowhere does Daumier, whose profession as a cartoonist kept him throughout his life continually alert to the pulse beat of the present, express himself in a more personal or uncompromising fashion. Don Quixote is for him the free man unencumbered by any allegiance, the man who leaves Sancho behind so that he may be alone with himself.

Nowhere is there any anecdotal embellishment of his deeds and adventures. They take place in an

135 VERNET Mazeppa; 1826.

139
FUSELI The Incubus.

140
BLAKE The Whirlwind
of Lovers; c. 1824.

158 HUNT Awakening Conscience; 1854.

136 MUNCH Puberty; 1894.

137 MUNCH Ashes; 1894.

143
BURNE-JONES King Cophetua
and the Beggar
Maid; 1884.

141
BLAKE Vision of the Daughters of Albion
(frontispiece); 1793.

142 KLIMT Water-nymphs; 1907.

144 TOULOUSE-LAUTREC *Au Cirque Fernando;* c. 1888.

area of complete isolation. The landscape is utterly desolate, there is no sign of man anywhere. The haggard figure is riding through a wilderness with no human world waiting beyond it. In this open space there is no answering voice, no echo, no dialogue. Let us remember – as is essential if we are to assess the picture's protesting force – the actual date when it was painted; it was just after the middle of the century, the time when the masses were given a voice, when people were dreaming of the greatest good of the greatest number and basing their hopes of international brotherhood on the progress of science. It is in the midst of all these optimistic expectations that we see Don Quixote insisting on the superiority of loneliness.

Another figure in which the artist recognizes himself is that of the author of the *Divine Comedy*. Carlyle describes him in his third lecture in *Heroes and Hero-worship*. His face, whose features Giotto has preserved for us, he calls 'the mournfullest face that ever was painted from reality.' Tenderness contrasts in it with isolation and 'proud hopeless pain... The face of one wholly in protest, and life-long unsurrendering battle, against the world.'

In order to know what manner of man the exiled Dante was, the nineteenth century had no need to look backward to the Middle Ages. There is in some notes of Delacroix a description of Byron which bears a remarkable likeness to Carlyle's words on the Florentine. He is pictured as the fugitive whom society and an all-powerful public opinion have banished, the man rejected to whom no mercy is shown, the Cain of our time. Some decades later Rilke was to take a rather similar view of Cézanne, who also had to endure the sneers of his fellow citizens, and to describe him as a man subjected to public ill-treatment.

The nineteenth century possessed a great wealth of Dante-interpretations. He was a favourite subject for painters of scholarly and educational pictures and he was also a favourite theme for the monumental illustrations in which the Romantic movement took a peculiar delight.[35] Cornelius made a kind of commentary on him on the ceiling of the Casino Massimo. Doré adapted him to the taste – now coarser and more eager for sensation – that characterized the latter half of the century, while the English Pre-Raphaelites made him the idol of their complex-laden sensitivity and treated him as the very symbol of ill-starred love. This unfortunately caused them to relapse into sentimental *genre* painting. Rossetti, who more or less identified himself with Dante, shows the poet being painted by Giotto – surely a symptomatic encounter between two artist-saints of the Pre-Raphaelite movement.

The most passionate and in many ways the most brilliant of all Dante pictures is by Delacroix. It shows the poet, accompanied by Vergil, being ferried across Acheron by Phlegyas (plate 81). It is a conception that vaguely suggests a classical *Walpurgisnacht* (there comes to mind a more disciplined, and also more distant, portrayal of horror: Dürer and Celtes in the midst of 'The Martyrdom of ten thousand Christians'). It is no mere chance that Delacroix, who once appeared as Dante at a fancy-dress ball, should, in this very century in which Dante was rediscovered, have painted the only picture which went beyond mere illustration and truly contrived to symbolize the dual role played by the artist. It contrived to do this because it was really a self-portrait. Himself an outlaw, a homeless man, the artist must take upon himself the sufferings of a nameless humanity that clings around his own neck. It is in this sense that he, by partaking of their agony, becomes their redeemer. Delacroix's 'Vergil and Dante' is Delacroix's 'Ecce homo'. Similarly, the man whom Daumier, in this own 'Ecce homo', placed before the raging crowd, is secretly their brother; their sufferings are his own. Behind all these different manifestations there is the same idea: the artist believes himself to be the redeemer of mankind and, like Shelley's Prometheus, is an innocent sufferer on their behalf.

Prometheus looms very large in the century's imagination – the rejected one who seeks to help and is for that very reason mocked, jeered at, and martyred: Prometheus fastened to the rock and torn by the eagle. It was in this form, in the image of one who obstinately persisted in his own pain, that since the *Sturm und Drang* period men had visualized the creative Titan. The nineteenth century believed that he could manifest himself in any one of the three forms in which, according to Baudelaire, man may rise to true greatness – the poet, the priest, and the soldier. The imagination of the day, which somehow felt a need for mythical figures, tended to attribute vast stature to all three of these. The poet became a world-creator, a tamer of chaos who also endowed it with form; the priest preparing the sacrifice became a saint; the soldier who made a sacrifice of himself became a hero and a Messiah.

The Bonaparte cult illustrates the trend. In the tenth chapter of *Le Rouge et le Noir* Stendhal lets his hero climb a mountain. The knowledge that he is standing alone and high above men makes young Sorel feel happy and gay. Then from a still higher peak there rises a sparrow-hawk which draws its vast circles in the sky. Julien envies the bird's easy strength, he envies its detachment and freedom. The chapter ends with the words, 'Such was the destiny of Napoleon – would it one day be his own?'

The rocks, the wilderness and the untamed birds of prey – all these were symbols that accompanied the image of the superman. Byron's Manfred compares himself to the lion and the eagle; Chenavard's figure of one rising from the dead is accompanied by an eagle lifting its wings, while Christian iconography sees in the eagle a symbol of the Son of God's ascent into Heaven. The kingly bird was a part of Napoleon's insignia during his lifetime; after his death what had once been the sign of imperial status began to suggest a fallen majesty whose wings had been broken but whose spirit rose upward to immortality. Napoleon's banishment to St Helena seemed to make his already legendary figure even more remote, and enhanced its appeal by connecting it with yet another suggestive idea which the special circumstances of his exile provided – the island rock. No other setting could have provided a happier stimulus to the artist's imagination. Napoleon[36] sitting upon a rock, lonely beneath the stars, comes near to being a god enduring punishment, a god who has endeavoured to help mankind and is now expiating his impious daring upon a rock that is his prison. His image begins to seem something wholly beyond the confines of our earth. The conquered god stands high above men and his greatness promises to be imperishable.

Rude eloquently represents the deceased emperor awakening to immortality (plate 12) – we see him chained to a rock, around which plays the sea, while at his feet there is an eagle that will never rise again (1845-47). Seen after this fashion Napoleon's death is transfigured into that of a sacrificial victim. While Byron was comparing him to Prometheus bound,[37] enthusiasm in France rose to even greater heights. For Couture[38] the island of St Helena was a French Golgotha; and in 1855 Gautier, standing before Ingres' 'Apotheosis of Napoleon', was moved to the wildest of panegyrics as he expatiated on the resurrection of a hero-god. He discerned in the picture a fitting companion piece to the 'Apotheosis of Homer'. The painter, as he saw it, was according divine status to the greatest poet of antiquity and the greatest warrior of modern times. The body of Napoleon now lacked all human stigmata; even the diamond nails which had nailed him to the rock had left no mark...[39]

The fate of exile ties down the restless man, who had once marched across an entire continent, to a single place. Gradually this causes him to forget his expansive urge to be doing great deeds and allows other equally Promethean features to come into prominence – his endurance in self-sacrifice, his greatness in suffering, his lonely absorption in thought. A painting of Gérome, 'Napoleon and the Sphinx', helped men's minds to see him in this way. Literature did not lag behind, and by comparing him with Oedipus made the image even more compelling.[40] In the picture by Delaroche we see even more clearly this emerging image of lonely greatness lost in thought, meditating on the affairs of all mankind. By the end of the century that same image had cast off all its historical trappings and reappeared more power fully than ever as Rodin's 'Thinker' looking down into the abyss of humanity (plate 159).

Rodin had at first intended to treat this piece of sculpture as representing 'The Poet'. He was clearly referring to Dante, this being the obvious interpretation of the great figure which originally dominated the grandiose but unfinished 'Hell Gate'. Even, however, after the statue had been taken out of its original setting and treated as an independent work of art, its spiritual significance still remained; and we still feel this great and lonely man is looking down into the abyss of humanity. Those whom he beholds down there, caught up as they are in the hellish intoxication of the senses, are his own creatures; and what weighs upon that brooding mind is that their inexorable fate is also that of their creator, who had striven to emulate the gods. There is something devilish that weighs down this Prometheus, something of the demonism of Lucifer himself – the shadow of a burdened conscience.

He might almost repeat the contemptuous words that Friedrich Görres put in the mouth of Napoleon: 'All men on earth are little more than a rabble and those who hold themselves in the highest esteem should be looked upon as the very dregs ... When I looked down from the Kremlin and saw the sea of fire which was Moscow, my heart was moved with keen delight, for I saw before me a resolution and a will. Something had happened, in spite of all, in that empty time, and the flame called forth my praise in a thousand tongues. What Nero cunningly contrived as a madman's game, that and much more had become for me a most serious matter. I should have liked to have sat in the midst of those flames upon a bronze throne and warmed the spirit within me, the best part of which had become hard and stiff from the frosty cold.'[41]

In Moreau's conception of the Promethean figure there is a considerable shift of emphasis. His 'Prometheus' (1868) (plate 16) shows no rebel, no disturber of the people. No chains appear to weigh him down. The symbolistic painter has changed his penance into something different. He towers upward, remote from man, and the lonely figure seems to encompass the whole universe with his knowledge. If one is to gather the world thus into oneself, is it not sufficient to traverse it with one's thoughts, to take possession of it with the eye of the spirit? Thus argued the more retiring and exclusive aesthetic philosophy of the symbolists. It made the outraged god more gentle, it gave him a quality of clarity and calm that was no longer wholly of this world, the quality of one who freely accepts his fate. Even critics of Moreau's own day were already speaking of his work as 'the Prometheus with the head of Christ'.[42]

Klinger's 'Brahms Fantasy' (1890–1894), a series of etchings, underlines the dramatic and Titanic elements of the Prometheus-myth and brings them into conjunction with the lot of the artist and the fate of mankind. Hölderlin's *Song of Fate* put into the mouth of Homer, the minstrel, introduces the eternal symbols of human uncertainty – water, the cliff, and the precipice. The fundamental thought is pessimistic; there is a curse on man, and all his acts bear the imprint of destruction. The last sheet of the series shows Prometheus set free on a forward-jutting rock, his face in his hand, his whole attitude eloquent of pain. The bending of his body – a posture used throughout the century from Blake to Munch to convey the brooding mind – and the wrenching apart of the legs both express despair. Deep beneath him there rise out of the waves the jubilant Oceanidae. In the hour of his liberation the first redeemer is more lonely than before, and in this he is like Rodin's 'Thinker', though he lacks the latter's Satanic melancholy.

A displeasing dissonance goes through the greater number of Klinger's creations. They are seen too sharply and there is in them an overabundance of conscious thought. Much as Moreau overloads ethereal bodies with precision of detail, Klinger seeks to unite a penetrating near-sighted naturalism with the monumental qualities of a vision. His art rarely does more than produce a rather startling effect, though sometimes his sheer technical skill and lavish use of material do produce a contrast that is really interesting. We can see this in his statue of Beethoven which glorifies the Titanic artist-god. The coloured metals and stones which surround the white body provide it with a kind of frame, with the emphasis on movement and materiality, and this in turn most effectively emphasizes the pale spirituality of the central figure. The eagle is no longer seen as a means of inflicting torment, it is the symbol of a genius that knows no earthly fetters, and also the carrier of divine inspiration. Klinger's 'Beethoven' is therefore related not to the Prometheus symbol alone but to one of the themes of Christian art – St John upon Patmos. The degree to which this work was in tune with the requirements of the religion of art is shown by its essentially religious mode of presentation in the Vienna 'Secession' in 1902, where it seemed to turn the whole building into something like a hallowed place.

To conclude these observations on the suffering Titan and his symbolic significance, I have chosen Daumier's 'Ecce homo' (circa 1850) (plate 54). It is only after the eye has grown familiar with the other incarnations of the creative spirit – suffering, persecuted and yet proud – that it is ready to look on this painting, which is one of the most profound creations of the century. Everything is contained within it – the wanderer, the last man, Don Quixote misunderstood, Dante surrounded by the damned, and Prometheus in his chains. In the midst of a chaotic sea of humanity we see the silhouette of a man – motionless. All the other figures are frantic with excitement, greedy hands stretch out to seize, bodies push forward, crowding against each other, and press dangerously against the platform on which the man stands exposed. This nameless, unprotected man whose loneliness is savoured by the crowd as though he were in a play – does his slender outline really belong to our chapter on religious iconography? He is a whole world apart from the picture of Christ with which the nineteenth century was chiefly concerned, from Cornelius and Ingres with their traditional cult of beauty, from the humanitarian gentleness of Fritz von Uhde, and from the cold archaeology of Millais and Klinger who cared for little save exact historical reconstruction.

Daumier's 'Ecce homo' unites within itself all the other figures that symbolize the Great Man thrust back into lonelines. This man, covered with insults and abuse, represents the noblest manifestation of the remote being who is only a visitor to our earth. In a much more complete fashion than Dante and Prometheus with their bowing down before men, he breaks the isolating spell of a proud and deliberate self-withdrawal, for he alone has the strength to open his heart to men and be their brother. The complacent detachment of the creative artist, saint-like among the elect, has disappeared and turned into a passionate desire for participation in all that is human.

On the threshold of madness, that headlong fall from proud, brilliant isolation into pitiful anonymity, Nietzsche experienced this revelation. He signed his last messages of madness once as Dionysus and once as the Crucified. In his letter to Burckhardt of the 6th January 1889, the whole frame of his personality breaks into pieces and his self seems to dissolve. He himself is every name in history. Yet this is no self-glorifying megalomania but its despairing abdication:

'Before all the virtuous I would be guilty,
I would be called guilty and all the great guilts shall be mine.
Before all the trumpets of fame
Let my ambition be as a worm,
Among such I desire
To be the lowest.'

approved, has all too often been interpreted – quite wrongly – as a form of flight. Yet what the artist fled from was not man but a distorted image of man – the empty phrases of the Philistine, the outward show of the self-righteous, the sprawling well-fed comfort of the mediocre, who, like Sancho, nurse their leisurely digestion, while Don Quixote is always turning to face the unknown.

Even as he fled from the distorted image of man, so he sought with increasing ardour for the true one, with which he, a homeless wanderer, could identify himself; he sought it in the undisguised savage, the savage as nature made him, in the man wholly mastered by instinct, and in the madman who lived in a world that was entirely his own; and, because he was in fact seeking for himself, he sought it in the criminal who, unprovoked, challenged the world at large, and in the poor who for that world care nothing at all. Thus the wheel came full cycle. Art that was without a hold to cling to sought in the world around it for those who had no hold upon themselves. Hence, too, the abandonment of reason. The huge tensions of instinct require instinct to comprehend them. Mere reason is inadequate for the task.

One can expand the argument further. If a man wishes to enter into the unfettered freedom of the lawless, he must cast off all those laws that impose an established tradition, all that makes for the common acceptance of an established code. Similarly, to reach a point beyond the effective sphere of bourgeois morality, the artist must renounce the aesthetic values which that morality determines and which are really under its authority, the values – such as they are – that it holds in genuine esteem and preserves in the shape of empty etiquette. In the nineteenth century the 'middle-class public' is the advocate of the canons of absolute beauty, of lofty ideas, and of rational and clearly intelligible meanings – and it is this public that is the artist's enemy.

2

This brings us to that ultimate estrangement, that ultimate separation from the true self, the phenomenon of madness, which for the nineteenth century had an obsessive interest, and which it would be worth our while to examine in greater detail.

'The Dream of Reason brings forth Monsters'. So wrote Goya beneath one of his 'Los Caprichos' etchings (plate 44). The sluice-gates are open and a flood of nocturnal visions weighs down the helpless man whom no sense of rule or moderation protects any longer. The world which reason had constructed for him with such consummate artifice breaks down, its order is no more, and no teaching or principle of religion now has binding power. Chaos breaks out triumphant. Goya was seeking to defend himself against all that was thus oppressing him, and he recognized that he was himself in danger of being devoured by this horror. He wrote: 'Deserted by reason, the imagination breeds impossible monsters. United with it, it is the mother of the arts and of all their wonders'[4]. Goya's drawings and paintings give scant evidence of obedience to such precepts. He breaks his marriage vows to reason and without halt or compromise courts this carnival of the irrational. He does not flee from the temptations of the instincts but seeks them in wild and fevered dreams, so that he may taste to the full their overwhelming power. Romantic indeed is such an imagination, for, contrary to all the rules of classical aesthetics, it notes down, without inhibition of any kind, all its vast hallucinations, and elevates the experience of its dreams to become the only indisputable reality.

Even the artist who obeyed the classical rules permitted his figures to dream, though what he set before our eyes had already been emasculated by the alliance which imagination had made with reason, and had been made to conform to the canons of beauty. Even 'Ossian's Dream' (plate 80), though for an artist like Ingres it is an extreme concession to the obscurantism of the Romantics, is, when compared with Goya's works, a well-ordered historical painting whose figures have obediently

145 COURBET *La truite*; 1873.

146 CÉZANNE *La pendule noire*; 1869–71.

147 VAN GOGH Gaugin's chair; 1888.

148 MENZEL The studio wall; 1872.

submitted to rigorous stage management. These figures undeniably have an existence of their own within the general design of the picture, an existence that is entirely independent of the dreamer. The mythical singer illuminates by the spiritual light of his imagination the vague twilight of the Nordic Olympus and calls the figures into being. In the Goya, however, the artist who, one seems to feel, is in some prison cell, is visited by the shadows of the night, but the birds which flutter around him have come uninvited. Poe's raven whom we see in Gauguin's portrait of Mallarmé is a creature of just this kind.

From the 'Dream of Reason' a direct road leads to Mazeppa, fettered and attacked by the birds of the wilderness; and another leads back to *Sturm und Drang* – to Fuseli's 'The Nightmare' (plate 47), and even to Goethe's *Tasso* in which those lines spoken by the imprisoned poet are so strikingly reminiscent of Goya:

> Das häßliche zweideutige Geflügel,
> Das leidige Gefolg' der alten Nacht,
> Es schwärmt hervor und schwirrt mir um das Haupt.
> Wohin, wohin beweg' ich meinem Schritt,
> Dem Ekel zu entfliehn, der mich umsaust,
> Dem Abgrund zu entgehn, der vor mir liegt?*

Yet another road leads to Cézanne's 'Temptation of St Anthony'. In this picture, which is a disguised self-portrait, we reach the point where almost all the variations on the theme of human temptation are connected with one another and their common iconographic origin becomes discernible. In them all we see a secularized version of man's confrontation with the powers of instinct, whose symbols are woman and the beast. Since temptations have now forfeited any place in a clear-cut religious scheme, the subjective imagination is left to experience, interpret, and portray them much as it pleases; but the same demons still rend the human heart and establish an affinity between their present victims and those whom they have previously tormented. 'In *Saint-Antoine* I myself was Saint Anthony, and him I forgot,' declares Flaubert.[5]

There is one other human temptation that especially concerns us here, that of acedia, the melancholy that can easily grow into the mortal sin of despair. This was the besetting temptation of the 'Saturnian' type of man, personified in Christian iconography by St Anthony (whose 'temptations' were really crisis states of depression).[6] Saturn is the planet whose orbit takes it into positions furthest apart and the Saturnian type includes men at the opposite poles of melancholy: prisoners, beggars and madmen as well as philosophers and hermits.

If we bear this in mind, we gain a new insight into the real nature of that inner and almost religious compulsion that made Goya paint criminals, hooded monks, prisoners, and inmates of the mad-house; we begin to understand this as part of the mental process that made him shut out the real world and live wholly in that of his imagination. Yet the picture becomes even clearer if we extend Nietzsche's view of the criminal to all those who have the feeling of being 'outlawed, unworthy, and unclean to the touch', to that section of humanity that is for ever hovering on the edge of the secure and ordered world. We can then realize the kind of relationship that united the artist with all those others that stand outside the pale of society. In letting that relationship become to an ever-increasing extent the inspirational mainspring of his pictures – because it helped him in his essential business of self-portraiture – he contrived to create out of all the horror and despair in the world an artifical hell that

* *The ugly twin natured fowls*
  The pestilential company of old night,
  It swarms around me and glides about my head.

Whither shall I direct my step
To escape the loathsomeness that whirrs around me,
To avoid the abyss that lies before me?

was more than a substitute for the real one. The resultant inferno, made more hideous by its very complexities – for in it tempter, tempted, and damned were inseparable – was manifestly of this present world and for that very reason there was no escape from it. In the nineteenth century madness, crime, sensual orgies, and the collective misery of these 'wanderers' were felt to be manifestations of a hell that was everywhere immanent and so a worthy subject for the painter. Artists of every kind – save only those idealists who were pious devotees of the cult of beauty – contributed toward the trend which represented a secularized version of the Christian concept of man unredeemed and at the same time gave that concept a larger meaning.

Here too we must penetrate beneath disguises – and this is as necessary in the case of the Romantic working with traditional symbols as it is in that of the realist who hides his intentions behind what is apparently a *genre* picture. Delacroix paints a naked woman at her toilet. Behind the mirror there lurks the Devil 'in the guise of a wealthy rentier, furnished to the point of extravagance with elegant horns',[7] and we see towering up a heap of gold. The same scene is somewhat differently observed in Manet's 'Nana' (plate 127), a certain worldly-wise discretion being employed. The Devil is here an elegant man of pleasure, a tempter who himself submits to temptation by 'Madame World'.[8] In Delacroix we have a hot demonic sensuality, in Manet a more or less commercial partnership which does not fear the light of day. 'Our urges are transformed into demons with whom we must do battle.' Nietzsche's concluding sentence in his already quoted remarks on man's search for his true self (die Verinnerlichung des Menschen) could be applied to Delacroix; of Manet it would be truer to say that the demons were transformed into urges – which can be satisfied.

This marginal group of the mad, the criminal, and the destitute, is distributed among various circles of hell. Sardanapalus (plates 132, 133), who in the hour of his death commands an orgy of murder, is – in another sense of the word – as lawless as the slave, the homeless wanderer and the street-acrobat. He is the very head of the hierarchy of those whose actions are wholly arbitrary and dictated by purely subjective whims. Like Nero, he needs human beings to feed his desires, he rejects society, he is an outlaw from it by choice. The anonymous outsider, however, does not have any choice as regards his lot, but simply endures it. The active type attains its summit in the Superman to whom humanity submits because he proclaims himself to be its destiny; the passive type culminates in Dostoievski's 'Idiot', who pleads for brotherhood.

3

'The culminating point of true egoism, utterly detached from the substantial world, is madness itself, which is the imagination wholly free from reality'.[9] That was how a historian in the middle of the century judged the eccentricities of imaginative power that marked the Romantic movement.

The Romantics, like men in the *Sturm und Drang* period before them, felt madness to be inherent in any situation of extreme dramatic conflict; they saw in it a clash of forces, a trial of strength, an explosion of energy: the tragic stigma of great personalities for whom surrounding circumstances had become a prison. For the Romantic imagination which sought everywhere for the unusual, the unconventional, and the extraordinary, madness was nothing other than the visible emergence of the irrational forces of life. Tasso, Ophelia, Lear, and Hamlet are literature's great examples of this subjective revolt that turns into despair and ultimately insanity. The madman is really that more profound and better endowed human being whose self-development society is eager to crush, though for the critic of Romantic subjectivity he is a fugitive from the world who has withdrawn into his own egoism and in doing so has become oblivious of the very substance of life.

For the Romantic, as for his opponent who declares the misunderstood artist to be merely mad, the borderland between genius and madness becomes a kind of common ground on which the demarcation line between the normal and the exceptionally gifted man can be drawn. In the years when Delacroix was having to endure the slights and ridicule of the critics – the editor of the *Journal des Artistes* was asking for his commital to the asylum at Charenton – his mind was occupied with the figure which seemed to foreshadow his own destiny. In 1814 he painted 'Tasso in the lunatic asylum', which was in many ways a kind of secularization of the mocking of Christ.[10]

The passive brooding madness which is the object of uncomprehending stares, the madness whose satisfaction is in self-abasement, and whose hunger, stimulated by self-loathing, is for the dagger in its own heart and the sensual delight to be derived from pain – this represents one aspect of the Romantic movement. For although the endurance of suffering yields a spiritual profit if religious faith is present to absorb and transform the pain, its effect is exactly the opposite if the tortured man is left uncomforted and unredeemed, if sheer weariness does not release him from the labyrinth of depression, if despair destroys both body and sense and his cries remain unanswered. For then the suffering seeks release in a wild reaction of sheer madness, in downright destruction and the merciless dishonouring of humanity. The instincts erupt to the surface, the cruellest lusts clamour for satisfaction, the darkest passions proclaim their dominion. Man, suffering as he is through himself, through his unredeemed condition, and through the world, revenges himself upon that world by destroying it. He spreads death and horror about him, he sacrifices his own desperate world, he desires to produce Dionysiac pain so that in it he may forget his own. All this must be borne in mind when we think of the great madmen whom the Romantic imagination produced, when we think of Goya's 'Saturn' (Kronos) (plate 46), of Count Ugolino, of Blake's 'Nebuchadnezzar' – the very symbol of reason gone mad – of Delacroix's 'Medea', and of the 'Death of Sardanapalus' (plate 132). All of these are something more than mere villains and malefactors in whom an over-heated imagination has personified the revolting and the horrible. They are figures symbolizing the pain and fear of the world.

Saturn devours his children because he fears they will emasculate him. Fear that turns to greed is the real motive for his act, fear of the uncertainties of the future. The begetter deals death to his own creatures, he calls back the life which he himself had called into being. Here is the culminating point of absurdity, for here madness does not merely flee from the substance of life, it destroys it so as to free itself from the threat that hangs over it. Life devouring its own fruits is the most terrible manifestation of the nihilistic impulse taking its revenge on creation.

Goya's 'Saturn' is the very embodiment of monstrosity. We see the ultimate survivor in the act of destroying the human race, the dreadful negation of the Creator, a figure that is the antithesis of Prometheus the begetter of new forms of life – we see the annihilator of the world who thrusts all creation back into the devouring maw of chaos. Yet this madman is himself an injured thing, a pitiful creature by reason of the very lack of measure and moderation which he displays; his mis-shapen body is marked with the colours of death and corruption, his eyes are wide open in his agony, his hair stands on end, his emaciated limbs are weary and all their strength has departed. He is himself a victim of the horror he inspires. What will happen when the last of his children has been devoured? There will be complete emptiness all around him – the eternal, unbroken night of despair. Here is something that even Goya's imaginative genius may have been unable to grasp, something that reminds us of the vision of Baudelaire: 'Boredom with a yawn devours the world'.[11]

Few themes from Dante's *Inferno* found more illustrators in the nineteenth century than Count Ugolino in the Tower of Hunger – Ugolino whose own sons offered themselves to him for nourishment and who in the end, blind and broken-hearted, began groping for their bodies[12]. By and large it was the pathos of the sufferer that was emphasized. The count became the symbol of the humbled spirit, the victim of political injustice. Such an interpretation overlooked the hero's sinfulness, it purged him of the crime which he had himself committed, and in doing so robbed his personality of an important dimension.

It was not this man's complete submission to God that Carpeaux stressed in his famous bronze group, but his inner conflict. There was nothing here of suffering humbly endured, nothing of the quality which dominated the visions of Fuseli and Blake. What Carpeaux saw was a man who had lost his way in the world, a doubter who saw no way of escape, a haggler who clung stubbornly to his own pain. Some demon seems to have made a great rift in this Ugolino and bitter memories of the past darken his anguished figure. He seems not to notice the sons who are pressing their bodies against his own. A new and sublimating quality has become discernible. Indeed beauty, as Baudelaire defines it, 'something both ardent and melancholy'[13], has become embodied in him. Something of this quality of grief concentrated into an inner glow seems to have passed from Carpeaux into Rodin's 'Le penseur de la "Porte de l'Enfer" '(The Thinker) who from a dizzy height, immobile, and seemingly unmoved, looks down onto the raging chaos of the damned, a knowing witness of their infamy (plate 159).

Another onlooker whose eye looks down in pain and satiates itself with despair, is the Assyrian king, Sardanapalus, who causes death to be dealt out to his women and his horses before being burned himself in his palace. The picture which Delacroix painted of the bloodbath which preceded this monarch's death (plate 132), concentrates the Romantic movement's demonic *eros* into a wonderfully effective spectacle, rich in gesture and movement. This is an apotheosis of the senses, a frenzy of both wild rebellion and surrender, a Witches' Sabbath of temptation and violence, recalling, as has been rightly said, the orgies described by the Marquis de Sade.[14] The proximity of death heightens the powers of life and gathers them together in a single tremendous collective discharge. The bodies of the women heave and subside in rhythms of the wildest ecstasy. They flare up, break away and collapse, as though drugged by the senses. It is a glowing orgy not of death but of life – life boils over and experiences its most exquisite delight in the orgasm of death. The frenzy of these last minutes of existence flows through these bodies and hurls them onto the brink of madness.

The Romantic movement admired Sardanapalus as a ruthless man of power who had the subtle inspiration to organize a spectacle of mass-murder on his own behalf. It light-heartedly overlooked the fact that this massacre was only the splendid overture to the drama of his own death. Yet it is difficult to confine our interpretation of Delacroix's 'Sardanapalus' to the idea of a mere sensual orgy and limit the raison d'être of the work to that of an erotic theatrical show. Certainly one of the ideas that led the painter to this choice of subject was the Romantic's conviction – which, long before Baudelaire, had been expressed by Novalis when he said 'that the real origin of cruelty is lust'[15] – that *eros* and crime are united by a secret complicity. Yet surely the mighty power of the artist's imagination had more than this to say. Delacroix, with his strange mixture of passion and melancholy, must also have been fascinated by the figure of Sardanapalus himself, the silent witness to all the noisy happenings in the picture, which are taking place at his own command. The drama being enacted in the hour of his death was really part and parcel of his entire life. It had occurred again and again. He had commanded whatever had at the moment touched his fancy and he had been compelled to recognize that nothing could satisfy him. It was not the Romantic's admiration of the strong man, but the essential sadness of the Romantic's view of life[16] that chose this Sardanapalus to express and represent its *ennui*. It is no mere chance that his attitude recalls that of Delacroix's Michelangelo sitting lost in thought (plate 58). Kierkegaard's 'Abyss of Melancholy', over which 'Le penseur' bends as he sits over Rodin's Hell Gate, is in the 'Sardanapalus' encountered once again, this time in the form of an invisible aura which surrounds the king and shuts him off from the world around him. A picture of this heaviness of the spirit whose ultimate stimulant is the wild raging of the senses was drawn by Kierkegaard in his study of Nero. It is emptiness and lack of fulfilment that cause the melancholy man to search continually for

149 F. M. BROWN The Last of England; 1855.

150 MERYON *Paris, La Morgue*; 1852.

151 DORÉ *Londres, Maison de Commerce*; 1876.

152 DORÉ Prison courtyard; 1876.

153 VAN GOGH Prison courtyard (after Doré); 1890.

154 VAN GOGH On the threshold of eternity; 1889.

155 MUNCH The death-chamber; 1894.

156 DAUMIER *Déplacement des saltimbanques.*

new sensations and new satisfactions of lust. 'It is,' says Rehm, 'the cowardly lust of melancholy to try to drug itself with empty pleasures and to seek in that drugged condition its ultimate distraction.'[17]

We can therefore trace a relationship between the unrelieved isolation of this perpetual spectator, resting upon his bed of state, and the drama going on in the foreground. Some words of Flaubert come nearest to the heart of the matter and most admirably express one phase of the bitter-sweet aesthetic philosophy of the Romantic movement. 'I want every single thing to have its bitter aspect: an unfailing catcall at the height of our triumphs, and sheer desolation infecting every enthusiasm.'[18] Thus speaks one who sees men wandering aimlessly around the empty hell of this world, one who knows that, wherever he goes, hopelessness, desolation, and despair march unceasingly beside him. A very closely related feeling was expressed by Kierkegaard when he declared that amid all the jubilation of the nineteenth century he could detect a note of secret contempt for humanity, a dark and unspoken despair at being a man at all.[19]

4

From Goya right down to Munch the loud terrified scream of despair pervades the art of the nineteenth century. The divine and overwhelming power of nature, which once moved the Romantics to shuddering humility, gradually becomes a deadly threat. 'Your self disappears, you are nothing, God is everything,' Carus cries to the man climbing a mountain.[20] 'A scream of terror before nature which grows red with rage and prepares to speak in storm and thunder to the foolish little beings who imagine they are gods, though there is little godlike about them.'[21] That is Strindberg's comment on Munch's 'Scream' (Schrei). The world seems to be bursting asunder, man calls upon a hostile and unfeeling nature to witness the misery of his last hours. His madness is fear of life and of death, he shudders as he sees the lack of any fulfilment in his own existence, and confesses that he has no power to find his way about the world.

Alongside this madness which is the fear of both life and death, from which world catastrophe might result, the nineteenth century discovered another and less conspicuous form of mental confusion, a spiritual disturbance, that was essentially static, speaking quietly to itself. Men withdrew from action and got lost in self-contemplation, a strange state which produced no tensions or conflicts outside the man himself. This introverted madness, with which monomaniacs and pathological eccentrics were afflicted, tended to hide itself, there being few visible features by which it could signify its presence. Only the most patient observation could capture it in a picture, for it produced no evocative gestures on which the artist could seize. Its discovery by art was left to the realists, to the conscientious eye-witnesses.

The actual discovery of this type was made at the beginning of the nineteenth century by Géricault. His five pictures of inmates of a madhouse rely on sober and conscientious clinical observation which seeks not the outward visible signs of mental decay but its hidden indications.[22] This economical and unpretentious procedure emphasized the bodily features revealing inner stress, without depicting grotesque dramatizations, expressions of savagery or pugnacity, or any extraordinary characteristics. Yet the secret desires of those portrayed can be discerned in their strained alert faces, in an inclination of the head that suggests eavesdropping and suspicion, and in their eyes, fixed on an imaginary object or staring into space. Géricault's romantic realism was in harmony with the psychiatric theories of the age which held that the insane felt fear, pain, and joy much more intensely than ordinary men; and it is noteworthy that the artist painted these pictures for a neurologist friend of his who entertained these views.

What is truly realistic in the artist's ideas is that they fix no arbitrary boundaries between sanity and its opposite, or between the 'healthy' and the unhealthy mind, and so leave the way open for the reintegration into society of the mentally sick. Since realism recognized no ideal of beauty, it was equally reluctant to recognize an ideal of health and looked on this as a figment devoid of any practical value; and just as it did not recoil from distorted form so long as it had life, so it accepted the man whose mind was distorted or unbalanced as merely representing one possible form of life among many.

Géricault's conception was, however, essentially Romantic because it perceived in the madman a more strongly expressed, demonic vitality and attributed to him greater potentialities for experience. The madman's deeds, his feelings, and his reactions are governed by his imagination, and this is sufficiently powerful to hold its own against empirical facts. An artist like Géricault, whose urge to be for ever observing prevented him from being a stranger to anything that was alive, instinctive, spontaneous, and real, could never have remained indifferent to the uncanny vitality of the possessed, particularly in so far as he was vaguely aware that he himself, who had often been suspected of madness, was a man whose general make-up was anything but normal.

Géricault examined the phenomenon of insanity without a trace of sentimentality, and refused to see in it anything very startling; he simply formed his general picture of the madman as a kind of solipsist who lived wholly within the world of his own arbitrary imagination. Géricault's successors inherited his method of analytical observation but applied it rather differently. Indeed, the art of the nineteenth century put a wider interpretation on mental derangement. It was less interested in actual clinical cases of madness, where there was an obvious need for medical attention, than in the clouding and blunting of the mind of man in the mass. Yet it still remained more or less on marginal territory and confined itself to those cases where it was first apparent that man's 'self-estrangement' and debased condition had turned him into a mere thing to be used, bought, and sold like any other piece of merchandise; and so it turned to the people of the streets, to the work-slaves and the prostitutes.

The accent now was not on the enhanced but on the diminished capacity for experience and feeling, not on the tense and over-excited look but on the look in which all inward fire has died, not on the over-heated but on the dulled imagination. People now appear before us as mere pieces of machinery, their gestures having neither real eloquence nor individuality; or again they seem to be withdrawn into stolid indifference and to make no gestures at all. The manner in which they sit around – in their bars, their places of amusement, and in railway carriages – would be much the same if the scene were a mad-house. For example, Manet, who started off by painting picturesque specimens of humanity in decorative costume, succeeded in a late work in depicting the dispirited spectator who feels removed from the surrounding world, though in the midst of a scene of fashionable commercialized amusement (plate 162). His barmaid is the menial servant of this amusement, in which she herself has no part. She stands there, absent in spirit, in a fictional world of mirrors in which a number of objects reflect one another, and in which there is light, brilliance, and movement. The girl is alone in this transformed world of social life. The stiff wooden way in which she stares full face out of the picture, has something of the marionette about it, though she is not wholly lacking in a dignity that would compel the impertinent to keep their distance. All of this contrasts sharply with the movement and easy-going atmosphere of her surroundings, and her eyes, which seem to be looking at nothing in particular, have the emptiness that goes with melancholy. In George Moore's *Memoirs of my Dead Life* there is a description of a waitress in the Latin Quarter which reminds one very strongly of this picture.

There is neither peace nor satisfaction for those who seek to escape from their inner emptiness into the emptiness of narcosis, and who endeavour to forget themselves in some vague distraction. Such efforts are bound to fail. Degas' two absinthe drinkers squat there as though in the midst of the cold hard lines of table and wall they were cut off from all the world, as though they were imprisoned by the very dullness of their senses, which have now become well nigh incapable of reacting to anything at all (plate 161). There is the same joyless, weary, and listless quality in the posture of the girls who serve as models for Toulouse-Lautrec. There is a kind of glaring disillusionment in the monotony of their mere presence, a presence that is never more than purely physical. They wait there aimlessly and without knowing for what they wait. How dull the creatures are, and how strange and hypocritical that misnomer that calls them 'filles de joie'.

There is no sign in the works of Toulouse-Lautrec of that 'lovely lost child' with the painted cheeks of whom Goethe sings in his *God and the Bajadere*. Nothing is here but the tired weary bodies that are a part of history's oldest form of slavery. The painter refrains from all romantic embellishment. His prostitutes belong to that circle of hell where those who are already damned in this our present world, are to be found. They differ but little from those other outlaws whose life is one long process of mere vegetation (plate 128).

5

Géricault's contribution to the iconography of madness is not confined to the analysis of physical features. He endeavoured to associate the unbridled power of the senses with a specific formal vehicle, a visual common denominator, and for this purpose selected the horse. It would be interesting to know whether he was acquainted with the ancient Roman practice of dedicating horses to the subterranean demon of phallic power in whose honour horse-races were held. One wonders whether he knew of the ghostly demon-horse of popular superstition. It seems hardly likely – and it is equally unlikely that Baudelaire knew of these things when he wrote that he would use the image of a wild horse that devoured its master to represent love.[23] Actually no knowledge of ancient sources is needed for the conception of such figures, for there are memories which superstition has preserved and which have been endowed with form by popular art. As a result, even enlightened ages have some knowledge of the suggestive power that certain creatures and certain objects once possessed. On these memories the painter and the poet can always draw.

The horse was used in the nineteenth century to convey a number of meanings. We see it as the embodiment of animalism pure and simple (Mazeppa), and as the demonic embodiment of *eros* – in such cases the role of the male partner is usually assigned to it. It is used as early as 1783 – in Fuseli's 'Nightmare' (plate 47), in which the horse is unmistakably a phantom whose sudden appearance hurls the senses into confusion and throws, or positively distorts, the woman's body into a posture of helpless surrender. The nightmare figure in *Faust* is the horse of Mephistopheles. In Fuseli's picture male lust is accompanied by the pale mask of a messenger from hell.

The French Romantics took particular delight in the noble war-horse – the recollection of Napoleon's campaigns was a factor in this – and in the youthful lines of the fiery race-horse. These have an exotic variant that Delacroix was particularly fond of – in the raging savagery of untamed Arab stallions, in the fighting spirit of their movements among and against one another, which translates all the force of their animalism into energy, thrust and collision. Under the urge to create plastic forms, Géricault, while in Rome, painted horse-racing scenes. Five years later in England he actually painted the Derby. This picture gives the impression of an eerie chase, the horses seem to be rushing along soundlessly, their bodies wholly removed from the earth – all this being set, and this was surely deliberate, against an ominous, stormy landscape.

The erotic significance of the horse in the 'Death of Sardanapalus' is obvious enough, though it is overshadowed by the theme of the general killing which the king has commanded, a killing in which horse and woman are to suffer alike. A more direct though less dramatic reference to the battle of the sexes – that process whereby lust and cruelty mutually intensify each other – is provided by the theme of Degas' 'War in the Middle Ages' of 1865 (plate 87). In this early work two of the painter's dominant themes, themes which are usually treated by him separately, are united within a single picture. We have women maltreated and misused – and here is the prototype for the washerwoman and the bent, bowed women whom Degas was later to observe at their toilet, women who have almost deliberately been made ugly; and we also have the proud male, eager to rape and rob, for whom woman is no more than an object that he desires to possess. The mediaeval archers seem to anticipate the jockeys – those perfectly trained creatures, whose supple bodies become one with those of their horses.

I would remark in passing that this master of barbed discretion – a quality that made Degas unique in a century given to explicit and unvarnished statement – never lost sight of the conflict between the sexes, though he carried it over into other settings. This dumb enmity, this strange interaction of fear on the part of the woman and coarse brutality on the part of the male, this hostility that almost anticipates Strindberg, is in one of his pictures (one of 1814) transferred to thoroughly bourgeois surroundings (plate 126). A hotel-room was ultimately to suffice for that which nine years previously he had had to make a detour via the Middle Ages to find (plate 87). If we compare the two pictures, we see that each setting stresses one aspect of the process in question. Distance in time permits the representation of open and undisguised brutality, but causes the inward spiritual tension to be ignored, though this, too, is implicit in the situation. When the whole occurrence takes place in a modern hotel bedroom, the main emphasis can obviously no longer fall on physical action, and this must of necessity give place to psychological analysis. The violation of woman has become a commonplace affair, it is no longer a matter of brutal force but a permanent condition. For that reason the 'inner significance' of this canvas, which is known as 'Intérieur (le viol)', is greater than that of the historical picture, even though the latter shows us the actual deed of violence in a far less disguised form.

The fin de siècle knew nothing of the swift light-footed charm of the horse that the Romantics of the beginning of the century could still delight in. Toulouse-Lautrec whose crippled body compelled him to be a man perpetually on the side-lines, exaggerated the heaviness of the horse's limbs, making the whole body into a monstrous thing and endowing it with gigantic dimensions. His race-horses are prehistoric monsters – fabulous creatures that carry man away with them. The erotic tension with which the figure of the horse is associated was transferred by Toulouse-Lautrec to the circus arena and clothed with pregnant irony (plate 144). The woman-rider in 'Au Cirque Fernando' is the little capricious woman who lets the horse – i.e. the man – have his will and lets herself be seduced, as was Europa by the bull. Yet the triumph of the man who directs his ringmaster's act with crackings of his whip, is really a defeat; he has made the woman obey him and now she rides around him in circles. Who is the winner in this duel and which of the two surrenders to the other – the man, the 'slave of the slave'[24] (Baudelaire), who must continually turn with the rider if he is not to lose her, or the woman, who is under orders to circle around the man?

6

Both the *Sturm und Drang* period and the Romantics praised the royal criminal and gave their applause to the worst abominations of the despots of antiquity. Their admiration for the ruthless type, what Heinse called the 'starker Kernmensch' – the man strong to the core – meant contempt for a dull and feeble age which muzzled all the instincts. But the man of action who was determined to live his life to the full changed into the adversary of ordered society, in other words the criminal. The Romantics inclined to attribute the responsibility for the collision between the criminal and the law to bourgeois law itself, which they seem to have thought guilty of positive provocation. Before he had

157 RODIN Balzac; 1867.

158
RODIN
Les bourgeois de Calais; 1884–86.

159 RODIN *Le penseur de la "Porte de l'Enfer"*; 1879–1900.

put himself beyond the pale of society by his crime, it was the dead hand of the law that had hindered the criminal – who was simply a human being – in his true self-development. The criminal does wrong only because of the wrong he feels himself to have suffered, and in this he is very like the artist whom the public covers with ridicule and subjects to public mockery. So Byron in his different 'outlaws' is simply representing himself.

Decades later, when Romantic crime had long ceased to provide a subject for a picture, Gauguin was to paint a self-portrait of which he was to say that it recalled Jean Valjean of *Les Misérables* and was an embodiment of the 'despised impressionist' who carried the yoke for the world.[25] In yet another picture Gauguin portrayed himself as one of the crucified thieves next to a yellow Christ. To this the companion picture in idea is the self-portrait with a halo (plate 66). The self-identification with the thief corresponds to the identification with the Redeemer. In 1889 Gauguin painted a 'Christ upon the Mount of Olives' in which the features of Christ were his own. Two years later Ensor, making the symbolism unmistakably clear, portrayed himself in his own 'Ecce homo'. There is a certain relevance here in some words of Strindberg, uttered some years later still, when he spoke of Munch as the victim of the 'hangmen critics' who pursued their calling like public executioners. There is a connection between the images of the criminal and of the Saviour which depth-psychology has striven to illuminate. Jung regards the criminal as a redeemer who by doing evil takes the burden of evil from ourselves.[26]

Goya and Géricault, the two most sharp-sighted interpreters of murder and violence, combined two essentially 'modern' ideas, each of which is to some extent the opposite of the other. They testify to the eagerness of the masses for the sensational, the extraordinary and the repulsive, an eagerness of which among others the artist was the servant and the tributary, and which was ultimately to be satisfied by cold-blooded visual reporting; but they also expressed the perplexity of those same masses (plate 45). We have seen how in the human creature, mutilated and dishonoured, the artist dimly recognised his unknown brother. From this it was not a far step to see in the criminal, whose execution he attended, a symbolic figure closely related to himself.

If we consider this dialectic, we can see our way clear to approach Goya's 'Saturn' (plate 46) the most monumental of all the figures in which the criminal is portrayed. In his despair of the world, which well nigh renders him unconscious of the quality of his own deed, we see this monster devouring man. This is surely the most wide and comprehensive motivation that crime can show. It is also the most terrible in so far as it endows this deed with all the elemental power of a symbolic act and so transfers it to a domain that is 'beyond good and evil'.

In his *Aesthetics of Ugliness* Rosenkranz, a pupil of Hegel, says that the decisive condition that led to the 'poeticizing of crime' (die poetisierende Behandlung des Kriminalverbrechens) was the rise of the proletariat to be a factor in world-history. The fourth estate possessed in the criminal class its martyrs and its avengers. Literature freely indulged in such imputation of nobility to the criminal, but it seems hardly to have inspired the visual arts to follow its example, save for one notable exception – Daumier's Robert Macaire cycle. Here however we enter, as it were, a different part of hell, and are dealing with one of its more grotesquely active figures.

Macaire, the swindler of the masses, who has learnt all the tricks of his trade, is a late descendant of the fraudulent beggar, who can be traced back to the popular literature of the Middle Ages.[27] In both cases success depended on the arts of disguise; the beggar simulated frailty, he changed his voice or pretended to be blind, while Macaire is the accomplished jack of all trades, who tries his luck in a hundred different parts – as a lawyer, a marriage broker, a stockbroker, an architect, a dentist, a town-crier, a hypnotist or a distinguished recipient of alms. He, too, stands outside the conventions of society, he is an outlaw, an adventurer, who belongs nowhere but knows how to make capital out of his marginal existence, and how to make fools of society. He is the very embodiment of the modern mass-deceiver who, thanks to the very fact of his cynical contempt for man, manages somehow to fascinate the public. In his *Metamorphosen des Teufels* (Metamorphoses of the Devil) Görres has described this man of many faces who contrives 'to be all things to all men, to adapt himself to men of any and every sort, and so by skilled adjustment to open every door with his master-key'.[28]

Like his mediaeval prototype Macaire promises people paradise on earth, good fortune, wealth, and material success. This endows his figure with a further symbolic dimension; this despiser and seducer of men, this costumed dandy – for it is the essence of the dandy that he is always bored and always playing a part – is none other than Satan in modern dress and, as such, is the visible essence of a restless, empty and uprooted type of man, whose life is a sham and whose shams are crime itself. To quote Rosenkranz again: 'Among the people of today, restless, exhausted, impotent and greedy for pleasure, among this bored and surfeited folk, among these elegant cynics whose education was pointless, who yield to every weakness, among these irresponsibly vicious people who flirt with pain, there has developed an ideal of the satanically blasé which in the novels of England, France, and Germany claims to be regarded as possessing the quality of nobility and does so with all the greater effect in so far as its heroes travel a great deal, eat and drink well, wear the finest clothes, smell of patchouli and have the good manners of accomplished men of the world. But this nobility is nothing other than the latest anthropological manifestation of the satanic principle.'[29] In his Robert Macaire cycle Daumier unmasks the hypocritical elegance and the demonic rootlessness of the so-called 'man of the world' and so enriches the Devil's iconography with a contemporary type.

7

Those embodiments of human greatness in tragic isolation – the Wandering Jew, Don Quixote, Prometheus – are also the representatives of a common destiny. Ruskin said once that the English take pleasure in the description of Ugolino's pangs of hunger though it would not be difficult to find a multitude of such figures – not counts, it is true – perishing of hunger in their own villages.[30] The social or political conscience was beginning to see the literary content of the picture through the spectacles of the present. The artist painting as an eye-witness recorded the present while the historical painter, who did not consider the present worthy of pictorial representation, remained in the past. Géricault's 'The raft of the "Medusa"' (plate 70) contains in the left-hand corner a group of despairing people who remind us of Ugolino's fate. The artist could claim to have based himself on fact. He had learned from eye-witnesses who had seen the rescue of the survivors that the latter had kept alive by eating the flesh of the dead.

The theme of those who in this world had been outlawed and damned was regarded from a number of different angles. The historical painter, preserving all his customary care for accuracy of circumstantial detail, might well transpose his subject into distant biblical times, as did Cormon in 'The tribe of Cain', while the student of present reality went on board an emigrant ship (plate 149). In both cases the state of outlawry is connected with a particular event and a precise and clearly defined period of time. Daumier, for whom past and present flow into one another to be experienced as a single whole, could dispense with both history, biblical or other, and with pictorial news-reports, nor did he see any need for involving himself with the exploits of chivalrous heroism. He simply painted refugees and in them he lets us see the fate of the wanderer which is timeless and universal.

Proud as it was of its own age, the nineteenth century was always eager to compare its own greatness with that of past times; Cézanne was called a Greek, Millet's gleaners were pronounced Homeric, and Courbet's peasant women likened to the figures of Greek Tragedy. Moreover, the earthly hell of

to the conceptions of bygone literature – particularly those of Dante. The serial
s peints par eux-mêmes contains in its third volume a chapter on the circles of
t modern city. Dante, too, the author declares, had his eyes on his own time
rno. 'I threw myself with utter despair into the reading of Dante,' says a letter
the mid-fifties, 'whose *Inferno,* thanks to the London atmosphere, became for
ality'.

ttention to the contemporary people of the streets, Mayhew, in his *Cyclopaedia,*
ory of the nomad peoples, hoping by his description of historic and non-Euro-
understanding of the vagabonds and outcasts of his own day. Mayhew was re-
me human categories as Daumier was drawing and painting at that time, the
singers and acrobats, the people of the fairs that wandered aimlessly from place
ovide the crowds with cheap and pitiful illusion, a few beggarly tricks mechani-
y sensation that seeks for a fleeting moment to distract them. The showman yells
ng man' to the public's notice, the superman as the masses conceive him, the
othing; a human being is put on show for the rest to gawk at (plate 52). A harle-
on of intense greed upon his face is crying out to the crowd, like death beckoning
Death'; a hand draws a curtain aside and there is nothing behind it save a ghast-
awings by Daumier in which a clown cries out his despair to all around him,
to hear, and his voice seems to be torn from his inmost soul. These jesters are the
in which what was once a ritual act is put on view in a showman's booth. To put
s to expose them and so the showman's booth becomes a torture chamber. These
e whipping post, and the waiting crowd, with ugly desire in their eyes, calls im-
s.

they have played their wretched parts, there is an end to their empty gestures,
and there is no more of that fleeting mastery over men that even the shabbiest of
ners must exercise. Weary, despised and humiliated, these people go their way
th their poor little bundle of possessions under their arms, to start afresh some-
6). The human desert of the homeless receives them. At the middle of the century
aris were estimated at thirty thousand.

'The cruel loneliness in the midst of a human desert'[31] was for Stendhal one of the distinguishing signs of the modern age. This way of feeling about life was not confined to the wandering people of the fairs; it was the painful mark of an age in which the relations between one human being and another had become distorted. It was something that affected even the famous stars of the entertainment industry when the footlights were left behind and all the illusion of the stage, whose very centre they were, gave place to the sober realities of every day. They go their way – both the people who a little while ago were thundering their applause and the dancer who was its recipient – and know one another no longer. None has given a more convincing portrayal of this situation than Toulouse-Lautrec in his picture 'Jane Avril sortant du Moulin Rouge' (plate 163). An incisive outline circumscribes the used-up exhausted body. Its footsteps are hesitant and have a certain pointed quality about them. The earth seems positively to withdraw itself beneath them. There is something sliding, falling and precipitous in this picture that expresses the inner collapse of someone very tired who has lost her foothold and is letting herself go.

Edgar Quinet's comparison in which he likens the masses to the Wandering Jew and Prometheus, hits the mark very well. He knows the two constituent characteristics of the nineteenth century's earthly hell. Man is an outlaw who is also in chains. He is free to wander, but is inwardly bound. He has no resting place, 'no house, no home, no wife, no children'[32] – and yet he is a prisoner of the multitude, a slave of collectivism, for whom there is no escape. In all the important pictures of despair which the century produced we find these two coalescing strata of meaning: the restless inner disquiet incapable of freeing itself in any kind of action and stubbornly continuing in passivity, and the helplessness of the exile with the spread of deathly stillness all around.

But in the 'Raft of the "Medusa"' (plate 70) (1819), Géricault, with his Romantic's appetite for contrast, joins light with shade and combines a flash of hope with a despair so listless that it seems as though nothing could stir it; it becomes in part at least a picture of hope. The waving, gesticulating, pyramid-shaped heap of humanity is welcoming a brighter future in the figure of the distant ship and discerns in it its own liberation from the misery and abasement of the present. These ecstatic gestures of joy are really directed towards a greater and more powerful France, a France that has once more won back her pride. The critics of the day were not slow in attaching this political significance to the picture, though Géricault himself repudiated it.[33]

In the figures of these shipwrecked people, who have once more found courage in their hearts, a liberated nation is gathering itself together and, by a mighty effort of will, is throwing off the lethargy of the Restoration. A decade later Rude in his 'Marseillaise' was to elevate this vitality to a monumental expression, while Delacroix in 'Liberté guidant le peuple' (plate 72) made an allegory of it, showing an erotically kindled will to life triumphing over death.

Daumier's 'Uprising' (circa 1860) (plate 75) on the other hand, endows the whole subject with the ruthless hard-fistedness of ordinary folk claiming their rights. Once more the eyes of this painter are sharper and more free from illusion than those of any other. The dream of justice and brotherhood that once called a wildly excited people to the colours has in Daumier's picture vanished, and the nation has relapsed into its various conflicts of interest. There is here no irresistable forward charge, no revolutionary patriotism. Patriotism has, as it were, split into two, into the patriotic phrases of the possessing classes on the one hand, and on the other into the rebellious rage of those who have no possessions at all.

Thus within a few decades the joyous gestures of that company of the shipwrecked had turned into their opposite. Géricault had allowed those desperate people to believe in a rescue and so find their way back to humanity. Daumier's rebels have no tangible aim, no visible object of their faith and hope. Do they really know why they have come on the street at all? The arm raised in Géricault's painting is a signal that tells of release. It is both a signal and a summons. In Daumier it is a threat and a challenge, denoting a battle in progress, and that is all. Daumier is free from the ironic pessimism of a Rethel who represents death as an agitator, a demagogue mouthing democratic slogans, who like Robert Macaire can impersonate any character the occasion requires.[34] In his bitterness there is a kind of resignation. To understand it one must view his 'Uprising' (plate 75) in the same context as one sees his 'Un wagon de troisième classe' (plate 160) and his 'Refugees' and relate this triptych of the humiliated and debased to his 'Ecce homo' (plate 52). If we set these pictures over against one another, we see the tragedy of a people that seeks for its redeemer and then denies and insults him when he appears in their midst.

In Dostoievski's story of the Grand Inquisitor Christ reappears among men and becomes the prisoner of his own priest.[35] Out of the mouth of the Grand Inquisitor, to whom the word of God has been entrusted but who really stands in the service of Antichrist, there is uttered against Him the terrible accusation of heresy. There is a grimly grotesque picture which we might well regard as related to the same order of ideas: Ensor's 'L'entrée du Christ à Bruxelles en 1889' (1888) (plate 53). Christ here rides upon an ass, gentle and unassuming in the midst of a great crowd. Lemurs and goblins dance around Him. Soldiers march in front of Him. Are they granting Him the protection of the authority which rules in His name, as in the Corpus Christi procession? Or are they leading Him away as their prisoner, as they did once before? In either case He is mocked. Some dance around Him with flags and slogan-bearing banners, while others misuse His message for their own purposes. His open enemies are hardly more dangerous than His hidden ones whose hypocritical submission really implies a secret contempt of Him. This empty-minded world of lies and deceit, this cynical excitement about civilization, these enthusiasts for the brave new world, who are the lineal descendants of Robert Macaire, are all depicted by Ensor as a loathsome Danse Macabre in a Shrove Tuesday Carnival. The crowd, that 'human desert' which indulges in its filthy sport with the returning Christ, is well aware of its treason. It huddles together in fear, like the fear of hell; the bodies press against one another, bereft of leadership, while from the idiot's mask of animal exuberance comes the gape of despair.

Ensor's masks are really disfigurements. They can no longer be removed from the faces that wear them; they have eaten deeply into those faces and destroyed their features from within. Since Goya, the mask has ceased to serve the harmless dalliance of a ball; it is a covering which people draw over their true selves so that they may both express and conceal their despair. Finally it becomes a part of the face itself and actually replaces it. The mask gives way to a face that is merely masklike. In Goya's 'Carnival' (1815) the mask is a symbol of fear itself, of the man driven into a corner (colour plate v). These dancers are rooted to the spot and it is despair that causes them to raise their arms as it is with the rebels in the picture of 'Murat's troops executing inhabitants of Madrid on 3rd May, 1808' (plate 67). The carnival is being taken to the grave and the time – to quote Malraux – is over when people believed themselves free and were merry because they forgot that they had just been wearing the faces of the dead.[36] Here we have again that Ash Wednesday mood, sustained by shrill gestures made with difficulty, that marks all those pictures of despair that the nineteenth century produced. It is the mood of great bitterness spoken of by Flaubert – hopelessness in the midst of enthusiasm.

We can get at the essence of the phenomenon of the faceless and characterless human mass that made its appearance in European art at the beginning of the nineteenth century if we simply let it convey to us the idea of fear, a fear that has taken complete hold of men's minds. Man in despair flees from himself, but man in fear runs with the crowd, adopts its gestures, for it removes from him the pattern of his personal self and he can thus hide away in anonymity. And yet escape into the crowd is but another form of being alone.

This gives us the key to the third plate of Goya's 'Disparates' (sometimes called 'Proverbios'): some dozen muffled figures squatting like birds of the night on an enormous bare branch. Man is literally exposed, deprived of all connections. Goya gives shape, in a far more radical fashion than any of his Romantic contemporaries, to the essence of the modern mood – a sense of isolation from which there is no redemption or escape. To express this feeling of being utterly lost, the Romantics surrounded man with the vastness of nature. They set him among the emptiness of mountains (Friedrich) or abandoned him to the infinite expanses of the sea. In its macabre foreground, Géricault's 'Raft of the "Medusa"'–which by the way was painted in 1819, the year of the 'Disparates'–is just such a picture of the fate of shipwrecked men who are being handed over helpless to the elements. Delacroix's 'Dante and Vergil' (plate 81) transposes the earthly hell of human helplessness into the domains of a visionary half-world.

In later years when the fire of his early passion glowed dimly on in a brooding unrest – again and again his diaries speak of 'ennui'[37] – Delacroix once more tackled this theme of shipwreck in his 'La barque de Don Juan' (plate 71). The subject of this picture is that moment in Byron's poem when the lot is drawn which condemns to death one of the ship's company who is to serve as nourishment for the rest. The actual literary reference however is of secondary importance. Indeed when the picture was exhibited Delacroix simply named it 'A shipwreck'. The real theme is the despair of this collection of people. They are near to madness, driven by the waves, without direction or aim, and there is no will to steer them. They are chained to each other and driven into the pathless void – Prometheus and the Wandering Jew.

Compared with Goya's people upon the branch, the exposed and forlorn situation of these shipwrecked folk may seem to be conventional and almost insignificant, for the people in this picture are still surrounded by reality. The Spaniard contrives to intensify the lost condition to the maximum degree by showing it naked and separate from the surrounding world. The void is total in which these figures have contrived to nest, the silence is total that lies above them, their removal from the earth is total – there is no abyss or precipice at their feet. Once again we can see how Goya's whole manner of building up his picture symbolizes this quality of exclusion.

Fear disfigures a man, it both empties and ravages his face. A great bawling lump of people – half-wits, madmen, criminals and cripples – who howl meaninglessly and plod around like animals, but get nowhere – that is how Goya paints the 'Pilgrimage to san Isidro' (plate 54). One thinks of Brueghel's 'The Blind'. Yet there is no parable here of the blind leading the blind to point a moral. Goya's heaps of humanity are bundled together by desperate and devastating fear; he creates a collective body of men from which none can free themselves. Brueghel's falling diagonal line emphasizes movement and the attraction of depth; Goya's pilgrims on the other hand are rammed fast in the earth, though they seem almost to be slowly vanishing into an invisible hollow in the ground. Only one of these faces is looking at something directly. It is the face in the very centre of the picture, lurking and motionless, and is the picture's core. The determination in those eyes – 'ardent and melancholy' – is unforgettable; it comes from depths which defy description in human speech.

One has to get one's breath if one stands for some time before this picture. It is a De Profundis without its like in the whole of nineteenth century art; and there is all the misery of separation from God in the fact that this Inferno is called a pilgrimage, that it is none other than the 'pious pilgrim' whose step has become uncertain, whose wild gaze has lost the power of beholding truth, the power of apprehension by the light of faith. The object which sent these men on their pilgrim's way has completely disappeared from their conscious mind.

There came into being at the end of the century another band of pilgrims and the road they took was a very different one. I speak of Rodin's 'Les bourgeois de Calais' (1884–1885) (plate 158). Goya's heap of humanity is a monument of scorn for the religious community as such and – in a very comprehensive sense – a parody and denial of all communion between men. Rodin's burghers are prisoners preparing themselves for death but they have freely offered themselves and accepted their fate, paying this price so that their city might be spared. Their way of sacrifice unites them into a community of faith, their manly resolve tames the fear which the individual may experience. Thus the figures – and this was Rodin's intention – express the modest anonymity of the sacrifice, 'as it actually happened at that time'.[38]

The chronicler of this tragic episode, writing in the middle of the fourteenth century, tells us that these six men came from among the most distinguished of the citizenry. 'Clothed only in a shirt and with a hangman's noose about their necks and carrying the keys of the city and of the citadel in their hands' they went forth from the beleaguered city to hand themselves over to the English king. Rodin made full use of the symbolism that is implicit in this story. He drew attention to the ethos of citizenship and in doing so deeply offended the well-fed and complacent bourgeoisie of his time. He cast the hair shirt of penance over the bourgeois, cut him off from family and property and set him among the outcasts. He thus endowed a historical event with the religious depth of a parable. These citizens 'who are preparing to take up their cross' are re-living the sacrificial death of Christ. Historical actuality is here transfigured into timeless martyrdom. The suffering human beings at the fringes of society, plunged into want and despair, have in the art of the nineteenth century replaced the saints of the Bible.

8

The latter part of the nineteenth century moved away from the lapidary intensity of Goya to the extent that it clothed the vision of man damned and despairing with the colours of time and place. The hell of this present world is thus related to the destinies of rank and class and begins to be connected with specific situations. Four works exemplify this: Daumier's 'Un wagon de troisième classe' (1862) (plate 160) which comes nearest to the timelessness of Goya, Toulouse-Lautrec's 'Salon' (1894) (plate 128), Munch's 'The death-chamber' (1894) (plate 155), and Doré's 'Prison courtyard' (1876) (plate 152), made famous thanks to Van Gogh's interpretation (plate 153) – four variations, each different from the other, on the theme of man's imprisonment, four 'waiting rooms'. The shabby railway carriage, that transportable cage of those condemned to life, is the modern Charon's barque. A remark of Van Gogh's comes to mind about the inmates of the asylum of Saint-Rémy: 'The room where people pass the time on rainy days is like the third class waiting room at some village, all the more so since there are a couple of worthy lunatics who always have a hat, stick, spectacles and travelling clothes (as people do in bathing resorts by the sea) and play the role of passengers' (25 May, 1889).

Similarly, the cheap luxury of Toulouse-Lautrec's 'Salon' suggests a kind of artificial cell, shut off from the world, in which people spend their lives waiting in empty boredom. The only 'openings'- are mirrors and these provide an optical illusion that merely complicates matters. The room is not only shut off from the world, it is now a labyrinth from which there is no escape. Munch's 'Death-chamber' is the last stage of the 'waiting room', being at the very edge of life. It is a bare little place in which life slowly ebbs away. Finally, within the narrow confines of Doré's walls the prisoners walk in a never ending circle. Two birds have flown down into the yard, but nobody notices them; the eye has become dulled and, like the spirit, can no longer rouse itself. It was during his internment in Saint-Rémy that Van Gogh put this interpretation on Doré's work and found his own fate represented there.[39]

Frightening indeed is the exclusion from nature in these works: the railway carriage is like a prison, the salon is a kind of temple of artificiality, the death-chamber and the prison yard are 'terminal stations', hermetically sealed from all outside. Here we have quite literally the inescapable despair of the historical world which turns away from nature; here is the stage on which is enacted the weary Inferno of modern civilized man. This is a world created by the hand of man which bars itself in against the greater and more primeval world of natural life.

IX   Still Life

I

Movement stimulates, rest satisfies, and so there comes about
that fulfilment in the soul that we call beauty.
Stifter, Der Nachsommer (*The Indian Summer*)

THE mind that sees things in historical perspective sees man opposed to nature; the mind that thinks in terms of myths and symbols sees him allied with her. The two opposing patterns of life that derive from these viewpoints are reflected in two clearly defined human types.

In the sixth chapter of his *Heinrich von Ofterdingen* Novalis contrasts these two types. The man of action, the shaper and controller of events, keeps his eyes steadily fixed on a distant goal and 'for that reason has to harden his spirit against the impact of a new situation, against the distractions of a multiplicity of objects... Things are quite different with those quiet, unknown people whose world is their spirit, whose activity is contemplation, whose life is an imperceptible building up of their inner powers. No unrest drives them outwards. It is enough for them to possess what they possess in peace, and the mighty spectacle going on outside them does not tempt them to play a part in it... Their lot is a simple life'. To their sensitive minds the great world presents itself 'in its more intimate and unimportant manifestations'. Everywhere they – the poets – renew their 'honourable service to mankind and to their chosen gods: the stars, spring, love, good fortune, fruitfulness, health and happiness'. No foolish desires impel them. They breathe in the scent of the fruits of the earth without consuming them.

In the real world such a contrast between action and contemplation is rarely encountered in a clear-cut form. Men tend to alternate between the two, and thus the artist also reveals the characteristics both of the hero and of the poet. The hero is the man of genius, tragic, beset by problems, and always at odds with the world; the other type is the tactful and cautious wooer to whom the world surrenders of its own free will. Both are men of passage who wander through the places where we live; the poet is always at home, the hero never. The poet is *en rapport* with all things. He has overcome the conflicts of isolation; often, indeed, they lie wholly outside his experience. He knows nothing of the unrest that affects the man who is cut off from his fellows. His world of the imagination demands but little. Without effort he accepts the world and its 'intimate, unimportant manifestations', nor does it ever enter his mind to do otherwise.

A cleavage that corresponds to the distinction drawn by Novalis can be found in the history of art. Since the Renaissance, European art has seen the world from two points of view. The one is historical (in the widest sense) and concentrates on the human figure; it receives both nurture and instruction from the academies. The other is concerned with the unhistorical and commonplace, and includes in its purview the world of nature. The south of the continent has concentrated on the important subjects of secular and religious history. The north has busied itself with the surroundings of ordinary life – that is, with still-life, the interior, and landscape.

Without making anything like a rigid analysis, I want to say something here about the different creative methods of the two kinds of artist whose task it was to present these two different worlds to the eye. The heroic temperament is more easily and more intensely moved, and to it extraordinary and dramatic events make their appeal. It chooses themes of great 'external significance', and these themes tend to produce certain distinctive qualities of form. The utmost strictness of formal design, a composition that is thoroughly thought out and deeply deliberated, is best suited to the various subjects

160 DAUMIER *Un wagon de troisième classe*; c. 1862.

161 DEGAS *L'absinthe (dans un café)*; 1876.

162 MANET *Un bar aux Folies Bergères*; 1882.

163 TOULOUSE-LAUTREC *Jane Avril sortant du Moulin Rouge*; 1892.

of historical painting. Great subjects call for complexity and variety of creative means, and are not amenable to the spontaneous sketch.

The artist concerned with the impressions he has of things close at hand works quite differently. His contemplative eye lets itself be guided by the world of mere appearances. His creative power is most fully released when he is turning all that is intimate and uncomplicated to his own uses. Novalis speaks of spring, love, happiness and fruitfulness; in such terms he paraphrases the symbolic message which the artist gives to the world that to him seems so near and so companionable. If the expressions were not so shop-soiled, one could speak of a world in a continual process of 'becoming', or again of a world of universal harmony and contentment.

Compared with those of historical painting, such commonplace themes are less exacting in the matter of composition and arrangement. If art is to be found behind every hedge, as Constable believed,[1] and the painter should paint with the circumspection of a naturalist – then a composed landscape is something very like a forgery. Those painters who satisfy their creative needs by the simple observation of reality must obviously be indifferent to the aura of glory that surrounds the man of genius. That is why we so often find that the realists and Impressionists compare their creative activity to the processes of natural growth which we take for granted. The artist in fact regards his own powers as essentially analogous to the forces of the organic world.[2]

The sensual warmth and natural richness of still life – if I might include in that expression all the subject matter of the contemplative painter – demand a form of expression that is direct and wholly free. This world about him that the artist perceives needs to be interpreted through the medium of warm sensual colour. 'Colour, which is vibration, is able, just as music is, to reach to that which is most generally existing and most difficult to pinpoint in nature: the force at the heart of things.'[3] These fine words of Gauguin, which incidentally recall a certain passage in Runge,[4] endow the world of colour that the nineteenth century created with its appropriate degree of symbolism. The artist's aim was not to reproduce nature's processes of growth and flowering, it was to recreate them with his brush-strokes. It was to re-enact in colour the creation of the physical world, so that the day of creation might be said to dawn once again.

In dealing with the painters of 'still life', as I am using the term, we touch on an aspect of nineteenth century art for which there was obviously no room in the preceding chapters: the more friendly kind of art that captured the sympathies of the public. It is with this kind of art and its themes that I now wish to deal. The critics surely underestimated these men who communicated the natural and uneventful sides of existence, when they contrasted them in their intellectual simplicity with the painters of literary and historical subjects, pointing to them as examples of pure painting unspoiled. It is not true that for such painters as these the nature of their subject was a matter of indifference as, in the case of Manet, Zola had declared it to be.[5] It is not true that they were wholly preoccupied with 'pure seeing' or that, when painting, they thought of nothing save purely technical processes. Even a work of *bonne peinture* clearly has its own meaning and a theme of high symbolic significance. What they were setting their faces against was the expression of the historical view of the world. Over against the essentially masculine personality of the Great Man, they set their dominant theme of femininity. In place of loneliness they set companionship; in place of the earthly hell, the ideal of the earthly paradise.

In order to keep the consideration of these themes firmly on the ground, let me first make some observations on landscape, still life and *genre* painting.

Friedrich's 'Wreck of the "Hope"' (1821) (plate 14) is a symbolic picture of the highest order. Its symbolism finds expression in the title, and especially in the name of the ship which seems to have been chosen by the painter himself. As in Géricault's 'Raft of the "Medusa"' (1819) (plate 70), the scene is the breaking of man by hostile and overwhelming natural forces. Géricault transforms the catastrophe into a rescue at the very last moment. But Friedrich writes *finis* beneath it; the elements hold man inexorably in a deadly stranglehold. His deeds, his energy, his courage – all are in vain. Nature takes her revenge for the wounds which man has inflicted on her. He has interfered with her where she had remained undisturbed; now he himself is hacked to pieces by her. The ice-floes have so hemmed the ship in that its shape can hardly be seen at all. The fragile work of man's hand has something inexpressibly wretched and insignificant about it in the midst of this elemental world which destroys without leaving any trace of its destruction. The fragmentation produced by the violence of nature endows the picture with certain formal and intellectual qualities. Here we touch a deeper level than that of mere loneliness and death. What is forced on our minds is the tragic alienation between nature and man in his historical context, even though he traverses the cosmos as hero and conqueror.

The man of history, whose restlessness shuts him out from the security represented by 'still life,' experiences nature in a way that expresses itself in conflicts. The 'Wreck of the "Hope"' is a symbol of this feeling about the world, this dialogue with the forces of nature that knows only the opposing poles of victory and defeat. Delacroix has given expression to all this with great force in various passages of his *Metaphysical Fragments*.[6] These passages contain a confession of faith by one who is essentially a man of history and they also show the reverse of the coin which is a resigned admission of his impotence. Man 'oppresses and is oppressed, he burns, and rends, and consumes, and he in his turn is crushed and despatched'... 'If we take this false premise as our point of departure, the contention that everything must be related to our frail and transitory existence, then we are entitled to see in natural catastrophes contradictions in the divine will'.

The 'Wreck of the "Hope"' is also illuminating in another way. It illustrates a quality of the restless, brooding type of mind that will never never be satisfied with 'pure seeing' or the simple optical 'impression'. Such a mind forms an abstract conception of nature, set against a background of infinity, and regards it as its task 'to marry the finite to the infinite'. To carry out this vast purpose is beyond its powers, to bring the two things into a unity is something 'eternally unattainable'. And it is this disharmony – the quotation is from Schlegel's essay *Von der Schönheit in der Dichtkunst* (Concerning Beauty in Poetry) – 'that gives man the appearance of continual ill-fortune, imperfection and alienation'.

The longing to bridge the gap caused by this alienation is clearly discernible in this picture and Friedrich's majestic detachment has endowed it with nobility. It is his awareness that he is dealing with things that are incommensurable that makes his painting devotional, though in a secular way. The uncompromisingly religious feeling that informs his whole life's work was never to appear again in quite that form. For all that, the feeling of being a stranger and the resultant sense of desolation experienced by the man of history continued to influence nineteenth century art and made a deep impression on a wide range of landscape painters. Certain cloud-studies by Delacroix, Constable, Stifter and Menzel with their peculiar quality of evanescence and imprecision, are symbols of the vastness of nature and of that 'incomprehensibility' by which she eludes man's grasp. Helpless and unsatisfied he confronts these natural powers, in whose transience he sees a reflection of his own destiny. With uncertain steps he traverses bridges and paths which offer him a way through the threatening elements. He seeks in castles and lighthouses (Blechen, Hugo) a refuge like that of an island prison but finally achieves his isolation in the dungeons of Böcklin's 'Isles of the Dead' – paraphrases by a late Romantic of Friedrich's monastic cemeteries. In his destitution he carries his melancholy to the shores of the sea (Munch).

Instead of devoting himself to understanding nature, the lonely man sees her through the spectacles of alienation. He is insensible to the organic powers that thrust forward into life and sees nature as something wounded and frail. He sees abysses and deserts, angry surf, storm and thunder clouds, broken and frozen forms, and in them he sees a reflection of his own mood. Friedrich's elegiac landscapes with ruins convey the message that all is vanity. The artist's eye with its desire for change even possesses the power of destruction. Friedrich's imagination sees buildings which are in a perfect state of preservation – the Church of St James in Greifswald and the Meissen Cathedral – as though they were in a state of decay. Such anticipation of a ruin is characteristic of a tragic view of history whose sceptical outlook feels all the works of human hands to be threatened by destruction. Hubert Robert paints the ruins of the great gallery of the Louvre, and Sir John Soane shows us the relics of the Bank of England. Flaubert's imagination sees Paris after an earthquake[7] and recalls the paintings of John Martin whose 'The Last Man' (plate 17) belongs to this same category.

Threatened, and uncertain of his own creative power, man looks with fascination at the destructive power of nature. Artists like Friedrich look upon the quiet crumbling of over-grown ruins and delight in the very feel of such decay. Others are drawn by the rages of nature, by her wild dynamic discharges. Pictures of rushing torrents and floods, such as those of Turner, Martin and Ensor, are just such responses to the call of chaos. They have their counterparts in the poems of Edgar Allan Poe. Like the giant wave in the drawing by Victor Hugo to which he gives the title 'Ma destinée' (plate 20), the raging suns of Van Gogh are a passionate appeal to the elemental, to which man offers himself as a sacrifice – a romantic gesture of submission to the burning source of power.

3

It was necessary to review first the various phases of that tragic sense of disharmony, of alienation and of chaos which the art of the nineteenth century records and thus more easily pass on to a description of that other way of experiencing nature, in which man was released from his tragic separation and permitted cautiously to feel his way into the great unity of the natural world. To the landscapes of loneliness vast distances are appropriate, they involve extension of space beyond all measurable bounds. In it man wanders around homeless and unhoused. The other landscape where the spirit of companionship and harmony is supreme, has features that definitely please. It is limited in its dimensions and is a true living space for man.

Once more let a poet draw the graphic distinction between the two forms of imaginative experience – between friendly nature and cosmic drama. Stifter's preface to *Bunte Steine* (Coloured Stones) (1852) contains a declaration of faith in the quiet power of nature that preserves the world and the moral law that preserves man, and he reconciles man with the cosmos through this intimate process of interaction. 'The gentle movement of the air, the murmur of water, the growth of crops, the waves of the sea, the green of the earth, the brightness of the sky, the shimmering of the stars, these things I consider great. The thunderstorm as it approaches in all its majesty, the lightning which splits houses in two, the storm that whips up the surf, the mountain spitting fire, the earthquake that buries entire countries, these things I do not consider greater than those mentioned above; indeed, I consider them smaller for they are only the effects of much higher laws.'

'The gentle law' is another expression descriptive of the spirit of what I have called 'still life'.

Both phrases call to mind the ideal image of a nature that is intimate and undistorted, whose voice proclaims the enduring fullness of life. An attempt had already been made in the first decades of the century to deduce the whole character of nature from her smaller and less significant manifestations. Weary of the tensions of history, artists were being more and more attracted by forms of landscape that breathed a spirit of comfort and imparted a sense of protection and security. As appreciation grew for things near at hand and unpretentious, the values thus affirmed led the artist towards new forms of landscape-painting. Home, the village, the suburban garden, the small town, all these and more began to attract his notice. New types of picture came into being. The scene glimpsed for a moment in passing, the casual view from a window, provided intimate settings in which nature could be observed. As man sees the landscape, so he sees himself reflected in it – confiding and guileless, pleasantly simple and innocent. The *genre* picture and the landscape with figures imparted to human relations the qualities of goodness, gentleness and warmth of heart. Something childish – the child is the idol of the period! – is to be found in these men and women whose life is fulfilled in the circles of their families and their friends. A sabbatical calm endows the lives even of the peasants and the poor with beauty. We see a harmless, unsuspecting, happy world that never passes beyond its chosen ambit of sober pleasure in its own existence.

To fulfil this gentle law of nature and to embed human life therein, after stripping it of its passions and desires, is the ideal of bourgeois sensibility. This is a European ideal which takes a different form in France from that in Germany, a different form in England from that in Austria. The German-speaking countries possess no Corot, but they do possess the poems of Stifter whose pure nature poetry may well be compared with the works of the French master. One might add that both – and almost exactly at the same moment of time – attain a pictorial closeness to nature that foreshadows the work of the Impressionists of the second half of the century. Yet the fresh and happy unconcern of the eye which determinedly selects whatever subject happens to please it and sets that subject down with the maximum spontaneity – as we see it in the sketches of Stifter, Menzel, Blechen and Wasmann – not only remained without any kind of successor in Central Europe but was first completely overlaid by the sentimental playfulness current at this period among the German-speaking peoples, and then thrust aside as a merely marginal experiment. The bourgeois felt a need for a friendly and sympathetic reflection of reality and found a more agreeable fulfilment in the whimsical 'small-town poetry' of Spitzweg than in the impressionistic sketches of a few individualists. He liked nature to be straightforward and pleasant, or shrouded in the gossamer of fairyland. He took pleasure in the strangely devotional atmosphere of the woods that was so successfully caught by Richter and Schwind, an atmosphere untouched as yet by any revolutionary storms. Rübezahl and Genoveva, hermits and wood spirits had of course to be present to echo the mood of the landscape itself. In the end, just as in ordinary life people set out to achieve a simple pious domesticity, so nature was made to acquire the gentleness of monastic contemplation. The monastery, the hermit and the pilgrim became the symbols in in which God-fearing men saw the earthly paradise embodied.

In Western Europe, in France and England, the discovery of nature as a protective force, beneficent to man, was made along rather different lines. The poetical accessories are only rarely found; they occur, for instance, in certain woodland idylls of Corot where they form, as it were, an accompanying chord to the landscape itself, and where things seen and things imagined are woven into a kind of web. A ring of dancing nymphs mingles with the coloured light, which binds all the figures together. This sort of picture of nature reveals her gentle aspect and it is the directness of the artist's perception of nature that makes possible the intermingling of all the picture's constituent parts.

The movement introduced into France by Corot and the Barbizon School, inspired originally by a stimulus that had first come from England, attained its noon-day maturity with the Impressionists and its final transfiguration in the later work of **Monet** – in particular the water-lily pictures. We can disregard the strict classification into schools and boldly call all these painters Impressionists. For they really were devoted to the 'impression' in the sense that they left the ordering of nature to the powers within herself, to the changes of light, the passage of the seasons and the time of the day. Such artists did not start off with any positive assumption concerning nature, they simply allowed themselves to be influenced, to be 'impressed' by her. The idealist of the old school, who allowed his imagination to construct grandiose landscapes, gave pride of place to what he considered to be permanent in nature; nature seen after that fashion is something formed by the power of the masculine will, an ideal abstraction of reality. The artist on the other hand who was determined to preserve in his picture that 'direct impact upon the senses' which Hegel despised, painted nature as a colourful event, an atmospheric spectacle of continual change. He gave her feminine features, he succumbed to what Cornelius called 'the wanton allurement of colour'. The magic that radiates from a landscape of Renoir or Monet is evidence of this connection between colour and the sensual, almost feminine appearance of nature. Such magic must surely derive from the fact that the senses of these artists experienced the impression of colour with all the intensity of a seduction and it is this seduction that their brush relates. It gives back to nature her flattering tenderness, it thanks her for the benison she has allowed the eye to feel, and indulges in a blossoming of sensual joy. There is a fine passage in Kierkegaard that throws light on the whole relationship: 'Woman grasps the finite, she understands it through and through; that is why she is lovely, and essentially every woman is lovely. That is why she inspires delight, and no man does that. That is why she is happy, happy as no man can be or ought to be. That is why we can say that the life of a woman is happier than that of a man. The finite can make people happy, the infinite as such never does this.'[8]

The happier world is made according to the measure of man, it encloses him as the fruit encloses the nut, it holds him in its grasp as the power of the female does the male. He can abide in it and can find his way within it without effort. It does not overtax his powers by vast immeasurable distances. It does not tempt him into remote and dangerous places. Its dimensions are such that a man may linger in it or wander on in leisurely fashion. It is true that its more distant views played a liberating part in bringing the Impressionist landscape into being. But a survey of the latter's development shows that it was the foreground and the ideas which it suggested that carried increasing weight. The landscape becomes a park or a garden, the sea becomes a lake, the stream a pond, the long line of houses in a boulevard gives place to a group of buildings around a square. Nature here is all within easy reach of the eye and within the compass of a short walk – even when it seems to melt away in strands of mist. There is no violence to distort it, no extravagance to break its moderate bounds. Within it man is secure.

In Corot's 'Le pont de Mantes' (plate 38) the bridge leads across a river whose quiet surface is like standing water. Although much of the subject matter in the landscape is man-made, it nevertheless breathes an atmosphere of perfect harmony. The whole picture is a kind of bridging, a combination and understanding, between form and form. The outlines of the bridge and of the houses fit perfectly into the general composition. The horizontal lines are parallel to the frame; thus they remain in the flat and join with vertical ones to create an effect that is pleasing to the eye. The four trees in the foreground are all in a vertical plane; two touch the sides of the picture, three are cut off horizontally. Thus we get a strip-like arrangement extending over the whole picture, which can be viewed either vertically or horizontally. All the constituent elements of the picture are wonderfully interwoven. The light and shade upon the actual bridge correspond to the dark outline of the trees, as these are set off against the lighter tones of the water. The rhythm of the upright parts, the trees, the piers and the chimneys, combines with the broad vista of the shore, with the spans of the bridge, with the roofs and with the line of the horizon. One hesitates to designate this interweaving of light and dark, of forms that tower upwards and forms that glide away, as a composition at all, although it is not difficult to detect symmetrical correspondences in this apparently artless interpenetration of one object by another. Two trees are placed directly in the centre and combine with the two at the sides in an alternating sequence of gently swinging and robustly upright forms (a-b-a-b); in the wide intervals are the two houses, each equidistant from the central axis and the edges of the picture. A spirit of harmony emanates from the whole and there is a complete absence of conflict.

The human figure in the picture, worked in so subtly at the boundary between water and shore that it almost escapes notice, melts more and more into the coloured structure of the landscape. The 'open air' painter always proceeds unmistakably from the hard to the soft, from the clearly defined to the indefinite. As the brushwork becomes more fluid the effect of 'coloured moisture' increases and the whole texture of the picture becomes more homogeneous; all the phenomena of nature appear to be flowing in a gentle stream. The world as the Impressionists see it – particularly Pissarro, Sisley, Renoir and Monet – is Neptune's offspring; water is the power which gives it life. The way in which these artists seek to mollify and preserve nature is shown by their treatment of the changing face of water. The element whose infinite extent had once spelt terror, as in Géricault and Delacroix, now with its gently gliding motion becomes a symbol of beneficence.

Courbet shows us two women by the water's edge lying in the shade of a great tree (plate 122). The figures are full of colour and have about them a holiday air. Together they seem to have melted into an oval shell of ruches, lace and the folds of their dresses. They are enclosed in the moist satisfying coolness of meadow and foliage. Nature is constricted to form an arbour, grows up on all sides and encloses the human beings. The small gap that remains open between the earth and the leaves is filled by the water. One of the two recumbent figures holds a bunch of flowers near the centre of her body, the other has opened her dress and nestles against the moist ground. The sensual abandonment and animalism in her gesture, almost embarrassingly emphasized by the look of exhaustion on her face, reminds one of the slave girl at the feet of Sardanapalus. Gauguin's South Seas women cower down in a rather similar fashion, but here there is a complete ritual surrender.

The picture is an *allégorie réelle* of the fruitfulness of woman and nature. The body that thus allows itself to sleep with the earth is a symbol of the earth's inexhaustible fruitfulness, a Gaia in metropolitan dress, a figure representing the dark, luxuriant natural forces of secret organic life.

Courbet had a robust devotion to the physical, which caused many to decry him as a materialist. He nevertheless prepared the way for that immaterial quality which was later to be the peculiar mark of the figures painted by Renoir and Manet. One does not see this in his 'Stonebreakers' (plate 168) but rather in his bathing and recumbent figures and in the slumbering 'Woman in a Hammock' (1844). In his 'La balançoire' (1876) (plate 205) Renoir gave what was definitely the ideal pictorial form to this detachment from the earth, which corresponds to the gentle merging of his figures into the coloured atmosphere. We get here a vision of floating incorporeality that symbolizes the manner in which the Impressionists conceive of man's intercourse with nature. He does not wound her, he allows her to play around him, he glides along over her; his rowing boats and sailing boats are simply material symbols of this way of experiencing life. When Renoir paints skaters, they are scarcely distinguishable from strollers on the boulevard.

Note also the holiday air of these people with nothing to do. The figures of Courbet and Millet are closely concerned with nature; they work, plough, sow and reap. The people of the Impressionists do nothing in particular and obviously enjoy it. They remain on the surface of nature, though they let themselves become shrouded and transformed by her atmosphere. The people standing around the swing are immaterial apparitions, they float over the earth and the earth itself is a coloured emanation of warmth and coolness, of light and moist shadows. Rich gradations of blue impart to the whole picture the quality of a submarine landscape. The carefree and unencumbered quality of these lives is symbolized by the woman who nestles against the swing, like some blossoming plant, without ever setting it in motion. All is inactive and relaxed. The people here are enjoying their rest, knowing they are in harmony with the world. They have neither will nor purpose but are surrendering to the fleeting moment as though is would last for ever. Any activity would break the spell.

Once again, nature encloses man; he is inside her body, screened on all sides by a roof of leaves through whose covering the light slowly trickles down. Nature becomes an 'interior', like the body of a mother nursing an unborn child – and later, with Bonnard and Vuillard, the 'interior' resolves itself into a landscape of potted palms and flowered wallpaper. The man-made world of hard objects is softened with colour; it blossoms into a flowering, leafy home, whose inner space increasingly radiates a sense of comfort (plates 200 and 203).

Another example of this floating, casual air with which the Impressionists endowed the friendly aspect of nature is Monet's 'La Grenouillère' (1869) (plate 183). We see a happy island, like the paradisial centre of all existence. Boats and footbridges all point or lead towards it and it seems to float between water and air, without anchorage in the earth and without weight, as though the gentle waves could work their will upon it. Man and nature are wholly in harmony; both are loosened, rested and relaxed. The water is completely domesticated, so that man can settle upon it and take his ease. It is the element that is most nearly akin to the Impressionists' whole feeling about life. Unresisting, it receives into itself the whole phenomenal world, mirroring it back in countless different reflections. Its flowing movement is a symbol of passive surrender to any impelling force. It seeks no known goal and, like the Impressionists themselves, is governed by no pre-existent form. Water is the element of playful improvisation and is the epitome of that with which the Impressionists were reproached, namely, the dissolution of matter into an indeterminate visual phenomenon.

In the water-lily pictures (colour plate VIII) Monet combines two dominant ideas, water and the thick growth of flowers and leaves, into a pictorial carpet full of tropical luxuriance. Nature unceasingly generates life in the most manifold forms and lets it ripen to paradisial splendour. Out of the water, the primal source of all life, blossoms an over-rich vegetation; drenched with moisture, the landscape has no finite horizon. It has about it the inexhaustible quality of organic life which envelops man. The luxuriant growth on every side coalesces to form a closed interior scene. The over-ripe, aromatic and saturating colours endow this garden with an exotic impenetrability. Nature embraces man and brings him under her spell.

That these water-lilies possess a peculiar symbolism nourished by archetypal memories is clear from Bachofen's remarks on swamp procreation. 'In this spectacle which swamp life presented to the astonished gaze of the first men, the whole mighty power of terrestrial creation was plainly to be seen. No seed fructified the womb of the earth, no plough opened any furrow; of its own power matter sent out into daylight, fully formed, that which it had prepared in the depths... there seemed to be exhibited here the prototype of all earthly life. In the vegetation of the swamp and its everlasting cycle there was revealed the law to which the world of animals and men had to submit. There was the same coming into being out of the womb of matter, the same return into the darkness thereof: the same preservation of the eternal youth of the race through the eternal dying of the individual.'[9]

4

Cézanne too painted the enduring essence of nature, as Novotny has shown – the eternal process of birth and growth[10] – though he used other and richer means. It is not easy to persuade people of this, since today the Impressionists are regarded as antithetical to Cézanne, as the painters of a surface world that is kindly and full of joyous feeling, as men who occupied themselves in pursuing fleeting impressions and in noting down atmospheric charms.

In the art of the nineteenth century Impressionism plays a connecting rôle. Earlier I pointed out that since the French Revolution the artist had been confronted by the necessity of making a choice between the present and the past. In either case, whether he was depicting history or recording his own time, he concerned himself with the event of a particular moment (the historical painter achieving this through meticulous and scientific documentation). In this pre-occupation with the moment of time the position of Impressionism was the extreme one, since, more consistently than the early Impressionists of the forties, it concentrated more and more upon the fleeting moment and sought the spontaneous evocation of an unrepeatable impression. The Impressionists' experience of the world started with the unique event, but gradually grew richer. The eye that had once been intent upon the transitory turned to lingering contemplation and as a consummation of this process there came into being the full vision of nature and her unchanging and permanent powers.[11] In the more restful works of their maturity, the Impressionists no longer concerned themselves with a single point of time, and similarly in their composition they avoided the quick sketch or restricted view, which was another way of laying hold of the transient. They no longer painted situations that lasted only for an instant, but revealed the coloured glory of organic life in which man knows himself to be at one with nature.

The declared programme of the Impressionists should not mislead us here. The capture of the fleeting moment was not the fundamental concern of these artists at all, but the lasting fullness of life. Many people, with a side-glance at the solid structure of Cézanne, speak of the dissolution and weakening of the whole composition, overlooking the fact that regarded positively this dissolution is really a way of achieving unity between objects by allowing them to melt into one another. If we employ traditional concepts, this means that Impressionism sublimated and idealized the world of phenomena. It discovered the pictorial formula for two ideals which can be traced to the very beginnings of the century. One of these is the Romantic's conviction that, as Carus says, 'life is not a thing apart and alone, a reality that exists by itself', but rather that all the powers of nature, since they continually intermingle, were from the outset permeated by one single life.[12] The other is the bourgeois ideal of 'still life', the life that is guided by a gentle law. Even contemporary defenders like Philippe Burty were able to discern that what this disquieting form of painting was really concerned with was 'the general aspect of things'.[13] In Monet, the painter of sunshine who was exalted by Aurier as a priest of light,[14] they saw a pantheistic poet.[15]

We should remember this when, in connection with Renoir and Monet, people speak of Cézanne's treatment of the landscape. After he had brought under inner control his wild and violent sensuality Cézanne belonged to those painters of 'still life' of whom Novalis said that their life was fulfilled in contemplation and in the 'formation of their inner powers'. Cézanne said of himself that his art lay 'parallel to nature'. This much-quoted phrase can only mean that the painter felt the processes of his own art to be moving in the same direction as those of nature herself. Cézanne did not wish to reveal the world as something in a standstill state of existence, motionless and complete, but as a process of struggle, directed towards a fulfilment and an end.

There is some relevance here in a remark of Cézanne's that has been handed down to us by his young critic friend Gasquet, though it has no doubt suffered some embellishment since it was first uttered. 'Try to understand that I treat my whole canvas as one single unity embracing many elements. I bring together, in one gesture, all these scattered elements, taking from left and from right, from here and from there and from everywhere, tones, colours, subtleties, I isolate them and then I fuse them. They become lines. They become objects, rocks, trees, without my volition.'[16] Compared with the work of the Impressionists, the dynamism of these pictures is more controlled and tightly

packed, their quality is less engaging, their total effect is harder and more crystalline. And just as the earthy outlook of Cézanne differs from that of the Impressionists, who were essentially devoted to water and the sea, so his vision of nature shows a more intensive formal concentration. In my view, therefore, the art of Cézanne should be regarded less as a reaction against Impressionist fluidity, but as deepening and stabilizing it, both in form and content.

Cézanne's 'evolving' forms derive from a deeper geological stratum than those of the Impressionists' delicate brush-work. His gropings after a shape reach more deeply into primordial formlessness, into the essential nature of colour itself. Their transient and provisional character does not reveal any uncertainty in the artist's vision, but results from the fact that he feels colour to be pre-existent to any object he portrays. So far as his mature and balanced forms are concerned, these are superior to those of the Impressionists by reason of their strictness and compactness. There is therefore a greater intensity of creative effort in his art. It is more primitive and also firmer; it is therefore more comprehensive and more complex, and also much more strained than that of the Impressionists and achieves its purpose more slowly. And yet his aim is a related one; it is fulfilled in endowing the 'process of growth and becoming' with permanence and endurance. The flowing calligraphy of the Impressionists' brush tends also to harden, in their own style, into a rich and balanced unity, as in the coloured saturation of the water-lily pictures, which raises the mere 'impression' to a point of permanence and endows it with its 'religious character'.[17]

Cézanne's experience of nature was not a sociable one and this unsociable quality, of which the formal expression is a certain stiffness and clumsiness, probably distinguishes him more strongly from the Impressionists than anything else. Nature in Cézanne is not prepared to receive man; she is often impassable and proudly distant. Sometimes her meditative solemnity reminds one of the landscapes of Friedrich. Yet Cézanne never painted any picture that could be called devotional. The lonely, isolated figure of the worshipper is wholly absent from his work. The stillness in his pictures never has a tragic colouring and has nothing to do with the romantic pathos of solitude. Nature unfolds herself with a gesture of splendid self-sufficiency and is revealed alone. Man has no possibility of active intervention; he has been withdrawn from nature (not wholly excluded) and has at the same time been attached to her as an observer. A comparison may make my meaning clearer; whereas the Romantic sought to bring the finite quality of his subject as near as possible to the infinite quality of nature, Cézanne from the very beginning accepts this infinite quality as a constituent part of his picture. Yet he refrains from making the picture an occasion for the development of a purely subjective mood. Kurt Badt is certainly right when he says that Cézanne's sympathetic feeling for nature derives from a quality of observation that 'has no intention behind it, but is confined to the recognition of what is there'.[18]

Yet, if he is fully to master nature, the artist must go beyond a mere act of apprehension. He must make her take shape upon the canvas; only thus can he become conscious of reality in a way that he can never achieve by any mere process of thought. It is by such ideas as these that Conrad Fiedler, Cézanne's contemporary and the patron of Marées, describes the process of 'Sichtbarkeitsgestaltung', or making the visible take form, in his essay *Über den Ursprung der künstlerischen Tätigkeit* (On the Origins of Artistic Activity).[19] One cannot help feeling that these remarks have a particular relevance to Cézanne. 'It is only by some such activity that the visible quality of any object can be forced loose from the object itself and appear as a free and independent form.' This development, the attainment of autonomy by the creative form, is the very centre of the art of Cézanne. In it the artist's desire to attain simplicity and to free himself from every inhibition is united with his high resolve to win back the status of the great masters of the past.

The strain which such an effort involves is plainly apparent to anyone who looks at Cézanne's work. The interpenetration of organic and monumental forms has no longer that careful and self-evident arrangement with which Corot knew how to compose his pictures. How difficult it is in an age that tends towards stylization for an artist to impart to the elements of a picture, after building them into their final form, the purity and innocence of natural growth, is clear if we compare the 'Pont de Mantes' (plate 38) with Cézanne's 'Les marroniers du Jas de Bouffan' (plate 39). The architectural function which Corot divides equally between the bridge and the tree trunks is in Cézanne largely entrusted to the row of trees. Everything is categorically clear; the process of composition is naked before one and plain to see. Man remains outside the picture in meditative contemplation and the sheer simplicity of nature prevents him from seeking a home in her recesses, or from being caught and held by her moods. Cézanne's nature never offers the protection and warmth of thick foliage. She merely exposes to view her architectural design.

How unmistakably solemn is the formal quality of that leafless avenue! The slender vertical lines of the trees form a kind of framework for a Mediterranean nature sanctuary. They are in full harmony with the houses in the background. And it was another of these cathedrals of nature that was later to enfold the women's bodies in 'Les grandes baigneuses' and to impart to their company the dignity of a ritual gathering (plate 118). One's thoughts go to another 'religious' landscape, Friedrich's monastic cemetery in winter. The romantic procession of monks is withdrawing from cold hostile nature into the ruins of the church. Friedrich is celebrating the transitoriness of man. Cézanne's group of women is celebrating inexhaustible life to which the leaning branches are extending their protection.

5

Like landscape, still life can express opposite poles of experience: transience and permanence, danger and security, death and life. In the category of still life with a tragic note we must place the dismembered limbs painted by Géricault (plate 45), a *nature morte* in the most precise sense of the term, and the masks on Menzel's studio wall (plate 148), which cannot be explained merely in terms of an artist's interest in the effects of light and shade. They are ghostly properties of the theatre of life, half way between the living and the dead, a warning of mortality. Using the thematic and formal language of pictorial realism, they point backwards to the demoniac creatures of Goya and forward to Ensor's masquerades.

The tragic still life, which must of necessity concern itself with the fate of man or beast, shows traces of violence and wounds and is often accompanied by that demoniac feeling belonging to the no-man's land between life and death. We see Courbet's trout in the moment of frantic resistance against death, a symbol of demoniac vitality, that even as it expires seems to have a threatening quality (plate 145). Here we can actually feel the powers of life making their final stand. But the end of the century, resigned and tired of life, no longer sought to conjure up the pain of the robust animal, only the silent flickering out of existence, the withering of a slack body (colour plate x).

Among those pictures of still life that pose a question and are a kind of *memento mori*, we must also place Cézanne's 'La pendule noire' (1869–1871) (plate 146). Here a certain seriousness conveyed by the close arrangement of lifeless objects tends to make us thoughtful. The vertical surface of the table cloth, broken at regular intervals by monotonous folds, has a repellent effect. The huge shell whose symbolic function was in later pictures taken over by a skull, possesses the impenetrable quality of a sphinx's head which will reveal its secret to no man. From the face of the clock, which has no hands, there stares at us the empty circling of time.

From these disquieting pictures of still life we must distinguish those others which portray, not transience, but security and duration. Their subjects are largely traditional, such as flowers and fruit. The repetitive objects of mass-production gave the artist a desire for something genuine whose inherent strength would increase his own. Rilke must have had this in mind when he spoke of the bottles in the still life of Cézanne as 'saints'. Here still life has taken over the empty place left by the religious picture.

Another example of the sanctification of a lifeless object is Van Gogh's 'Gauguin's chair' (plate 47). The painting is an act of homage to the reality of an artless hand-made article of common use in whose company a man passes his life. This chair, which seems to have the impressiveness of a human face, is a sure place of rest. It invites a man to take his ease and has the strong reliability of a friend. Van Gogh has caused simple, solid objects to speak to us and has clothed their very poverty with a symbolic, even an epic, significance. He is deeply moved by them and it is as though he felt them to be his brothers. These inanimate things seem to him, as they did to Cézanne, to possess a kind of piety, which attracted him almost more than did any merely human association.

The ennobling of the unimportant can, however, have something quite different behind it. It can derive from a delight in the artificiality of things. Degas certainly moved in this direction and if we compare him with the elemental, almost religious art of Van Gogh he seems to have about him an air of sophistication. He loves obliqueness, the transposition of objects, a certain witty refinement, an unexpected but felicitous association; and it is typical of him that he should join the spectacle on the stage to the spectacle in the stalls (plate 196). He is attracted by artifice assuming the mask of the natural and that is why he is interested in a milliner's shop. He transforms a paper ornament into a bunch of flowers that can never wither. The work of artifice wants to be taken for a work of nature, only to be made by artificial means into something really different. That is how he means us to see his dancers. Their gestures are the result of intense physical discipline, but they are meant to appear spontaneous and unremarkable; the fact that they are being made by ordinary human creatures is disguised by a mask-like and anonymous smoothness. In fact, these creatures of an artificial world remind one of flower arrangements, with grease-paint and tinsel added. (Gauguin had already observed this.[20])

The inner connection between *plein-air* painting and still life is not hard to grasp. If all phenomena are inter-connected and a common breath of life animates all natural forms, a certain 'still life' quality is found in all categories of painting – the portrait, still life, landscape, and *genre*. Of course, since man too is related to all these interconnected aspects of life, he has to pay a price. He is no longer the most prominent among the constituent elements of a picture but a single phenomenon among a number of phenomena. Yet he is always present, if only by implication; both interior and landscape are adjusted to him and ready for his visit. They are conceived according to the human measure and have every indication of comfortable habitability.

Such a picture of 'still life' is Menzel's 'Room with a balcony' painted in 1845 (plate 199). It is a masterly and typical expression of this new sense of intimacy and candour. The 'wafts of air' of which Stifter speaks with such reverent admiration have here become 'wafts of light', which open the enclosed room and fill it with something like a sense of promise. Perhaps the secret of the picture is its strict economy. The room is astonishingly empty; such furniture as there is, is either grouped around the mirror (the two chairs) or reflected in it (the sofa with the picture hanging above it). A bright light is all we can see of the balcony or the world outside. The shimmering curtain reveals and conceals at the same time. What it promises remains only a surmise. The essence of the outer world has been brought into the room and assimilated, without its visible attributes. Only the life-giving force of the spacious world beyond remains – light, the source of strength and movement. Outside there might be a garden or a street or a courtyard; it would neither dim nor enhance the gentleness of the light. One could imagine a man sitting on the chair, reading perhaps, but this would only introduce a note of distraction into the serene clarity of the picture, and turn it into a *genre* painting. Actually, anybody

164 F. M. BROWN Work; 1850.

165 MILLET *La bergère*; 1867.

166 PUVIS DE CHAVANNES *Le pauvre pêcheur; 1881.*

167 MILLET *Les glaneuses*; 1857.

168 COURBET The stonebreakers; 1849.

169 MENZEL The rolling-mill; 1875.

170 DAUMIER *La blanchisseuse.*

171 DEGAS *Les blanchisseuses portant du linge*; 1876–78.

172 LIEBERMANN Old woman with goats; 1890.

173 VAN GOGH The sower; 1888.

174 DEGAS *Repasseuses*; c. 1884.

attracted by the picture to stand and gaze will find himself sitting on that chair by special invitation.

Another picture that seems to be offering an invitation is Monet's 'Le déjeuner' (plate 203). It is indeed remarkable how with the Impressionists one always feels oneself surrounded by hospitable attentions. Monet's picture has a joyous sensuality about it that is almost epic and yet it has also a kind of meditative reserve. It shows us a garden rounded off on all sides, a secure world in which every day is Sunday. Once again our gaze, which can nowhere travel very far, encounters the kindly protection of an enclosed landscape. The meal is over, yet the deserted table still has tempting things upon it. As in 'La Grenouillère', with its islands of boards on to which all the figures converge, an oval is the central point of the picture, radiating an air of discreet festivity in all directions. Still life, figure painting and garden landscape – all these elements are here drawn together to form an epitome of the life that is truly 'still'. By this I mean the life that both satisfies physically and preserves a man's inner balance. These qualities are inseparable characteristics of the world here portrayed.

6

Monet's picture was painted in 1872, one year after the Franco-Prussian war. The seventies were not a happy time for France; the political upheaval had left behind a legacy of discomfort, doubt and pessimism. The country's economic recovery was slow. The people's *joie de vivre* seemed to be clouded over, if not crushed. Nothing of all this is to be seen in the work of the Impressionists. The war and its consequences seem to have left them untouched. This fact is well worth noting, all the more so since privately these artists were by no means lacking in patriotism. Everything that was confused, or at war with its surroundings, darkly adventurous or grossly sensual, everything that was in a bad sense 'exciting' was, as Stifter has pointed out,[21] excluded from their art. The war and history in general had as little place in it as had death, disease or natural catastrophes.

That is how the legend of the happy age of the Impressionists came into being. Rarely could any painters who claimed the right to paint everyday reality have been less concerned than these to be eye-witnesses of current events. The evidence is easy to adduce: in 1877, just one year after Renoir finished his 'Moulin de la Galette' (plate 204), Zola published *L'Assommoir*, a grimly accurate portrait of his age. What Renoir and his friends were painting was the poetic manifestation of the ideals of bourgeois democracy. They painted a world that had recovered it kindliness and joy, but it was the world of a dream.

One might summarize the view of life behind this work in a phrase: the abolition of frontiers (Entgrenzung). This means, first of all, that the brush has blurred and destroyed the outlines of objects, their boundaries. Objects living and lifeless, in motion and at rest, light and dark, are made to melt chromatically into each other. It also means that etiquette, conventions and differences of rank have fallen away and that the world throws aside all that makes for stiffness and separation. It further implies that it is not the individual in isolation that counts but the whole, that it is not the unique, sensational happening that concerns the painter, but a process involving the abolition of distance, so that everything becomes connected with everything else.

This ideal world, at peace with itself, radiant, comforting, and calm, is shown to us in the picture of the Impressionists with such verisimilitude, that we cannot but believe that the reality of the seventies and eighties consisted entirely of racecourses, parks, boulevards and sailing boats.

The phrase 'the abolition of distance' must be broadly understood. Not only has the isolating contour between objects in a picture been forgotten, but the observer's physical distance from it as well. Renoir is a master of the art of bringing the observer into the heart of a picture. The rhythm of dancing couples laps round him like a wave; as he gazes, he becomes a part of the curves and texture of clothes and hats, foliage and chandeliers. All these together are like a moving sea of flowers, here and there shot through by coloured light. A '*jardin des voluptés*' indeed – but a natural, not an artificial one; not a sham paradise made out of carefully selected stage properties like the World Exhibitions. Distance means transience; nearness, permanence. In these pictures there is always nearness, security, and harmony; the glance that speaks, the embracing of bodies, the marriage of colours. One hesitates to apply to canvases like these the abstract ideas they evoke; organic life, democratic intercommunication, the myth of womanhood, the earthly paradise.

X Woman as Myth

I

'MAN is more mineral, woman more vegetable' (or organic), says Novalis.[1] Man can move with ease within a rigid structure of thought, his conceptions of life tend towards a systematic, crystalline finality. Woman is averse from such divisions in the mind and prefers a more primitive interpenetration of ideas. Her nature rises from the darker depths of life and is a source of unity rather than separation. In this there are revealed the primordial conditions of human experience and we again observe action and contemplation as two opposite ways of life. 'Against war,' says Bachofen, 'we set the motherly figure of peace; against battle, reconciliation; against man's wanderings, the permanence of home; against the verdict of arms, the peaceful verdict of justice; against conquest, the care for one's own possessions; against violence, harmony.'[2]

I have shown elsewhere that it is not difficult to relate this symbolism of the sexes to the way in which in the nineteenth century the artist shaped his world, and so to throw some light on the sources from which he derived his power. In this century, there was both a masculine and a feminine way of experiencing nature. We find this symbolic character of nature vividly expressed in an address by Cornelius, contrasting the landscape of India with that of the Rhine. He describes nature in India as being 'more rich in sensual charm than our own. The cradle of the human race could hardly be other than that. The happier the note struck by the outside world, the clearer will be the echo coming back from within ourselves. Yet though such gentle playfulness on the part of nature and such a joyful method of teaching us our first lessons was necessary and beneficial for our race, it is no longer suited to its manhood. Indeed, it turned of its own free will and destroyed its former playthings, so that it might attain to freedom of the spirit. An everlasting memorial of that manhood is provided by our castles, churches and cathedrals, and on their brow of stone is written bitterness towards a race that has grown degenerate and has once more, thanks to its precociousness, become a feeble child.'[3] We have here two distinct types of landscape: a feminine one that gently unfolds itself and like a mother imparts the sense of security that comes from the proximity of familiar things, almost playful in its moods, with a kind of organic unity that suggests new life; and the masculine one, suggesting a man stepping out boldly towards far places, his acts performed by the conscious will, with a longing for great heights and a tragic striving for the summit.

Among romantic painters, Runge typifies the feminine element, the organic unity of new life, while Friedrich represents the masculine – what Novalis calls the mineral element. Runge takes fo his subjects the nearby, fresh and growing forms of nature, her mature manifestations and sometimes even the frozen and inaccessible. Runge painted children, flowers, springs, while Friedrich painted trees, mountains, desolate glaciers, the burial grounds of nature. Like Blake, Runge surrounds his tender human figures with a protection of leaves and blossoms; Friedrich shows man unprotected, his relation to the gigantic forces of nature being one of tension. Water for Runge means the life-giving, gentle spring, gushing out from the depths of the earth; for Friedrich, it means the majesty of great rivers and the sea, the very symbol of distance and infinity. Runge's children blossom literally from innocent plants, and form part of the daily cycle of life (plate 209). Friedrich's lonely human beings face the evening of existence and after death become one with the silent blocks of stone that form their world.

In the art of the early nineteenth century, Runge's feminine and organic view of the world is wholly unique. His spiritual kinsmen are to be found among the poets and philosophers of the romantic movement.[4] Schlegel calls the truly feminine principle a 'point of balance and rest'; he praises the devout way of looking at nature that Christian revelation has brought about, thanks to which she is now visualised in the form of a woman. Rousseau's view of nature had already endowed her with an essentially feminine and sensitive quality. It was left to the Romantics to Christianize her, while religion, being unavoidably affected by this trend, itself assumed feminine features. Schleiermacher calls it the 'motherly body in whose sanctified darkness my young life was nourished.' For Görres too it is essentially feminine. Since art and religion now establish a neighbourly relationship, the Romantic's common denominator of femininity is made also to apply to the processes of creation. 'It is the deeply hidden and inexpressible element that constitutes the essential charm of art. Its very nature is the feminine principle; it has no need of truth', says Görres. For Adam Müller poetry is essentially feminine. It is the woman who by her own power gives shape to the material that nature provides. It is in woman that, for the romantic imagination, the dark mysterious sources of life are gathered together. The simple, the elemental, the point of balance and rest, the primeval unity of life – in woman are all these to be found.

The wishful speculations of the Romantics found later confirmation in Bachofen's new interpretation of Greek myths. His work must of course be taken in its entirety. As a piece of historical research it is supported by very considerable marshalling of evidence; but it is also distinguished by the imagination of a poet. It therefore provides a particularly suitable accompaniment for a certain phase of nineteenth century art in which the artists dimly recalled a world over which the female or mother element seemed to predominate.

A study of Bachofen shows us the female principle manifesting itself in two distinct forms: Aphrodite and Demeter.[5] Both are archetypes with which nineteenth century art was concerned.

The courtesan type of mother goddess is the designation applied by Bachofen to the Asiatic Aphrodite to whose whim man is subjected. Cleopatra, Dido, Omphale, Semiramis and Delilah are cited as typical oriental queens determined to enslave men by means of their seductive arts, and the prototype of the courtesan reveals a full and uninhibited natural spontaneity. All restraint is cast aside; physical and political emancipation go hand in hand. Life assumes an increasingly sensual character. 'In place of elaborate state organization', to quote from Bachofen, 'the laws of democracy and of the masses' hold sway. As organized rule disappears in the brilliance of a life rich in material goods and lively in matters of the mind, strength of will gradually vanishes and morals decay. While Demeter leaves man his manhood, the courtesan reduces him to abject subservience. The cult of Aphrodite was served by the licentious slave festivals of Asia and the Babylonian Feast of Sacaea. 'The full freedom of life unchecked by any human law determines the customs and all the arrangements. All social and official regulations that might inhibit the rule of nature are suspended. For five days, from the rising of Orion to the 16th day of the month Loos, the rule of the goddess Mylitta is supreme. All the bonds of slavery are broken during this period because they are displeasing to the Great Mother. All artificial social distinctions are suspended. The Sacaea is a feast of universal freedom and equality… the lower orders receive back from the hands of the Goddess the rights of which they have been robbed and are permitted the free expression of their joy.' The Goddess represented by a courtesan dedicated to her serv-

175 RUNGE The artist with his wife and brother; 1804.

176 COURBET *"Bonjour, M. Courbet"*; 1854.

177 GAUGUIN *"Les misérables"* (the artist with a portrait of Van Gogh); 1888.

178 FANTIN-LATOUR *Hommage à Delacroix*; 1864.

179 FANTIN-LATOUR Verlaine and Rimbaud (detail from *Le coin de table*); 1873.

180 RENOIR *Le cabaret de la mère Anthony*; 1866.

181 MARÉES In the loggia; 1873.

182 CÉZANNE *Les joueurs de cartes*; 1890–92.

ice awaits the King of the Festival, chosen from the ranks of the slaves, so that she may present to him the insignia of his short-lived power. 'With endless joy the people watch the proffered spectacle. Camping in tents, they abandon themselves to all the pleasures of love. In the riot of nightly orgies every man is Omphale's servant in female dress, every woman the image of the seductive goddess Anaitis.'

Demeter's cult rises superior to this. It strives for discipline and chaste behaviour. Its foundation is the strict marriage law. What corresponds to it in natural life is agriculture, as opposed to the uncontrolled luxurious vegetation of the swamp, which corresponds to the orgiastic feast. 'Both stages of life rest on the same fundamental principle, the importance of fertility; the difference between them lies in their opposite conceptions of natural motherhood.'

2

I have given a concentrated account of Bachofen's theories by describing the mythical figures around which his interpretations centre. In doing so, I have succeeded in plotting out the ground from which nineteenth century art derived its symbolic figures of womanhood. On this territory the artist did not stand alone. Though no bonds of spiritual brotherhood connected him with them, he found himself on common ground with those who sought substitutes for religion and elevated woman to be Priestess, Goddess and Saviour in their various cults of the Brotherhood of Man. All these last appeared to be striving for that same mingling of classes which was one of the marks of Matriarchy. It is possible, if we are willing to continue to adhere to Bachofen's terminology, to distinguish two systems of symbolism, both of which made use of the idea of womanhood in their political Utopianism. One of these recalls the cult of Demeter; Daumier's 'Republic' is an example. The other symbol, Aphrodite's courtesan, can be discovered in Delacroix' figure of 'Freedom', leading the people to the barricades (plate 72) – the 'Goddess Revolution' (Richard Wagner). The latter has her champions among the Saint-Simonists, the former is near to the cultural aspirations of Auguste Comte.

Baudelaire's idea that the power of the Church rested on her womanliness[6] points to the tactical reasons which persuaded Comte to place the cult of woman higher than the cult of humanity in his positivist catechism. 'The ordinary family has always been the foundation of the true Church'[7] and Comte gives very explicit directions for the pictorial form which the cult figure of the 'Grand Être' should assume. The symbol is to be a mother bearing her son in her arms. The sex with the greater religious susceptibility is to cherish the active male. At the end of the century Zola in his novel *Fécondité* was calling for a religion of motherhood.

The Saint-Simonists as part of their deification of woman proclaimed her right to freedom from the moral constraint she endured in the past. A woman is to grow conscious of her priestly power and dignity. A female Messiah is expected. The new religion will be a religion of love. The ritual union of the sexes will no longer involve the subordination of one to the other, but will be made as the result of free choice in perfect equality and in harmonious agreement. The uninhibited union of all with all was justified as a feast of divine love. Comte's cult of motherhood calls to mind the wise discipline of Demeter. The 'Divine Services' of the Saint-Simonists are like the ancient slave festivals which allowed both men and women to take any partner they desired. (Remember too what the Marquis de Sade had in mind: a community of women for men and a community of men for women – society thus based on the 'libre jeu des institutions'.)

The ideal of free love must be accounted as yet another of the visions of the religion of humanity. It is essentially a romantic ideal, deriving its power from the passionate desire for community and harmony between all men. So urgent are these feelings that they ignore the limits placed by morality and social convention and see the act of love as typical of all human relations. 'Friendship is partial love,' declares Schlegel, 'and love is universal friendship, coming from all sides and extending in all directions.' (Elsewhere we find the assurance that no objection could be raised to a marriage *à quatre*.[8])

Love is universal friendship – it is not surprising that, in the century that made man its god, this theme received impressive symbolic treatment. The increased longing for love is one of the avenues of escape devised by man so that he may break out from the isolation of the 'human desert' and mingle with his fellow creatures. Since this longing cannot be satisfied within the restricted dialogue of conjugal love he endows all human relations, and even nature, with an erotic radiance. He seeks natural, open, unrestricted forms of association to give expression to his universal desires. This will be apparent if we glance at two themes, the implications of which the century expended considerable energy in elucidating: the harlot and the earthly paradise.

The image of the harlot takes many forms. We encounter her in mythical or literary trappings, historically or exotically costumed. We see other versions of her in the weary features of the women of the street and again in the cold pride of the man-devouring Sphinx. However, it is not so much with the outer characteristics as with the inner significance that the artist is concerned. One critical attitude concentrates on the harlot's mercenary services and insists on the fact that she has become a piece of merchandise, and so alienated from her true self. But another raises the prostitute from her slave status and endows her with the dignity of a Priestess; not because she must, but because she wants to, she belongs to every man who desires her. This interpretation is governed by the conviction that such a woman's readiness for love is both boundless and genuine.

Bourgeois morality consigns the harlot to the limbo of the debased and insulted. The artist does the same, but he reverses the meaning of the judgement. For him the outcast is the exemplary type of man and as he sees things symbolically the very fact that the harlot has no human ties binds her to all humanity. Since she is no man's property, she belongs to all. This means, of course, that it is she to whom every man belongs, that her readiness to surrender ends with the triumph of woman over man. These two aspects of the prostitute, her humiliation and her power to humiliate, often mingle with one another in the artist's representation of her.

In Baudelaire's view[9] the harlot's unconstrained submission brings her close both to the artist and to God. All of them are beings expelled and exposed, banished from the safe paths of life, sacrificing themselves to a humanity that denies them. The artist justifies his creative task as an apostolate, as a ritual act of consecration; he offers himself to every man and his work is a surrender to a partner who has no choice. God is the all-loving, whose resources of love are inexhaustible, whose readiness for sacrifice knows no bounds. Baudelaire's comparison, which borders on blasphemy, has a deep symbolic quality. In their acts of self-sacrifice, he sees the harlot, the artist and God as beings with a high mission – to redeem humanity: but the sacrifice is rejected. The Messiah is nailed to the Cross, the artist is derided and the harlot despised.

There are, of course, other levels on which the harlot is close to the artist and his symbolic figures. The artistic type of man, feeling he belongs to all and to none, refuses to be held by any human ties or responsibilities.[10] Self-exiled, he is also placed by society beyond the pale. 'The artist', says Fernow[11], 'is only accepted on sufferance; like the Jews, he has no civic rights. The academies are his ghetto.' The harlot is the female counterpart of the man without rights and without a home. She is like the Wandering Jew, who can nowhere find rest or fulfilment; and like the eternally unsatisfied Don Juan who seeks to forget in pleasure his despair and his inability to love. (Wagner's Kundry in *Parsifal* personifies the demonic, wandering woman, condemned to restlessness since the crucifixion of Christ.)

Whereas the universal longing for love finds its cult-symbol in the prostitute, it has in the earthly paradise an anonymous community in which everlasting bliss reigns supreme. There is a connection between these two imaginative conceptions. The multitude that pays homage to the priestess-courtesan demands some symbol for its erotic hedonism. In other words, where no love is sinful, the law of natural life determines the free form of human society. The ennobling of the harlot is followed by the ennobling of free love. We find the connection between these two orders of ideas at their highest and most spiritual level in the work of William Blake.[12] In his poetry, Blake exalts the selfless and carefree state of belonging to one another, the bucolic community of the golden age which knows neither jealousy nor self-love. He compares love to the free wind that blows down from the mountains. It is 'The Whirlwind of Lovers' that mingles the different pairs in an endless marriage (plate 140). Blake's illustrations to Dante, to which this drawing belongs, are in parts full of highly controversial polemics. They correct Dante's whole outlook on the world. It may well be that it is in this sense that 'The Whirlwind of Lovers' is to be interpreted. In this work of his old age, it seems to me, Blake is reverting to a theme which he treated in his youth, namely the rehabilitation of that love which is offensive to traditional sexual morality. It was not the sinful lovers, lashed by infernal storms, whom Dante met in the second circle of hell, but creatures whose ardent passion united them with the consuming flames. Out of the constricting material world which forbade their union they fled into the infinite, where they could belong to each other for ever. Paris who abducted Helen, Tristan who loved the wife of King Mark, Paolo who desired Francesca, the wife of his brother – all these outlawed persons were brought by their passion into conflict with custom, morality and convention. Fetters were laid upon their desire, and for that reason, according to the provisions of the orthodox moral code, their passion was a sin and a crime. In the eyes of a society poor in love and hardened by egoism, jealously guarding its possession, these lovers are 'criminals', as Nietzsche understood that word; but in Blake's view they are among those whose passion was prevented from unfolding freely by laws that are alien to life. Constraint and convention kill the joys of love, jealousy and hypocrisy guard the marriage bed, and debase the wife to the level of a prostitute and a slave. Where human relations are subordinate to regulations imposed from without, crimes and excesses become common. 'Prisons are built with stones of Law, Brothels with bricks of Religion'.[13] Abstract, analytical reason represses desire so that it shuns the light. It locks the joys of the senses in the brothel.

Blake's poetry, born of a world of sophistry and burning with revolutionary fire, protested against the hypocritical morality and false shame that cast suspicion on the senses and repressed the instincts. This protest passed through a number of phases. In the last decade of the eighteenth century, when Blake was championing the egalitarian trends of the French Revolution, the hope for an earthly paradise was at its strongest. Blake looked back to a primeval golden age and his imagination pictured its renewal in the future. Coming generations, he believed, would be permitted to taste again without restriction the joys of an all-embracing love. In his later work he seems to transfer the fulfilment of love's desire to another world. A symbol of unrestricted union, no longer hindered by any earthly or material obstacles, is the vision of the kiss which blazes forth behind the figure of Vergil (plate 140). Like flowers winding about each other, the two figures are intertwined in an embrace as though recalling a time when there was no division of sex and anticipating one when the division would again disappear.[14] The kiss is the 'point of balance and rest,' where the freeing of the senses is transformed into a redemption, and desire, to which the whirling bodies are restlessly subjected, is finally stilled. The finale of the *Flying Dutchman* contains a similar apotheosis of love: 'In the glowing red of the rising sun one sees above the wreckage of the ship transfigured bodies of Senta and the Dutchman rising out of the sea locked in each other's embrace and floating upwards. Senta raises up the Dutchman, presses him to her breast and points with her hand and with her eyes towards heaven'. Such a description might well apply to a sculpture by Rodin, who might be called a Wagnerian in the plastic arts.

Painting in the nineteenth century finds a place for 'Woman' in various categories of art. The historical painter bases his imaginary eye-witness report on the anecdotes of the history book and shows us the trial of Joan of Arc, the death of Elizabeth of England and the arrest of Marie Antoinette. The realists prefer inner to outer significance. The shepherdesses of Millet (plate 165) possess that introspective, dreaming purity which the official representations of Joan of Arc fail to convey — one thinks of Ingres' picture in the Louvre with its plethora of stage properties. Daumier's 'La blanchisseuse' (plate 170) carries on her shoulders the burden of motherhood and all the weight of social rejection, borne with the dignity of Hagar in the Bible. It is easy to interpret Leibl's 'Three women at church' (1878–1882) as representing youth, maturity and age (plate 93). They are all types of women that might belong to the cult of Demeter and their life is aimed towards preservation and protection. They live quietly and uneventfully and cherish their inner thoughts. This protective power is communicated to the actual form of the picture and translates its realism into a symbol. So completely is the simple and familiar preserved here, so tangible does it seem, that the observer experiences an essentially religious feeling of a loving care by which he himself is protected.

The feminine and organic principle is supreme in pictures of every type. Monet's water-lilies typify the splendour and richness of the luxurious growth of the swamp. The bathing women of Renoir and Courbet are descendants of mythical water sprites (colour plate VIII; plates 117, 114). And in this context it might be remembered that Wagner suggested a relationship between music, water and womanhood. He called harmony the 'feminine, maternal' element of music and the musician (composer) a man who walks across the ocean.

Another painter should be mentioned here: Arnold Böcklin. Endowed with a rich, sensuous vision, he too portrayed woman symbolically — 'the Descent to the Mothers'[15] — but his poetic imagination was stronger than the power of his eye and he differed from Courbet in that he painted not the descendants of mythical creatures, but the mythical creatures themselves. He gives the feminine principle a realistic external significance, in order to identify more clearly the symbolic content (plate 115). His Naiads and Nereids have something about them of the *allégorie réelle*. There is a contrast between the realism of their well-shaped bodies and the imaginary world to which they belong. Thus there is fundamentally a double meaning, not an ambiguity, in these symbolic allusions. Böcklin is pleading for an unconstrained relationship between the sexes, free from bourgeois conceptions of morality. There is a message in his art and a knowledge of the conflict in civilized man between what he wants to do and what is permitted him.[16] For this reason, he does not paint the people of his time and their conflicts, but fills his stage with mythical figures who act as substitutes. While other painters transfer the conflict of the sexes to a hotel room (Degas, plate 126) or to the compartment of a railway carriage (Menzel), Böcklin represents it in the silent estrangement between Odysseus and Calypso. Böcklin's picture of humanity reveals the extreme contrast between the hero and the primitive creature of nature, between the Magna Mater and the temptress of the sea. Odysseus is a symbol of man's eternal desire to wander and shows that the hero is doomed to tragic isolation. To live the physical life to the full is only possible by transformation into one of the lower creatures of nature. For this too Böcklin needs a mythical form, namely that of the nymphs and fauns. Thus he seeks to catch the feelings of the time when in the words of Floercke 'there was as yet no mind to distinguish between earth, plant and animal, since an unbreakable unity still existed between the organic and the inorganic'.[17]

Although Böcklin introduces into his primordial world some figures from the mythical repertoire of idealistic art, he handles natural forms in a far coarser and more brutal fashion than his contempo-

raries in France, whose themes were less literary and remote. Compared with the crude subservience to instinct that these women of the sea exhibit, the bathing women of Courbet and Renoir do not shock or surprise us, despite their vigorous animalism, but keep a certain reticence. They too plead the cause of the natural life, but it lies nearer to them than to the German mind, which burdens even the simple and naïve with a complex of problems and pays for its longing for 'depth' with a tendency toward coarseness.

The 'terrible mother' too is widely personified in the nineteenth century. The artists concentrating on 'external significance' choose prominent figures from mythology and history, the others are satisfied with the types that are ready to hand in their own world. Manet's 'Nana' (plate 127) is a cold objective companion piece to Rodin's 'Everlasting Idol', once named 'The Host'. Woman is always the object of adoration whether her body is in a harlot's quarters, adorned with faded violets, as in Flaubert's *November*, or is clothed in robes and jewels, for the performance of an office both erotic and priestly, as with Moreau and Peladan.

The conflict between the sexes – wooing, seduction, jealousy – is also visualized on different levels. Scenes from the repertoires of the idealist painters are mirrored in a profane setting. Munch's 'The Dance of Life' (plate 218) and Toulouse Lautrec's 'Maxime Dethomas au bal de l'Opéra' (plate 129) are modern conceptions of the Judgement of Paris. Before we encounter it in the setting of ordinary life, we can find the conflict of jealousy dramatized by mythical characters. Blake's title-page for the *Vision of the Daughters of Albion* (plate 141) gives shape to a theme which was to recur in Munch's 'Jealousy' – a woman between two men, bound by law to the man who owns her, while her unsatisfied heart goes out to the man she loves.

At the beginning of the century there was a preference for the sphinx-like type – the woman full of knowledge, the smoothness of whose body suggests a sinuous flexibility like that of a snake, while her cynical nudity offers itself with calculating coolness. The Romantics, especially the French Romantics, presented women in sensual exotic splendour. The Symbolists followed their example, but they toned down the erotic ecstasy to something statuesque and majestic, and are in this close to the Classicists. The women of Gauguin and Moreau have the unapproachable quality of idols. Thus every trend possesses one symbolic female figure or more. A historical survey which endeavoured to find its way among the different stylistic groups might thus be able to classify the various 'isms' by arranging them around their respective ideals of womanhood. Such a procedure would, however, be contrary to my purpose which seeks expressly to ignore formal differences and stylistic labels and to trace throughout certain common elements of experience. Thus we encounter connections which cut across all 'isms'. Bachofen's distinction between Demeter and Aphrodite as opposing mother-figures provides us with two essential prototypes, in terms of which the nineteenth century can be interpreted, though there are certain intermediate types which link the two together. The first is the child-bearing and protective mother in whom the life-giving forces of nature find their expression. The other is the seductive courtesan, the unfathomable woman of riddles. (Depth psychology distinguishes between the archetypes of the 'good' and the 'terrible' mother.)[18]

4

The ambiguous symbolic content of Runge's 'The Morning' (plate 209) is not easy to disentangle. To interpret Aurora as feminine 'genius' is not enough. We come nearer to understanding the picture's message if we remember that Runge always endowed flowers with human feelings. Men and plants complete each other; they are outwardly different, but inwardly creatures of similar kind. 'As there is spirit in flowers, so there is also in trees,' Runge wrote to Tieck.[19] Schlegel expresses the reverse idea, and speaks of the 'eternal plant of humanity which forms itself in stillness'.[20] It is this relation of mutual interaction systematized in Schelling's 'philosophy of identity', that provides 'The Morning' with its different layers of content. The picture is a devotional one. The baby on the sward – he is like the Christ child in Runge's 'Flight into Egypt' – grows like a flower out of the fruitful earth and has his place in the most elementary kind of plant life. A symbol of this material power of Nature, who can without outside aid bring forth man from within herself, is the floating female figure. She is the mediator between 'our dear Mother the Earth' and the immaterial sphere of light, which is the metaphorical expression of the fatherhood of the god of light (Apollo). The unearthly brightness betokens the victory of the spirit and of the male principle, over the female principle of nature, but the victory is not final. Out of the zone of light there grows the lily, a new spiritualized kind of matter to which man entrusts himself once more. Between the first innocence of the baby on the sward and the second innocence of the lily and its creatures, lie the various transformations of man and the various stages of his development in each of which he must spend a part of his life. There is the earth which brings him forth, the woman who guards his natural growth, and the light to which his longing is directed. In no sense, therefore, is 'The Morning' an allegory of the passing of a day. What it seeks to express is the work of creation, and the myth of man whose way is determined by cosmic laws. It is possible that Runge in 'The Morning' was endeavouring to set down a comprehensive symbolic statement of his artistic intentions, since on one occasion he compares the artist to a woman who is bringing up her child to a divine union with the world. On that supposition, the floating figure would be the genius of art, who is both wife and mother. In the final analysis, 'The Morning' is a religious picture since the mighty manifestation of light points to Him of whom men must make neither picture nor image. 'For God was before the light and is greater than the light and the light was before the sun, for light is the nourishment of the sun and the light shines in the darkness and the darkness comprehended it not. Then God gave to man colour and the joyous light burst forth from the depths of the spring and now the earth brings forth the children of men and we have seen His day and walk happily up and down upon the earth. Inwardly our longing is for the light and our dear mother the earth holds us fast, and we cannot but love the earth and she greets us with every flower'.[21] Perhaps the dazzling power of the light also represents a turning point in human existence, namely that culminating point of conscious life, that tremendous tension of the mind which 'causes the mind to flee from the landmarks it has found, so that we can no longer attain to the consciousness of ourselves as integrated beings until we have returned to the earliest sincerity of feeling or until we have become children again. The circle, in which we always become dead at least once, is experienced by every man, and the more often a man experiences it the deeper and more sincere his feelings become'.[22] That is why the lily grows out of the light and why out of the lily, to complete the circle, there comes the state where for the second time we are as children, and in that state man once again becomes simple. We meet similar ideas in Blake's illustrations to his *Gates of Paradise* (first engraved 1793). The plant of humanity sleeps like a worm upon a leaf, or like some flower of nature it is drawn out of the ground by a woman. The innocent joys of childhood recall Paradise Lost.

Perhaps we should interpret the symbolic content of Runge's picture on two different levels, though they will interpenetrate. One of these levels is that of *matter* and here we are concerned with feeling or instinct, with a mood that is essentially natural – that is to say feminine. The other level is that of the *spirit* which is master of all the forces of nature and reveals to them the almighty power of creation. The encounter with the spiritual however is followed by a return to the primordial state. Existence thus proceeds in a circle. Man is born 'without consciousness or knowledge', he receives 'a supreme intimation' of the infinite before his spirit, released from its tensions, flies back to God. After that man must start again 'with his first childlike feeling'.

335

In addition to plant life, water is one of the symbols of female fertility[23] and also of caressing womanhood (as Swinburne puts it in 'A Swimmers Dream': 'Softer than sleep's are the sea's caresses, Kinder than love's that betrays and blesses'). Among the 'motherly waters' (Novalis) which thus expressed the idea of bringing forth life, of protecting and guiding it, are the spring, the pond and the brook. Blake's 'The River of Life' (plate 210) must also be reckoned among these. Much in his symbolic picture with its wealth of meaning – paraphrasing a passage in *Revelations* – reminds us of Runge's 'The Morning', above all the vertical arrangement of the composition, and the plant life which provides a framework and gives the whole a rhythmic balance. On the edges of Blake's picture are paradisial shores to which the tree of life vouchsafes its fruit. The river gliding between gentle meadows is a translucent road that leads man to God. The kinship with Runge is not merely in the formal composition, but also in the content, and this becomes apparent as soon as we realize that the figure leading the children is female (this interpretation is confirmed by other works showing children being led by women).[24] As with Runge, woman thus has the rôle of mediator and guide.

Blake's supple linear rhythm is clearly related to the feminine principle and to the gentle and ethereal lines of the female figure, as it is also to flowing water and growing plants. Thus the predominant features in the 'River of Life' are the characteristic movements of the female form: a sense of floating as in a dream, the easy and unconstrained charm of the bodies, the sprouting branches of the trees. The pale river is no male and masterful stream. It reminds us of that magical metaphor which Novalis uses in *Heinrich von Ofterdingen* where he speaks of the white blood of the mother.

The rhythm of growth passes into the rhythm of flowing water and moves towards the glowing ball of the sun. The finite material world returns to the infinity of the divine light. Freed from the restrictions of earth, man unites his soul with God. The multiplicity of matter is transformed into the eternal unity that was from the beginning, and all separation disappears. Novalis, who so often comes very close to Blake (both had certainly been to some extent inspired by the mysticism of Jakob Böhme) has sung of this everlasting happiness in one of his *Hymns to the Night*:

Getrost das Leben schreitet
Zum ew'gen Leben hin,
Von inn'rer Glut geweitet
Verklärt sich unser Sinn.

Die Lieb ist freigegeben
Und keine Trennung mehr.
Es wogt das volle Leben
Wie ein unendlich Meer.

Die Sternwelt wird zerfließen
Zum goldenen Lebenswein,
Wir werden sie genießen
Und lichte Sterne sein.

Nur eine Nacht der Wonne,
Ein ewiges Gedicht!
Und unser aller Sonne
Ist Gottes Angesicht. *

Blake, Runge and Novalis – in the mystical imagination of all three the contradiction between matter and spirit, between earthly happiness and supermundane redemption continues to be worked out. A common feature of the mythological form of their work is the tension between the world of the mother and that of the father. The mother stands for the origin of life. Her womb is 'the dark green

---

* *A rough translation is as follows:*

Confidently life passes on to life eternal,
Enhanced by an inward glow our senses are clarified.

Love is made free nor is there any longer separation,
The waves of life in its fullness move like an infinite sea.

The world of the stars will be dissolved to a golden
We will enjoy it and be bright stars.   *[wine of life,*

Nothing now but one long night of joy!
A vision eternal – and the face of God is the sum of us all.

185 MONET *La Grenouillère*; 1869.

184 BOUDIN The Empress Eugenie on the beach at Trouville; 1863.

185 DEGAS *Voiture aux courses*; 1873.

186 MANET *Musique aux Tuileries* (detail); c. 1860–62.

187 MANET *Le balcon*; 1868.

188 MANET *Chez le père Lathuille*; 1879.

189
RENOIR
Lise; 1867

190 SEURAT *Un dimanche d'été à la Grande Jatte*; 1884–86.

depths of the sea'. She is 'the loving mother goddess growing up among the full golden sheaves' and to her, 'the loveliest of goddesses', is dedicated the ecstasy of love. Above the security of this primeval mother-world, which is also a part of our present life, there is raised up the father-world. The god of light and fatherhood overcomes the female, sensual material myth of nature. In the twin-poled cosmogonies of the Romantics the contrast between man and woman is made evident in the two great world principles. This dialogue continues throughout the century, although it sometimes narrows down to a mere conflict between the sexes, and as a result forfeits some of its cosmic symbolism. There is some shifting of emphasis; the river of life which woman first sends forth into the world is directed by woman back towards herself. The nineteenth century confirms Bachofen's remark that 'the earliest conditions of the races of men once more break through to the surface at the end of their development'. Those who have returned to the mother principle remain caught in its binding embrace. The overwhelming power of the irrational releases them from the strict decrees of the Father God. In reaching back towards the great mother, the nineteenth century's creative talent makes its protest against the rationalized world of modern civilization. From a world that is for ever resolving itself into abstractions and whose very institutions are governed by such abstractions, which masks itself behind historic affectations, man seeks once more to return to one whose ties are organic, to a world of wholeness. He seeks to escape from the everlasting pre-occupation with artifice and analysis and longs for the primordial and unthinking spontaneity of the Golden Age. He rates the myths of the forces of nature higher than any sentiment that such an essentially masculine rationalization as the concept of progress can inspire. He desires once more to taste of a life that is entire and undivided. The instincts by whose power he allows himself to be guided, turned their back on all that is conceptual and well-ordered; a deep distrust of civilization itself is the force which drives him forward and by which his inhibitions are resolved.

5

As to the artists, their feeling for the essentially feminine outlook on life and the world goes hand in hand with their practice of depicting everything through colour and at the same time imparting to colour a new fluid quality. Colour itself becomes part of the picture as one of the actual powers of nature and places before the artist's eye a world that in Runge's words 'holds enclosed within itself a veritable miracle of life'.[25] Indeed, as so often happened, Runge's deeply searching mind pointed the way to the future, not with pictures, but with words. After the early Impressionist open air school, this hope that it might be possible to establish an analogy between the materials used by the artist and the forces of nature themselves was most consistently realized in France. There painting produced a formal equivalent to this feminine view of the world, transforming the world of tangible objects by weaving it into a continuous texture of small open particles, that is to say particles of paint clearly discernible on the canvas, and abolishing the boundaries between objects by a combination of chromatic transitions. Colour is recognised as one of the elemental substances forming the world. It unites the near with the far, the hard with the soft, the harsh with the tender. It causes things to melt into one another, it reconciles them and effects a brotherhood between them. Thus there blossoms forth a flowing, growing, homogeneous world of phenomena, the constituent parts of which are all of equal rank. The same affectionate delicacy of feeling with which the brush is applied to the flower is devoted also to the portrayal of an apple or a face. The inherent dignity of objects resides in their colour. This kind of painting which culminates in Impressionism is unmistakably 'democratic', not because of its sympathetic interest in the reality of life 'here and now', but because of a levelling tendency inherent in colour. It is democratic in the sense that appertains to all matriarchal ways of life, for these too care little for public affairs. 'Women', says Novalis, 'know nothing of the life of the community. It is only through their husbands that they are connected with the State, the Church or the public at large.'[26] Such matriarchal ways of life, as Bachofen has pointed out, accept the ruin of political organization and the decay of civic order as the price that must be paid for making life more beautiful and more satisfying to the senses.

Despite the fact that the social class of which it was representative misunderstood it, Impressionism is the 'voice' of the spirit of the liberal bourgeoisie, which withdrew from its public duties and sought to create an earthly paradise within its private world. Social life as Impressionism reflects it is private, anonymous and hedonistic. It is part of a world that knows neither social duty nor moral precept, but is held together by a joyful common feeling with a somewhat erotic tinge and by a harmless and pleasing confidence that unites men, things and nature into a single colourful organism. In all its phases, in its formal means of expression and its relation to material things, this is a woman's world. But we no longer have here the woman of Millet and Courbet whose home is in the woods and the fields; we have woman seen with a metropolitan eye, carrying her refinement as though to the manner born – woman unconstrained, and so casting her spell upon the artist for whom constraint is something from which he must at all costs flee, and who thus comes to see this same world with a feminine eye. Since the preserving of life is one of womanhood's motherly tasks, this feminine spirit moved the artist to attempt an actual preservation of reality in his pictures as distinct from mere reproduction. This explains why Impressionism, having begun with the declared intention of seizing hold of some transient and momentary phenomenon, ends with the transfiguration of the myth of nature. The water-lilies and haystacks of Monet and Renoir's goddess-like figures of women are the visible proof of this.

In Monet's series of landscapes, the plein-airists' mere delight in the pleasures of the eye becomes something deeper – a mighty vision of the symphony of nature unfolding. Even his 'Rouen Cathedral' (plate 206) takes on the rhythm of growth of some luxuriant creation of nature. If we view these pictures as a connected series, we feel that they express both the changing and the permanent element in nature. Every minute of light brings the glow of some new kind of colouring, every time of day or year works a change in what we see. Yet it is only the impression that is transitory. The object behind it, though in process of continual metamorphosis, continues throughout time.

The mystic view of nature of the late Impressionists shows much kinship of spirit with the dreams and visions of the Symbolists. Whoever enters the Water-lily Room of the Paris Orangerie, and allows himself to be enveloped by Monet's long paintings (all representing variations of the times of day), finds himself in a world whose very texture is watery and organic and which in the truest sense of the words is impenetrable and mysterious. The words which the Symbolist Redon uses to describe his own imagination might well describe the vision of Monet's submarine landscapes.

'The sense of mystery... it comes when one is in a continual state of doubt, when one sees things from two, or three, aspects, and more are hinted at (images within images), when forms are on the point of taking shape, forms that differ according to the spiritual state of the observer. All things are more suggestive when they are just about to become visible.'[27]

Two vital processes connected with this watery world are especially associated with womanhood – preservation in stillness and spontaneous birth, the hidden maturing of the fruit and its final effortless emergence. The artist's imagination has always been conscious of this dual aspect and endowed the female figure with the form of both a fruit and a vessel. The container hides that which it contains until it is ripe for coming forth, and this fruit of the body is projected by the artist's imagination on to the vessel that contains it. The preserving body itself becomes a fruit.

An excellent example of this is Ingres' 'Venus Anadyomene' (plate 112). The figure here shows that even an essentially linear art, which refuses to concede to colour any independent value of its own, can attain to the creation of a symbolic form of womanhood. The foam-born Goddess, a descendant of the Great Mother of Asia, is the embodiment of fruitfulness born of the sea. She is herself both fruit and also a protector of fruit. The melting fluid outline of her body still has the original quality of freshness and shyness that it must have possessed when first awakening to life, and yet the slender oval shape brings to mind the vessel-like quality of the female form. The surrounding line of the picture, which echoes the human body, emphasizes this dual aspect of vessel and fruit and rounds off the feminine form of the composition, creating an indissoluble unity. The rhythm of round, enveloping shapes, characteristic of all forms, leads the mind by association towards what is essentially female in physical life: the egg, the embryo, the womb, the breast, and hair. (We can see something of the same thing in Runge's 'The Morning', where the artist is obviously striving to achieve a rounded fruit-like form.)

Redon's Venus, whose outline was possibly suggested by Ingres' picture, is a plant and a water creature (plate 113). The shell is laid around the body like the cup of a flower to protect the body's plant-like blossoming, in which the shell itself has a part; the mother of pearl oval is part flower, part transparent foam. More obviously and more openly than in Ingres, the round form suggests fundamental security and a connection with the inner world of the embryo in the mother's womb. Ingres isolates man in his domination over nature, organic and inorganic. Redon, 'the revolutionary Symbolist', believes in the formal unity of all living things. Life for him is an unceasing transition from one form to another, and his imagination enlarges the created world by filling it with strange, mongrel creatures outside all human experience. Behind the multiplicity of phenomena, Redon is always searching for the unifying principle, that primordial, persisting essential form which Goethe believed he could find in his *Urpflanze*.

To accentuate the protection accorded to Venus as she enters the world, Ingres uses the oval outline, Redon the shape of the shell. The formal smoothness of the Classicist, which leaves nothing to suggestion, both emphasizes the noble line of the mythical figure and at the same time makes her almost naturalistically life-like. But Redon keeps the visual presentation of his imaginary concept in a state of suspense – hence the ambiguity both in the form and in the symbolism. His Venus is at one and the same time both rising and disappearing. The shell seems to be both expanding and contracting. The body only just born could be that of an Ophelia over whom there is closing the 'rejuvenating flood' of death.[28] Beginning and end are in balance, the circle of life seems both to open and to close and nature takes back its creature in the very act of bringing it to life.

6

'Death's rejuvenating flood' – Novalis uses this image in the fourth of his *Hymns to the Night*. It is one of the metaphors the poet uses to bring together in shadowy union his dark visions of night, water, death and motherhood. Water is no longer the power that brings forth life, but the cold womb of the mother of death; night is the almighty World-Goddess. The poet's phrase provides a transition to the nocturnal personifications of the female principle, by means of which man is confronted with a stern and merciless ruler. Myth has already drawn a distinction between the good and the evil mother, between the mother who brings forth life and the mother who destroys it. Like water, woman can symbolize two opposing ideas. In the cycle of life she represents both the source and the final goal to which the river flows, she is the origin and the end of life, the first and the last refuge of man.

The romantic-classicist tendencies of the century identified the 'terrible mother' with the unfathomable powers of fate, though without noticing her erotic attraction. Among the figures endowed with this significance are Ingres' Sphinx, Goya's Fates, Blake's Hecate and Carstens' Night (plate 208), and we still get an echo of them in Hodler (plate 215) and in Segantini's 'Evil Mothers'. At about the same time Fuseli and Goya began portraying the fashionable cocotte and the venal woman of the streets. The scenes which the artist's imagination selected as the setting for erotic desires were the Orient, the theatre and the cabaret, and the night-life of the metropolis in general. The exotic, the unfamiliar and the artificial had at this time a special hold on the mind – anything out of the way that could still be found here and there in a humdrum civilization. Against this background there gradually emerges the polymorphic image of the great temptress who wears a seductive mask and conceals her deadly grasp. This figure had a mediaeval ancestor. Zola's Nana, of whom Flaubert wrote so admiringly that she was a half-mythical creature of Babylon,[29] the cynical cocotte who ultimately succumbs to small-pox – what else is she but a reincarnation of those figures of 'Madame World' in the mediaeval cathedrals, whose front is fair enough, but whose back is full of worms and toads.

The figures of the great harlots always have about them an air that suggests night and death. They are wrapped in impenetrable calm, their immobility is almost mask-like and suggests the life-lessness of an idol. Their cruelty which seems to gleam in every limb is that of some sinuous beast of prey as it fixes its eyes on its victim. Salome and Olympia, the perverted princess and the sickly child of the great city; Messalina and Nana, the royal strumpet and the bourgeois mistress; Pauline Bonaparte and Yvette Guilbert, the Sphinx and Syrian Astarte – they have many names and they enter the world of our imagination embellished by literal, mythological and historical memories of the most varied kind, but they all possess but one body. They are transformations of one and the same arche-type, daughters of Aphrodite; the courtesan of myth.[30] The cliché *femme fatale*, worn out though it is, still describes better than any other phrase, if one remembers its original force, the idea of the inevitable and irreversible ruin that these creatures of erotic desire bring in their train. Admittedly, these figures are children of the male imagination, but they are also symbols of manhood enslaved, seeking torture in love, cruelty in lust and in woman a cold-blooded tyrant.

Whether these women follow their calling in exotic or antique costumes, as goddesses or actresses, odalisques or barmaids, the same mysterious ambiguity attaches to them. They are seductive, yet remote; they entice and yet they threaten; their embrace offers security, but it is the consuming embrace of the vampire, the cold clasp of the grave, the frozen stillness of the lust of death, from whose spell there is no escape.

The *tableau à clef* in which we can trace a number of thematic threads leading to the future is Ingres' 'Oedipus and the Sphinx' (1808). Without question, it is the male figure here that not only carries the formal emphasis, but also declares the picture's meaning. Oedipus has the clear, masculine intellect that brings light into darkness, comprehends the world, and puts to flight the chimeras of fear. The whole line of his body, so clearly revealed, guarantees certainty. Although the dialogue of his hands indicates that the riddle has been answered (one hand points towards himself, the other emphasizes his reply to the Sphinx), yet his features still express uneasiness, as though with his very answer he were expecting a reply to a question of his own. A companion picture to the Oedipus painted three years later is that of Jupiter with a worshipping Thetis nestling against him (plate 5). This is a much more forthright expression of a view of the world that endows the male with unchallengeble sovereignty. The Oedipus picture is more complex, with its layers of meaning; there is neither adora-tion nor subjection, but an interchange of question and answer.

Only a strong unbroken manhood, conscious of its historical past, can have the last redeeming word in this dialogue, and so free human dignity from the monster's threat. When man loses his way under the spell of woman and becomes the prisoner of his instincts (the Sphinx is one of the symbols of lust),[31] the Sphinx brings ruin upon him and her riddle death. He becomes the prey of the 'terrible

mother'. Thus it comes about that the powerful figure of woman, threatening and questioning – in Ingres still forced to one side – generally supplants the figure of the male, as during the course of the century he forfeits his ability to reply to her riddles, loses the sense of his historic rôle and capitulates before her questions, to which woman continues to retain the key. As Zeus did with Themis, so man must learn from woman the laws of nature.[32]

Goya's 'Recumbent nude' (plate 119) – *Maya* – and Manet's barmaid at the Folies Bergère (plate 162) are Sphinx-like beings of this kind, as are the 'Messaline' (plate 195) of Toulouse-Lautrec and his blond sphinxes too. I should also like to include here one of the century's most famous pictures, Manet's 'Olympia' (plate 121). At first sight this picture seems anything but profound or literary. On the contrary, it seems to have a certain challenging and primitive directness, to be almost deliberately artless. By primitive I mean the new revolutionary means of expression through simple, almost commonplace brush work, the painting of harsh contrasts in colour and line without a connecting link between them, the omission of any modelling of the body – all in fact that is conveyed by a saying attributed to Courbet that Olympia was like a playing card.[33] Yet when I say primitive I am also seeking to describe the girl herself: the directness of her attitude as she lies there, the absence of any reticence or concealing artifice, her stiffness, her cool and contemptuous look, her professional shamelessness.

There is only one other picture in the whole of nineteenth century art that shows the naked body in so cold, brutal and yet so enticing a fashion. It is Goya's 'Recumbent nude' (plate 119) – 'the naked *Maya*'. The question whether Manet knew this picture when he painted his Olympia is still unanswered, and is, as far as we are concerned with it at all here, only of marginal importance. It is more instructive to identify the degree of formal passion peculiar to both these pictures, which are so strongly spiritually akin. Goya works with the simplest of means. A couch in a barely suggested room, and a smooth body on green velvet and white silk, turned towards the observer – and so detached from what it is lying on that it appears almost vertical. A taut, animal intensity lurks in these limbs, which seem in places almost stiff and lack a uniting, rhythmic outline. This results from the fact that the legs are in strict parallel and the arms are clutched behind the pillow; the arms turn and form a right-angle with the rest of the body, and at the same time emphasize the different directions in which the two breasts are pointing, by repeating the line in the elbows. The two arms enclose a rhomboid that is like a mouth; one could almost interpret it as a vaginal symbol. Passionate desire has here been directly projected into a formal equivalent.

'Olympia' has not this ruthless consistency of physical display, uninterrupted by any accompanying figure. The *Maya* is a beautiful, dangerous little woman, Olympia a cheaply adorned Paris prostitute who is borrowing an exotic perfume from the negress. In her expression there is a complete lack of embarrassment that comes from long practice of her profession, but no triumph, no flickering fire. This weary shop-soiled sphinx has her companion at the extreme edge of the picture – the black cat. It is hardly likely that Manet was induced to add an animal to the two figures through any considerations of colouring or composition. The reason that led him to do so must be sought elsewhere.

The cat is not simply an Imago of the female principle,[34] but one of the symbols used by the nineteenth century instead of the Sphinx. In his famous poem, *Je suis belle, ô mortels*, Baudelaire compares the enthroned woman with a misunderstood Sphinx. In another passage of the *Fleurs du Mal* he equates the cat first with woman and then with the Sphinx; thus the symbolic circle is closed on all sides. These poems are not the only evidence of the symbolic 'cult' of the Paris aesthetes around the middle of the century. It was just at this time that Champfleury wrote a history of the cat which went into several editions and in which Manet was represented with an illustration, while Baudelaire published his translation of Poe's tales in which the cat appears several times as a demonic monster. Without doubt Manet knew that with his black cat he was doing something more than create an interesting effect, and that he was painting a key figure of which, so far as I can see, little notice has hitherto been taken. For Manet, the faithful observer of every-day facts, the Sphinx was an impossible theme. He was compelled to resolve into its constituent parts a figure that myth had made half human and half animal – woman and beast – and to present these as two separate figures. It is no longer Oedipus to whom the question is being addressed, but the painter himself.

In the figure of Oedipus there is expressed yet another idea: the admiring devotion of the man who looks up to the woman. Question and desire, humility and uncertainty, are expressed in a single glance. This glorification of the 'virago' is of romantic origin and can be traced from Fuseli's courtesans (whose literary equivalents can be found in Heinse) to the female figures of Klinger, the perverted imagination of Felicien Rops, Toulouse-Lautrec's circus rider and Munch's Madonna, that strange devotional picture glorifying decadent love. The cult of the strong woman who reduces man to subjection gives the figure of woman monumental proportions, but it also makes a demon of her. Woman becomes unapproachable; the sorceress is petrified by her own magic, and none can come near her.

The archetype Sphinx is beset with loneliness and, as Baudelaire rightly saw, she is misunderstood. Her pride is a mask, behind which she hides her disappointment that none can answer her questions. In this the Sphinx resembles the royal courtesans of Asia whom Bachofen described in his *Legend of Tanaquil*. Both have made man a slave of their whim, both either give him a crown or destroy him as they see fit, without in either case belonging to him. Together with the ruling power of the male, both have inherited the male's other characteristics: his loneliness, his restlessness, his perpetual dissatisfaction. Salome and Cleopatra, the Queen of Sheba and Messalina, who with her wild excesses belongs to every man and therefore is no man's possession, all these are profoundly tragic figures. In the nineteenth century's hierarchy of symbols they stand on the same level of isolation as Don Juan, Daumier's Don Quixote (colour plate 1), Kierkegaard's Nero, or Ahasuerus, the Wandering Jew. One has only to read Baudelaire's analysis of the *femme errante* – and here one thinks of Jane Avril (plate 163) – to be conscious of these interconnections.

Rodin's 'Everlasting Idol' shows with solemn over-emphasis the meeting of man with woman and the consequence thereof – two-fold imprisonment, unredeemed. Mutual understanding is impossible, union an illusion. The man surrenders helplessly to his idol, the woman gazes past him into the distance which belongs to her alone. If she were to speak from her lonely eminence, then her words might well be like those of the poet.

> Je suis belle, ô mortels! comme un rêve de pierre,
> Et mon sein, où chacun s'est meurtri tour à tour,
> Est fait pour inspirer au poète un amour
> Eternel et muet ainsi que la matière.
>
> Je trône dans l'azur comme un sphinx incompris...[35]

Again Oedipus confronts the Sphinx, yet neither the questioner not the questioned knows the valid answer.

7

The Great Mother is one of those primordial conceptions in which the art of the nineteenth century is rooted. In the sensual warmth of the world of motherhood the creative artist was to find the security that cool reason and an historical consciousness could not afford him. Two types of womanhood especially occupied the artist's imagination. One of these is really a reversion to the Good Mother and stands for nature pure and simple. Its portrayal is bound up with the whole process of nature's growth, blossoming and ripening, of which it is the living symbol. The Great Mother is wholly absorbed in her existence as a physical creature.

She is not particularized, since she is herself connected with all living things. She is an anonymous creature, who stops short at the threshold of individuality. It is while she is at hand to exercise her influence that the art of the nineteenth century achieves a happy understanding between man and nature; it is under her guidance that the artist finds his way into the unclouded felicity of true harmony and companionship, which is the earthly paradise.

The other Sphinx-like archetype stands in opposition – not embedded, as it were, in the processes of nature, but a symbol of loneliness. The Sphinx stands outside all human order and relationships, which means that, like all that is extraordinary and abnormal, she belongs to Nietzsche's criminal category. Alone with her questions she lives, like Prometheus, within her rocky prison, beyond redemption. In his *Atta Troll* Heine gave a defence of Salome which, provided we take for granted the romantic mingling of lust and cruelty, might well apply to every other manifestation of the *femme fatale*. Has any woman, he asks, ever asked for the head of a man whom she did not love? If we discount the irony, this question is the Romantic's confession of the eroticism of death which turns the act of love into a sacrificial ritual or a Black Mass. 'I loved her and destroyed her' says Manfred – the lustful murder is the final phase of the embrace, even as death itself is permeated by lust and eroticized. 'Mêlons des voluptés à la mort' – so speaks the dream figure of a woman in Chateaubriand's *René*.[36]

This is the fate of the Sphinx – destruction of others or self-destruction. In the trial of strength between man and woman only one can remain the victor. To this time-honoured and uncompromising conflict modern romantic man adds fresh variants. He extends the mutual abuse of the sexes over a lifetime. Art now takes over new fields of experience – the estrangement of man and woman, the decline of feeling as association becomes a habit, the exhaustion of both partners by boredom, monotony and sheer emptiness – all of which leads ultimately to the leap into the abyss and to combined self-destruction.

Nineteenth century art thus succeeds in reawakening a mythical figure – that of the 'terrible mother' – though it fills in her outline with the problems of our shattered contemporary life. Like the man whom she enslaves the Sphinx-like *femme fatale* bears the stigma which Stendhal declared to be the fundamental experience of modern times: loneliness in the midst of a desert of humanity, loneliness that persists even within the conjugal embrace – a double isolation. The century, in so far as it is honest with itself, is sceptical and the reverse of naïve.[37] Behind its pleasures it experiences the weary indifference of ennui, behind its joy the bitter aftertaste of the *semper eadem* – the monotony of repetition. This pessimism, once a purely male attribute, is now impressed on the woman – not, of course, on the innocent unthinking creature of nature, but on the all-knowing Sphinx whose questioning look has a two-fold meaning – temptation and its companion boredom. The harlot is Don Juan's counterpart (compare again Wagner's Kundry), as she seeks a partner to release her from her ennui.

The 'terrible mother' differs from the Good Mother in that she can be analysed psychologically. Painters and poets – probably for the first time – were in the nineteenth century confronted by the problem of woman, while in the practical world of affairs the 'woman question' began to be discussed.[38] What till now had been the privilege of the Great Man, is transferred to woman – namely, isolation. The situation is not without paradox. Woman most quickly becomes the equal of man at just that point where she feels herself to be oppressed and misused by him – at the point of inner despair. The psychic and inner emancipation preceded the legal one and was largely its efficient cause. In a word, woman had first to attain the full spiritual possession of her own personality before she could demand juridical equality of rights.

191 DAUMIER *Le drame*; 1856–60.

COROT

192 COROT Ophelia; 1871.

193 MANET Faure as Hamlet; 1877.

194 DEGAS *Mlle. Fiocre dans le ballet de "La Source"*; 1866–68.

195 TOULOUSE-LAUTREC *"Messaline"* à l'Opéra de Bordeaux; 1900.

196 DEGAS *Le ballet de "Robert le Diable"*; 1872.

197 TOULOUSE-LAUTREC *Au Moulin Rouge*; c. 1892.

198 SEURAT *La Parade*; 1889.

As to art, in the first half of the century it had no response to make to woman's awakening consciousness. The episodes of Paolo and Francesca and of Count Ugolino, scenes from the *Divine Comedy* that were most frequently made the subject of illustration and similar pictures of ill-fated love, held a monopoly. Their points of psychological interest were never fully exploited. It is only towards the middle of the century that jealousy, estrangement and conflict were reckoned worthy of pictorial representation. Blake's title-page, referred to earlier, which shows woman between her lawful owner and the man she loves, is a significant anticipation and points to a theme to which some decades later the Pre-Raphaelites were to devote themselves – forbidden love which social convention looks upon with contempt and drives into concealment, the suppressed and fettered instinct which can find no fulfilment. Quite as English as the idea of persecuted and baulked desire, is the moral volte-face at the halfway point. The flight from convention ends in self-accusation. In Holman Hunt's 'Awakening Conscience' (1854) (plate 138) – the picture was painted two years before the publication of *Madame Bovary* – this problem is spun out to the proportions of an essay. The seducer seduced declares herself guilty; she foresees the future, which Ruskin describes with moving words in his remarks on the picture – poverty, an outcast's life, wandering upon the streets.[39] If one accepts the statement by this champion of the Pre-Raphaelites, that with this work art has taken its place beside literature, one cannot but be aware of the formal weakness revealed by the picture in the contest with the written word. Its complete and explicit detail never lets the form of the picture come alive at all. The picture's importance consists in one fact alone – that, for the first time and with unconcealed directness, it openly brings a new theme before the public: the awakening consciousness of woman – *si triste dans la volupté* – who has been suddenly endowed with knowledge, and feels that the man who holds her in his arms is miles away from her. More primitive and innocent is the strange look, suggesting second sight, of the beggar maid to whom King Cophetua looks up (plate 143).

We see it again, in the setting of the Annunciation, in Rossetti's 'Ecce Ancilla Domini' (plate 96). This virginal Sphinx, who for the first time has become aware of man, is typified in Munch's 'Puberty' (1894) (plate 136), from which a direct road leads to his 'Scream'. (From Burne-Jones' 'Blessed Damozel' there is a direct line of spiritual experience leading to Munch's 'Girl on a bridge'.)

Munch, whose iconographic 'family tree' still needs fuller examination, is the connecting point for a number of threads. He inherited from the Pre-Raphaelites the type of chaste and somewhat melancholy maiden. Continental painting in the seventies and eighties prepared the way for him in portraying the sullen marital conflict. One recalls Degas ('Bouderie', 'Intérieur' (plate 126), 'L'absinthe' (plate 161)), Menzel ('Railway Carriage') and Böcklin ('Triton and Nereid' (plate 115), 'Odysseus and Calypso').

Munch aims at something more than an analysis of desertion or parting ('The morning after' (plate 130), 'Jealousy', 'Ashes' (plate 137)); he seeks rather to combine symbolically the different tensions between the sexes. Yet, perhaps unconsciously, he revives that favourite theme of the temptation of man, to whom woman offers herself for the choice – the Judgement of Paris. How close his interpretation of the theme comes to that of a painter engaged on illustrating mythology, is shown by a comparison with Klinger's 'Judgement of Paris' (1886–1887). The spirit of both belongs to the *fin de siècle*; both pose the same question – the riddle of woman. Two contemporaries seem to give two closely related verdicts. Haendcke[40] writes on Klinger's work: 'Naked Hera approaches Paris with open arms, Athene half shows him her back, Aphrodite comes close to him half concealed in a red cloak. Three types of women, the sophisticated *grisette*, the virtuous maiden, the mature woman, proud of the honour due to her'. Compare what Schiefler[41] says about Munch's etching 'Woman' (1895): 'In the middle, thick-limbed, the woman governed by sensual impulse; to the right the woman in black in mystic mood; to the left a virginal figure, the embodiment of the childish, flower-like nature of woman.' (If we forget the sharply-drawn psychological characterization, then the three figures, like Leibl's 'Three women at church' (plate 93), might symbolize the three stages of life.)

Some years later in the 'Dance of Life' (1899-1900) (plate 218) Munch combines the symbolism of the stages of life with that of the 'Judgement of Paris'. The decision has been made; like Paris, the man has decided in favour of the allurement of the senses, the seduction of the middle stage of life. The maiden and the old woman suffer the fate of the rejected. And there are onlookers whom life has passed by. The pair that enquiringly hold each other's hands will be driven by the whirlwind of the instincts. In the ecstasy of their embrace they will seek the fusion of their desires and the breathless storm of passion, at the end of which wait disillusion and estrangement.

The misunderstood loneliness of women, to which man is blind, whether he approaches his partner violently or in humility – this is the final line that the century draws under the battle of the sexes. There is nothing of the sacred equality and harmony prophesied by the Saint-Simonists, nothing of that other dance of life found in the Moulin de la Galette. There is no illusion now, but bitterness, mutual recrimination, the awakening conscience, jealousy, mistrust, estrangement and a speechless co-existence that knows no more to say.

XI   The Earthly Paradise

*All peoples have visions of this kind, down to the most humble
picture of a land of idleness - so wretched are the circumstances
in which the ordinary individual has to live.*

Jacob Burckhardt

I

THE time when man was in 'direct communication with heaven' had passed. In the nineteenth century faith lost the extra dimension that took it into another world and transferred heaven and hell into the present one. Men believed that the promise of paradise, of happiness and contentment, could be made good here and now. The prospect offered by religion of a life after death gave place to an ambition that could be satisfied on earth. But although the nineteenth century hoped again and again for an earthly fulfilment, and looked forward with frantic enthusiasm to the coming of the Kingdom of God, in doing so it did not make a pseudo-religious act of faith as in Büchner's 'comfortable religion', adapted to a collective desire for happiness; it merely sought to give to human life, from which God's presence had been removed, abundance, a mission, significance and justification, in an earthly paradise existing now. Though he no longer had a place in a world beyond, man was still determined not to have lived in vain. The hope of an earthly paradise went hand in hand with the fear that life should prove wholly without meaning.

The hope developed in various ways. The opposing forces of history and life, characteristic of the century, were once again at work and presented antithetical conceptions of the earthly paradise. I propose to illustrate this by contrasting two contemporary writers: Castagnary and Burckhardt. In his *Philosophie du Salon de 1857* Castagnary, the friend of Courbet, laid the foundations of his humanitarian realism, as he then conceived it. He starts out from the conviction that the development of art is analogous to that of man. There is an identity between the artist and society even though the artist always remains himself. Once art glorified gods and heroes, now it must be devoted to the apotheosis of man. To express his views in a clearer and more visual form, the prophet of realism did not shrink from allegorical embellishment; he placed the following words in the mouth of man, who was assumed now to have attained full consciousness of self: 'Beside the divine garden from which I have been expelled, I will erect a new Eden ... At its entrance I will set up Progress ... and I will give a flaming sword into his hand and he will say to God, "Thou shalt not enter here". And thus it was that man began to build up the human community.'

The nineteenth century briefly occupied this *cité humaine* of progress in the artificial paradise constructed at the World Exhibitions. It dreamed of it in the communal life of the Saint-Simonists and the Fourierists. Castagnary, for whom the earthly paradise was a paradise of progress, claimed for the artist the ability to create out of his own experience of the present a new humanitarian vision of happiness and contentment which would be no less compelling than that of mythological art, though it was to make no use of the latter's forms and themes.

Burckhardt[1] thought quite differently. In a lecture given at Basle in 1876, he praised Homer's Phaeacian island of Scheria, a land of bliss, as an example of antiquity's wonderful creative imagination. 'We should thank the gods', he said, 'that a great poem of the past should anticipate such a happy state of affairs, for modern poetry no longer possesses the means to do it.' Later he said: 'It is a good thing that past ages have relieved us of the labour of portraying a more sublime world in poetic terms. Our "emotion" would trip us up a thousand times.'

There were, as we have seen, both conservative and revolutionary conceptions of the Golden Age;[2] in the latter man actively takes possession of the world, in the former he is given over to idleness and pleasure. There are memories of a peaceful state of nature and visions of a communal spirit leading man on to ever higher stages of civilization. The socialist utopias exalted the active planning of human happiness, but the dreams of purely subjective bliss were satisfied with the voluntary choice of a rich life lived to the full, and their escapist worlds were modelled on the legendary extravagances of antiquity. The disciples of the religion of reason hoped for a return of man's early unclouded natural state; their opponents, repelled by the industry and activity of modern civilization, sought to revive the elemental existence of exotic worlds. Those who believed in the past, according to their individual tastes, swore by antiquity, the Middle Ages, or the Renaissance, while the champions of the present proclaimed a classless paradise won by active effort. Every religious, artistic or social creed had its ideal of harmony and contentment, though not every one of these ideals was susceptible of artistic interpretation. The artistic conception of the earthly paradise was always most convincingly 'at home' when it needed no literary or ideological programme, when in fact its vision of happiness, harmony and brotherhood was based on some powerful but essentially artistic idea, on some formal ideal of natural perfection.

2

At the beginning of the century two periods of the past competed for recognition as the paradisial age – antiquity and the Christian Middle Ages. In both of these the artist who sought assurance from the past saw both an ideal condition of human happiness giving unity to life and the epitome of a truly artistic culture. In those days, he argued, the artist was a significant member of human society with his sphere of work clearly defined and his thematic and formal repertoire universally accepted and so guaranteed. Both the antique and the mediaeval paradise offered the artist the natural spontaneity in which he believed.

In 1782, François Hemsterhuis published his dialogue *Alexis or The Golden Age*.[3] In it, following Hesiod, the author described that first age of the world when there were as yet no seasons. The earth stood steady in its course. Day and night were of equal length, every climatic zone maintained a constant degree of warmth. 'Nature, undisturbed and constant, offered man far more nourishing fruits and herbs, species which were later to be destroyed through the rapid succession of the seasons. Man and beast found their nourishment close at hand, and none was subjected to the melancholy necessity of feeding on the blood and entrails of a fellow creature ... Every human being considered himself the happiest creature on earth and so all ambition and all desire to acquire wealth or to embark on conquest were rendered impossible ... And the total ignorance of evil removed from morality both its strain and its sense of triumph, which today seems to us so bright and glorious ... In those days man, for whom all evil and all fear were absurd, passed from life as though from waking to sleep, or rather the opposite, and laid his body aside as does the growing fruit the blossom that announces its coming.'

Then the moon approached close to the earth and brought all the elements into confusion. True, man became once more conscious of beauty, but there was less harmony amongst things and the new beauty was more uncertain and more insecure than the previous one. Since that time only beasts are happy upon earth. Hemsterhuis saw in the philosophy of enlightenment the surety for a return of the Golden Age. Like Fichte in his *Grundzügen des gegenwärtigen Zeitalters* (Fundamental Character of the Present Age) he saw human history ending with the attainment of perfect rationality. This will occur when man has attained 'a healthy and correct equilibrium between his desires and the objects lying within his immediate sphere of effectiveness'. This is, word for word, the formal programme that the classicism of the nineteenth century was seeking to realize, an enlightened beauty subject to reason and moderation: not a vague, unconstrained creative urge, but static, comprehensible forms; no wild excess, but clear definition; restrained, not passionate, expressions of emotion – an equilibrium of capacity and will. The earthly paradise of the classicist is culture – and a vision of form.

I give two examples of this – Schinkel's 'The Blossoming of Greece' (1825) and Ingres' 'Golden Age' (begun 1843) (plate 207). Schinkel painted a panorama of culture, an informative historical painting in which the artist's formal vision of paradise had to give place to a descriptive philosophical programme. It is a picture of activity, not of unencumbered enjoyment; a transient moment of history, not a state of nature that lasts forever. The 'blossom' has in this case been made by human hands and lacks that air of being naturally at rest within itself, of organic security.

Ingres painted no vision of cultural activity, but a friendly gathering. Pressed close together, clinging to the earth or standing upright, these people form a harmoniously interwoven group, with flowing lines streaming through the whole. The painter received the commission in 1859 to decorate the great hall of the castle of Dampierre with a representation of the Golden Age. The dominant ideas of the work are described in a number of letters.[4] 'A heap of beautiful idlers! I have interpreted the Golden Age just as the poets of antiquity imagined it. The people of this race did not know old age at all. They lived long and always in beauty. So there were no old people. They were good, just and loved one another. The fruits of the earth, the water of the springs, milk and nectar provided their only nourishment. Thus they lived, and their death was a falling asleep. After death they turned into good spirits, and cared for mankind. Astraea frequently visited them and taught them to love justice and to practise it. Thus they lived and in Heaven Saturn joined in their happiness.'

Another letter describes the three centres of the composition, each of which represents one of the three seasons of antiquity. The middle one is devoted to peace and the summer; the left half, in which Astraea appears, represents the spring and justice; while in the right we see the ripe fullness of autumn. With this there corresponds a formal rhythm, moving from left to right and gradually dying away. The spring group comprises slender, linked figures suggesting upward growth; the dancing figures representing summer open out from one another to form a circle; in the right hand group the ripe fruit of humanity is reunited with the earth, their surfeited attitude as they lie there contrasting with the vertical group opposite. One can also read the composition from right to left; the recumbent figures would then represent the union of the sexes – the uninterrupted pairing of man and woman, united with water and the earth – while the group around Astraea would symbolize man erect, whose sense of justice has awakened.

This 'Golden Age', whose ideological programme is possibly based on Hemsterhuis, is an altar picture for the cult of antiquity. Ingres, who treated the ancient manner of art and life with almost religious reverence, was really painting a picture in which he expressed all his longings and religious faith; he put on canvas his dream of beauty, harmony and grace which his own surroundings seemed too uninspired to realize. The theme suited his temperament and he gave it all that lay in his power: the leisurely companionship, the restful stillness and the restrained yet purely animal life that marked an age 'when man and beast were on the same level'. Rarely did this artist with his knowledgeable and calculating mind achieve a similar degree of unconscious naturalness of form.

3

Novalis at the beginning of his fragment *Christendom or Europe* (1799) has a vision of humanity with an equally religious colouring. It is fascinating to observe how curiously this acceptance of a Catholic world order foreshadowed the utopias of those who believed in social progress, and how closely connected at one central point – that of the religious cult of love – was the Messianism of the French social reformers with the Romantic vision of the New Jerusalem, while at the same the ideal of the English reformers – as with Novalis – also centred round the picture of mediaeval society in which all men were brothers. In all these utopias modern man was taking up arms against the trend that was threatening to make him a mere anonymous member of the mass. The man of the nineteenth century was in need of this Fata Morgana of an earthly paradise, since the world about him was growing uglier every day.

Novalis developed two conceptions of his paradise. One was cosmic and organic – this we can trace throughout his *Heinrich von Ofterdingen* – the other was political and historical, its social theory being contained in his *Christendom*. 'Those were beautiful and brilliant days when Europe was a Christian land, when One Christendom dwelt in this part of the world that man had constructed. A great common interest united the most distant provinces of this broad spiritual kingdom ... Though lacking great worldly possessions, a single head united and guided the great political forces ... A numerous fraternity, which stood open to any man to join, was placed directly under him; it carried out his directives and strove zealously to strengthen his beneficent power ... With what lightness of heart could every man complete his daily task, since through these holy men his future life was assured, every wrongful act was forgiven, every ugly incident in his life wiped out and its stain removed ... Peace went out from them, and they preached nothing but love for the holy and lovely Lady of Christendom who, equipped with divine powers, was prepared to save every one of the faithful from the most terrible dangers.' Thus it was that in those days people lived with light hearts and full of the fear of God. Death was not for them a painful thing, since it promised reunion with those they loved. Arts, sciences and commerce flourished. Yet man was not yet ripe for this glorious kingdom. Concern with worldly affairs and self-interest laid hold of him, personal whims and desires complicated the hitherto simple conditions of life and loosened the communal bonds. Greed and the desire for material well-being drove out the nobler aspirations. Man now seemed 'more concerned with his immediate interests. And so the lovely blossom of youth, faith and love made room for the coarser fruits of knowledge and possessiveness'. Novalis fixed his exalted hopes upon the future, which after the destructive centuries between the Reformation and the French Revolution would restore universal and hierarchic order to mankind. 'At present we have only crude and disconnected hints of this, but they reveal to the historian's eye a universal character, a new kind of history, a new humanity, the sweetest embrace of a young surprised Church and a beloved God, and even the conception of a new Messiah in a thousand hearts simultaneously.' The fragment ends with the promise: 'Only have patience – it will, it must come, the holy time of everlasting peace, when the New Jerusalem will be the capital of the world'.

Christianity is the true religion of love. In Novalis' fragments[5] there are two further revealing aphorisms: 'Our whole life is a form of divine worship', and again, 'The Christian religion is the truly sensual religion. Sin is the great attempt to entice the love of the Deity.' The West European Social Reformers also exalted love as the force that would bind together in harmony the new universal order. But their mechanical belief in progress took from Christianity the idea of fulfilment in the next world in order to achieve it in this one – in the earthly paradise.[6] Fourier insisted that instead of suppressing the instincts, we should free and enrich them (Blake developed similar ideas in his poetry), and he saw human life governed by passions, which could be divided into three classes and twelve categories but were capable of forming a harmonious union. The basic passion for him was the Christian love of one's neighbour. 'Since God wishes to draw us towards Himself through pleasure and mutual attraction we can conclude that any ordering of Society incapable of combining utility with pleasure and luxury deviates from the paths laid down by Him.'[7]

Saint-Simonism is another such 'comfortable religion'.[8] Science, industry and religion formed a trinity of progress. Work and leisure were harmonized with one another, the former bringing weariness, the latter recreation. Because of a desire to do service to the community, purely utilitarian activity, which Novalis regarded as the great source of impoverishment in human relations, was exalted as the chief end of life. With the help of a refurbished Christianity, transformed into a 'moral and social doctrine', this new ethic of labour was to realize the purpose of human society, the material advancement of the poor. 'We are marching towards the Holy City, the New Jerusalem which Christians have beheld, but God has left to us to build. Peace upon earth! The day is coming when God will reign both in Heaven and upon earth, in the flesh and in the spirit, when the natural sciences will be formed into dogma, and the arts will not be profane pleasures but the expression of divine morality, when industry will be the true cult of the eternal ...'.[9]

With his 'systematic cult of humanity' Comte developed this idea of a 'Church of Intelligence'.[10] From Catholicism he took over the cult of the 'Great Mother' and claimed a right of inheritance against its churches and cathedrals. He followed the Christian principle of order, but did away completely with its religious content. Man's mature and scientific age is to find its fulfilment in the positivist 'natural' religion of humanity.

In the Communist Manifesto there is yet another prophecy of a paradise upon earth. It contains, as Löwith penetratingly showed,[11] an eschatological message. The final crisis of the bourgeois capitalist world corresponds to the Last Judgement, the world-historical role of the Proletariat, by which the whole of mankind is saved, corresponds to that of the Chosen People. The differences of class were to be resolved by an 'association' in which the free development of every individual was to be the condition of the free development of all. The 'Reign of Freedom' which results from this is a Kingdom of God with God left out.

The Romantic cult of the Middle Ages had its home in England in the second half of the century. It became the foundation of a reformist movement embracing the whole of life. Ruskin and Morris, its two apostles, spread the gospel with active religious zeal and sought to build a bridge between the Christian Utopia of Novalis and the socialist brotherhood of the future.[12] Their work reconciled – rather paradoxically perhaps – the poetically transfigured feudalism of the past with a vision of a planned and aesthetically governed Golden Age. The nineteenth century's laissez-faire philosophy, which led to social and artistic chaos, was repudiated, the organic and creative organization of the mediaeval builders' chapels was admired, and the Gothic age praised as a time when all men had a share in art. At the same time these reformers worked earnestly for a radical purification of taste, a new coherence of style and new collectively organized works of art. Morris dreamed of the London of Chaucer, 'small, and white and clean', and his socialist city of the future, described in *News from Nowhere* (1891), seems like an idyllic small town – low and pretty houses on the banks of the Thames surrounded by gardens of flowers, friendly dwellings radiating comfort and happiness. About the time when this paradisial ideal was committed to paper, British town-planning was evolving similar solutions in its garden cities.[13]

The intention and the achievement, the radical desire to change and the aristocratic conservatism, were fundamentally irreconcilable. It is true that Morris repudiated the purely sensual appeal of art for art's sake, yet the beautiful products of his own Kelmscott Press were obviously designed for a small circle of enthusiasts. One understands the nature of this fine idealism if – again somewhat paradoxically – one disregards the aristocratic exclusiveness of its actual products and only takes it at its face value as a purely ethical conception. Then its message is revealed as one of earthly happiness, in which art assumes the task of spreading happiness and joy.

Ruskin preached that art is the expression of man's joy in his work. He declared that he did not want to make an artist of a carpenter, but rather to make the carpenter more happy – and this is the central idea of his aesthetic Messianism. Following his teacher, Ruskin, Morris coined the inspiring formula: 'Art is to be made by the people and for the people, as a happiness to the maker and the user'.[14] Art was not only to beautify life by being combined, as it once was, with utility, but was to be a bond between creator and user. Artistic activity, rid of aristocratic preciosity, was to be at the service of the brotherhood of mankind. It was to free those who engaged in it from boredom and unrest. This was a doctrine of idealistic utilitarianism.

The connection between the artist and the social reformer took various forms. In England, where there was a revival of the applied arts, it was closer and more fruitful than in France, where plans for social reform in the first half of the century – though there is special relevance in the Saint-Simonist doctrine to the World Exhibitions – found little echo or corresponding vision in the artist's imagination. The points where art and life touched one another in France were of a more general nature. Saint-Simon and Fourier proclaimed the advent of a world harmony in which there would be physical well-being, sensual pleasure and freedom from all conflict – a brotherly reunion of all men in an open democratic society. The trend in nineteenth century art that expressed a sense of *joie de vivre*, showed the same spirit; its formal expression became constantly looser and more open – more picturesque, in fact – and revealed markedly sensuous features. This increasingly feminine outlook was directed towards the whole world of external objects, which to the artist appeared to be in a state of continuous intermingling, and thus to be a complex of coloured, homogeneous 'impressions'. The similarity between objects seemed more important than their differences and they had all to be considered as of equal value.

Art as a symbol of the joy of life – this essential ideal of Morris and Ruskin connected them with French Impressionism. In England the ideal was accompanied by an ambitious attempt to achieve a uniform style; on the continent it developed into the spontaneous expression of visual sensations. Both movements attempted, like those of social reformers, to master one of the problems of the nineteenth century. They sought to reconcile art with life, private with public needs. They sought to win back both for life and for art complete fulfilment and homogeneity. Art, says Morris, is to be merged with life, all are to have a part in it, all are to delight in it. 'Fellowship is life, lack of fellowship is death'. This too is a dream of the earthly paradise.

4

The Golden Age dreamt of by the Romantic individualists was very different. Work, utility, the common good and progress – none of these had a place in their visions. Idleness, beauty with no trace of utility, and a purely private delight in being alive were all that mattered. Aristocratic exclusiveness, not democratic mixing, was the ideal of the men who sought to live after this fashion.

A year before Fichte expounded his ethic of labour in *Der geschlossene Handelsstaat* (The Complete Industrial State), in which he declared that man could only attain prosperity by work and could not expect it from nature,[15] Schlegel in his *Lucinde* (1799) had exalted paradisial idleness. 'Man's desire for rest is a relic of that divine image which he has lost ... O idleness, thou art the breath of life for innocence and enthusiasm – the saints breathe thee in, and blessed is he who possesses and cherishes thee ...' And later: 'It is the right to be idle that differentiates the distinguished from the common; it is the true principle of aristocracy. The highest form of the full life is pure vegetation; and the more godlike man and his works are, the greater is his likeness to the plants'. The cult of leisure should be made into an art, a science, a religion, 'for work and industry are angels of death which prevent man's return to paradise.'

Some decades later this *dolce far niente* became the refuge of the bored and the blasé who had

gambled their lives away and were seeking to escape from themselves. Such people did not know why they were in the world at all – like Kierkegaard's 'aesthetic man' – and sought to forget their own emptiness and lack of character in a purely vegetable existence. 'I know what you want better than you do yourself', are the words which Büchner puts into the mouth of his Prince. 'We have broken our clocks and forbidden all calendars; we count the hours and the months only by the clock of the flowers and the growth of blossom and fruit.' And Valerio, the wise fool, tells a story of a future state of bliss. 'A decree will be published that anyone found to have blisters on his hands will be put under guardianship; that whoever works himself sick will be punishable as a criminal; and that anyone who boasts of earning his bread by the sweat of his brow will be declared mad and a danger to human society. Then we shall lie in the shade and pray to God for macaroni, melons and figs, for musical voices and classical bodies, and a "comfortable religion".'

A year later, in 1845, Théophile Gautier published his famous preface to *Mademoiselle de Maupin*. A weary hedonism, thirsting for new sensations, mocked at virtue in the name of vice, and represented progress as meaningless. What had the so-called 'perfectibility' of man brought us that we did not have in as good or even better form before the flood? If, however, anyone succeeded in inventing a new pleasure, he would deserve a prize, 'for pleasure', says Gautier, 'seems to me to be the purpose of life and the only truly useful thing upon this earth. God willed it so, Who created women and pleasant scents, light, flowers, wine, spirited horses, greyhounds and Persian cats, and did not say to His angels, be virtuous, but – be full of love'. Man was created for pleasure, and what distinguishes him from the beasts is not that he can read newspapers and keep records, but that he can make love at all seasons of the year.

When Couture exhibited his 'Rome in her decline' (plate 82) in 1847, Gautier found in it a confirmation of his ideal of uninhibited enjoyment, but he also recognized that here pleasure had been carried to the point where it turned into weariness, where the orgy became a battle and excess became boredom.[16] The aesthetic hedonist, whom at about this time Kierkegaard monumentalized in the figure of Nero, became weary of himself because of his inner emptiness, which he sought to get rid of through novel and ever varying sensations, but from which there was no escape. The 'paradis terrestre', as Rimbaud pointed out, turns into a 'paradis de tristesse',[17] that is to say, into one of those 'artificial paradises' in which despairing sensuality finds its home.

In Couture's picture there are two themes – the flaring up of passion and its dying away. Makart's 'Plague in Florence' (1868) selected one of them – and that the more dramatic – and speeded up its tempo till it became a raging orgy of death. Feuerbach in his 'The Symposium' (1873) (plate 85) makes an idealized reply to the famous picture by his Parisian teacher and gives a more positive expression to the dual note struck in the latter. He dignifies Couture's tired, surfeited figures and gives them the thoughtful tranquillity of a group of philosophers; and those who with uncertain gestures were making one last effort to rise are transformed to give a proud welcome to Alcibiades. There is a significant accord between the two opposing ideas; expansive love of life faces a dignified gathering of wise men. The truth of Hölderlin's saying that he who has thought most deeply loves that which is most truly alive, is here depicted with classic nobility. Feuerbach's strength and restraint, the thoughtful profundity of his composition, held in check any tendency towards lively spontaneity.

5

Feuerbach's vision of antiquity and Makart's of the Renaissance are aesthetic ideals. The late eighteenth century saw these visions of paradise, but in the nineteenth they underwent a twofold change. The concepts of history and life again indicate the two methods of interpretation. One method sought to capture a living principle; its aim was to free the old 'models' of their purely formal significance and conceive of them as vital and natural sources of creative inspiration. It was in this sense that Cézanne and Marées regarded the art of the past as providing them with models for their work, and it was in this way that Renoir reacted to the art of Raphael. The other approach did not seek to get to the inner meaning behind the form, but confined itself to the surface features of antiquity and the Renaissance. It concentrated on matters of archaeological detail, on the minutiae of cultural history, on literary and mythological tradition. This was the approach of Cornelius and Ingres, of Couture, Feuerbach and Makart.

The art to which Heinse, Fuseli and the young Goethe were receptive, in which they could perceive a perfect harmony between beauty and energy, between spontaneous expression and self-conscious artistry, lost its simple and direct appeal in the course of the eighteenth century; its content and subject-matter became the centre of a conflict. Originally, before the ancient world had been divided into categories by the dry-as-dust scholars, eager hopes were centred not only on a humanist educational ideal, but on the rebirth of the natural man, 'strong at the core', of whom Nietzsche was to speak a century later, and on a new flowering of the arts; but in this dream there already lay concealed a destructive tendency, the germ of an aesthetic cult of the past, the first stirrings of the attempt to escape from social reality, as in one who says: 'How glad I shall be when I can once more move among men who go naked and among whom I can go naked myself'.[18] Such a dream of an earthly paradise where there is no concealment set its hopes upon a happy community free of all insincerity and artificial conventions. Unfortunately it refused to admit that contemporary civilization had any beauty, greatness or power whatsoever, and so created an unbridgeable gulf between the wicked, restrictive present and the paradise of the past. The further the century progressed, the more slender grew the hope of a living re-creation of antiquity, and even its official representatives, so to speak, namely the historical painters, confined themselves to stylized recollections, academic poses and erudite reconstructions. These leading figures of the nineteenth century, with their reactionary prejudices, doubted the vitality of their own age and sought to recapture the lost integrity of life by wearing borrowed costumes. Their reconstructions of an artificial paradise and their dramatic presentation of history actually affected the present. Art, of a theatrical and rather precious kind, had an influence on life, but only to make it ridiculous; since men had no faith in the ordinary life of the time, it had to be disguised in the trappings of the past. Thus during the Second Empire Prince Napoleon had a Pompeian house[19] erected in the centre of Paris in which he 'played at antiquity' (plate 84), while Makart in a rather less distinguished fashion, though on much the same level of culture and intelligence, arranged riotous artists' parties in his sumptuous studio, at which the guests indulged their high spirits in Renaissance or Baroque costume (plate 109). All this play-acting was devised to obliterate the boundaries between art and life, between fiction and reality, and to send life to the schoolroom of history. Félicien Rops' luxury yacht and Swinburne's house in Chelsea (a 'Palace of Arts' of the kind that Morris had dreamed of), and the castles of Ludwig II, all these substitutes for the real world must also be counted among the century's visions of paradise, even though what was once a genuine veneration of antiquity and the Renaissance as sources of new and vital inspiration, was here perverted into an artificial pose wholly unrelated to life.

Even at the end of the eighteenth century there was already an awareness of something that Gauguin was later to reduce to a formula[20] – the rejuvenating power of the barbaric. There was a search for primitive language, primitive poetry and primitive people. Nature has departed from us and hidden herself, said Herder[21]. Thus, following Rousseau, people expressed their dissatisfaction with civilization by rejecting it, and looked for the natural (one of the most important nineteenth century images) in two spheres – in antiquity and in exotic lands. The historically minded escaped into the past, the lovers of the exotic into distant countries. The latter remained within the present, but gave it an extreme geographic extension; the earthly paradise was removed to territories that had not yet been touched by civilization or by any of its institutions. At the end of the eighteenth century and the beginning of the nineteenth, when nature and antiquity were held to be identical, both lines of escape seemed to coincide. Nature, the refuge – since Rousseau's pessimistic analysis of culture – of those who could no longer find a foot-hold in their own surroundings, led these dissatisfied spirits directly to antiquity, which was regarded as nature's most superb manifestation.

The strange thing is that even the hostile camps of the nineteenth century continued to believe in this identity between nature and antiquity, despite the fact that they administered the formal heritage of antiquity in very different ways. Ingres would have nothing to do with idealism and considered himself a humble servant of nature. One of his pupils attributed to him the merit of having rediscovered nature's inexhaustible richness.[22] Castagnary compared Millet's 'Les glaneuses' (plate 167) to Homer; Rivière called Cézanne a Greek.[23] It was only later that the formal breach was felt to be irreparable. Puvis de Chavannes, says Gauguin,[24] 'is a Greek, I am a savage'. Antiquity and nature began to exclude one another. His radical point of view justified Gauguin. Puvis de Chavannes' vision of paradise took its constituent parts from the Mediterranean world; the undeniable greatness of his pictorial ideas, to which Gauguin owed much of his inspiration, fell short of any final formal concentration. An embarrassing trace of classicism can be perceived round the outlines of his figures, like a restricti frame, and it prevents their complete harmony with nature. Cézanne, Gauguin and Marées, who had greater powers of construction at their command, overcame this obstacle and achieved a far higher degree of naturalism.

Here I must say a word concerning a new romantic quality of experience which since the end of the eighteenth century had obtruded itself between lofty idealism and the commonplace – the picturesque. This is connected with the primitive and the natural, and therefore with the earthly paradise. The picturesque always becomes a necessity when aesthetic taste (which must be assumed, for it is an aesthetic phenomenon) demands lively colours, when the commonplace has begun to weary us, when things that are natural and close at hand no longer satisfy us and we begin to seek a change. The picturesque does not exist without its contrary – the unpicturesque, the charmless, the inexpressive. It is only when the world exhibits blind spots of indifference to what is set before it that the picturesque begins to assert itself and tries out its more expressive make-up, though it often happens that the real world is actually more brightly coloured and is then seen to be more genuine and more natural. This was true of the exoticisms of the nineteenth century. They provided new sources of sensual pleasure for the dulled eye of civilized man, and also new insights into natural forms of life. And it was the romantic movement that made the artist especially interested in 'races which civilization, as it presses in upon them, has not yet deprived of their original character nor stripped of their national rights'. As an example of this Heine points to scenes from the Tyrolese mountains and from rural life in Italy, where the artist can find 'that ideal nature, that primitive nobility of appearance and those picturesque costumes for which the artist's heart longs.'[25] These are the picturesque manifestations of the earthly paradise.

Exoticism and orientalism sought to experience the present in its unspoiled freshness and to bridge the gap between the ideal and the real. The weaker elements tended to indulge merely in ethnological anecdotes; for the stronger talents the picturesque represented literally a pictorial, that is to say an essential gain. Delacroix returned from his Moroccan journey not only with new themes, but with a freshened palette. Deeply conscious of the growing ugliness and narrowness of the civilized world, the artist sought for one that was more open and more natural. When he managed to find it, his manner of giving form to his ideas became more open and more free.

199 MENZEL Room with a balcony; 1845.

200 VUILLARD *Intérieur*; 1899.

201 MONET *Le Boulevard des Capucines*; 1873.

202 RENOIR *Paysage*; c. 1873.

205 MONET *Le déjeuner*; C. 1872–1874.

204 RENOIR *Le Moulin de la Galette*; 1876.

205 RENOIR *La balançoire*; 1876.

206 MONET Rouen Cathedral; 1894.

Just as some artists were historically minded and reached back in time to antiquity and the Middle Ages, others made a geographical journey to the countries at the edge of Europe – to Spain, Italy and the Balkans – or went to the Near East, to Morocco or to distant islands. Stendhal[26] admired the Italians because they had not yet been captured by the 'modern ideal'. At about the same period Delacroix travelled through North Africa and discovered in the Arabs the descendents of Homer[27] – but Ingres reconstructed his pictures of antiquity from traditional sources. In the middle of the century Semper[28] was compelled to confess that the splendid colours of Algerian carpets were superior to anything that Europe could show in the way of applied arts. The judgement that he formed at the London Exhibition reduced to a formula the artist's ideal of the earthly paradise (the ideal of a natural perfection) – and it was as valid for the applied arts as it was for painting. 'What we must learn from the non-European peoples is the art of hitting on those simple and understandable melodies of form and colour which instinct provides for man's handiwork in its simplest form, but which are far more difficult to grasp and hold on to when richer means of expression are available.' It is in this direction that some decades later Gauguin was to make his search for natural perfection; form and content would both reveal the fullness and original freshness of paradise.

6

In his account of the Salon of 1831 Heine wrote: 'Our modern evening dress has about it something so fundamentally prosaic that it can only be used in a painting by way of parody'. Three decades later Manet's contemporaries might have felt much the same about the two men in his 'Déjeuner sur l'herbe' (plate 123). This picture produced a considerable shock-effect, since within a narrow compass it brought before people's minds one of the most acute controversies of the century – namely the relation of the naked to the clothed. Manet, both in form and content, had produced a dialectical picture, a picture of unreconciled contrasts, which confronted the natural world of woman with the artificial and civilized world of man.

If we introduce into this pictorial idea that of the earthly paradise, then the painting becomes a kind of *allégorie réelle* whose contrasting elements both challenge and support each other. If we start by looking at the nude female figure, then we see the two men as examples of a 'modern' reality, which is intended to remind us that the nakedness of the female partner is revealed not in a vague 'somewhere' but in the middle of the nineteenth century. As against this, if we start by looking at the men, then the woman has the effect of a pictorial theme which removes from the situation its transient character and its existence in a particular period of time, and raises it to the level of timelessness.

Such pictorial conceptions could never set a fashion. They remain exceptional, for their inner balance is inimitable. The last decades of the century simplified the problem and decided in favour either of the clothed paradise or of the naked one. A number of masterpieces achieved success along each of these two separate lines, and when we compare them with one another, we are able to forget the contrast so provocatively stated by Manet. The reason for this is that Impressionism preferred to suppress rather than emphasize any kind of dissonance. As Impressionism reconciled man with his surroundings, so also it reconciled him with the dress that his epoch happened to prescribe. Renoir's and Monet's people wear their clothes not as tight artificial integuments, but as pleasing and colourful adornments of the body. The Sunday visitors to the Grande Jatte have become entirely one with their clothing and, so to speak, melt into it (plate 190). The conflict between nature and civilization, between natural product and artefact, has been resolved in a truly monumental formal conception. The cylinder-shaped trousers and coats possess a ceremonial solemnity, banal though they are in themselves; and yet they have a certain similarity to the tree-trunks, a comparison which of course holds good in reverse. Even more than such formal analogies, the unbroken surface-texture of colour binds all the pictorial elements together so as to evoke a sense of permanence. In his own way Morris also sought at about this time to ennoble the banal clothes of civilization. What was in his mind can be seen in the pictures of Burne-Jones, Puvis de Chavannes and Marées – 'women not upholstered like armchairs'.

As against this, the naked human form no longer seemed so defiantly bare. 'Les grandes baigneuses' of Cézanne (plate 118) and the great compositions of Marées (see plate 213) show man and woman as creatures of nature. These figures have stripped off all surface eroticism and exchanged it for a pleasing naturalism that is not open to question. The effect is essentially chaste, for this is not civilization's tribute to love, but nature's. These are visions of paradise regained; they are not escapist pictures, but simple statements of the nature of man.

One feels that this last third of the century gives the idea of the earthly paradise a new direction. It identifies man's natural existence with a natural and straightforward formal expression. It seems to be striving towards a natural perfection of life and art – and this is the real message of the Golden Age. If we abstract the idea of the earthly paradise from its literary and mythological settings and seek the common factors in its different manifestations, we shall find the following characteristics: a life dominated by instinct rather than intellect, warmth of sensual perception, timelessness, permanence, the natural state, fellowship without effort or conflict – in a word, equilibrium.

We have thus indicated the point of view from which the artist of the second half of the nineteenth century conceived the earthly paradise. Of course the subjective motives which were at work should not be underestimated. Being no longer a member of any community, the artist sought to create in the earthly paradise a new bond among men – a thing impossible in his actual surroundings. He wanted a binding relationship in which he would be secure. The real motive for Gauguin's flight was a longing to strike roots somewhere, and he described this in a letter to his wife.[29] He wanted to be surrounded by a new family and to live in harmony with nature and with his art. He tried to bring art to the point where it was taken for granted as a normal manifestation of a full life, and so to forget the gap that existed between art and life.

The earthly paradise provided a theme in which a natural form matched a natural existence. It became for the artist a symbol of the rediscovery of man's original creative endowment. Marées wrote in 1869: 'I am confident that, after a process of purification, which may well be hard, man will once more return to his true uninhibited state, and so rightly reveal that which nature has granted him.' Four years later he wrote: 'A true artist remains above all else a product of nature: that is why he is so rare.' The life work of this painter was an uninterrupted endeavour to be simple again, to be a part of nature, to free himself from all artifice or virtuosity, to throw off the heavy weight of his artistic training and of the medium he had learnt to use, and to make what he had really learnt his own in such a fashion that nobody would ever call his full personal possession of it into question; he sought to regain the original innocence that was lost with original sin. That is why the Golden Age is truly the dominant theme of his art. It is the epitome of all that is genuine and devoid of artifice, of sincere trust between one man and another which needs no moral code to prescribe it.

A similar way of looking at the world is expressed by Cézanne: 'Genius would consist in bringing into the open the friendship of all things, all with the same aspirations and the same desires'. That was what Impressionism was already aiming at. Its very enthusiasm for nature moved it to weave men, things and nature into a single comprehensive web of colour, like the paradisial community in which differences are obliterated. Earlier still, in the fairy-tale and atmospheric world of Corot, we find, for the first time in nineteenth century art, human figures gently merging into nature, the landscape fading away in bright colour, and a rhythmic union of all parts of the picture from which glows the magic of paradise.

The 'friendship' that Cézanne sees embraces not only the atmospheric appearance of things but their structural unity. His aim was to make objects transparent without losing their essential solidity. With his insight into the inner structure of the world, he sought to discover a new formal structure parallel to that of nature. When Cézanne spoke of the great labour and anguish of realizing what he set out to do, he was referring to the slow rediscovery of paradise, where everything is simple and free, and art spontaneously echoes the harmony of the universe.

Gasquet has handed down to us the expression 'the virginity of the world'. If indeed these words were originalliy uttered by Cézanne, we can surely say that no artist has ever coined a more telling phrase to describe his work.

Even when set beside the superb high noon of the Impressionists, Cézanne's art brings renewed youth to the world and goes much further than they in suggesting its primeval state and primitive spontaneity. His paradise has the quality of the untouched and the innocent. His people are still without speech, their gestures unsophisticated and chaste. The 'Grandes baigneuses' (plate 118) form a ritual community; they recall the matriarchal stage of human development and the earliest dialogue between man and nature. The man stands apart on the other bank, shut out from all participation. The implications of this picture remind one of the bitter ending of *News from Nowhere*. The author recognizes that he was only a guest – 'as if I had no business amongst them'. Cézanne restores to his figures – including the friends who sat for him – the anonymity of early man. This is what gives his art, whether the subject be landscape or the human figure, its air of reverent stillness; it has the quality of 'still life'. Cézanne was indeed always attracted by lifeless things, for they possess something that man must slowly win back for himself – the peace and strength of simply existing, the natural perfection promised by the earthly paradise.

7

The earthly paradise is a static vision of humanity. In it life holds its breath, its busy events are stilled. Nothing happens: man is simply there, surrounded by an everlasting present indistinguishable from any past or future. He does not recognize the passing of time and knows neither age, nor decay, nor any seasons. He neither remembers nor looks forward. His is eternal youth, an everlasting existence that has no history.

It is clear therefore that the account of an earthly paradise represents a certain conception of natural man. It has two aspects: first, it postulates an elementary, unselfconscious man without any historical setting; and secondly it is a concept most easily expressed visually in an elementary, underivative way that does not depend on any style. The question of man's 'whither' or 'whence' remains unuttered.

I spoke earlier and at some length of the two contrasting world views that lie behind the concepts of 'nature' and 'history'. The many different pictures with a historical perspective were gathered together, in a special chapter, into one iconographic group. They exalt the Great Man, the man of action who makes the world his own; they tell of the founders of religion, of artists, discoverers and inventors. But these human epics present a picture of continual change. History never stands still, it knows no Golden Age that lasts for ever, it has no final certainty. Unlike nature, it cannot repeat itself but is always moving on towards new developments, producing new situations and new agents to act in them. It brings to the man who claims eternal fame for his deeds a knowledge of their transience but also of their uniqueness. The historical painter, if he aimed higher than merely to illustrate a picture book, could not evade the questions of man's 'whence' and 'whither'. Indeed they weighed heavily on historical painting. They complicated the outlook of the optimists, who believed in the straight course of progress, and cast them into doubt. Numerous sceptical voices began to be heard in the second half of the century prophesying the relapse of European civilization into chaos and barbarism. The historical principle seemed only relative and was like a ship without rudder or compass.

In these circumstances historical painting made use of the only means by which it could give a clear significance to historical events. It equated them with the vital processes of nature and arranged them according to the phases of youth, maturity, age and death. Chenavard, in many respects a supreme exponent of a disciplined system, adapted his historical calendar to the four ages of man, for by this alone could he assure himself that what had a beginning was moving towards some kind of end. By this means alone could he endow the fluctuating processes of history with an organic coherence. It was this that produced a shift of emphasis. History was no longer the final court of appeal. It surrendered its authority to life, with whose cyclical course it identified itself. It is a significant and indeed almost symbolic coincidence that Chenavard's Pantheon decorations, in which the historical portrayal of man reaches its culminating and critical point, should have come into being at the same time as Courbet's 'L'atelier'. Before he surrendered his encyclopaedic pictorial concept and contented himself with the portrayal of the history of manners, the historical painter realized that he must find a place for a new truth of faith, and so he attempted for the first and last time to strike a balance between history and life, between the idea of progress, the consciousness of decadence, and the natural cycle. While Chenavard used his imaginative power to obtain this comprehensive view, the realists, who took no account of man's historical origins, posed the question of his destiny and purpose anew. Courbet's 'L'atelier' was not the first picture of the century that used the ages of man to answer this question of 'whence' and 'whither', but it was the first that made of this idea a picture of mankind whose symphonic development gave it equal rank with the erudite arrangements of the historical painters.[30] Liberated from the processes of history and seeking a new relationship, man took nature as his symbolic model. He did not seek to master her but to receive her maternal blessing, hoping that in her he might find security and a home.

The earthly paradise was the best expression of this deeply felt understanding between man and nature and provided its most ambitious and also its most apt framework. In order to represent the equation of man with nature in the life process, limited by birth and death, it was only necessary to divide paradisial man into different age groups, to extend the pure, imperishable being that knows no seasons into a future and a past – not with the purpose of reintroducing the time of clocks and calendars, but to reintegrate the life of man with the rhythmic processes of nature. And so the mythical took the place of the historical picture of mankind.

From Ingres to Renoir the earthly paradise had only one temporal dimension. It was reserved for youth. Cézanne too in his 'Grandes baigneuses' glorified the virginity of the world, the 'innocence of growth'. It was only when the earthly paradise gave place to the natural stages of life to which man is subject, that it was seen in a wider context and gave symbolic form to the whole content of life and not merely to a precious dream of harmony. Thus deepened and endowed with a new power, the vision of the earthly paradise could well become a picture of humanity, and the artist might entrust to it the question that Gauguin wrote on one of his paintings, 'Where do we come from? What are we? Whither are we going?' (plate 217).

8

Hans von Marées is one of the painters of the simple innocent life. His art was not concerned with what is unknown or puzzling but with what is 'as far as possible known to all men'. Wölfflin has preserved a saying of his: 'We should all become children again in our view of the world'. The view of the world that his pictures communicate is one in which a slow development is preferred to 'the epidemic of haste'. Marées' people are always sunk in stillness, whether they are tarrying in the garden of the Villa Borghese, sitting before an inn in the forest, or in a Roman vineyard. But out of these idylls there emerge two complementary and interpenetrating pictorial ideas, each of which adds depth to the other – the Ages of Man and the Golden Age. It is therefore no mere chance that at the end of the seventies Marées illustrated these two almost at the same moment of time, in two great compositions. The 'Ages of Man' and 'The Golden Age' (plate 213) are so closely related to one another that we could almost reverse the titles.

At the beginning of this prolific decade of his life – the last but one – Marées painted a picture of humanity with even more varying layers of content and an even greater formal richness, in which the abundance and beneficence of life are richly spread before us: the fresco in the library of the Zoological Station in Naples. It was his intention to paint a series of great pictures 'which in an interconnected manner were to show the charm of marine and seashore life'.[31] We shall surely not be guilty of an unjustified literary interpretation if we see in this work the evidence of a deeply thought-out view of the world, expressed here wholly in visual terms. It may not have lain within the artist's intention, or been a part of his set programme, to establish a common denominator between the men of science and the Italian fisherfolk, but in spite – one might better say because – of this he succeeded in creating a flawless unity of life, a continuity of form and thought that can allow itself to set the naked body next to the clothed. Simple existence is joined with the life of thought, rest with action, age with youth, achievement with vigorous effort, the protection afforded by woman with the action enjoyed by man. Around all is laid the shield of nature, promising fruitfulness, security and nourishment.

On the south wall are two groups of figures that have been transferred to a paradisial orange grove (colour plate xv). On the left of the picture are two women and a boy, on the right are four figures of whom two are naked – a sitting child, a recumbent boy playing with an orange, a youth standing erect and plucking an orange, and an old man digging the ground to give the soil fresh growth. The homage paid to woman is set off against the male knowledge that change is the price of continuity. With rare discrimination Marées makes the two women represent the mature middle years of life (they remind one of Courbet's 'Demoiselles au bord de la Seine'), while the earlier and later stages are reserved for the male. The woman brings the fruit, but it is the man's portion.

The interconnected themes on the other three walls join up with this one. The fundamental accord of thought and action is again discernible, and is relevant to the scientific institution itself. On the long wall there is a rowing boat, with a group of fishermen on one side pushing their own boat into the water and on the other five men at a table under a pergola together with two women (plate 181 shows a sketch for this). The scientists and the fishermen are bound to one and the same element – water. Both live with and by nature. At a time when there was a flowering of scientific analysis and scientists were busier than ever arranging and cataloguing phenomena, Marées made his naturalists into a relaxed group of men and gave them the dignity of philosophers, though in a letter he showed himself enthusiastic about their ceaseless quest for the unknown. They are sitting with some artist friends around a table; like the latter, they seem to direct their calm gaze not at fleeting phenomena but towards a deeper search for the essential principles of nature in all her aspects. It is for this reason as well that they have been given into the care of the two women.

The rejuvenating and enlivening influence that Marées, on his own showing, found in the Italian landscape and in Italian life, could no longer be found anywhere in Europe by Gauguin, who was eleven years his junior. Gauguin's journeys to Martinique (1887), and to the islands of Oceania (1891–1895, 1895–1903), have been considered a form of flight. In reality they were the opposite of that. It was not an extravagant adventure in foreign lands, but a search for human relationships and harmony with nature. The restless fever that drives men into remote places speaks a different language from the art of Gauguin, in which there is a longing to be at peace, to strike roots, and a passion for spiritual equilibrium. The restless spirit can be found in those words of Nietzsche that tell of a determination driving men not towards the harbour but towards the open sea. 'Do we know whither? We know not yet towards what we are being driven, once we have thus severed ourselves from our ancient soil. Yet that very soil has bred in us the strength that now drives us forward into distant places, into adventure; it is that strength that impels us towards the boundless, the untried, the undiscovered – and so we have no choice. We must be conquerors since we no longer have any land which is home for us and where we are moved to preserve what is ours.'

Gauguin is no such conqueror, he is no Faust, nor does he seek 'the boundless and untried'. What he seeks is something firmly based, clearly defined by unwritten tradition, a proven, valid life unconfused by Progress, a primitive life unspoilt by civilization. He seeks a landscape that can offer him shelter. Here was a man who was turning his back on the 'father-world' of European civilization and seeking to find his lost paradise in distant and exotic places – in the secure warmth and protection of the 'mother-world'. The Eve whom Gauguin set in his Garden of Eden bears, as has recently been shown,[32] the features of his mother. In the letter to Strindberg, written a few months before his second and final departure for Tahiti, he grows enthusiastic over the natural, spontaneous nakedness of his barbaric Eve and contrasts her with the lovely but shameless woman of civilization, who turns man into a woman-hater. (Was there not the unrelieved bitterness of a Strindbergian tragedy in Gauguin's own wrecked marriage?)

The 'return to the Mothers' is also the return to the origins of Art. That 'virginity of the world', which Cézanne's meditative gaze perceived in his riper works, was felt by Gauguin to reside in the essentially female world of tropical nature, from whose barbarism he hoped for a rejuvenation of his artistic power. The longing for the earthly paradise took several forms with him: there is the yearning for the 'mother-world' and the dream of a simple human community; there is the search for the source of art to which primitive spontaneity is restored and whose processes are similar to those of nature herself.

Gauguin speaks in various letters of the paradise he hopes to find in the South Seas. In the first chapter of *Noa-Noa* his friend and collaborator Morice uses certain striking words which have been doubly underlined in Gauguin's manuscript transcription. The words sound like the title of a picture – 'Le Rêve du Bonheur'. Are they a quotation? Are they a fragment recollected from a conversation with Gauguin? Do they refer to a picture which has been seen somewhere or other? We cannot exclude the possibility that they have some reference to the work of a Salon painter, since Gauguin himself connected his most comprehensive pictorial concept – 'D'où venons-nous? Que sommes-nous? Où allons-nous?' (Where do we come from? What are we? Whither are we going?) (plate 217) – with the competition for the 'Prix de Rome'. 'What will the students of the Academy make of this theme?', he asked in a letter to Daniel de Monfreid.[33]

Evidence that Gauguin's pictorial themes are not incapable of an academic interpretation is not difficult to find. Dominique Papety, an eclectic of no inconsiderable importance, painted in 1845 a

'Rêve de Bonheur' of which engravings issued by the firm of Goupil enjoyed a wide popularity. Four years later he painted 'Le Passé, le Présent et l'Avenir'.[34] There is no suggestion here of an actual influence or the adoption of an idea; least of all is there any question of Gauguin's being dependent on academic models. What is suggested is merely that the division which separated him from the official painters is a matter of 'how' and not of 'what', of the formal mastery of the pictorial idea, not of the idea itself. If we look at the matter from this latter angle, we can see a correspondence between the great 'Where do we come from?' on the one hand and the 'Dream of Happiness' and 'Past, Present and Future' on the other.

The picture was painted at a time of crisis which almost drove Gauguin to suicide, and it may well be regarded as his spiritual testament.[35] It touches the cardinal question of the nineteenth century, that 'small circle' of ideas on which everything depends. 'Who are we? What purpose do we serve? From whom? Whither? The great spheres of philosophy dance around this small circle without touching it at any point of its periphery' – said Gutzkow in 1856.[36] Delacroix, one of the century's greatest tragic artists, declared that man had no means of giving a valid answer to the riddle of the universe. After observing an ant-heap he wrote in his journal: 'We are of all sorts and kinds – animals, human beings, plants – all locked up in this great box which is called the universe. We have the effrontery to believe that we can read the message of the stars. We presume to have knowledge of past and future, which are hidden from our view, and we understand not a thing that is before our eyes'. The nearness and familiar character of the 'small circle' within which man is in harmony with nature, this territory, so close at hand and small in extent, became for Gauguin great and all-comprehending, of equal rank with the 'great spheres of philosophy' – and yet in a different fashion; for his brush communicated visible things and not abstractions, symbols and not recondite reflexions, myth and not speculation. It is myth, says Bachofen 'which carries within itself the origins of things – and myth alone can reveal them'.

In a letter to Daniel de Monfreid Gauguin described the figures in the picture without explaining them. The important thing here is the reference to the two wandering figures behind and to the right of the seated nude figure seen from the back – the figures 'who dare to think of their fate'. It is they who are asking about the whence and whither. Like Dante and Vergil, they wander through the world enquiring and interpreting. What seems to them dark and mysterious is taken for granted by the other inhabitants, who ask for no explanation and live 'without knowledge'. The two wandering creatures are shut out from the general community, like the two onlookers in the 'Grandes baigneuses' of Cézanne (plate 118). A later letter to Morice makes this even clearer. 'Two weird figures behind a tree in clothes of a melancholy colour. Beside the tree of knowledge, they strike their painful note which actually comes from that knowledge.' Their 'knowledge' separates them from the simple creatures, who enjoy the fact of just being alive in a virginal natural paradise.

There is admittedly a contrast between this paradise into which Gauguin has set his foreground figures and the symbolic portrayal of transience for which these figures are used. The same letter throws light on the significance of the three groups in the picture: 'Whither are we going? An old woman near to death. A strange stupid-looking bird marks the end. What are we? Ordinary life. The man of instinct asks himself what it all means. Whence do we come? Spring. Child. The common life'. The central figure reaching for knowledge is distinguishable by its questioning gesture from the 'simple creatures' on the left and right, for whom life poses no questions; but it is also distinguishable from the wandering pair, for the knowledge for which it strives is a bright certainty, not something that oppresses the soul. It is this figure then that asks the three questions and it is this figure that answers them.

207 INGRES The Golden Age (detail); 1862.

208 CARSTENS Night with her children; c. 1795.

209 RUNGE The Morning (first version); 1808.

210 BLAKE The River of Life; c. 1805.

211
BURNE-JONES
The Golden Stairs; 1880.

212 PUVIS DE CHAVANNES *L'hiver*; 1889–93.

215 MARÉES The Golden Age; 1879–85.

214 BÖCKLIN *Vita somnium breve*; 1888.

215 HODLER Night; 1890.

216 HODLER Day; 1900.

217 GAUGUIN *D'où venons-nous ? Que sommes-nous ? Où allons-nous ?* 1897.

218 MUNCH The Dance of Life; 1899–1900.

Let me however say a word about the picture's other layers of meaning which are somewhat easier to grasp. I see in it – especially in the right half – an appeal to motherhood and its protective warmth.[37] From this there proceeds – if we read the picture from right to left – a number of changing manifestations of womanhood. Unlike the three types of women in Munch's picture, they remain psychologically undifferentiated, with the freedom and innocence of savages. They are not 'beyond good and evil', as Nietzsche has it, they have never heard of them. They represent the stages of life of a simple creature from birth to old age. Nature follows man. When he awakes to life, her strength too begins to blossom. When he raises himself up in the middle of life, she offers him her fruits, which have now ripened. She accompanies his old age, herself becoming withered and bare.

But we do not exhaust the full meaning of the picture by simply observing the intimate relationship between the earthly paradise and the ages of man. My own belief is that there is a central stratum of meaning, which provides an answer to the questions asked in the title, and that this lies deeper. I believe that Gauguin's vision of natural perfection – though he may not himself have been conscious of it – was feeling its way back to the basic starting points of human nature, and that Gauguin was dimly aware of future harmonies in this human nature of ours, though such perception could not be given visual form either through the earthly paradise or through the ages of man.

In 1888 Gauguin wrote to the sister of his friend Bernard, a girl towards whom he entertained very passionate feelings. He advised this seventeen-year-old girl to regard herself as a 'sexless hermaphrodite'. 'The soul, the heart, all that is divine should not be the slave of matter, i.e. of the body'. Sexlessness was one of the images which exercised great influence on this artist whenever, having either grown weary of his own sensuality, or mastered it, he once more yearned for harmony and natural perfection. That the division into male and female brought a rift into the cosmic order is a very ancient belief of the human race. That it produced a certain irreconcilable relationship of mutual opposition between men and women was something Gauguin had learned from his own bitter experience. The harmony of undifferentiated unity, of which in Europe he could only dream, was some years later to be experienced by him as a visible reality among the people of the South Seas. He now encountered a race in whose physical make-up the distinguishing marks of sexual differentiation were much less evident. Gauguin in his writings is continually insisting that Maori women are so much like men that the two sexes can often be mistaken for each other. Once when a youth was guiding him through the forest, he experienced in a matter of seconds the revelation of bisexuality, an experience that both moved and confused him. These visions have taken visible form in the central fruit-picking figure of the picture here under consideration. It is here that the key to an understanding of the whole picture is to be found. This figure is searching for the secret and is itself the means of revealing it. Alone among all the figures it is neither woman nor man – and in the commentary to be found in Gauguin's letters this ambiguity remains.

The dream of the hermaphrodite is very ancient indeed. Did Gauguin come across it in some literary source? Did he know of the mythology of Blake according to which male and female were one in primeval man? Did he know of the theories of Ballanches which prophesied the end of sexual differentiation? Or were these ideas first aroused by the decadents of his Paris days – say, by Moreau?[38] All these questions should probably be answered in the negative. They merely show that Gauguin was not the only one in this particular century who entertained such views. What was more powerful than anything that he may have read in the writings of poets and philosophers was his own memory of the archetype of primeval undifferentiated sex, that primal state where the single individual was double-sexed and this double-sexed character was his pledge of immortality. And to this recollection of man's original state ('Where do we come from?') there was added the truly Romantic belief – which Gauguin shared with Blake – in the perfection of man through the ultimate fusion of the male with the female, in the vanishing of all differences between the two and in the rediscovery of immortality. This natural perfection, which was older than the earthly paradise, would again be granted to man with all its power of reconciliation.

9

In 1876 Burckhardt had in his lecture denied that contemporary poetry – and presumably also contemporary painting – had the power to describe 'a sublime world' with the resources at its disposal. Yet at that very time Renoir was painting his 'Bal au Moulin de la Galette'. A few years previously the frescoes in the Naples Library had appeared. In the following decade Seurat produced his magnum opus, 'Un dimanche d'été à la Grande Jatte', Renoir his 'Grandes baigneuses', and Gauguin the masterpiece we have just discussed.

By these works the century proved that it could free itself from traditional forms and from worlds of purely literary fantasy, and that it was capable of shaping for itself the vision of a natural and ideal humanity and of doing so without being tripped up by its own emotions, as Burckhardt had feared. The richness of the new form of painting burst the confines of the normal canvas and artists quite deliberately exploited all the possibilities of largeness of scale. The actual content of their work justified this process, for these pictures plead for an open communal existence, for harmony between man and nature. That is what makes the mural, the essentially public form of painting, so appropriate. What was denied to the learned compilations of the historians was successfully achieved in these pictures of humanity: a monumental power combined with the vigour of life.

XII   The Divided Century

Can one have the right or authority to deny that a century has
any independent creative power, without insulting oneself and
doing the nineteenth century an injustice?   C.D. Friedrich

I

IN the nineteenth century a hierarchic system of values was in collapse. Dogmas were called in question, absolute standards replaced by relative ones. The power of faith, on which previously a whole world had reposed, disappeared and an entire order whose guarantee that faith had been, broke asunder. With it was lost the ability to create and preserve a style. With the break-up of the whole, the constituent parts lacked any common denominator and claimed autonomy and equality. A vertically ordered system of value relationships gave way to a single horizontal plane upon which the opposing forces carried on their debate. In a word, the whole hierarchical scheme was replaced by a battle of dialectics.

This overwhelming break in the development of the human spirit presented art too with an entirely new situation. The artist was no longer restricted by an accepted style, but had to recognize the relative nature of all values. 'We understand everything, we live everything', says Nietzsche, 'we no longer have any feeling of enmity within us.' Yet such a view was bound sooner or later to lead to another. If in the sphere of artistic form every epoch is its own master, there is no reason why this large-minded philosophy should apply to the past alone, in which everything must be understood and nothing condemned. There followed therefore a universal and insistent demand that the present must be wholly itself and nothing but itself.

The artist saw that his work was subject to question; that is to say, in the truest sense it was worth asking questions about. Art became self-conscious and like every discipline with an autonomous system of values it became its own problem. No one described that condition with greater precision than Hegel in the introduction to his *Aesthetics*. 'Our particular manner of artistic production has ceased to satisfy the highest needs of our spirit. We have got beyond the stage of adoring works of art and paying them divine honours. The fine arts have been outflanked by the processes of analytical thought.' Art was something pertaining to the past and had ceased to be the highest need of the spirit. The age was not favourable to it; 'the fair days of Greek art are over, like the golden period of the late Middle Ages.' The knowledge of this fact weighed more heavily on the artist than on anybody else. His whole mental training made it impossible for him to withdraw from his analytical world into artistic isolation. The artistic consciousness was broken and disquieted. If it was to come to terms with itself, it was compelled to a quite unprecedented degree to engage in self-examination. Indeed the artistic consciousness became its own subject in works of art. It was only in the writings of philosophers that this new art, free of any extraneous purpose and belonging wholly to itself, was correctly evaluated. Hegel's justification of a science of art – a product of the Romantic's passion for comparisons! – could have been formulated in other terms: autonomous art is in constant need of interpretation and commentary.

The days were over, then, in which art was content simply to exist and ask no questions about itself, finding its justification in the tasks assigned to it. Once it had become autonomous, it had no other function but to ensure its own survival, no other justification but self-analysis. 'Art', says Fernow, 'released from both the prop and the compulsion of religion must henceforth rely upon itself.' Once it had accepted the fact that it had no external support or control but had to provide its own subject matter from within, its self-sufficiency became absolute. Art substituted its own self in place of the values and ideas to which it was once subservient. The creative act replaced the confession of faith and the artist now considered himself to be the only true measure of humanity. It was inevitable that he should dramatize his personality with the gestures of the priest, the martyr or the criminal. It was thus that he compensated himself for the knowledge that he stood in isolation, cut off from all normal relations with men.

The link of a universal style had been broken. The dogmas of absolute beauty had lost their general validity. What this meant to the individual is shown once again by Schelling: 'Like everyone whose work lies in the sphere of the mind or the spirit the artist can only follow the law that God and nature have written upon his heart, he can follow no other. No man can help him, he must help himself. Nor can he borrow from without, since what he does not create for his own sake would immediately appear worthless. That is why no one can give him orders or prescribe the way he should go.'

Since this was its guiding principle, art became increasingly a process of self-portraiture, self-analysis and self-clarification. 'Every picture is more or less a reflection of the character of him who painted it.' So wrote Friedrich,[1] while Runge, ever ready for far-reaching and ambitious undertakings, declared: 'My wish is to represent my life in a series of works of art'.[2] This desire of the artist to bring his essential self into the work that he created was new, and his contemporaries were aware that it constituted an unprecedented claim. Difficulties in mutual comprehension now arose between the artist and his public. Blake calmly declared that most people saw things differently from himself: 'I see Every thing I paint in this world, but Every body does not see alike.'[3] The certainty that he would not be understood made the artist nervous and over-sensitive but at the same time proud and obstinate. 'What I call "art",' says Runge, 'is so constituted that even if I were to tell people outright what it all meant, nobody would understand me and people would consider me either raving mad or plain stupid.'[4] Young Delacroix, when rebuked because of his impetuosity, answered the Director of the Beaux Arts: 'The whole world will not prevent me from seeing things as I wish.'[5] These statements come from the first third of the century; in its second half they were to become both more numerous and more violent. The artist whose subject is himself has quite a different vision and experience from those of his public. Since he is responsible to no client and is guided by no tradition, since the choice of both content and form is his personal decision, he must 'only set to work on that which truly touches his heart and inspires him to portray it' (Fernow). He must speak only in the language that is his own; everything else is false – lies, coercion and compromise. In the nineteenth century, great art demanded from its creator a statement of ethical principles. To a much greater degree than ever before, it was the fruit of searching self-questioning, the achievement of the few. It had to be so. It was not arrogance nor a desire to be original that drove the artist into isolation, but his conscience and his refusal to compromise. It was not the public that thrust him into a ghetto, but his conviction that his art would only be valid if it came out of himself, from an inner compulsion.

Since however there was no longer anything to show in what general direction art was tending, 404 every artist began to insist that he alone was right. As a result art became split up into great individual achievements, but lost what till then had been its essential characteristic – a dignity transcending personalities. Art, in the sense in which earlier ages understood it, in the nineteenth century ceased to exist. There were only artists, who made every effort to develop their own individual and unmistakable language. For the first time abstract conceptions such as Nature, Reality, Beauty and the Ideal became postulates subject to polemical debate. Artists, stimulated by self-examination and the theories resulting from it, adopted extreme positions and held them intransigently. The diligent imitation of reality overshot the mark and landed in the territory of the photographer; and on the other hand the intense desire for subjective expression haughtily turned its back on physical facts. There was no general agreement that would make it possible to prescribe anything in the nature of an elementary grammar for the artist. There was no focal point at which the near and the distant, the material and the abstract, could be gathered together into a unity. Small wonder that every artist sought a different hold to which to cling. One became a student of nature and only concerned himself with the world of experience and its imitation. Another became an ardent pilgrim along the paths of history. A third, relying wholly upon himself, concentrated on the provocative assertion of his own peculiar style. A fourth cared for nothing but what Ruskin called 'the innocence of the eye'. In a hundred different ways the artist sought to arrive at an understanding of himself and his art.

3

In no circumstances should we underrate the importance and intensity of this new purely subjective mode of experience. To the artist the world was his own peculiar problem and he used it as a pretext for his own self-revelation. He used art as a tool which, if he was to handle it successfully, must bear the imprint of his personality. This may savour of arrogance but there was greatness in it, for it opened the way to new depths of expression.

Admittedly there was danger in the revolutionary choice of subject and artistic form – in that very danger, the nineteenth century found the true sources of its power, but also the limits of its potentialities. Autonomous art depends on the effectiveness of two impulses: one towards self-revelation, the other towards experiment. It is an art which develops dialectically. It is for ever upon the road and never reaches its goal, for it is perpetually seeking to discover all its potentialities.

If we say that European art in the nineteenth century had entered the epoch of self-revelation, in the field of form this means either that it was recapitulating its own historic development, or that it was endeavouring to find new and untried ways of artistic creation. We can see that the hostile armies, though moving in different directions, were fundamentally seeking the same assurance. This new art, which provided its own subject matter, was throughout the century pursuing an ideal that took many different shapes – its lost spontaneity. One group believed that it could be found in the art of antiquity, another in Gothic; the realists sought it in the empirical world, the Impressionists in free brush work.

There was involved in all this a continual dialectic. The artist who was free to experiment inevitably became a partisan, with a set of declared beliefs to which the autobiographical and self-revelatory character of his work naturally bound him; yet at the same time he was searching for a form he could directly and sincerely accept, and rejected the empty formulae of routine. It is the dialectic inherent in this that imparts to the century its restless and shifting features.

The nineteenth century recognized no hierarchy of subject matter any more than it acknowledged an absolute standard of beauty. All subjects and all forms were treated as of equal rank and of equal value. 'We paint Gods and Madonnas', says Vischer in his *Kritische Gänge*, 'heroes and peasants, just as we build in Greek, Byzantine, Moorish, Gothic, Florentine, Renaissance or Rococo styles, but never in a style that is our own. We paint what the world demands of us. We are lords of everything, and nothing. There is no centre, no main principle, no main course among all the side-dishes, sweet-meats and pastries under which our table groans. Lost in thought, the artist makes his choice from all the material that ever was and cannot see the wood for the trees.'[6]

This diagnosis applies to all camps, including the Romantics, the realists and the Impressionists, for even for these, in theory at least, all things were equally worthy of representation. Even the Symbolists claimed that they found a symbol in everything they saw. All these potential forms of art, however, equal in rank with one another, were subject to a process of mutual interaction. They continually challenged one another. Idealism and realism were always changing places, as were *Pleinairisme* and Symbolism. Meanwhile every movement formulated its aims with the greatest strictness of definition, and every thesis thus already contained its potential antithesis; yet there was no bridging element that could possibly produce a synthesis. The nineteenth century only knew style in a plural sense, as a repertoire of possibilities.

Here lay the cause of that restlessness that marked every attempt at a new form and of that radical, often intolerant faith that supported it. Here also, however, lay the cause of the hasty rejoinder by an opposite party, the rapid growth of disgust with what had been achieved, and the wasteful discarding of ideas. In a century in which, as Marx says, 'Everything seems pregnant with its contrary', the process that was once spoken of as development became subject to breakneck acceleration. Since something new had always to be produced, solutions already found merely brought about new problems.

This restless tendency to experiment had a two-fold result. It sharpened the apprehension of the secondary problems, the formal grammar of line, colour and tone, and at the same time brought the artist's work into the full light of conscious analytical thought. This is not difficult to understand; since there was no such thing as accepted style, no hierarchy of formal values, every means of expression, the decorative line as much as pointillism, had the right to claim for itself absolute value. Since all categories of painting had an equal claim, each of them – landscape, still life and figure-painting – had a right to be proclaimed as the highest. (The same spirit of acrimonious controversy is observable in the century's ideological struggle; every philosophy, whether social or metaphysical, insisted that it was the only acceptable substitute for the defunct religion of the past.)

These tendencies imposed a new caution and conscientiousness on the artist's efforts, but they also inhibited and burdened him. They distorted his vision of the whole and imparted to the creative act a quality of restlessness and insecurity. Art was in process of seeking to understand itself; no approach could therefore any longer present itself to an artist as self-evidently right. Even the return to nature and the descent into the instinctive and unconscious had all the signs of deliberate choice. They resulted from the growing realization of a need for roots. Behind every such act there was reflexion, self-knowledge and an assertion of personality. As Nietzsche says, 'He who acts is no longer without knowledge.' That is why the artist's attempt to express his inner self often took the form of an experiment, and a would-be confession ended in something very like exhibitionism. The abnormal liveliness of the artist's mind induced him to play a part and to express his personality in terms of a distinctive style: so the picture of that personality was often marked by a distorting emphasis. The confession assumed the explicit crudity of a poster, but the artist when he bared his heart knew exactly what he was doing and why. We can find examples of this in the greatest figures of the century, in Goya, Ingres and Courbet. For the century inclined – and this applies to all parties concerned – positively to thrust its gestures at the observer. It is in this that it revealed the quality of its artistic consciousness.

4

Among the observations which Semper brought back home from his visit to the London Exhibition in 1851 is the following, which concerns buildings in the United States. The American house, he says, is really no house at all 'but a framework for furniture'. Concerning the Crystal Palace, he had the following to say: 'This glass-enclosed vacuum is suitable for anything people want to put inside it. I say this without any *arrière pensée* or desire to provoke argument; it was the task of the architect to construct just such a glass-covered vacuum. This building is as it were the embodiment of the tendency which our age is bound to follow'.[7] Semper's perception was correct; his diagnosis of architecture is symptomatic of all the arts. The art of building, which had once consisted in the inseparable union of the constructive and the plastic part, had become split into the constructions of the engineers on the one hand — who were concerned with the realistic use of materials and tectonic utility — and on the other into the extravagant displays of the academic architects, whose buildings were designed mainly for optical effect. The Crystal Palace avoided all solidity; it was a framework enclosing a space, obeying the 'inner compulsion' of its own constructional form. Free of all plastic, ornamental, and representational features, this manner of building established the principle of radical, unconcealed veracity. It did not seek to seem more than it was. On the one side, then, we have the puritanism that concentrated on space and structure and on the other the architecture of display, using the styles of the past, in which all is appearance, facade and superficial illusion.

This division had already begun with the experiments of the Romantics, with Soane in England and Schinkel in Germany, through the selection of certain historic styles and their application externally to the body of a building. This brought about a disturbance in the organic relationship between the inner and the outer part, between the kernel and the shell. The kernel was thought of as existing independently and the shell as something added which could be lifted off. The ideas of both engineer and academic architect were made plain beyond any doubt; the one made the constructive process explicit by laying it completely bare, the other reconstructed the history of architectural styles. The engineer was honest enough to draw the inescapable conclusion from his premise and build a 'vacuum'. The academic architect, though he was reluctant to admit it, was equally ready to proceed to a logical conclusion and apply his stylistic formulae to a theatre, a museum or a railway station.

There is much to be learned from the example of architecture. It illustrates with particular clarity the dichotomy that in the nineteenth century affected all the arts. The same process that in building confined the ornamental and representational elements to the surface, superfluous to the structure, can be seen at work in the applied arts, separating the useful from the artistic. The charm of sumptuous ornamentation became an end in itself and completely concealed the purpose that objects were designed to serve. Meanwhile the pure, unadorned and honest form of the industrial product was determined by the 'inner compulsion' of its function and purpose and remained content with a utility unembellished by art. From the middle of the nineteenth century onward an attempt was made to bring about a reconciliation between the two extremes — artistic concealment on the one hand (in 1851 you could in London have admired a Gothic piano!) and on the other artlessly unclothed functionalism.

The conflict with which we are here concerned had its origin in the fact that the partnership that had lasted for centuries between beauty and truth had been determined. This is particularly noticeable in painting and the plastic arts. Appearance and idea, the charm of sense and the sterner beauty of morals which had once co-operated as a single effective unity, now turned their back upon one another. Those who felt the urge towards sincerity, which had the force of a religious faith, mocked at harmony and balance. They accepted the reproach of being formless, chaotic or even clumsy, for they preferred the direct undisguised gesture to anything conceived by academic ingenuity. The vital form was what really mattered – and it was just this that tended to be suppressed in the conservative camp, where homage was paid to nicely chosen derivative ideals of beauty.

The supporters of the two opposed conceptions were nevertheless united in one respect – namely, in their readiness to demonstrate the fundamental nature of their beliefs and purpose, though they might do so with differing emphasis. It is by this that we recognize the dedicated artist, who likes to talk about himself and his art. Like the academic architects, the academic painters drew attention, clearly and deliberately, to their historical formulae and their generally eclectic methods, and openly paraded their stylistic erudition, which they had obtained at second hand. And just as the architects concealed the body of a building behind their masks and disguises, the painters hid the process of painting behind a smooth and lifeless aesthetic formula.

There is a similar connection between the engineer-architects and the free style painters. Both were eager to demonstrate their processes and to reveal the actual method of construction – in the framework of their buildings or in the conjunction of the spots of paint applied by the brush. The act of creation was not suppressed or modestly concealed, even though a statement of its final purpose might be evaded or the question left completely open. The stages by which a work of art takes shape were freely disclosed and made plain for all to see. From this resulted the artistic discovery that was to have the most far-reaching effect on the future – that is to say, on our own time. This discovery transferred the true significance of a work of art from the final form it assumes to the process whereby it comes into being.

If we compare the two tendencies of the nineteenth century, which are discernible in all categories of art, we are left in no doubt as to which of them showed the more intensive creative power; or in which of the two the gain has been greater and more pregnant for the future. It was not the servile or at best reverent trustees of our past heritage who gave the century new creative impulses (how could they do this with their eyes glued to yesterday?), but the artists who felt that a moral obligation underlay their efforts to achieve sincerity of expression. They were far more concious of form than the eclectics, for all their assiduous attempts to reproduce the essence of a style. The latter were still seeking to effect a compromise with the ghosts of past styles and they merely wasted their efforts in trying to awaken the dead. For it was already plain that new solutions to the problems of form were not to be found in the old stylistic formulae but in the judgement of the individual artist. In the nineteenth century the power to create a style was with the individual alone. It began with him and came to an end when for the last time he laid down his brush. All efforts at formal codification were therefore bound to fail. They could only result in verbal directives that lacked the breath of life; and that was true not only of the academicians who perished in their own formulae, but also of all those who tried to lay down a code of procedure for the free, open-handed painting of the period and so to reduce what was vital and spontaneous (one has only to think of the dogmatizing of the pointillists) to a mechanical process or a set of rules for a game.

5

The processes described above – the free choice of forms and experiments with them, the ceaseless argument, the isolation of individual parts of an artistic problem and their confrontation as mutually exclusive opposites – represent the formal aspects of the artist's self-expression. Beside them was the whole iconographic complex described in previous chapters. It was not only in the forms that he chose or worked out for himself that the artist revealed himself; his personality with all its problems and ideals is also preserved in the content of his pictures. In the nineteenth century the choice of subject made possible a profound insight into the personality of the man who made the choice; for – in a way unknown in any previous century – this act, in an age of 'art for artists', depended entirely on the individual. Whatever he painted, he was always painting himself. He declared his destiny, his longings and fears, his conceptions of the rôle of art and of the tasks of the artist. Whether he obtained his thematic inspiration from the present or the past, whether he expressed a purely personal point of view or depended upon literary sources, whether he was re-awakening archetypal memories or commenting on contemporary events, he always – more fundamentally and subjectively than artists of previous periods – took his subject matter into the very centre of his personal experience.

In the cult of the Great Man the artist was seeking to found for humanity a new religion of heroes. In his moments of extreme self-confidence, he cast himself for the rôle of the Messiah. It was not the victorious and successful that attracted him most, but the restless and purposeless wanderers and the outcasts who had nowhere to strike their roots. Small wonder – for in these men he recognized the destiny decreed for his own art. His art was 'a vagabond, who knows everything and tastes everything and takes nothing seriously'.[8] Vischer's diagnosis appeared in 1842; a year later the following sentence could be read in Kierkegaard's *Either-Or*: 'Every aesthetic view of life is despair.' It is impossible not to hear the romantic overtones of this sentence. They echo right down the century, for again and again the artist was made aware of the tragic fact that his whole activity had no purpose outside itself, that it was utterly useless and that he himself led only a marginal existence. That is why he felt so close to those like himself with no ties or purpose – Don Juan and the Wandering Jew, the harlot and Don Quixote, Sardanapalus and the rejected Prometheus. Since the normal securities that society offers to its members gave him nothing to cling to – and in any case he despised them – he sought brothers and comrades to share his ghetto life or his vagabondage, who like himself lived a marginal life, though they lived it far more intensively than the well-meaning folk who represented law and respectability. He found such brothers among criminals, madmen or figures like Mazeppa, among prisoners and clowns.

Yet the man who had thus broken with the world sought something more than a tragic apotheosis that would release him from earthly life. He yearned for some link with the world around him and for the resolution of that enormous tension that kept him from it. Sometimes such men, confident that history would do them justice, professed a 'religion of genius' that they claimed was valid for all time. Others sought to remove the barriers surrounding the artist's life; they allowed him to share in humble anonymity the life of ordinary folk. In the great historical pictures, art was elevated to the status of a substitute religion. In those dealing with contemporary social life, such as 'L'atelier', it adjusted itself to ordinary everyday circumstances.

It was the worker whom the artist picked out as the man with a genuine and unspoilt attitude to life, and he put him on a pedestal; for unlike the aesthetic type of man, the worker was not a mere spectator looking at real life from the outside, but a direct and effective participator in it. He found another ideal in the exotic races, who showed him a vision of the primordial vitality that civilization has lost. And in his search for the natural and primitive, he sought with an almost religious fervour to penetrate into the processes of nature; the simple life was to restore his lost innocence and contact with nature was to release him from the conflicts of the world of civilization. Finally, in the poetic transfiguration of the ordinary life of a great city the artist tried to forget that he no longer had any part in the community that binds together the people of this world.

The symbols of the simple and the natural are most concentrated in the myth of womanhood; and they are all gathered together in the dream of an earthly paradise where the artist's fairest wish becomes a reality – a vision of natural perfection, harmony between art and nature, and sweet simplicity. Art had set out to regain Paradise Lost.

If I insisted earlier that these dominant themes were common to all the movements and trends of nineteenth century art, the impression thus created of a closed iconographical circle should not cause us to forget that there were different stages of intensity in its manner of presentation. It might be superficial and conventional, or it might be fanatical and possessive. The final and decisive factor was the mastery of form. One can find the same themes among the darlings of the Salon as among the rejected and misunderstood, but the levels of formal expression will be different to the point of being irreconcilable (plates 82, 128). What, in an age governed by a homogeneous stylistic tradition, was no more than a difference of quality, now appeared as a conflict of opposites that could never be resolved. Those who concocted official taste and sought their guarantees in history would never commit themselves to a form in which they fervently believed and rarely got beyond mere illustration. The great thoughts of the century could only take pictorial form when men did not shirk the risk of expressing them in a wholly subjective language.

In an epoch whose demand for pictures not only favoured the flatness of a cliché but actually insisted on it, the world of art suffered a grave loss of substance. The wide use of pictures, increased by the discovery of photography, gave employment to both painter and draughtsman. As illustrators, they could not resist the temptations of prolixity, learned profundity and long-winded descriptions. In such a century as this, only the strongest personalities were able to preserve and renew the essential power of painting, deeply rooted in myth. All others were lost in their dramatizations, their archaeological stock-taking, their excursions into the history of style or their minutely detailed naturalism.

6

I should like to end this book with a further quotation from Hegel which is particularly apposite. It is the function of art, he says, to reveal truth and present the reconciliation of opposites: the universal and the particular, the spiritual and the sensual, duty and instinct, objective reality and subjective thought.

This clash of contraries, for which Hegel held our intellectual education and the modern mind responsible, forces man to live in two different worlds that are perpetually at war; it causes him to be 'tossed from one side to the other, incapable of finding satisfaction in either of them'. 'For on the one hand we see man caught in the toils of ordinary reality and of things earthly and temporal, driven by his necessities and desires, oppressed by nature, imprisoned by matter, enmeshed by sensual purposes and pleasures, governed and carried away by his natural passions and appetites. On the other, he raises himself to the sphere of eternal ideas, to a realm of thought and freedom, conforms his will to general laws and directives, strips the world of its lively and blossoming reality and turns it all into abstractions; his spirit asserts its rights and dignity by denying those of nature, thus repaying her for the misery and sufferings he endured at her hands. This dichotomy between life and the conscious mind offers a challenge to modern education and modern thought; it challenges them to resolve the contradiction.'

This challenge can be heard throughout the entire century – from Schiller's famous letter right down to Huysmans' 'spiritualistic naturalism'. It affects all spheres of thought and life, for the conflict and dichotomy are discernible everywhere. History is divorced from life, the natural from the spiritual, myth from the World of Truth, action from thought. A similar division is evident in social life and theory; the individual is divorced from the mass and private from public life. Thinkers who derive their ideas from Hegel – Kierkegaard and Marx – reveal in their writings the dialectical conflict. Kierkegaard exalts the existence of the individual as the decisive factor and the sole reality; he makes his complaint against the age that 'no man is ready to be an individual existing on his own'.

With Marx the individual loses his identity in his social relationships, the only decisive factor being the class. (Burckhardt too sees the individual encompassed by the amorphous mass.)[9]

All nineteenth century art that is worthy of the name is marked by this dichotomy. Though the generality of artists fail to achieve a synthesis, the efforts of an individual artist who has managed to effect a happy fusion of all his powers are at times crowned with success. Such a man occasionally contrives to master the condition of 'being tossed hither and thither' of which Hegel speaks – revealed in the period's restless experimentation and its 'discontent'[10] – and to express such mastery in a pictorial form in which apparently irreconcilable elements are synthesized and resolved.

The concentration of perception into an idea, the universal that shines through the particular – that is how the problem presents itself to the philosopher. Art has a similar, or at least a parallel problem. I have spoken of it as the tension between the male and female principles, because in that form it is most easily recognizable. Continual attempts were made to reconcile these principles and bring about a union of male and female. Yet only very rarely was that continuous union attained through which a true marriage can bring about a higher unity, creating what Novalis calls 'harmonious beings'.[11]

For such success is only vouchsafed to him who wrestles with himself to attain it. It depends entirely upon the individual, since there is no general agreement to direct him (Goethe's 'ground bass'), on which he can build a new unified method of presentation. He never achieves the final condition for an objective standard for art – the continuing union of opposites, the conversion of the subjective into the natural harmony of a generally accepted style.

'None is a measure for all. Each is a measure for himself and for such spirits as are more or less related to him', says Friedrich.[12] It is here that the century comes up against the limits of its power. So long as the subjective law of 'inner necessity' remains established – so long, that is to say, as art continues to be mainly for artists – the division that for two hundred years has affected the mind of European man can only be healed by and for the individual.

Postscript

I HAVE already explained that I could not hope to achieve comprehensiveness in this book. It was not my intention that the reader should see the century's huge mass of material spread out before him, but rather that he should be able to recognize the structural patterns underlying the whole. I was governed by these considerations in my selection and arrangement of the illustrations. The juxtaposition of illustrations sometimes makes explanations in the text unnecessary (it is not always the most striking pictures that demand interpretation).

The reader will be conscious here and there of the absence of familiar names. The fact that the book does not present a complete panorama should not be thought to imply that the author has scorned the abundance of his material, but rather that he has contrived to view it from a distance. Just as in every whole any growing parts are contained and delimited, so, it seems to me, this enquiry of mine has an inner consistency and logic – even if the enquiry is by no means complete. Without losing its essential character, it could still be organically developed. There is no lack of problems requiring further examination.

It may be held against me that I, an art-historian with none of the credentials of a specialist, have frequently quoted from poets and philosophers. I confess that if I have been governed anywhere by mere inclination, I have been governed by it here. I have called on Novalis, Baudelaire, Flaubert, and Nietzsche in particular to be my witnesses; but I could easily have called on other no less representative figures. The notes that accompany the text are restricted to a minimum. I have not made an exhaustive record of all the literature of which I have availed myself, but merely one of the works from which I have taken quotations, or borrowed thoughts and suggestions. I have found the works of Gaston Bachelard, Karl Löwith, Walter Rehm, Mario Praz, and Wladimir Weidlé especially rewarding and useful in showing me where my path lay.

My way of looking at the nineteenth century in this book may seem unusual. Similar attempts on the part of art-historians are anything but numerous. I owe much to the too little known work by Hermann Beenken, *Das 19. Jahrhundert in der deutschen Kunst. Aufgaben und Gehalte* (Munich 1944); and I have been stimulated by thoughts expressed in Hans Sedlmayr's *Verlust der Mitte* (Salzburg 1948), (English edition: *Art in Crisis*), though I have remained unconvinced by its arguments. Kurt Badt's magisterial study, *Die Kunst Cézannes* (Munich 1957), has supported many of my own feelings on this subject, and given me a great wealth of new insights. It was only after completing my manuscript that I learnt of two works that sought an answer to much the same questions as those I had posed myself. They are: Lorenz Eitner's 'The Open Window and the Storm-tossed Boat' (*The Art Bulletin* 1955) and Bettina Polak's *Het Fin-de-Siècle in der Nederlandse Schilderkunst*, 1955. In the United States Joseph C. Sloane has written a work entitled *French Painting between the Past and the Present; Artists, Critics and Traditions from 1848 to 1870* (Princeton 1951). I mention this very painstaking work here because its point of view is diametrically opposed to my own. Sloane writes (p. 210): 'The break which was to separate the present from the past was sharper here (i. e. in subject-matter) than in the domain of style, where earlier modes continued to exert a steady and powerful influence right down to the present, while traditional ideas about content became virtually anathema to the avant garde.' I have been anxious to prove the exact opposite of this. That is why I have tried again and again to make formal analysis the servant to iconographic illumination, and sought by this means to circumscribe the 'visible form' of works.

The writing of the book took place under favourable circumstances in as much as the publishers were anxious to produce a work on the nineteenth century. The result of this was a particularly intensive and fruitful piece of collaboration, for which I owe especial thanks to Herr Gustav Stresow who has spared no pains in making the author's wish-image come true and producing a most beautiful and artistic book.

Dr. Hans Melchers and Dr. Walter Romstoeck have each contributed energetically to the project's realization. I should like to thank them for their critical examination of the manuscript, their help in the collection of the illustrative material, and their expert assistance in the arrangement of the pictures.

I dedicate this book to my wife without whose presence it could never have been written.

Palaiseau-Villebon, June 1959   W. H.

Notes

I THE ARTIST'S STUDIO

(1) See: René Huyghe, Germain Bazin and Hélène Adhémar, Courbet – L'Atelier du Peintre, Paris 1944

(2) La foi nouvelle cherchée dans l'art de Rembrandt à Beethoven, Paris 1850

(3) Cf. Meyer Schapiro, Courbet and popular imagery, in: The Journal of the Warburg and Courtauld Inst., IV, 1940

(4) Personalien und Prinzipien, Berlin 1908, pp. 125, 128

(5) Goethe, 'jubilee' edn., vol. 27, p. 253 (cf. Beenken, Das 19. Jahrhundert in der deutschen Kunst, Munich 1944, p. 134)

(6) Novalis, Werke, ed. by Ewald Wasmuth, Heidelberg 1953–1957, vol. 2, fragm. 1473

(7) loc. cit., fragm. 1369

(8) Julian Schmidt, Geschichte der Romantik in dem Zeitalter der Reformation und Revolution, Leipzig 1848, vol. 2, p. 414

(9) Salon de 1859, in Œuvres complètes, Paris 1954, Bibl. de la Pléiade, p. 780

(10) Schriften, Munich 1914, vol 2, p. 100

(11) Menschliches, Allzumenschliches, II, I, 177 (Werke, ed. Schlechta, Munich 1954, vol. 1, p. 806)

(12) See: Studien zur Kritik der Moderne, Frankfurt 1894

(13) Ein Beitrag zur Kritik der politischen Ökonomie, 1947 edn., p. 268 (refd. to by Löwith)

(14) Vorträge 1844–1887, Basle 1919, p. 379

(15) L'Eau et les Rêves (1942), Paris 1956, p. 26

II NATURE AND HISTORY

(1) Nietzsche, Unzeitgemäße Betrachtungen, II: Vom Nutzen und Nachteil der Historie für das Leben, 1 (loc. cit., I., p. 211)

(2) Troeltsch, Der Historismus und seine Probleme, I, Tübingen 1922, p. 101

(3) Das Mutterrecht (1st edn. Stuttgart 1861), Basle 1948, p. 57

(4) loc. cit., p. 48

(5) A. Tabarant, Manet et ses Œuvres, Paris 1947, p. 70

(6) Burckhardt, Werke, VII, p. 162 (refd. to by Löwith, Jacob Burckhardt, Der Mensch inmitten der Geschichte, Lucerne 1935)

III ART WITHOUT CERTAINTY

(1) Cf. Gaz. des Beaux-Arts, 1958, p. 163 (fig. 3)

(2) Wind, The Revolution of History Painting, in: The Journal of the Warburg and Courtauld Inst. II, 1938/39, p. 116

(3) Cf. Jean Locquin, La Peinture d'Histoire en France de 1747 à 1785, Paris 1912; Werner Hager, Das geschichtliche Ereignisbild, Munich 1934

(4) Schadow, Aufsätze und Briefe, 2nd edn., Stuttgart 1890, p. 32

(5) Cf. Wind, loc. cit., p. 123

(6) Weidlé, Die Sterblichkeit der Musen, Stuttgart 1958, pt. 2, ch. 5

(7) Aufsätze und Vorträge, I, Leipzig 1957, p. 191

(8) Hetzer, loc. cit., pp. 188, 191

(9) C. D. Friedrich detests 'the empty bravura of the brush' and 'the unnatural and boastful effort to achieve richness and fullness' (Bekenntnisse, ed. Eberlein, Leipzig 1924, pp. 152, 156). There are similar comments by Runge and Blake

(10) Quoted by Pevsner, The Englishness of English Art, London 1956

(11) Goethe's essay appeared in the Propylaean, vol. 3, pt. 2, p. 167. Schadow's rejoinder: loc. cit., p. 47

(12) Nach Falconet und über Falconet, 1775

(13) Norman Schlenoff, Ingres – ses sources littéraires, Paris 1956, p. 141

(14) Cf. Meinecke, Die Entstehung des Historismus, Munich 1936; Troeltsch, Der Historismus und seine Probleme, Tübingen 1922; Löwith, Jacob Burckhardt, Der Mensch inmitten der Geschichte, Lucerne 1935

(15) Löwith, Von Hegel bis Nietzsche, Zürich (and New York) 1941, p. 269

(16) 'Mon intention . . . était de peindre les mœurs antiques avec une telle exactitude que les Grecs et les Romains, en voyant mon ouvrage, ne m'eussent pas trouvé étranger à leurs coutumes'. (Le tableau des Sabines exposé publiquement par le Cen David, Paris VIII)

(17) Waterhouse, Painting in Britain 1530–1790, London 1953, p. 199

(18) Adolphe de Bouclon, Canova et Napoléon, Paris 1865, p. 52

(19) Stendhal, Hist. de la Peinture en Italie, II, Paris 1825, p. 186

(20) Werke, ed. Suphan, VIII, p. 63

(21) Hetzer, loc. cit., p. 184

(22) Bouclon, loc. cit., p. 52

(23) loc. cit., p. 112

(24) August W. Schlegel, Cf. Sulger-Gebing, Die Brüder A. W. und F. F. Schlegel in ihrem Verhältnisse zur bild. Kunst, Munich 1897, p. 42

(25) Memoirs of the Life of John Constable . . ., 2nd edn., London 1845, p. 350. The degree to which the allegedly unprejudiced eye of this artist was dependent on pre-existing models on just those occasions when real spontaneity might have been presumed, has recently been shown by Gombrich (Art and Illusion, London 1960, p. 174)

(26) Friedrich der Landschaftsmaler, Dresden 1841 (new edn., Berlin 1944, in the series Dokumente zur Morphologie, Symbolik und Geschichte, p. 8)

(27) Hinterlass. Schriften, I, Hamburg 1840, p. 6

(28) Carus, Lebenserinnerungen und Denkwürdigkeiten, II, Leipzig 1865, p. 210

(29) Goya's series of etchings is entitled 'Los Caprichos'

(30) Malraux, Goya, Cologne 1957, p. 53

(31) With regard to Fuseli's place in the history of art, see Zeitschrift f. Kunstgeschichte, 1952

(32) Walter Rehm, Experimentum medietatis, Munich 1947, p. 34 (there are refs. here to parallels between Goya and Jean Paul)

(33) Leben des Künstlers Asmus J. Carstens, Leipzig 1806, p. 251

IV THE INNER COMPULSION

(1) Fernow, loc. cit., p. 253

(2) Einleitung in die Ästhetik, ed. Hotho, Werke, X, 1, p. 10

(3) Cf. Castagnary, Les libres propos, Paris 1864, p. 57

(4) Considérations sur la Grandeur et la Décadence des Romains, 1734 (Meinecke, loc. cit. 1, p. 159)

(5) Werke, ed. Suphan, VIII, p. 188

(6) Meinecke, loc. cit., II, p. 373

(7) Burckhardt, Werke ,VII, p. 162 (refd. to by Löwith)

(8) Cf. Blake: 'Everything that lives is holy' (Visions of the Daughters of Albion, 1793)

(9) Schlenoff, loc. cit., pp. 195, 197

(10) Lettres, ed. Malingue, Paris 1946, p. 46

(11) loc. cit., p. 110

(12) Œuvres complètes, Paris 1954 (Bibl. de la Pléiade), p. 643

(13) Œuvres litt., loc. cit., I, pp. 71, 113

(14) Delecluze called 'Dante and Vergil' (1822) 'une vraie tartouillade' (cf. Maurice Tourneux, E. D. devant ses contemporains, Paris 1886): Rewald, The History of Impressionism, New York 1946, p. 26

(15) Champfleury, Histoire de la Caricature antique, Paris 1865, p. 193

(16) Hegel, loc. cit., pp. 4, 13

(17) Journal, ed. Joubert, I, pp. 187, 193, 198, 199, 235, 242, 274, 315, 392, 418, 460; Œuvres litt., I, pp. 121, 169: cf. Baudelaire on 'le fini' (Salon 1845)

(18) loc. cit., I, p. 160

(19) Über das Verhältnis der bild. Künste zu der Natur, Munich 1807, pp. 57, 61

(20) loc. cit., p. 677

(21) Brecht, Heinse und der ästhetische Immoralismus, Berlin 1911, p. 39

(22) Werke, ed. Suphan, XXXII, p. 86

(23) Hurd, Letters on chivalry and romance, 1762 (Meinecke, loc. cit., I, p. 277)

(24) Schadow, loc. cit., p. 54

(25) On the concept of 'artist's art': Worringer, Fragen und Gegenfragen, Munich 1956, p. 141

(26) S. Rudolph, Die Krise der Kunst in Malerbriefen aus dem 19. Jahrhundert, Lorch 1948, p. 346

(27) Ernst Förster, Peter von Cornelius, Berlin 1874, II, p. 25

(28) Silvestre, loc. cit., II, p. 97; Ch. Blanc, Grammaire des Arts du Dessin, Paris 1867, introduction

V PICTURES OF HUMANITY

(1) p. II

(2) Des tendances de l'art au XIXe siècle. Revue univ. des arts, I, 1855, p. 82

(3) Grillparzer, Der arme Spielmann

(4) Werke, VII, p. 162 (refd. to by Löwith)

(5) London labour and the London poor. A Cyclopaedia of the Conditions and Earnings of Those that will work, Those that cannot work, and Those that will not work, London 1851, 3 vols. Publications like Mayhew's must have affected Courbet and Chenavard very differently. (It is shown below that they represented two opposing approaches to life.) Chenavard, the traditionalist, regarded the Great Man as the chief formative factor in history, and would have had little interest in other social forces. He would probably have regarded the working classes as a static and unchanging element in society, as Le Ploy did, in distinction to Marx for whom they were 'the firstborn sons of modern history'. Actually, however, there is little sign in Courbet's art of his views being any nearer to Marx's; and to some degree this applies to all the realists – whose creations were often held to have a biblical or Homeric character. Courbet's breach with tradition lay in his method of artistic creations, and not in his general view of humanity.

(6) Th. Silvestre, Les Artistes français, II, Paris 1856 (new edn. 1926, p. 106)

(7) Hubert Schrade, Das deutsche Nationaldenkmal, Munich 1934; Hans Sedlmayr, Verlust der Mitte, Salzburg 1948

(8) Ges. Schriften, II, Munich 1854, p. 391

(9) Julius von Schlosser, Vom modernen Denkmalkultus, in: Vorträge der Bibliothek Warburg, 1926–27, p. 15; Alfred Neumeyer, Monuments to 'Genius' in German Classicism, in: The Journal of the Warburg and Courtauld Inst., 1938/39, p. 159

(10) Förster, I, p. 213: cf. H. v. Einem im Wallraf-Richartz-Jb., 1954, p. 104

(11) Margarete Howitt, Friedrich Overbeck, Freiburg 1886, II, p. 56

(12) Die Malerei und das Neue Testament, 1885, in: Vorträge, Basle 1919, p. 283: cf. Förster, I, p. 13

(13) Die Welt als Wille und Vorstellung, bk. III, §. 48

(14) Camille Lemonnier, Les Peintres de la Vie, Paris 188, p. 153

(15) Werner Danckert, C. Debussy, Berlin 1950, p. 200

(16) Th. Silvestre, loc. cit., p. 98; Théophile Gautier, L'Art moderne, Paris 1856 ('Le Panthéon'); J. C. Sloane, P. Chenavard, in: The Art Bulletin, 1951, p. 240

(17) loc. cit., § 48

VI MANKIND ON SHOW

(1) Sources: The official catalogues of the World Exhibitions; the collected volumes of the Cabinet des Estampes of the Bibliothèque Nationale, Paris (Va 278 d, Va 275 a, Va 275 b, Va 275 c, Va 275 d); literature: A. Démy, Essai historique sur les Expositions universelles de Paris, Paris 1907; Raymond Isay, Panorama des Expositions universelles, Paris 1937; C. H. Gibbs-Smith, The Great Exhibition of 1851, London 1950. In Verlust der Mitte, Sedlmayr treats the exhibition as one of the 'principal new problems'.

(2) Nietzsche, Jenseits von Gut und Böse, 223 (loc. cit., II, p. 686)

(3) Isay, loc. cit., p. 38

(4) Gibbs-Smith, loc. cit., fig. 179

(5) Œuvres, XIII, p. 136; XVI, p. 197. In his Etudes de la Nature (Paris 1784) Saint-Pierre reduces the numerous shapes occurring naturally to five basic geometrical forms; he compares the circle with the stars and so calls it the fairest of forms. In this he comes close to Ledoux and Boullée. (On the cosmic aspect of monumental architecture, see Neumeyer, in: The Journal of the Warburg and Courtauld Inst. 1938–39; Sedlmayr, loc. cit.: 'Das architektonische Denkmal')

(6) Cités ouvrières . . ., in the periodical Phalange, Paris 1849; Victor Considérant, L'Avenir. Perspective d'un Phalanstère ou Palais sociétaire dédié à l'humanité.

(7) Ansichten über die bildenden Künste . . ., Heidelberg u. Speyer, 1820, p. 97

(8) Hermann Beenken, Schöpferische Bauideen der deutschen Romantik, Mainz 1952, p. 67

(9) Démy, loc. cit., p. 131

(10) Hans G. Evers, Tod, Macht und Raum als Bereiche der Architektur, Munich 1939, p. 221

(11) Henry-René d'Allemagne, Les Saint-Simoniens 1827 à 1837, Paris 1930

(12) J. A. Möhler, Ges. Schriften und Aufsätze, II, Regensburg 1839, p. 49 (refd. to by H. Sedlmayr)

(13) d'Allemagne, loc. cit., p. 307

(14) Hinterl. Schriften, II, p. 219

(15) Anton Henze, A. Gaudis Sühnetempel der heiligen Familie. Festschrift für Martin Wackernagel, Cologne-Graz 1958, p. 194

(16) Plate 21 in A. G. Meyer, Eisenbau, Esslingen 1907 (cf. Champury in L'Art, XVIII, 1892, p. 20)

(17) Lützow, Zeitschrift f. bildende Kunst, 1879/XIV, p. 197

(18) Usener im Wallraf-Richartz-Jahrbuch, XIV, 1952, p. 217

(19) Quoted by Wladimir Weidlé, Die Sterblichkeit der Musen, Stuttgart 1958, p. 161
Also Schinkel conceived the idea of a painted 'history of architecture', i. e. a painting representing architectural landmarks of all epochs and countries. (G. F. Waagen, Kleine Schriften, Stuttgart 1875, p. 376)

VII THE GREAT MAN

(1) Peter Brieger, Die deutsche Geschichtsmalerei des 19. Jahrhunderts, Berlin 1930

(2) Beenken (Das 19. Jahrhundert in der deutschen Kunst, Munich 1944) distinguishes between the need for pictures and the need for art.

(3) Heine (on Delaroche), exhibition of paintings of 1831

(4) W. Friedlaender, Napoleon as Roi thaumaturge, in: The Journal of the Warburg and Courtauld Inst. IV, 1940

(5) A. Chuquet, Stendhal, Paris 1902, p. 369

(6) Cf. Mitchell, Benjamin Wests 'Death of General Wolfe' and the popular history piece, in: The Journal of the Warburg and Courtauld Inst. VII, 1944, p. 20

(7) Exhibition of 1831

(8) Wagner's The Revolution appeared in the Volksblätter on 8. 4. 1849 (Collected Works, vol. XII p. 245,). For Wagner the goddess Revolution possesses features of the good and the bad mothers. She brings both promise and punishment. He calls her 'the ever-rejuvenating mother of humanity, the creator of a new world', an earthly paradise; and identifies her with life itself, 'whose cycle leads through death and destruction'.

(9) Gutzkow, Die geistige Bewegung, 1852

(10) Martin, Die Erschießung Kaiser Maximilians von Mexiko von Edouard Manet, Berlin 1948 (Der Kunstbrief), p. 21

(11) Louis Bouilhet, Dernières chansons, Paris 1872, introduction; Correspondance, Paris 1891–1893, III, p. 386; IV, p. 81

(12) Quoted by Aurier, Œuvres posthumes, Paris 1893, p. 180

(13) Paintings by: Vetter, Munkacsy, Granet, Meissonier, H. Vernet, Meissonier, F. Gérard, Poittevin, Robert-Fleury, Robert-Fleury, Delaroche, Alexandre Hesse, Girodet-Trioson, Cogniet, Ingres, Ingres

(14) Œuvres litt., loc. cit., II, p. 52

(15) Illd. in Adhémar, Daumier, Paris 1954, § 87

(16) Manet raconté par lui-meme et par ses amis, Geneva 1945, pp. 58, 164

(17) K. Lankheit, Das Freundschaftsbild der Romantik, Heidelberger kunstgesch. Abhandlungen, NF 1, Heidelberg 1952

(18) Otto Rank, Don Juan – une étude sur le double, Paris 1932

(19) Badt, Die Kunst Cézannes, Munich 1956, p. 64

(20) Cf. Jacques Roos, Aspects littéraires du Mysticisme Philosophique au début du Romantisme: William Blake, Novalis, Ballanche, Strassburg 1951, p. 308 – 'Jesus and his Apostles and Disciples were all Artists'. (Blake, Works, 1939 edn., p. 580)

(21) Jullien, Fantin-Latour, Paris 1909, p. 80

(22) loc. cit., p. 1220

(23) ed. Joubin 1950, I, p. 362

(24) Correspondance, I, p. 197; III, p. 88; IV, p. 28

(25) Entweder-Oder, pt. II

(26) loc. cit., p. 11

(27) Lemonnier, Les Peintres de la Vie, Paris 1888, p. 6

(28) L'Art Moderne, Paris 1856, p. 283

(29) Rehm, Clemens Brentanos Romanfragment 'Der schiffbrüchige Galeerensklave vom Todten Meer', proceedings of deutsche Akad. d. Wiss. zu Berlin. Phil.-hist. Kl. 1948/4, p. 40.
This desire for loneliness and exposure to the elements finds a strange echo in the imaginative voyagings of the architects of the French Revolution. A passage from Boullée's Treatise on Architecture is worth noting in this connection: 'Que l'on nous peigne l'homme au milieu des mers, ne voyant que le ciel et l'eau; ce spectacle, donné à l'homme, est vraiment celui de l'immensité. Dans cette position, tout est hors de notre portée. Il n'y a nul moyen de faire des comparaisons. Il en est de même d'un Aérostat qui, planant dans les airs, et ayant perdu de vue les objets de la terre, n'aperçoit que le ciel dans toute la nature. Errant ainsi dans l'immensité, dans cet abyme d'étendue, l'homme est anéanti par le spectacle extraordinaire d'un espace inconceable'. (Boullée, Treatise on Architecture, ed. Helen Rosenau, London 1953, p. 48). The passage is remarkably close in spirit to Friedrich's 'Monk on the sea shore'.

(30) F. H. Lehr, F. Pforr, der Meister des Lukasbundes, 1924, p. 268

(31) Cf. catalogue, The Romantic Movement, London 1959, p. 231

(32) W. F. Otto, Dionysos-Mythos und Kultus, Frankfurt 1933, p. 97

(33) Das Inselschiff, 1923, p. 195 (refd. to by Rehm)

(34) Cf. Helene Deutsch, Don Quijote und Donquijotismus, in: Imago, XX, 1934, p. 444

(35) Ludwig Volkmann, Iconografia Dantesca, Leipzig 1897; Irene de Vasconcellos, L'Inspiration dantesque dans l'art romantique français, Paris 1925

(36) Painting by Delaroche (in possession of the British royal family)

(37) Kraeger, Der Byronsche Heldentypus, Munich 1898, p. 32

(38) Th. Couture . . . par lui-même et son petit-fils, Paris 1932, p. 83

(39) L'Art Moderne, Paris 1856, p. 302

(40) Ballanche symbolizes Napoleon in the figure of Oedipus (Antigone, Paris 1814)

(41) Ges. Schriften, Munich 1854, I p. 397

(42) Paul Flat, Le Musée Gustave Moreau, Paris 1899; Leon Deshairs, G. M., Paris 1913

VIII THE EARTHLY HELL

(1) W. H. Riehl, Die bürgerliche Gesellschaft, Stuttgart 1851, p. 299

(2) Œuvres, VIII, 1853, p. 156

(3) Götzen-Dämmerung, loc. cit., II, p. 1020

(4) A. L. Mayer, Goya, Munich 1923, p. IX

(5) Correspondance, II, p. 73 (refd. to by Badt)

(6) André Chastel, La Tentation de Saint-Antoine ou le

Songe du Mélancolique, Gaz. des Beaux-Arts, 1936, p. 218; Rehm, Experimentum medietatis, p. 190

(7) Rosenkranz, Ästhetik des Häßlichen, Königsberg 1853, p. 283

(8) Cf. Baudelaire, loc. cit., p. 1221 (Venus as the Devil)

(9) Julian Schmidt, Geschichte der Romantik in dem Zeitalter der Reformation und Revolution, Leipzig 1848, p. 388

(10) Joubin, Gaz. des Beaux-Arts, 1934, I, p. 247

(11) loc. cit., p. 82 (refd. to by Rehm)

(12) F. A. Yates, Transformations of Dante's Ugolino, in: The Journal of the Warburg and Courtauld Inst. XIV, 1951, p. 92

(13) loc. cit., p. 1195

(14) M. Praz, La carne, la morte e il diavolo nella letteratura romantica, Florence 1948, p. 147

(15) Novalis, ed. Wasmuth, fragm. 1229; Nietzsche, loc. cit., I, p. 839 (Grausamer Einfall der Liebe)

(16) Cf. Rehm, loc. cit., p. 102

(17) Quoted by Rehm, loc. cit., p. 187

(18) Correspondance, II, p. 183

(19) Rehm, loc cit., p. 53

(20) Neun Briefe über Landschaftsmalerei, Villingen 1948, 2nd letter

(21) Revue Blanche, I. VI. 1896 (quoted by Hodin, Edvard Munch, Stockholm 1948, pp. 56–57)

(22) M. Miller, Géricault's Paintings of the Insane, in: The Journal of the Warburg and Courtauld Inst. IV, 1940/1

(23) loc. cit., p. 791

(24) loc. cit., p. 201

(25) Lettres, ed. Malingue, p. 140

(26) Cf. Anthony Blunt, The criminal-king in the 19th century novel, in: The Journal of the Warburg and Courtauld Inst., 1937, p. 249

(27) E. von Kraemer, Le type du faux mendiant dans les littératures romanes depuis le Moyen-Age jusqu'au XVIIe siècle, Helsingfors 1944

(28) Ges. Schriften, IV, p. 300: cf. Jean Paul, Vorschule der Ästhetik, I, Hamburg 1804, p. 185 (der Teufel als Hanswurst)

(29) Rosenkranz, loc. cit., p. 382

(30) Yates, loc. cit., p. 101. With regard to the use of Dante and other literary sources to describe the earthly hell of the present (see paragraphs that follow in text), there comes to mind Marx's comment after visiting a match factory: the scene in this factory, he said, was more terrible than any of Dante's imaginative descriptions of hell. John Martin seems to have been filled with similar feelings when after a journey through Britain's 'Black Country', he painted 'The Great Day of His Wrath'. His son later said of him that 'he could not imagine anything more terrible, even in the regions of everlasting punishment. All he had done, or attempted in ideal painting, fell far short, very far short, of the fearful sublimity of effect when the furnaces could be seen in full blaze in the depth of night. (F. D. Klingender, Art and the Industrial Revolution, London 1947, p. 114)

(31) Stendhal, Hist. de la Peinture en Italie, II, Paris 1825, p. 154: the same expression is used by Baudelaire (loc. cit., p. 892)

(32) Friedrich Halm. Klinger used this verse as a motto for his Brahms-Phantasie

(33) Géricault raconté par lui-même et par ses amis, Geneva 1947, p. 222

(34) Th. Heuss, Alfred Rethel: Auch ein Totentanz, Stuttgart 1957

(35) Cf. Rehm, loc cit., p. 72

(36) Malraux, Goya, p. 133

(37) Journal, loc cit., I, p. 290, II, pp. 215, 230

(38) Bünemann, Rodin: Die Bürger von Calais, Stuttgart 1957, p. 6

(39) Leymarie (Van Gogh, Paris 1951, p. 129) declares that the resemblance of the departing figure to Van Gogh is intentional.

IX STILL LIFE

(1) Letters to Leslie, London 1931, p. 57

(2) 'Tout romancier devrait être aussi innocent que le pommier' (Champfleury, Le Réalisme, Paris 1857, p. 21); 'Monet would like to paint as a bird sings' (Charles Morice, Quelques Maîtres Modernes, Paris 1914, p. 17); 'Symbolism also sees a relationship between the poet's work and the organic grow thof fruit' (Michaud, loc. cit., p, 54): cf. Gauguin-Morice in Noa Noa (ch. I, Songeries), and Cézanne's remark, 'L'Art est une harmonie, parallèle à la nature' (Gasquet, Paris 1921, p. 80)

(3) Lettres, ed. Malingue, p. 288

(4) For Runge colour is a 'force of nature' which 'has the same relation to the form as the tone of voice has to words', a world 'that has locked within it a wonder at life' (loc. cit., p. 80)

(5) Zola, Salons (ed. Hemmings-Niess), Geneva 1959, p. 91

(6) Œuvres littéraires, I, Paris 1923, p. 122

(7) Seznec, Flaubert and Graphic Arts, The Journal of the Warburg and Courtauld Inst. VIII, 1945, p. 182)

(8) Kierkegaard, Entweder-Oder, pt. II

(9) Bachofen, Versuch über die Gräbersymbolik der Alten (1859), Basle 1954, p. 373

(10) Novotny, Cézanne und das Ende der wissenschaftl. Perspektive, Vienna 1938, p. 89

(11) Pierre Francastel was probably the first to recognize the poetic and visionary content of impressionism (L'Impressionisme, Paris 1937, p. 9)

(12) C. G. Carus, Von den Naturreichen, ihrem Leben und ihrer Verwandtschaft, Dresden 1818 (new edn. in the series Dokumente zur Morphologie, Symbolik und Geschichte, Berlin 1943, pp. 10, 16)

(13) Philippe Burty, 1877, Venturi, Les Archives de l'Impressionisme, Paris 1939, p. 291

(14) Œuvres posthumes, Paris 1893, p. 222

(15) G. Geffroy, catalogue of exhibitions Bibl. Nat., Paris 1957, no. 97

(16) Gasquet, Cézanne, Paris 1921, p. 80

(17) Francastel, loc. cit., p. 197

(18) Die Kunst Cézannes, Munich 1957, p. 133

(19) Schriften über Kunst, I, Munich 1914, p. 322

(20) Avant et Après, Copenhagen (facsim. edn.), p. 74

(21) Stifter, introduction to Bunte Steine

X WOMAN AS MYTH

(1) loc. cit., fragm. 1022

(2) Versuch über die Gräbersymbolik der Alten (1st edn., Basle 1859, p. 217), Basle 1954, p. 259

(3) Förster, loc. cit., I p. 92. Markedly similar feelings are expressed through landscape symbolism in Shelley's Prometheus Unbound. The Liberator of Mankind is surrounded by a threatening rocky landscape. He desires to wed Asia who is also an embodiment of Venus and Nature; and dreams of an earthly paradise, of a nature that is soft and motherly:

    'Henceforth we will not part. There is a cave,
    All overgrown with trailing odorous plants
    Which curtain out the day with leaves and flowers,
    And paved with veinèd emerald, and a fountain

'Leaps in the midst, with an awakening sound...
And there is heard the ever-moving air,
Whispering without from tree to tree, and birds,
And bees; and all around are mossy seats,
And the rough walls are clothed with long soft grass;
A simple dwelling, which shall be our own;
Where we will sit and talk of time and change,
As the world ebbs and flows, ourselves unchanged.'

(4) The quotations following are taken from Julian Schmidt, loc. cit., pp. 421, 441, 469, 478

(5) In the passages that follow, certain ideas are reproduced from Das Mutterrecht and Die Sage von Tanaquil

(6) loc. cit., p. 1190

(7) Catéchisme positiviste ou sommaire exposition de la religion universelle, Paris 1874, pp. 104, 125, 127

(8) Lilly Jung, Dichterfreundschaft und ihr romantisches Gepräge, Dissertation, Berlin 1934, p. 44; Athenäums-Fragm., Minor 359

(9) loc. cit., p. 1189

(10) Rehm, loc. cit., p. 161: cf. Flaubert, Corresp., III, p. 80

(11) Leben des Künstlers A. J. Carstens, p. xx

(12) Cf. Roos, loc. cit., p. 112

(13) Complete Poetry and Prose, ed. G. Keynes, London 1956, p. 183

(14) The theme of the embrace is also found in Far Eastern art; the flower is used as a symbol for man there too (cf. Runge). (Blunt, The Art of W. B., in: The Works of W. B. in the Tate Gallery, London 1957, p. 19). For flower symbolism, see Schelling Blumenleben, Peng 1804

(15) H. Floerke, Böcklin und das Wesen der Kunst, Munich 1927, p. 17

(16) G. Schmidt, Böcklin heute, Basle 1951, p. 22

(17) Floerke, loc. cit., p. 27

(18) C. G. Jung, Symbole der Wandlung, Zürich 1952

(19) Hinterl. Schr., I, p. 27

(20) Lucinde (1799)

(21) loc. cit., p. 20

(22) loc. cit., p. 11

(23) Bachelard, L'Eau et les Rêves, Paris 1956

(24) Catalogue of the Tate Gallery, no. 23. Wicksteed identifies the principal figure as Christ (Blake's River of Life: Its Poetic Undertones, 1949, p. 70)

(25) Runge, loc. cit., p. 80

(26) loc. cit., II, p. 89

(27) A Soi-même, Paris 1922, p. 97

(28) Cf. Bachelard, loc. cit., p. 111

(29) Corresp., IV, p. 366. Nietzsche's view is that the 'heroic shell' (der heroische Balg) should be stripped from Wagner's figures – his heroines would then look so like Madame Bovary that it would be impossible to distinguish one from the other (Der Fall Wagner, loc. cit., II, p. 922)

(30) The basic method of representing the femme fatale in the nineteenth century is indicated in the work of Mario Praz, to which reference has been made

(31) Jung, loc. cit., p. 296

(32) Gräbersymbolik, 1859, p. 217

(33) 'C'est plat, ce n'est pas modelé . . . on dirait une dame de pique d'un jeu de cartes sortant du bain' (A. Wolf, Figaro, 1. 5. 1883): cf. Friedrich, Bekenntnisse, p. 107: 'The works of *** make one think of cards that are always being shuffled'

(34) Marie Bonaparte, Poe, Paris 1933, II, p. 579

(35) Gautier has an even clearer conception of the Sphinx as a terrible mother ('Le Sphinx', in: La Comédie de la Mort, Paris 1838, p. 201): cf. Réau, Iconographie de l'art chrétien, Paris 1955, I, p. 108 (The cat as incarnation of the Devil)

(36) Praz, pp. 79, 114

(37) Nietzsche, loc. cit., III, p. 510

(38) Jules Blois, L'Eve nouvelle, Paris (ca. 1895)

(39) Letter to The Times, 25. 5. 1854

(40) Max Klinger als Künstler, Strassburg 1899

(41) Verzeichnis des graphischen Werks von E. M., Berlin 1907, no. 21

XI THE EARTHLY PARADISE

(1) Vorträge 1844–87, Basle 1919

(2) Special use has been made of the following works: Ernst Bloch, Freiheit und Ordnung, Abriß der Sozial-Utopien, New York 1946; Alfred Doren, Wunschräume und Wunschzeiten, in: Vorträge der Bibliothek Warburg 1925/26, Leipzig 1927, p. 158; Hans Girsberger, Der utopische Sozialismus des 18. Jahrhunderts in Frankreich und seine philosophischen und materiellen Grundlagen, Zürich 1924; Karl Mannheim, Ideologie und Utopie, Bonn 1930; Julius Petersen, Das Goldene Zeitalter bei den deutschen Romantikern, Festschrift f. F. Muncker, Halle 1926, p. 117; Fritz Saxl, A Humanist Dreamland, Lectures, I, London 1957, p. 215

(3) Philosophische Schriften, Karlsruhe und Leipzig 1912, II, p. 217

(4) Schlenoff, loc. cit., p. 257

(5) loc. cit., fragm. 1761, 1799

(6) Löwith, Weltgeschichte und Heilsgeschehen, Stuttgart 1953 (ch. on Comte). The social revolution is the 'nineteenth century's version of the Day of the Lord' (Christopher Dawson, Progress and Religion, London 1945, p. 229)

(7) Fourier, Cités ouvrières. Des modifications à introduire dans l'architecture des villes, in: Phalange, Paris 1849, p. 29

(8) Henry-René d'Allemagne, Les Saint-Simoniens 1827 to 1837, Paris 1930, pp. 71–78

(9) Père Enfantin, 1829, quoted by d'Allemagne, p. 77

(10) Culte systématique de l'humanité, Paris 1849; Catéchisme positiviste . . ., Paris 1874

(11) loc. cit., p. 45

(12) Cf. Holbrook Jackson, Dreamers of Dreams, The Rise and Fall of 19th century Idealism, London 1948, pp. 97, 125, 140, 147, 155, 158, 159

(13) Sir Ebenezer Howard, Tomorrow, London 1898

(14) The Art of the People, 1879, Coll. Works, XXII, London 1914, p. 47. The general theory goes even further. It says that just as there is no restricted or exclusive representation of the people – 'the whole people is our parliament' – so all are involved in a work of art, and are, so to speak, co-creators. One is reminded here of Carlyle's remark, 'We are all poets when we read a poem well.'

(15) Werke, ed. Meiner, III, p. 453 (refd. to by Bloch)

(16) Couture, loc. cit., pp. 21, 23

(17) Une saison en enfer, 1873 (refd. to by Rehm)

(18) Brecht, loc. cit., p. 71 (from Heinse literary remains)

(19) Gautier, Le Palais pompéien, Paris 1866

(20) Lettres, loc. cit., p. 263

(21) Werke, ed. Suphan, VIII, p. 63

(22) Amaury-Duval, L'Atelier d'Ingres, Paris 1924, pp. 61, 187, 188, 213, 235

(23) Castagnary, loc. cit., p. 24; Venturi, loc. cit., II, pp. 315, 316

(24) loc. cit. p. 300

(25) Exhibition of 1831

(26) Histoire de la Peinture en Italie, Paris 1825 II, p. 206

(27) Letter dated 29. 2. 1832

(28) Wissenschaft, Industrie und Kunst, Brunswick 1852, p. 26

(29) loc. cit., p. 184

(30) The concept of the historical picture is inherited by sections of society today. Courbet calls his 'Funeral at Ornans' a 'tableau historique' (Silvestre loc. cit., II, p. 134); Riviere says the same of Renoir's 'Bal au Moulin de la Galette' (Venturi, loc. cit., II, p. 309)

(31) Briefe, Munich 1923, p. 67

(32) Dorra in der Gaz. des Beaux-Arts, 1953, p. 189: cf. Lettres, p. 263 (letter to Strindberg)

(33) Lettres à D. de M., Paris 1950, p. 119

(34) Ferdinand Servian, Papety, Marseilles 1912

(35) Leymarie in the catalogue to the Gauguin exhibition Paris 1949 Orangerie, p. 61

(36) Goethe im Wendepunkt zweier Jahrhunderte. H. R. Bookmaker has related the theme to Carlyle's Sartor Resartus (Synthetist Art Theories, Amsterdam 1959, p. 230)

(37) 'Je m'enfonçai vivement dans le fourré, comme si j'eusse voulu me fondre dans cette immense nature maternelle' (Noa-Noa): cf. Lettres, p. 144 (Cult of Venus)

(38) Blake, loc. cit., p. 559: cf. Roos, loc. cit., pp. 90 (Blake), 366 (Ballanche); Sloane, P. Chenavard, in: The Art Bulletin, 1951, p. 253; Praz, loc. cit., p. 303

XII THE DIVIDED CENTURY

(1) Bekenntnisse, loc. cit., p. 135 (cf. pp. 104, 110, 114)

(2) loc. cit., I, p. 7

(3) The Letters of W. B., ed. by G. Keynes, London 1956, no. 6 (1799)

(4) loc. cit., p. 29

(5) Silvestre, loc. cit., I, p. 29

(6) Vischer, Kritische Gänge, I, Tübingen 1844, p. 210

(7) Semper, Wissenschaft, Industrie und Kunst, Brunswick 1852, pp. 31, 63.

One aspect of the conflict, described in this section, between the artists who strove to conceal their techniques and those who emphasized them, may be illustrated by the case of Wagner who insisted on hiding away all the mechanics of opera production, including musicians and conductor. The exponents of the opposite school of thought are, of course, the Impressionists, who were intent on revealing the processes of creation. It is no mere chance that one of them was prepared to display the actual 'technical evolutions' of the orchestra on canvas (in the painting of which plate 186 is a detail)

(8) loc. cit., p. 211

(9) Löwith, Von Hegel bis Nietzsche, pp. 150, 152, 201, 202, 212

(10) Hegel, Werke (ed. Lasson), XIII, p. 153 (refd. to by F. Heer)

(11) Novalis, loc. cit., fragm. 1025

(12) loc. cit., p. 104

Acknowledgments

A.C.L. Brussels 4, 53; Adalbert-Stifter-Gesellschaft, Vienna 35; Alinauri-Giraudon, Paris 134; Anderson, Rome 26, 50, 54, 119; Archives photographiques, Paris 6, 25, 38, 56, 74, 82, 83, 107, 110, 124, 125, 150, 182; Art Gallery & Museum, Glasgow 184; Art Institute of Chicago 116, 144, 190, 197; Baltimore Museum of Art, Baltimore XII; Bayerische Staatsgemäldesammlungen, Munich 61, 86, 101, 172, 191, 213; Bibliothèque Nationale, Paris 8, 9, 106; Ann Bredol-Lepper, Aachen 11; Brooklyn Museum, New York 194; Sammlung Bührle, Zürich 97, 195; Photo Bulloz, Paris 16, 20, 23, 41, 55, 59, 62–64, 73, 94, 108, 111, 122, 128, 146, 156, 188, 204, 207; City Art Gallery, Manchester 131; Courtauld Institute of Art, London 162; Deutsche Fotothek, Dresden 91, 168; Durand-Ruel, Paris 201; Elsam, Mann & Cooper, Liverpool 17; Entwistle, Thorpe & Co., Manchester 164; Helga Fietz, Schlederloh (Oberbayern) XV; Gemeente Musea van Amsterdam 147, 173, 177; Gernsheim Collection, London 34; Photographie Giraudon, Paris VIII, 1–3, 5, 12, 33, 42, 45, 48, 49, 58, 68–72, 79, 80, 81, 84, 87, 98, 112, 113, 120, 121, 123, 132, 133, 145, 161, 165–167, 170, 171, 174, 176, 178, 179, 185, 187, 200, 202, 203, 205, 206, 212; Heinz Gleixner, Munich VI; Franz Hanfstaengl, Munich 96; Farbphoto Hinz, Basle 47; Institut für Bildjournalismus (Steichen), Munich 157; Kempter-Foto, Munich 1; Kleinhempel, Hamburg 14, 28, 76, 88, 93, 127, 148, 175, 209; Kunsthalle, Mannheim 78; Kunsthaus, Zürich 139; Kunstmuseum, Berne 215, 216; Verlag K. R. Langewiesche – H. Köster, Königstein i.T. II; Foto Marburg 32, 90, 99, 208; MAS Barcelona 46, 67; Metropolitan Museum of Art, New York 160, 183, 196; Minneapolis Institute of Arts 39, 43, 57; Museum and Art Gallery, Birmingham 10, 138, 140, 149; Museum Folkwang, Essen 52; Museum of Fine Arts, Boston 192, 217; Nasjonalgalleriet, Oslo 130, 136, 137, 218; National Gallery, London 22, 186; National Gallery of Art, Washington 66, 129; National Museum, Stockholm 180; Oslo Kommunes Kunstsamlinger 155; Öffentliche Kunstsammlung, Basle 214; Österreichische Galerie, Vienna 77; archives of the Österreichische Nationalbibliothek, Vienna 105, 142; Philadelphia Museum of Art 117, 118; Phillips Collection, Washington 51, 75, 126; Renger Foto, Essen 193; Rheinisches Bildarchiv, Cologne 31, 154; Roger Viollet (Charles Hugo), Paris 19; Rudomine, Paris 158, 159; Schweizerisches Institut für Kunstwissenschaft (Switzerland) 92; Verlag Albert Skira, Geneva V; Soichi Sunami, New York 198; Staatliche Museen Berlin, National-Galerie 27, 60, 85, 89, 115, 169, 199; formerly Staatliche Museen Berlin, National-Galerie 37, 95, 100; Städtisches Museum, Wuppertal 181; Rudolf Stepanek, Vienna 109; Stickelmann, Bremen 135; Verwaltung der Staatlichen Schlösser und Gärten, Berlin 13; Victoria and Albert Museum (Crown Copyright), London 15, 103; H. Wullschleger, Winterthur 18, 40; Württembergische Staatsgalerie, Stuttgart 21, 24.

Blocks by Brend'amour, Simhart & Co., Munich, except those for plates IV (A. Gässler & Co., Munich) and X (Jean Malvaux, Brussels). Thanks are due to Verlag Harry N. Abrams of Amsterdam for electros for plates IX and XVI, and to Verlag Albert Skira of Geneva for electros for plates III and XI.

N.B.: the references are to plate numbers.

Index of Artists and Illustrations

ALT, RUDOLF VON

b. 1812 in Vienna, d. there 1905. Pupil of his father, Jakob Alt. 1826, attended the Vienna Academy (landscape class and 'Historical School'). 1828–29, the first walking tours through the Alps. Later professional journeys took him through all the countries of the Austrian Monarchy, as they also did to Switzerland, Italy, Germany and the Crimea. 1897, Hon. President of the Vienna 'Secession'.

105 *The Vienna Hofmuseum* (after Gottfried Semper), 1878. Österreichische Nationalbibliothek, Vienna.
   Of the aforesaid grandiose project there were only carried out the two Hofmuseums (right and left foreground), the right wing of the new Hofburg (but not the corresponding left wing) and the right part of the adjoining quadrangle. The Triumphal Arch which was to span the Ringstrasse and connect the two museums with the Hofburg, remained on paper.

109 *Makart's studio*, 1885. Historisches Museum der Stadt Wien, Vienna.
   Makart's studio was open to visitors daily from 4 till 5. 'Every stranger who cared for culture had to see it, and if they had not much time they would prefer to omit the picture gallery' (Lichtwark).

BARDOU, EMANUEL

b. 1744 in Basle, d. 1818 in Berlin. From 1775 onwards a modeller in the royal porcelain factory.

11 *Kant*, 1798. Formerly Staatliche Museen, Berlin (sculpture section).

BLAKE, WILLIAM

b. 1757 in London, d. there 1827. Poet and painter. 1778, at the Royal Academy School. Of the Old Masters he preferred Dürer and Michelangelo, and of his contemporaries Fuseli, Mortimer and Barry. He despised Reynolds and criticized naturalistic landscape-painting. He earned his living as an engraver, and thus became acquainted with the Gothic, which decidedly influenced his linearism (copies of the sculptures in Westminster Abbey, 1773). The only exhibition of his work during his lifetime was in 1808, and it was vehemently rejected. (The first discussion of Blake's work in German appeared in Perthes' publication *Vaterländisches Museum.*) Blake illustrated Young's *Night Thoughts* (1797), Thornton's *The Pastoral of Virgil* (1821) and *The Book of Job* (1825). His own poems are also decorated with illustrative material that opens up new methods of book illustration (*Songs of Innocence* and *Songs of Experience*, 1787 and 1794, *The Marriage of Heaven and Hell*, 1790, *Jerusalem*, 1820).

7 *Newton*, 1795. The Tate Gallery, London.
   Blake saw in Newton an enemy of the imagination. In much the same way 'Nebuchadnezzar' embodied for him the animal quality of man dominated by reason. The circle is the symbol of measuring rationalism which reduces the infinite to something finite.

140 *The Whirlwind of Lovers*, c. 1824. Museum and Art Gallery, Birmingham.
   After Dante's *Inferno* (canto 5). One is reminded of Rodin's *Hell Gate*, and the final chapter of Mathurin's novel, *Melmoth the Wanderer* (1820).

141 *Vision of the Daughters of Albion* (frontispiece), 1793. The Tate Gallery, London.
   Albion is interpreted as the cosmic transmutation of Adam, and he has twelve daughters who accompany Oothon, Bromion and Theotormon. Blake carries on a polemic in his poem against the sinful moral oppression of love, and the placing of it under a kind of tutelage. Oothon, the gentle soul, is fettered to the back of Bromion, who has raped her. Theotormon, her lover, is sunk in despair. (In this people have seen the effect of the moral arguments of Bromion.) Cf. plate 115, Böcklin, *Triton and Nereid*.

210 *The River of Life*, c. 1805. The Tate Gallery, London.

BLECHEN, KARL

b. 1798 in Kottbus, d. 1840 in Berlin. Was a student at the Berlin Academy. Strongly influenced as a landscape painter by Friedrich and Dahl. Thanks to a recommendation by Schinkel he was appointed scene-painter at the Königstädtische Theater. A visit to Italy (1828–29) directed his attention to the atmospherical processes of nature. 1831, became Professor of Landscape-Painting at the Berlin Academy. 1835, visited Isabey and Vernet in Paris. One of his last works, *The rolling-mill at Eberswalde*, anticipates Menzel thematically, with whom he has a certain kinship in his impressionist attempts. Blechen died with his mental powers gravely impaired.

30 *Ruined Gothic church*, c. 1835.

100 *The palm-house on the Pfaueninsel*, 1834. Formerly Staatliche Museen, Berlin, National-Galerie (on loan from the Verwaltung der Staatliche Schlösser und Gärten, Berlin).

BÖCKLIN, ARNOLD

b. 1827 in Basle, d. 1901 in San Domenico near Fiesole. A pupil of Schirmer's in Düsseldorf. 1847, in Brussels and Antwerp, then in Geneva. 1848, short stay in Paris; he returned 'with a deep aversion to France and the French character within me'. 1850, his first stay in Italy, where he settled later.

60 *The artist with Death playing the violin*, 1872. Staatliche Museen, Berlin, National-Galerie.

101 *Pan among the reeds*, 1857. Bayerische Staatsgemäldesammlungen, Munich.

115 *Triton and Nereid*, 1875. Staatliche Museen, Berlin, National-Galerie.
   This pictorial idea is embodied in two versions. The Munich picture is naïvely described in a catalogue of the Schack-Galerie as an idyll. 'Next to him (the Triton) a Nereid leans against a rock and fondles a huge snake which is probably its playfellow at the bottom of the sea'. Georg Schmidt has recognized the real significance of the picture. He sees in it 'the woman between husband and friend'

('Böcklin could have been a Rodin in painting if the Germany of the time had tolerated such open expression of passion'). In the Berlin version there is no serpent, and the emphasis is on the longing for distant places exhibited by the man. Cf. plate 141, Blake, *Daughters of Albion*.

214 *Vita somnium breve*, 1888. Öffentliche Kunstsammlung, Basle.

BOUDIN, LOUIS-EUGÈNE

b. 1824 in Honfleur, d. 1898 in Deauville. His art forms the connection between the landscape-painting of the Romantics and that of the Impressionists. Isabey, Troyon and Corot, and above all, Jongkind, had a special influence on him. He was the first teacher of Monet at Le Havre. 1874, took part in the first group-exhibition of the Impressionists.

184 *The Empress Eugenie on the beach at Trouville*, 1863.
Glasgow Museum and Art Gallery: the Burrell Collection.

BOULANGER, GUSTAVE CLARENCE

b. 1824 in Paris, d. there 1888. Pupil of Delaroche. 1849–56, in Rome (Rome Grand-Prix).

84 *Flute-player rehearsing at Napoleon's Roman villa*, 1861.
Musée de Versailles.
The Palace of Prince Napoleon which was subsequently pulled down was in the Avenue Montaigne. Gautier – who is represented in the picture with a fine beard – describes it in a pamphlet as a 'dream' and a 'strict reconstruction' of Pompeian architecture. The busts represent the ancestors of the Bonaparte family. A frieze described the ancient myths of the creation of man. Other themes were, the Earth (Bacchus and Ceres), the Birth of Venus, Work (Daedalus), Pain (the Conquest of Troy). The Palace was renowned for its Turkish bath.

BOULLÉE, ÉTIENNE-LOUIS

b. 1728 in Paris, d. there 1799. Court architect; pupil of Lancret, Collins and Pierre, and of the architects Blondel, Hoffrand, Lebon and Lejeay. 1762, member of the Académie d'Architecture; 1795, Membre de l'Institut. He worked for a number of religious and private patrons. His official commissions included a new entrance for the Bourse (formerly Hôtel de la Compagnie des Indes), work for the École Militaire, a detention house – adapted from the Hôtel de la Force – and plans for a Royal Palace and for the rebuilding of the Bibliothèque Nationale (Rosenau, Boullée's Treatise on Architecture, London, 1953, p. 1). Few of his megalomaniac plans were ever carried out. Most of the designs surviving his death are in the Cabinet des Estampes, Bibliothèque Nationale, Paris.

8–9 *Design for a cenotaph for Newton*, 1784.
Bibliothèque Nationale, Paris.
A sarcophagus was to serve as the only adornment inside. Similar but less bold projects were later conceived by Délépine and Labadie.

BROWN, FORD MADOX

b. 1821 in Calais, d. 1893 in London. Studied in Antwerp, Paris and Rome (1837–1846). In Italy came under the influence of the Nazarenes (Overbeck and Cornelius), whose conceptions of art he later passed on to the English Pre-Raphaelites through his pupil Rossetti. He stood very close to the Brotherhood but did not actually belong to it.

149 *The Last of England*, 1855.
Museum and Art Gallery, Birmingham.
The two figures represent the artist and his wife. At the beginning of the second half of the century economic necessity drove many British people overseas. Brown himself thought of going to India. (He designated his painting a 'historical' picture, as Courbet did his *Funeral of Ornans*, and Rivière Renoir's *Le Moulin de la Galette*, plate 204.) Daumier's pictures of emigrants are usually put in the late forties.

164 *Work*, 1850. City Art Gallery, Manchester.
The scene is a street in Hampstead. On the right are Thomas Carlyle and F. D. Maurice, the leader of the Christian Socialist Movement and founder of the Working-men's College, in which Brown gave instruction in drawing. The 'religious' significance of this picture is conveyed in a poem of Brown's of 1865 in which he exalts work because it releases mankind from the devil.

BURNE-JONES, SIR EDWARD

b. 1833 in Birmingham, d. 1898 in London. As his intention was to go into the Church, he entered Exeter College, Oxford; there he formed a friendship with William Morris which lasted all his life. Ruskin's works and Millais' and Rossetti's pictures won him over to the profession of painting. A visit to the cathedral at Beauvais revealed to him the greatness of mediaeval art. He became Rossetti's pupil. He designed decorations for cupboards, pianos, organs, mosaics and tapestries for his friend Morris, and besides this a large number of stained-glass windows.

143 *King Cophetua and the Beggar Maid*, 1884.
The Tate Gallery, London.
The legend of the African king Cophetua who married the beggar maid Penelophon, is also used by Tennyson in his poem *The Beggar Maid*.

211 *The Golden Stairs*, 1880. The Tate Gallery, London.

CANOVA, ANTONIO

b. 1757 in Possagno, d. 1822 in Rome. Settled in Rome in 1780 (tomb for Pope Clement XIV). 1798, comissioned to do tomb for the Archduchess Maria Christine in the Augustinian Church at Vienna. 1802, invited to Paris to do a portrait of Napoleon. 1810, colossal statue of the Emperor commissioned (now in the Brera Gallery at Milan). 1815, invited to London to examine the Elgin Marbles.

26 *Pauline Bonaparte*, 1808. Galleria Borghese, Rome.

CARPEAUX, JEAN-BAPTISTE

b. 1827 in Valenciennes, d. 1875 in Château Bécon near Asnières. Influenced by Rude. 1846, began his academic studies. 1854, Rome Prize. In 1862, the plaster-of-paris model of his *Ugolino* was exhibited for the first time. This is conceived in the Romantic tradition of despair. The group, *La danse*, on the façade of the Paris Opéra was severely criticized after its erection.

110 *La danse*, 1869. Musée de l'Opéra, Paris. (A contemporary photograph taken at the first exhibition of this group).

CARSTENS, ASMUS JAKOB

b. 1754 in St Jürgen, near Schleswig, d. 1798 in Rome, where he had lived since 1792. Studied in Copenhagen. His criticisms of the Academy resulted in his being forbidden to receive instruction there. First Italian journey; 1788, to Berlin, where he refused the professorship he was offered at the Academy (1790). Was friend of the brothers Genelli. He loved Homer, Pindar, Shakespeare, and Klopstock, and, after Michelangelo and Raphael, considered Dürer to be the greatest of the later masters. 1792, went to Rome on a scholarship from the Berlin Academy.

In a letter to Minister Heinitz his artistic conscience moved him to make this statement, which has since become famous: 'I must further remark to your Excellency that I do not consider myself to belong to the Berlin Academy but to the human race.'

208 *Night with her children*, c. 1795.
Schlossmuseum, Weimar.
His rejection of 'Judaeo-Christian mythology' caused Carstens to occupy himself with pictorial ideas relating to cosmogony. He took an interest in the four elements, the four seasons, and the four ages of man, and also did work on a Golden Age. His *Birth of Light* (1795) is related in its thought to Runge's *Morning*, but he makes use of allegorical personification to express cooperation between the male and female powers.

CÉZANNE, PAUL

b. 1839 in Aix-en-Provence, d. there 1906. A friend of Zola, who was a fellow-student at the Collège in Aix. 1861, to Paris, where he met Pissaro and Guillaumin at the Académie Suisse. 1864, rejected by the Salon jury. Lived from 1873–1879 at Auvers-sur-Oise. Took part in 1874 and 1877 in the exhibitions of the Impressionists. In 1882 a portrait was accepted by the Salon. At the beginning of the eighties he grew more and more isolated. Return to Aix (1882). In 1886 the publication of Zola's *L'Oeuvre* produced an estrangement from the friend of his youth. 1895, exhibited with Vollard, later joined the Indépendants.

XII *La Montagne Sainte-Victoire*. The Baltimore Museum of Art.
36 *Les toits (View of Paris)*, c. 1880. Private owner.
39 *Les marronniers du Jas de Bouffan*, 1885–1887. The Minneapolis Institute of Arts.
64 *Self-portrait*, 1885–87. Collection Paul Cézanne Fils, Paris.
118 *Les grandes baigneuses*, 1898–1905. Philadelphia Museum of Art; W. P. Wilstach Collection.
124 *Une moderne Olympia*, 1873. Musée du Louvre, Paris.
A hot-blooded answer by a Romantic, aimed at Manet. The bearded man has the features of Cézanne; possibly the 'parody' is only a pretext and Cézanne is both making and holding back a very personal confession, since the observer's attention is directed to Manet through the borrowed title.
146 *La pendule noire*, 1869–1871. Niarchos Collection, St Moritz.
182 *Les joueurs de cartes*, 1890–1892. Musée du Louvre, Paris.

CHASSÉRIAU, THÉODORE

b. 1819 in San Domingo, d. 1856 in Paris. A pupil of Ingres, later influenced by Delacroix (journey to Algiers, 1846). His monumental chief work, the frescoes of the stairway in the Paris Court des Comptes points towards Puvis de Chavannes (1871, the greater part of it was destroyed).

83 *Tepidarium*, 1853. Musée du Louvre, Paris.

CHENAVARD, PAUL MARC JOSEPH

b. 1807 in Lyons, d. 1895 in Paris. Came to Paris in 1825. Studied first with Ingres, then with Delacroix. At the Sorbonne he heard lectures by Guizot and Cousin and took part in the gatherings of the Saint-Simonists and the Fourierists. Came to Rome in 1827, where he may have met Hegel, whose doctrine that the stages of consciousness for the individual are the same as those through which the general consciousness of mankind must pass, were of fundamental importance in his *Palingénésie sociale*. During his second stay in Rome he met Cornelius and Overbeck (copies of the frescoes in the Villa Massimi). Chenavard was accounted a witty conversationalist by Delacroix.

104 *La Philosophie de l'Histoire* (*Palingénésie sociale*). Musée des Beaux-Arts, Lyons.
Exhibited at the World Exhibition, Paris, 1855.

The main part of the Pantheon decorations – designed as a mosaic floor to go beneath the central dome. The lower quarter of the picture which represented the dissolution of human society, chaos and re-birth – the last being symbolized by a phoenix – may well have been lost. The following description follows Gautier: to the right and left of the figure of Christ, i.e. the Logos, the sages of the Apocalypse. On the right, the four cardinal virtues, which lead the deities of the Orient and the Mediterranean by the hand. On the left, the three theological virtues with the Nordic gods (Odin with the raven; a skeleton represents Hope). In the middle of the pillared section stands the symbol of all world religions. To the right of it, Zoroaster, Confucius, Homer, Plato, Solon, the Sibyls. To the left, figures from the Old Testament (Adam and Eve, Noah, Moses, the Prophets). On the left below, Mary, together with Jesus and John the Baptist, descending a stairway; below them, Saints and Fathers of the Church. In the corresponding part in the right half of the picture there is a representation of the end of the old world (Ptolemy, Alexander, Caesar, Attila; on the extreme right Charles Martell with Arabs). In the centre, the crowning of Charlemagne – symbolic of the mediaeval world. Below, on both sides, the great men of modern times from the Renaissance right up to Washington and Napoleon (Luther, Dante, Mozart, Spinoza, Cromwell, Peter the Great, Lavoisier are represented among others).

CONSTABLE, JOHN

b. 1776 in East Bergholt, d. 1837 in London. Although he attended the Royal Academy School in London, his conception of landscape was chiefly formed by the study of Ruisdael, Claude Lorrain, whom he called the most perfect landscape painter of all time, and the English painters of the eighteenth century. 1802, exhibited for the first time at the Royal Academy, of which he became a member in 1829.

15 *Stonehenge*, 1853. Victoria and Albert Museum, London. (Crown Copyright.)
A passage in a letter of Schinkel's of 1821 makes clear the nature of the attitude taken by the Romantics to the monuments of early Nordic times: 'Although it is true that the monuments of early Nordic times are formless, and that we often fall out over the question whether a further development is really possible from these beginnings, it is still undeniable that the large number of giant graves which are to be found at Rügen on all high places, the very curious mounds of earth which once surrounded Nordic sanctuaries, and the actual position of the latter in woods, by deep lakes, and on the high parts of the coast, harmonize with nature in this country in such a way that they form a strange but magnificent work of art, and exercise a strong influence on our minds.'

COROT, JEAN-BAPTISTE-CAMILLE

b. 1796 in Paris, d. there 1875. Starting from the academic landscape-painting of his teacher, V. Bertin, he developed a great sympathy in Italy for the pastoral themes of Poussin and Lorraine. His poetical *pleinairisme* is a prologue to Impressionism. He was a friend of Pissarro and a teacher of Morisot.

VI *L'atelier du peintre*, 1865–1868. Musée du Louvre, Paris.
38 *Le pont de Mantes*, 1868–1870. Musée du Louvre, Paris.
192 *Ophelia*, 1871. Museum of Fine Arts, Boston.

COURBET, GUSTAVE

b. 1819 in Ornans, d. 1877 in Vevey. First studied drawing with a pupil of David in Besançon. From 1839 onwards, in Paris: a pupil of Hesse and David d'Angers. 1844, represented for the first time in the Salon. 1848, meeting with Proudhon. 1853 and 1858, journeys to Germany. 1869, stayed in Munich, took part in the International Art Exhibition (influenced by Leibl and Thoma). Took part in the Paris commune riots, during the course of which he urged the crowd to upset the column in the Place Vendôme. From 1875 until his death, lived by Lake Geneva.

XI *Les cribleuses de blé* (*Women sifting corn*), 1854.
Musée de Nantes.

1–3 *L'atelier du peintre*, 1855. Musée du Louvre, Paris.
The full title is *Intérieur de mon atelier, allégorie réelle déterminant une phase de sept années de ma vie artistique*.
From left to right: the Jew, the priest, the veteran of 1793, the hunter, the cloth-merchant; behind these, two hunters and a reaper, the inquisitive man, the tomfool; the gravedigger, the prostitute, the unemployed worker, the Irishwoman (a memory of London), the boy, Courbet, the model, ('Truth'), Promayet, Bruyas, Proudhon, Urbain Cuénot, Max Buchon, Champfleury (sitting), the pair of lovers, the fashionable couple, Jeanne Duval (painted over), Baudelaire.

74 *L'homme blessé*, 1844. Musée du Louvre, Paris.
A self-portrait, which was rejected by the Salon jury in 1844.

114 *Femme à la vague*, 1868. The Metropolitan Museum, New York. Bequest of Mrs. H.O. Havemeyer, 1929; the H.O. Havemeyer Collection.

122 *Les demoiselles au bord de la Seine*, 1857. Petit Palais, Paris.

145 *La truite*, 1873. Collection Dunoyer de Segonzac, Paris.

168 *The stonebreakers*, 1849. Formerly Gemäldegalerie, Dresden. Burnt, 1945.
Courbet saw two stonebreakers on the road and invited them to come into his studio, where they posed as models. Proudhon compared the picture with a parable from one of the Gospels. Some peasants did in fact want to put it on the altar of their church.

176 *'Bonjour, Monsieur Courbet'*, 1854. Musée Fabre, Montpellier.
The painter meets his friend and patron, the collector Bruyas (cf. plates 1–3, *L'atelier*).

COUTURE, THOMAS

b. 1815 in Senlis, d. 1879 in Villers-le-Bel. A pupil of Gros and Delacroix. 1847, frescoes for a chapel of St-Eustache. Court painter to Napoleon III, teacher of Feuerbach, Manet and Puvis de Chavannes.

82 *Rome in her decline*, 1847. Musée du Louvre, Paris.
The picture, which was shown for the first time in the Salon of 1847, refers to a passage from Juvenal's Satires (VI, 292–3): 'Nunc patimur longae pacis mala; saevior armis / Luxuria incubuit victumque ulciscitur orbem.'
Nineteenth century interpretations of the picture that sought to see a topical relevance, concentrated on the contrast between the German and Latin peoples. The two Germans on the right of the picture are 'eye-witnesses' very much as Carlyle and Maurice are in Madox Brown's *Work* (plate 164), and Dürer is in Makart's *Charles V's entry into Antwerp* (plate 88), and also as the two figures are in Gauguin's *D'où venons-nous?* (plate 217) (cf. Seznec, *Gazette des Beau-Arts*, 1943, II, 221).

DAUMIER, HONORÉ

b. 1808, in Marseilles, d. 1879 in Valmondois. First studied with Lenoir, then at the Académie Suisse. 1830–1832, the first political caricatures. A contributor to *La Caricature* (1831–1835) and *Le Charivari* (from 1832). Met Balzac. In the forties produced his first paintings. 1852, Baudelaire writes a monograph

on Daumier. 1853–1857, friendship with the painters of the Barbizon school (Millet, Rousseau, Corot). 1859–1860, unsuccessful attempts to establish himself as a painter. Return to lithography. 1865, settles in Valmondois. 1878 first great exhibition with Durand-Ruel. .

1 *Don Quixote*, 1868. Bayerische Staatsgemäldesammlungen, Munich.
Cervantes' story was amongst Daumier's favourite ones. c. 1850, he painted his first picture of Don Quixote. In the second half of the sixties, probably stimulated by Doré's illustrations (1863), he grappled with this theme again. Daumier may well have experienced the conflict between the ideal knightly figure and the servile factotum within himself, for he possessed 'the soul of Don Quixote in the body of Sancho Panza' (Jean Adhémar).

51 *The strong man*. Phillips Collection, Washington.

52 *Ecce homo*, c. 1850. Museum Folkwang, Essen.
In 1849 Daumier received a commission from the 'Inspecteur des Beaux-Arts' to paint a number of religious pictures. It is questionable, considering the essentially subjective conception of the theme, whether the *Ecce homo* was to be a design for one of these commissioned works. Daumier's anti-clerical attitude (which his biographers continually stress, although really we do not yet know enough about it) would be quite in keeping with such a pictorial declaration of 'undenominational Christianity' (Strindberg). (The Amsterdam Rijksmuseum possesses a *Christ and his Disciples*; and in 1863 Daumier was painting an *Ascension* which has not survived.)

59 *The artist sitting before his work*, 1863–1866.
L.-R. Gramont, Paris.

75 *The Uprising*, c. 1860. Phillips Collection, Washington.

156 *Déplacement des saltimbanques*, c. 1866. Wadsworth Atheneum Collection, Hartford.

160 *Un wagon de troisième classe*, c. 1862. The Metropolitan Museum of Art, New York. Bequest of Mrs. H.O. Havemeyer, 1929; the H.O. Havemeyer Collection.

170 *La blanchisseuse*. Musée du Louvre, Paris.

191 *Le drame*, 1856–1860. Bayerische Staatsgemäldesammlungen, Munich.
This composition may have been inspired by an illustration of Grandville for Louis Reybaud's novel *Jérome Paturot* (1846). It has been impossible to discover with what particular play we are here concerned. The positions of the three actors vaguely recall Ingres' *Antiochus and Stratonice* (1840).

DAVID, JACQUES-LOUIS

b. 1748 in Paris, d. 1825 in Brussels. Pupil of Vien. 1776 journey to Rome, where he painted the *Oath of the Horatii*. 1784–85, court painter to Napoleon; 1816 emigrated to Brussels.

4 *The Death of Marat*, 1793.
Musées Royaux des Beaux-Arts, Brussels.
One of the four 'martyr pictures' that David painted of the heroes of the Revolution. It reproduces the artist's recollections of a visit which he paid to Marat on the evening before his murder. The picture was exhibited for six weeks in the inner court of the Louvre.

33 *View of the Luxembourg Gardens at Paris*, 1794. Musée du Louvre, Paris.
Painted from the window of the cell in which David was imprisoned from August to December 1794, after the fall of Robespierre. The picture was painted just before the beginning of a century in which the 'tranche de vie', i.e. 'the instantaneous, unique and suggestive (das Momentane, Einmalige und Motivische) ... was more than ever underlined' (Hetzer).

DEGAS, EDGAR HILAIRE GERMAIN (de Gas)

b. 1834 in Paris, d. there 1917. 1855, studied for a short time with Ingres' pupil, Lamothe. 1856–1857, journey to Italy. Study of the 'primitives'. Took regular part in the Salon exhibitions. Established contact with Gustave Moreau and Bizet. 1862, associated with Manet. 1872–1873, journey to New Orleans. 1874 to 1881, Degas took part in all group exhibitions of the Impressionists. 1884, meeting with Gauguin. In 1886 became estranged from the Impressionist circle.

62 *The artist with his friend de Valernes*, 1868. Musée du Louvre, Paris.
Evariste de Valernes was at the time at which this double portrait was painted, Degas' most intimate friend. A letter adressed to Valernes in which Degas speaks of his relations with people, a very rare thing for him to do, throws some light on this relationship.

87 *War in the Middle Ages (Les malheurs de la ville d'Orléans)*, 1865. Musée du Louvre, Paris.
The last of a series of five paintings which have as their themes ancient or historical events, and which were painted in the early sixties.

116 *Le bain*, c. 1890. The Art Institute of Chicago.

126 *Interieur (le viol)*, 1874. The Philadelphia Museum of Art; Henry P. McIlhenny Collection.
For a very long time critics suspected that this picture represented a scene from a novel or play, but it was only when Adhémar drew attention to Zola's *Madeleine Férat* that Degas' literary source was identified. Böcklin's *Odysseus and Calypso* represents a 'marital conflict' in mythological disguise in which the situation is the opposite of that in Degas' picture, for here the man is the prisoner of the woman.

161 *L'absinthe (dans un café)*, 1876. Musée du Louvre, Paris.
Degas called this picture simply *Au Café*. The scene is the café 'La Nouvelle Athènes'. Degas used the actress Ellen André and the engraver Marcellin Desboutin as models.

171 *Les blanchisseuses portant du linge*, c. 1876–1878. Howard J. Sachs, New York.

174 *Repasseuses*, 1884. Musée du Louvre, Paris.

185 *Voiture aux courses*, 1873. Museum of Fine Arts, Boston.

194 *Mlle. Fiocre dans le ballet de 'La Source'*, 1866–1868. The Brooklyn Museum Collection, New York.
Eugénie Fiocre danced from 1861–1874 at the Paris Opéra. Degas prepared a small clay model for the drinking horse.

196 *Le ballet de 'Robert le Diable'*, 1872. The Metropolitan Museum of Art, New York. Bequest of Mrs. H.O. Havemeyer, 1929; the H. O. Havemeyer Collection.

DELACROIX, EUGÈNE

b. 1798 in Charenton-Saint-Maurice, d. 1863 in Paris. Delacroix studied with Guérin and educated himself by looking at the Old Masters in the Louvre. Impressed by the English landscape-painters whom he encountered in the Salon of 1824, he travelled in 1825 to England. 1827, lithographic cycle for Goethe's *Faust*. 1832, journey to North Africa. 1843, lithographs for Shakespeare's *Hamlet*. 1855, Baudelaire makes the first important and penetrating analysis of his work. Monumental paintings in the Palais Bourbon, the Palais du Luxembourg, the Louvre and the church of Saint-Sulpice.

VII *The Chios Massacres* (detail), 1824. Musée du Louvre, Paris.

58 *Michelangelo in his studio*, 1850. Musée Fabre, Montpellier.

69 *The Chios Massacres*, 1824. Musée du Louvre, Paris.
A scene from the Greek war of liberation against the Turks, which aroused sympathy throughout Europe. Stendhal wrote as follows about the exhibition of this picture in the Salon of 1824: 'The public is so weary of the academic tradition, and of copies of statues which were fashionable ten years ago, that it stops and stands before the faded half-finished corpses, which M. Delacroix is offering it'. It is well known that Delacroix changed the landscape – under the influence of Constable.

71 *La barque de Don Juan*, 1840. Musée du Louvre, Paris.
The literary inspiration is to be found in the second canto of Byron's *Don Juan* (stanzas LXXIV and LXXV). The shipwrecked band are drawing lots, which will bring death to one of them. Don Juan is well over on the right, wrapped up in his cloak. No doubt recollecting *The raft of the 'Medusa'* (plate 70), Gautier wrote that the terrible nature of a shipwreck has never been more naïvely depicted.

72–73 *Liberté guidant le peuple*, 1830. Musée du Louvre, Paris.
The female popular hero was a favourite theme of the Romantics (cf. Maria Augustin, *The Maid of Saragossa*, whose part in Spain's battle against the French had been seized upon as a subject by Wilkie (1828) and Richard Westfall).

81 *Dante and Vergil crossing the lake that encircles the city of Dis, guided by Phlegyas*, 1822. Musée du Louvre, Paris.
Dante's *Inferno* (canto 8). This picture was copied by Corot, Courbet, Manet and Cézanne. Gros forced its acceptance on the Salon of 1822, where some conservative critics were scandalized by it.

132–133 *The death of Sardanapalus*, 1827. Musée du Louvre, Paris.
Inspired by some words of Byron (1821) dedicated to Goethe, Delacroix called this picture his 'massacre no. 2'. (Cf. plate 69).

DILLIS, JOHANN GEORG VON

b. 1759 in Grüngiebing, d. 1841 in Munich. Attended the Draughtsman's Academy in Munich. 1794, first journey to Italy. Subsequently long stays in Florence, Rome, and Naples. Was companion on one journey to Crown Prince Ludwig. Friendship with Angelica Kauffmann, J. A. Koch, and Thorwaldsen. Acted as a purchaser for the Munich Gemäldegalerien.

IV *View of the roofs of Rome*. Bayerische Staatsgemäldesammlungen, Munich.

DORÉ, GUSTAVE

b. 1832 in Strassburg, d. 1883 in Paris. Drew when he was only fifteen for the *Journal pour Rire*. 1854, was made famous by his illustrations for *Gargantua*. Illustrated the Bible, the *Divine Comedy*, *Don Quixote*, Balzac's *Fantastic Tales* and Eugène Sue's *The Eternal Jew*. 1868, made his first journey to London, where he was honoured with the founding of a Doré Gallery.

151 *Londres, Maison de Commerce*. Woodcut.

152 *Prison courtyard*. Woodcut.
Illustrations for *Londres* by Louis Enault, Paris 1876. In the text there occur these words: 'We must penetrate into the innermost reaches of the human hell, the social hell, at whose entrance one might well put the terrible words of the ancient Florentine poet...'

ENSOR, JAMES

b. 1860 in Ostend, d. there 1949. Studied at the Brussels Academy. 1883, broke through into the field of the fantastic and macabre. 1886, *The woman eating oysters* produced a scandal. 1929, raised to the nobility.

X *The skate*, 1892. Musées Royaux des Beaux-Arts, Brussels.

51 *'L'entrée du Christ à Bruxelles en 1889'*, 1888. Koninklijk Museum voor Schone Kunsten, Antwerp (on deposit).

FANTIN-LATOUR, HENRI

b. 1836 in Grenoble, d. 1904 in Buré. Studied with his father and Lecoq de Boisbaudran. Activity as a copyist in the Louvre. Entered Manet's circle. Several stays in England. Paintings and lithographs illustrating musical works of the nineteenth century (Wagner, Berlioz).

178 *Hommage à Delacroix*, 1864. Musée du Louvre, Paris.
The picture was exhibited in the Salon in 1864, a year after Delacroix's death. To the left, Fantin-Latour (with palette), Duranty (sitting), Cordier, Legros and Whistler (standing). On the right in front, sitting, Champfleury and Baudelaire, behind them, standing, Manet, Braquemond and Balleroy.

179 *Verlaine and Rimbaud* (detail from *Le coin de table*), 1873. Musée du Louvre, Paris.

FEUERBACH, ANSELM

b. 1829 in Speyer, d. 1880 in Venice. 1845–48, student at the Düsseldorf Academy (Schirmer). 1848–50, at the Academies in Munich and Antwerp. 1851, in Paris, where (1852–53) he visited Couture's studio. From 1856 to 1873 in Rome. 1873, called to teach at the Vienna Academy. Resigned his professorship; then 1876, in Venice.

21 *Iphigenia*, 1871. Württembergische Staatsgalerie, Stuttgart.

85 *The Symposium*, 1873. Staatliche Museen, Berlin, National-Galerie.
The composition and inventive qualities of the first version (in the Kunsthalle, Karlsruhe) have been compared with Schinkel, the Berlin picture with Semper. 'In the first *Symposium* he was going against his time, now it overpowered him, and made him a tributary' (Ahlers-Hestermann). Feuerbach was basing himself on a passage in Plato's *Symposium* in which the arrival of the drunken Agathon is described. Alcibiades, whom the newcomer is going to crown, stands in the centre. Next to him lie Aristophanes and Socrates who displays his right profile.

FRIEDRICH, CASPAR DAVID

b. 1774 in Greifswald, d. 1840 in Dresden. A pupil of Quistorps in Greifswald. 1794–1798, at the Copenhagen Academy, influenced by Abilgaard. 1798, in Dresden. Friend of Ludwig Tieck, Runge, Carus and Kersting. 1810, a member of the Berlin Academy; and in 1816, one of the Dresden Academy. 1824, professor of the Dresden Academy. 1835, had a stroke.

II *Chalk cliffs at Rügen*, 1820. Bequest of Oskar Reinhart, Winterthur.

13 *Monk on the seashore*, 1809–1810. Formerly Staatliche Museen, Berlin, National-Galerie (on loan from the Verwaltung der Staatlichen Schlösser und Gärten, Berlin).
'Nothing can be more sad and more discomforting than to be in this position in the world – the position of being the only spark of life in a realm of death, the lonely central point in a lonely circle. With its two or three mysterious subjects the picture lies there like an apocalypse, as though it were afflicted with Young's Night Thoughts; and, since in its uniformity and boundlessness it has nothing but the frame as a foreground, it is as though one's eyelids had been cut away when one looks at it' (Kleist). How little this unusual composition conforms to the traditional rules of beauty is plain if one considers Rosenkranz's definition of 'ugly monotony'. 'The monotony that is alleged to be ugly, is only thought of as such because of the neutral effect of absolute formlessness, the formlessness of a lead-coloured, smooth, stagnant sea under a grey sky when there is no wind to ruffle it.'

14 *The wreck of the 'Hope'*, 1821–22. Kunsthalle, Hamburg.
Painted in 1821, when there was much ice on the Elbe. An exhibition catalogue of 1822 mentions a 'second polar picture'.

27 *Monastery burial-ground under snow*, 1810. Staatliche Museen, Berlin, National-Galerie.
In this imaginative representation of the transitoriness of things, the forms of two architectural monuments – the choir of the Greifswald Church of St James, and the ruined monastery of Eldena – are fused together to form a single whole.

91 *The Tetschen altar*, 1808. Gemäldegalerie, Dresden.
The sculptor Kühn carved the frame according to Friedrich's directions. Below, in a wide panel, there was the all-seeing eye of God, surrounded by the Holy Triangle. At either side were ears of corn and bunches of grapes, which were to remind one of the body and blood of the Crucified One.
When the picture was exhibited in Dresden, Kammerherr von Ramdohr who was highly esteemed as an art-critic made it the target of a very intensive attack. The question he posed was whether it was a 'happy idea to use landscape for the allegorizing of a particular religious idea, or even for the purpose of awakening devotional feelings'. After criticizing the formal qualities of the picture, the absence of any internal structure in the rock, the unreality and inharmoniousness of the sky, and the neglect of perspective, Ramdohr answered this question in the negative.
'It is really an impertinence for landscape-painting to seek to worm its way into the church and crawl upon the altar.' Nor is Ramdohr wholly in the wrong when he objects to the aestheticizing and 'museumizing' of churches. 'Any relics of recognized saints, when set upon the altar, stir us far more than the most beautiful works of art, and the most savage caricatures have a far less disputable right to be preferred in this connection than the finest paintings imaginable'.

FUSELI, JOHN HENRY

b. 1741 in Zürich, d. 1825 in Putney. First visited London in 1764. From 1770 onwards was in Rome, where he remained for nine years. 1779, returned to London. Made the acquaintance of Blake. 1799, professor at the Royal Academy, where he was Keeper from 1804 until his death. Cycles of pictures illustrating Homer, Milton, Dante and Shakespeare.

18 *The Bard*, 1796. Bequest of Oskar Reinhart, Winterthur.

47 *The Nightmare*, 1783. Goethemuseum, Frankfurt am Main.

139 *The Incubus*, 1810. Kunsthaus, Zürich.

GAUGUIN, PAUL

b. 1848 in Paris, d. 1903 in Atouana (Dominica). 1871, bank official; first attempts at drawing. 1874, meeting with Pissarro, and a visit to the Académie Colarossi. 1880, took part in the Impressionist exhibition. 1883, Gauguin ceased to have anything to do with the stock exchange and devoted himself to painting. 1886, journey to Pont-Aven; made the acquaintance of Van Gogh. Visited Degas. 1888, second stay in Pont-Aven with Bernard and Sérusier. In the same year, meeting with Van Gogh at Arles. 1891–93 in Tahiti, where he finally returned in 1895.

XVI *Contes barbares*, 1902. Museum Folkwang, Essen.
In 1889 Gauguin painted a portrait of his Dutch friend Meyer de Haan, in which the subject of the portrait stares in front of him in a brooding fashion. On the table there is a bowl of fruit, and next to it two books: Carlyle's *Sartor Resartus*, and Milton's *Paradise Lost*. *Contes barbares*, painted

eight years after his friend's death, lets him enjoy the paradisial world of the South Seas, which he had never seen. The contrast in the earlier picture between the book and the fruit, that is to say between experience at first and at second hand, has been abandoned in favour of the nature myth.

66 *Self-portrait*, 1889. National Gallery of Art, Washington, D. C.; Chester Dale Collection.

98 *Ia Orana Maria*, 1891. The Metropolitan Museum of Art, New York; bequest of Samuel A. Lewisohn.

177 *'Les misérables' (the artist with a portrait of Van Gogh)*, 1888. Stedelijk Museum, Amsterdam.

In Pont-Aven Gauguin and Bernard planned to paint portraits of each other and send them to Van Gogh. The plan was dropped, and each painted a self-portrait and worked into it (in the background on the right) a picture of their friend. When Van Gogh received Gauguin's painting, he thought it was a prisoner he saw in it. An accompanying letter from Gauguin in which Gauguin compared himself with Jean Valjean, the hero of Hugo's *Les Misérables*, strengthened this impression. 'Is not this lawless man, with his love and strength, the picture of a present-day Impressionist?' Gauguin saw it as a collective portrait of all 'victims of society'.

217 *D'où venons-nous? Que sommes-nous? Où allons-nous?*, 1897. Museum of Fine Arts, Boston.

GÉRICAULT, THÉODORE

b. 1791 in Rouen, d. 1824 in Paris. A pupil of Carle Vernet and Guérin, his chief admiration was for Gros. In 1812 he exhibited in the Salon for the first time. 1816, journey to Italy. 1820–1822, stay in England. Died as the result of injuries received from a fall from a horse.

45 *Anatomical study*, 1818. Musée Fabre, Montpellier.

Clement, Géricault's first biographer, tells us that Géricault had rented a studio near the Beaujon hospital, and that the doctors there brought him 'corpses and amputated limbs which he used for a preliminary study for his *Raft of the 'Medusa'* (plate 70).

48 *The Death of Hippolytus*, c. 1815. Musée Fabre, Montpellier.

49 *La folle*, c. 1821–1824. Musée du Louvre, Paris.

One of ten separate studies of mentally afflicted people that Géricault painted for the physician, Dr. Georget, in the Salpêtrière, the Paris mental hospital. The pictures – of which only five survive – were probably intended as illustrations for Georget's work, *De la Folie*. Georget is accounted as one of the founders of social psychiatry.

56 *Portrait of an artist*. Musée du Louvre, Paris.

70 *The raft of the 'Medusa'*, 1819. Musée du Louvre, Paris.

On the 2nd July 1816, the 'Medusa' was shipwrecked off the west coast of Africa. Only fifteen people who managed to get on to a raft, were saved. Soon after the disaster there appeared a book, which was widely read, that described the whole affair in considerable, and even crass, detail. Géricault spoke with the survivors. He had a model raft made, and studied the corpses in the mortuary (plate 45, *Anatomical study*). The government suspected political implications, and would only sanction the unobjectionable title, *Scene from a shipwreck*.

GOGH, VINCENT VAN

b. 1853 in Groot-Zundert, d. 1890 in Antwerp (suicide). 1869 to 1876, employed by Goupil, the art-dealers, in The Hague, London and Paris. 1877–1879, a preacher in the Borinage. 1880, decided to become a painter. Studied at the Brussels Academy. 1886–87, in Paris. Meetings with Seurat, Pissarro, Toulouse-Lautrec, Gauguin and Bernard. 1888, with Gauguin

in Arles. 1889, in the sanatorium at Saint-Rémy. 1890, moved to Auvers-sur-Oise.

40 *Jardin de la maison de santé à Arles*, 1889. Dr. Oskar Reinhart, Winterthur.

65 *Self-portrait*, 1889. H. Tutein Noltheniu, Delft.

147 *Gauguin's chair*, 1888. Stedelijk Museum, Amsterdam.

153 *Prison courtyard* (after Doré), 1890. Museum of Western Art, Moscow.

154 *On the threshold of eternity*, 1889. Frau J. Kröller-Müller, The Hague.

173 *The sower*, 1888. Stedelijk Museum, Amsterdam.

GOYA Y LUCIENTES, FRANCISCO DE

b. 1746 in Fuendetodos, d. 1828 in Bordeaux. 1766, pupil of Bayeu in Madrid. 1771, short stay in Rome. 1775, in Madrid, where he made designs for tapestries. 1786, court painter. 1799, first painter to the King. He was reappointed to that office in 1814, although he had worked for Joseph Bonaparte. 1824, went to Bordeaux.

v *Carnival (The Burial of the Sardine)*, c. 1798. Academia San Fernando, Madrid.

44 *'The Dream of Reason brings forth Monsters'*, from *Los Caprichos*, 1793–1798.

One of the *Elegias morales* of Mélendez Valdes, who was befriended by Goya, has recently been named as a literary source by George Levitine. The *Caprichos* were later to arouse the enthusiasm of the French Romantics – Hugo, Baudelaire, Delacroix; it is possible that they even affected their dreams. Maigron tells of an unnamed Romantic who compared the thoughts that pursued him with the swarm of bats that has been startled into flight in the picture *(Le Romantisme et les Moeurs*, Paris 1910, p. 369).

46 *Saturn (Kronos)*, c. 1817. Museo del Prado, Madrid.

One of the murals in Goya's country house, the Quin del Sordo (House of the Dove) near Madrid, which the artist acquired in 1819. These painted nightmares were already known by contemporaries as 'pinturas negras'. 1878, they were removed and shown at the Paris Royal Exhibition. Later they went into the Prado.

50 *Lunatic asylum* (detail), 1800. Academia San Fernando, Madrid.

54 *Pilgrimage to San Isidro*, c. 1817. Museo del Prado, Madrid. The popular festivals on St. Isidro's Day were among the principal pleasures of the population of Madrid. In an earlier picture Goya had shown the merriment on the banks of the Manzanares. This later picture of the pilgrimage, that was in his country house, was sometimes also interpreted as a 'return from the Feast'. It contrasts sharply with the light-heartedness of the earlier composition.

57 *The artist with his physician, Dr Arrieta*, 1820. The Minneapolis Institute of Arts; Ethel Morrison van Derlip Fund. Goya added a special dedication to this picture in which he thanked his physician for the skill and care that had helped him to recover from a grave illness in 1819.

67 *Murat's troops executing inhabitants of Madrid on 3rd May, 1808*, 1814. Museo del Prado, Madrid.

Goya also painted the attack of the Mamelukes on the population of Madrid. It was this attack that began the suppression of the popular revolt.

119 *Recumbent nude (Maja desnuda)*, 1797–98. Museo del Prado, Madrid.

The figure in the picture has been identified with various people, chiefly with the Duchess of Alba, but all such attempts at identification repose on mere heresay and should be rejected. A far more important consideration is the fact that the painting of the nude was viewed with grave disfavour in Spain. Before Goya there is only a single example of a painting of a nude in the whole of Spanish art, namely Velasquez' *The Toilet of Venus* (the 'Rokeby Venus').

GROS, ANTOINE JEAN, BARON

b. 1771 in Paris, d. 1835 in Meudon. Pupil of David. Fled at the Revolution to Italy, where he later won the goodwill of Joséphine Bonaparte. At that time an honoured master, he welcomed the early works of Géricault and Delacroix. David, in exile, entrusted him with the management of his Paris studio. The failure of his *Hercules and Diomede* (1835) made his pupils desert him. In disappointment and despair he ended his life.

68 *Napoleon visiting people stricken by the plague at Jaffa* (detail), 1804. Musée du Louvre, Paris.

HODLER, FERDINAND

b. 1853 in Berne, d. 1918 in Geneva. Pupil of Barthélémy Menn in Geneva. 1878, journey to Spain. 1891–92, in Paris. Member of the Rosicrucian movement. 1904, exhibition at the Vienna Secession.

215 *Night*, 1890. Kunstmuseum, Berne.
   Writing about *Night*, Hodler remarks: 'Plus d'un qui s'est couché tranquillement le soir ne s'éveillera pas le lendemain matin'. The waking figure in *Night* is the artist himself.

216 *Day*, 1900. Kunstmuseum, Berne.

HUGO, VICTOR

b. 1802 in Besançon, d. 1885 in Paris. 1819, founded the *Conservateur littéraire*. 1841, member of the Académie Française. 1851, exiled by Napoleon III (Belgium, Jersey, Guernsey). 1871, return to Paris, and member of the National Assembly. 1876, Senator. Self-taught as a draughtsman, admired by Gautier, and compared with Goya and Piranesi. All the drawings left by him are in the Musée Victor Hugo at Paris.

19 *Victor Hugo on the 'Exile's Rock'*, Guernsey. Photograph by Charles Hugo.
   1905, a work by P. Gruyer on Charles Hugo's photographs was published. The reproductions of the photographs were accompanied by remarks of Victor Hugo's, such as: 'We are the despised ones and live in the abyss'. There is also mention in the *Châtiments* of the 'solemn rock' from which sound the 'eternal sighs of complaint'.

20 *Ma destinée*. Musée Victor Hugo, Paris.

HUNT, WILLIAM HOLMAN

b. 1827 in London, d. there 1910. 1844, entered Royal Academy School, where he met Millais and Rossetti. Of all the Pre-Raphaelites' work his is most strongly associated with religious belief. In 1905 he published his *History of Pre-Raphaelitism*.

138 *Awakening Conscience*, 1854. Collection of Sir Colin and Lady Anderson, London.

INGRES, JEAN-AUGUSTE-DOMINIQUE

b. 1780 in Montauban, d. 1867 in Paris. Pupil of David. 1806 to 1824, in Rome. Returned to Paris, where he had numerous pupils in his studio. In 1834 his *Martyrdom of St Symphorius* encountered violent criticism. His reaction to this 'ingratitude' was to return to Rome, where until 1841 he directed the French Academy. From 1841 onwards in Paris.

5 *Jupiter and Thetis*, 1811. Musée Granet, Aix-en-Provence.
   When this picture was exhibited in the Salon of 1811, it was regarded as an allegory on Napoleon. Ingres based his picture on a passage in the first book of the *Iliad*. Thetis implores Zeus for help for her son Achilles.
   'She rose from the waves at early dawn and ascended heavenward to Olympus. / There she found mighty Zeus sitting apart from the other gods / Sitting upon the highest peak of jagged Olympus / And she sat herself beside him, her left hand embracing his knees / While with her right she touched him under the chin.'
   The relief on the plinth represents the battle between gods and giants.

6 *Napoleon in his Coronation robes*, 1806. Musée de l'Armée, Paris.
   The picture was commissioned by the legislative assembly.

25 *Mademoiselle Rivière*, 1805. Musée du Louvre, Paris.

55 *Self-portrait*, 1804. Musée Condé, Chantilly.

79 *The Apotheosis of Homer*, 1827. Musée du Louvre, Paris.
   Commissioned by the Comte de Forbin, Director General of Museums, for the ceiling of a room in the Musée Charles X in the Louvre. The picture contains a collection of men of genius who are honouring another man of genius. There were precedents for the *Apotheosis* in the eighteenth century; one is the celebrated crowning of the bust of Voltaire on the stage of the Comédie Française, which has come down to us in the form of an etching.
   The texts of the Latin and Greek inscriptions were obtained by Ingres from the archaeologist Raoul-Rochette.
   At Homer's feet, the 'Iliad' sits to the left, the 'Odyssey' to the right. The figures in the left half of the picture are (from left to right) are Horace, Peisistratus, Lycurgus; Vergil, who is leading Dante; Raphael, hand in hand with Apelles – between them appear Sappho and Alcibiades; Euripides, Menander, Demosthenes; Sophocles and Aeschylus; Herodotus; Orpheus and Linos. In the foreground there are: Shakespeare, Tasso; Poussin (who appears disapproving) and Corneille; the head in profile behind has been identified as that of Mozart. The figures in the right half of the picture are: Aesop (squatting), Pindar, Hesiod (Anacreon?), Plato, Socrates; Pericles and Phidias; Michelangelo, Aristotle and Aristarchus; Alexander the Great. In the foreground: Racine, Molière and Boileau; Longinus and Fénelon; Camoëns and, behind him, Gluck.

80 *Ossian's Dream* (detail), 1813. Musée Ingres, Montauban.
   Painted for the ceiling of the bedroom in the Palazzo Quirinale, which was intended for Napoleon. Removed in 1836, the picture which was originally oval, was made rectangular by a pupil of Ingres.
   Ossian first became a fashionable subject in England, and the fashion was taken up in France towards the end of the eighteenth century. It is known that Napoleon always had a copy of Ossian with him in his field-library. Gérard, Girodet and Gros all painted pictures glorifying the Nordic heroes that made clear reference to the heroism of the Napoleonic age.
   Ossian's Dream depicts the blind Homer of the North in the foreground, while behind him there is a heavenly gathering of warriors. In the midst of them all is the Snow-King Starno; next to him there are a pair of lovers and Fingal with his sceptre. To the left of Ossian is Malvina, the wife of his dead son Oscar, who comforts the dreamer in his misfortunes.

94 *Louis XIII's vow*, 1824. The Cathedral, Montauban.

111 *Baigneuse*, 1808. Musée du Louvre, Paris.

112 *Venus Anadyomene*, 1848. Musée Condé, Chantilly.

120 *Odalisque*, 1814. Musée du Louvre, Paris.

207 *The Golden Age* (detail) 1862.
   Fogg Art Museum, Cambridge, Mass.
   A smaller version of the mural in the Château Dampierre (Seine-et-Oise), 1843–1847. The commission was given to Ingres in 1839. The artist Desgoffe assisted with the land-

scape background. *The Iron Age*, conceived as a companion picture, was begun by a pupil. It was to contrast with the peaceful existence portrayed in the other picture, and testify to the corruption of mankind and its entanglement in guilt and injustice.

KLENZE, LEO VON

b. 1784 in Bockenem, d. 1864 in Munich. Studied in Berlin with Hirt and Hilly, in Paris with Percier and Fontaine. 1816–1864, Architect to Ludwig I of Bavaria (Alte Pinakothek, Propylaea, Valhalla).

28 *Valhalla (at Regensburg)*, built 1830–1842. Kunsthalle, Hamburg.

Raoul-Rochette, the celebrated architect who was a friend of Ingres, gave an account in the *Revue des Deux Mondes* of the consecration on the 18th October 1842 – the anniversary of the Battle of Leipzig. The idea for it had come from Ludwig I of Bavaria; he had had the idea as early as 1807. The foundation stone had been laid in 1830. Raoul-Rochette calls the architectural construction one of the finest creations of modern art, and describes the relief frieze (by Martin von Wagner), which tells the story of the whole of German history. He also enumerates the busts of famous men which were already installed at the time of the opening. (The names of a number of legendary figures, or of people about whose features there is no exact tradition, are engraved on tablets in the upper part of the building.) The writer was less concerned over the presence of Catharine II of Russia than over the absence of Luther and Melanchton.

KLIMT, GUSTAV

b. 1862 in Vienna, d. there 1918. Studied at the Vienna Kunstgewerbeschule (school of applied art). From 1883 onwards, decorative murals and painted ceilings (Kunsthistorisches Museum in Vienna, stairway). 1897, co-founder of the Vienna Secession, which he left in 1905. 1917, honorary member of the Vienna Academy.

142 *Water-nymphs*, 1907. Privately owned, Vienna.

LEIBL, WILHELM

b. 1844 in Cologne, d. 1900 in Würzburg. Pupil at the Munich Academy (Ramberg). 1869, with Piloty very strongly influenced by the works of Courbet shown at the first international art exhibition in Munich. 1869–1870 in Paris, then again in Munich. Lived in a number of places in Bavaria.

93 *Three women at church*, 1882. Kunsthalle, Hamburg.

LIEBERMANN, MAX

b. 1847 in Berlin, d. there 1935. 1866–1868, studied under Steffeck; 1868–72, at the Weimar Kunstschule. 1873–1878 in Paris (1875, stay in Holland). 1878, settled in Munich, then in 1884, to Paris. 1898 elected to the Akademie der Künste.

172 *Old woman with goats*, 1890.
Bayerische Staatsgemäldesammlungen, Munich.

MAKART, HANS

b. 1840 in Salzburg, d. 1884 in Vienna. 1859–1865, in Munich with Piloty. 1869, summoned to Vienna where a studio was fitted up for him at the state's expense. 1879, professor of the Vienna Academy.

88 *Charles V's entry into Antwerp*, 1878. Kunsthalle, Hamburg.

When this picture was shown in 1878 at the World Exhibition in Paris, Lemonnier, a champion of the realists, deplored the empty 'apparatus'; while the conservative Albert Wolff spoke slightingly of a certain 'chic' virtuosity which had come half a century too late. Lemonnier's question why Makart had not painted the Vienna crowd was answered by the artist in his *Festival Procession* of 1879, in which the Vienna crowd were allowed to appear in the rôle of historical 'supers'.

MANET, EDOUARD

b. 1832 in Paris, d. there 1883. 1849, a pupil of Couture. Journeys to Italy, Germany, Holland and Austria. 1865, journey to Spain. His provocative paintings were defended by Baudelaire and Zola. 1867, one-man exhibition. About this time the young Impressionists were crowding around him. He became their spiritual leader, though he did not take any part in their group exhibitions. 1881, Légion d'Honneur. 1883, leg amputated.

XIII *Le balcon* (detail), 1868. Musée du Louvre, Paris.

41 *Les paveurs de la rue de Berne (The Roadmenders)*, 1878. R. A. Butler, London.

Manet painted the street-scene visible from his studio. The companion-picture is the *Rue de Berne decorated with flags*. (Sammlung Bührle, Zürich.) We can assume that in treating this theme Manet, who wanted to paint a cycle of subjects dealing with the life of a great city for the Paris Hôtel de Ville, was not merely concerned with the effects of light and colour, but also anxious to draw a contrast between the uneventful ordinary working day and the bright atmosphere of the festival. Both pictures give excerpts from the weekly life of a great city. The picture is really a 'caricature of manners' (Hogarth); here of course man is still the protagonist.

78 *Execution of the Emperor Maximilian*, 1867. Kunsthalle, Mannheim.

Ther are several possible ways in which the idea for this picture may have developed, an idea with which Manet began to concern himself immediately after the actual event. Whether Manet wanted to criticize the lack of political conscience, or whether his aim was to win that general recognition for his work which, as K. Martin says, it had hitherto been denied, is a very difficult question to answer. Was it with or without some ulterior motive that he clothed the Mexican execution squad in French uniforms? All we know is that in 1867 the police forbade the printing and further distribution of the lithograph of the execution. From the compositional point of view, a recollection of Goya's *Murat's troops executing inhabitants of Madrid* (plate 67) may well have influenced him.

Certainly Manet's *Execution of the Emperor Maximilian* marks a point of crisis in the development of the historical painting. For this picture, as Martin again points out, is a historical painting in which the purely historical element is overcome through the formulation of wholly new values.

99 *Dans la serre (In the conservatory)*, 1879.
Formerly Staatliche Museen, Berlin, National-Galerie.

121 *Olympia*, 1863. Musée du Louvre, Paris.

The title is derived from a poem of Zacharie Astruc, *La Fille des Iles*. It is said that Courbet declared the picture was like a playing-card: 'C'est plat, ce n'est pas modelé...' (*Figure*, 1st May 1883). When, later on, Gauguin copied Manet's *Olympia* he may have considered Courbet's criticism to be worth heeding.

123 *Le déjeuner sur l'herbe*, 1863. Musée du Louvre, Paris.

Pauli has shown that the group of figures is based on a motif of Raphael's which Marc Antonio Raimondi had handed down in his engraving of the *Judgement of Paris*. (Delacroix once observed that, as models, photographs were to be preferred to Marc Antonio's engravings.) On the right,

Eugène, the artist's brother; on the left, his future brother-in-law, the Dutch painter Ferdinand Leenhoff. The woman has the features of Victorine Meurend, Manet's favourite model in the sixties.

127 *Nana*, 1877. Kunsthalle, Hamburg.
The picture was painted before Zola began his novel. It was only in 1880, when the latter appeared, that it received its retrospective literary baptism.

162 *Un bar aux Folies Bergères*, 1882.
The Courtauld Institute Galleries, Courtauld Collection, London.
'The tangible reality is exclusively provided by the barmaid in the midst of her bottles, fruit, flowers and yet more bottles. The spatial zone beyond her, and the whole of the background is an intangible mirror-reflection. It is really there, but at the same time it is mysteriously deprived of reality' (Hans Jantzen).

186 *Musique aux Tuileries* (detail), c. 1860–1862.
The National Gallery, London.

187 *Le balcon*, 1868. Musée du Louvre, Paris.
The seated figure is the artist Berthe Morisot, who later married Manet's brother Eugène; standing behind are Jenny Clauss and the Dutch landscape-painter Antoine Guillemet; in the background Manet's son Léon Kœlla-Leenhoff is visible.

188 *Chez le père Lathuille*, 1879. Musée des Beaux-Arts, Tournai.
The actress Ellen André sat for the figure of the woman (compare Degas, *L'absinthe*, plate 161, Renoir, *Le déjeuner*, plate XIV). The adventurous young man was the son of one of Manet's acquaintances. It was the practice of the more sentimental school of *genre* painters to give such 'rendez-vous' pictures titles like *He and She*, or *A' Vital Question*.

193 *Faure as Hamlet*, 1877. Museum Folkwang, Essen.

MARÉES, HANS VON

b. 1837 in Elberfeld, d. 1887 in Rome. 1853–55, pupil of Steffeck in Berlin. 1857–64, in Munich; then in Italy till 1870. 1869, made journeys for the purposes of study to Spain and France. 1873 onwards, in Italy (Naples, Florence, Rome).

XV *The Orange Grove*, 1872–1873. Zoological Station, Naples.

61 *The artist with another painter called Lenbach*, 1863.
Bayerische Staatsgemäldesammlungen, Munich.

181 *In the loggia*, 1873. Städtisches Museum, Wuppertal.
(Sketch for the mural in the Zoological Station, Naples.)
Anton Dohrn, an independent scholar, had an international zoological research institute erected in Naples in 1872. For the decoration of a large hall he secured the services of Hildebrand and Marées. The latter was responsible for the murals, and the former did two busts for it – of Darwin and of the embryologist Baer – and carried out designs for the architectural arrangement of the space.
The scene in the loggia shows us the circle of friends: on the left, Anton Dohrn; standing behind him, Nikolaus Kleinenberg, the scientific director of the Institute; at the table the Scot Charles Grant, Marées and Hildebrand.

213 *The Golden Age I*, 1879–1885. Bayerische Staatsgemälde-sammlungen, Munich.

MARTIN, JOHN

b. 1789 in Haydon Bridge, d. 1854 in London. Exhibited for the first time at the Academy in 1811. 1825–27, produced illustrations for *Paradise Lost*. 1831–35 illustrated the Bible. His historical pictures enjoyed European fame; Bulwer and Gautier were among his admirers. In order to enhance the effect of the weird and monstrous, he painted some of his pictures on glass and set of artificial lighting behind them. He was interested in geology and prehistory. He developed projects for improving the qual-

ity of London's drinking water, for cleansing the air, and for the prevention of mine explosions.

17 *The Last Man*, 1849. The Walker Art Gallery, Liverpool.
The inspiration for this picture was the prophetic novel, *The Last Man* by Shelley's wife, Mary (1797–1851).

MENZEL, ADOLPH VON

b. 1815 in Breslau, d. 1905 in Berlin. In the main, self-taught. Only a short term of study at the Berlin Academy. 1855, a member of the Akademie der Künste and 1856 a professor there. 1898, raised to the nobility. Extended journeys to Paris, Italy, South Germany and Austria.

37 *View of an outlying quarter of Berlin*, c. 1847. Privately-owned, Berlin.

76 *Public funeral of victims of the March Revolution*, 1848.
Kunsthalle, Hamburg.
In a letter of the 7th April 1848, Menzel declares that he is 'plebeian in his views' (plebejisch gesinnt). He approached his task 'with a beating heart and full of enthusiasm for the ideas for which the victims had fallen'. Some months later he writes in a resigned tone: 'Once again we have expected too much of mankind. To the justifiable indignation about what had gone on above ground, there is now added indignation about what is going on down below.' This feeling of resignation may have been the reason for his leaving the picture unfinished.

89 *The Battle of Hochkirch*. 1856. Staatliche Museen Berlin, National-Galerie.
In the latest research work done on the subject – that of Konrad Kaiser – it has been emphasized that Menzel was not afraid of depicting one of Frederick the Great's defeats in this important picture.

148 *The studio wall*, 1872. Kunsthalle, Hamburg.
A phantom gathering of Great Men. Below on the right, is the mask of Goethe, and on the left, masks of Dante and Schiller, above them, the torso of the Venus de Milo.

169 *The rolling-mill*, 1875. Staatliche Museen, Berlin. National-Galerie.
The original title was *Modern Cyclops*. Menzel himself was enthusiastic about the richness in themes of the 'Cyclopean world of modern engineering' – of which he had been making preparatory sketches since 1870. 'And I don't just mean that bit of smoke', he remarked, as though he was alluding to pictures like Monet's *Gare St-Lazare* (1877). The scene is a great works at Königshütte that was given over to the production of rails. When the picture was shown at the Paris World Exhibition in 1878, it attracted a great deal of attention.

199 *Room with a balcony*, 1845. Staatliche Museen, Berlin, National-Galerie.

MERYON, CHARLES

b. 1821 in Paris, d. 1868 in Charenton. The son of an English doctor. He developed his skill in etching by making copies of Bléry and Zeeman. 1850, produced his first original work. Gautier and Baudelaire thought highly of his talent and powers of invention. He died in a state of mental derangement.

150 *Paris, La Morgue*. From *Eaux-fortes sur Paris*, 1852.

MILLET, JEAN-FRANÇOIS

b. 1815 in Gruchy, d. 1875 in Barbizon. Went to Paris in 1837, where he entered the studio of Delaroche and remained till 1844. 1844, exhibited in the Salon. 1849, settled in Barbizon and devoted himself entirely to peasant themes.

165 *La bergère*, 1867. Musée du Louvre, Paris.
167 *Les glaneuses*, 1857. Musée du Louvre, Paris.

430

MOLLER, GEORG VON

b. 1874 in Diepholz, d. 1852 in Darmstadt. Architect and architectural historian. Pupil of Weinbrenner. From 1810 onwards, director of buildings to the court of Hesse. In his *Denkmälern deutscher Baukunst* (Monuments of German Architecture) he produced the first authoritative and reliable representations of medieval buildings. He was reckoned 'one of the greatest experts in all Germany on the Gothic' (Goethe).

31 *Design for the rebuilding of Cologne Cathedral*, 1813. Stadtmuseum, Cologne.

After Goethe's panegyric on the Strasbourg Minster (1772), there appeared in 1790 Georg Forster's somewhat flamboyant introduction to the exalted architecture of the cathedral. The decisive impulse for the rebuilding came from Sulpiz Boisserée of Cologne who, in 1803, urged Schlegel, the theoretical spokesman for the Romantic movement, to make an important contribution on 'the fundamental principles of Gothic architecture', with special reference to Cologne Cathedral. In 1811 he won Goethe's support for the rebuilding of the Cathedral, and finally in 1814, the year of liberation, inspired the Crown Prince of Prussia with zeal for the same cause, and at the same time moved Görres to issue a most eloquent appeal for the completion of the cathedral as a symbol of the German unity achieved on 20th November 1814. In 1807 he had taken steps to ensure the safety of the building and in 1811 he had a report on its state made by Georg Moller. The engraving shown here is taken from Sulpiz Boisserée's superb work, *Ansichten, Risse und einzelne Teile des Domes von Köln* (Views, sketches and separate sections of Cologne Cathedral), Stuttgart, 1823, 1842, which had been in preparation since 1808. It gives a view of the interior looking towards the south-west, and has the title 'Cathedral Church of Cologne, the nave, as it should be when complete'. Drawn by G. Moller, 1813, restored by S. Boisserée, Engraved by Leissner.

MONET, CLAUDE

b. 1840 in Paris, d. 1926 in Giverny. Spent his youth in Le Havre where Boudin introduced him to pleinairism. 1859, entered the Académie Suisse, meeting with Pissarro. 1862, a pupil of Gleyre; friend of Renoir and Sisley; worked with them in the forest of Fontainebleau. 1865, exhibited in the Salon for the first time. 1870, to London; much impressed by Turner's paintings. 1872–1878, at Argenteuil. Took part in most of the Impressionists' group exhibitions. 1880, first one-man exhibition.

VIII *Étang aux Nymphéas (Pond with Nymphaea lilies)*, 1904. Musée du Louvre, Paris.

42 *Pont de l'Europe*, 1877. Musée Marmottan, Paris.

183 *La Grenouillère*, 1869. The Metropolitan Museum of Art, New York. Bequest of Mrs. H. O. Havemeyer, 1929; the H. O. Havemeyer Collection.

201 *Le Boulevard des Capucines*, 1873.

203 *Le déjeuner*, c. 1872–1874. Musée du Louvre, Paris.

206 *Rouen Cathedral*, 1894. Musée du Louvre, Paris.
Between 1893 and 1895 Monet painted twenty views of Rouen Cathedral.

MOREAU, GUSTAVE

b. 1826 in Paris, d. there 1898. Pupil of Picot at the Academy. 1858–1860, in Italy (meeting with Degas). 1885, journey to Holland. Influenced by the Quattrocentoists, Delacroix, Chassériau and the English Pre-Raphaelites. 1883, at the suggestion of Manet, an officer of the Légion d'Honneur. 1892, professor at the Academy (teacher of Georges Rouault and Matisse).

16 *Prometheus*, 1868. Musée du Louvre, Paris.

134 *L'apparition (Salomé)* c. 1876. Musée du Louvre, Paris.
E. Schuré thought he saw in the picture the victory of the powers of the spirit over the dark sensuality of the courtesan. Salome is paralysed by the steely glance of the dead apostle and – killed.

MUNCH, EDVARD

b. 1863 in Löiten, d. 1944 at Ekely near Oslo. 1882, school of draughtsmanship at Christiania. 1889–1892, in Paris; then until 1895 in Germany. In Paris was in contact with Pissarro and the Neo-Impressionists. In Theo van Gogh's house Munch saw works of the latter's brother and of Gauguin. 1892, exhibition in Berlin which produced a scandal. 1895–96, in Paris again. (Portrait of Mallarmé; article by Strindberg in the *Revue Blanche*.) 1902–1908, in Germany again. 1909, returned to Norway.

130 *The morning after*, 1894–1895. National Gallery, Oslo.

136 *Puberty*, 1894. National Gallery, Oslo.

137 *Ashes*, 1894. National Gallery, Oslo.

155 *The death-chamber*, 1894. National Gallery, Oslo.
Two of Munch's themes, that of the *Death-chamber* and that of the *Sick girl*, were anticipated by Robinson's photograph, *Fading Away*, of 1858. It is possible that the artist was familiar with this picture.

218 *The Dance of Life*, 1899–1900. National Gallery, Oslo.

NIÉPCE, JOSEPH NICÉPHORE

b. 1765 in Châlon-sur-Saône, d. 1833 in Gras. Inventor of photography. Had been interested since 1811 in lithography. 1824 succeeded in producing the first heliograph (a picture made with the aid of a camera obscura). 1826, associated with Daguerre.

34 *View from his window*, 1826. The first photograph in the world. Gernsheim Collection, London.

OVERBECK, JOHANN FRIEDRICH

b. 1789 in Lübeck, d. 1869 in Rome. Befriended Pforr in Vienna, and, after leaving the Academy, founded the Lukasbund with his friend (1809). 1810, moved to Rome. Overbeck was the spiritual mentor of the Nazarenes. He took part in producing the murals in the Casa Batholdy and the Casino Massimo.

90 *The Triumph of Religion*, 1833–1840. Städelsches Kunstinstitut, Frankfurt am Main.
Overbeck wanted to paint a 'divina conversazione' between divinely favoured spirits. In a commentary he spoke of a 'Magnificat of the Arts'. In this picture the Virgin Mary symbolizes poetry, the central art. The Martyrs and saints are to remind us of the inexhaustible riches of Christian pictorial themes. The stream of water coming from the fountain symbolizes the 'striving of Christian art towards the attainment of heaven.' The painters form three groups: the Venetian (to which are added Leonardo and Holbein), the Tuscan (grouped around Dante), and the Nordic-Italian (to the right of the fountain) which is to represent in visual form the harmonious understanding between the different groups (Lucas van Leyden gives Mantegna his hands, while Dürer stands between the two as intermediary). The two seated monks are to remind us of the early stages of painting. The left side of the foreground is taken up by the sculptors, the right by the architects. Overbeck would not allow the presence of 'any artists of the late Renaissance because from that period onwards an unecclesiastical naturalism, a paganized Christianity, was making its influence widely felt' (M. Howitt).

PAXTON, SIR JOSEPH

Landscape-gardener and architect, b. 1803 in Milton-Bryant (Bedfordshire), d. 1865 at Rockhills near Sydenham. Worked for the Duke of Devonshire and created the best laid out gardens in the world at Chatsworth, his seat. Was knighted for his plans for the Crystal Palace in Hyde Park and the realization of them (the Crystal Palace was later moved to Sydenham). Wrote a number of important works on horticulture.

102 *Crystal Palace*, International Exhibition, London, 1851

PILOTY, KARL THEODOR VON

b. 1826 in Munich, d. 1886 in Ambach. Pupil of his father and at the Munich Academy. 1847, Venice; 1852, Antwerp and Paris (influenced by Gallait and Delaroche). 1856, professor at the Academy, 1860, raised to nobility. Teacher of Makart, Defregger and Grützner.

86 *Seni and the corpse of Wallenstein*, 1855.
Bayerische Staatsgemäldesammlungen, Munich.

PRUD'HON, PIERRE PAUL

b. 1758 in Cluny, d. 1823 in Paris. 1784, received the triennial prize of the states of Burgundy. From 1791 onwards exhibited in the Salon. Painter to the Empress Joséphine. 1816, Membre de l'Institut.

23 *Joséphine Beauharnais*, 1805. Musée du Louvre, Paris.

PUVIS DE CHAVANNES, PIERRE

b. 1824 in Lyons, d. 1898 in Paris. Studied for two weeks in Delacroix's studio. then for three months with Couture. The frescoes of Chasseriau in the Court des Comptes provided the decisive stimulus that led him to concern himself with murals. The most important cycles are to be found in the Panthéon (1874–1878), the Sorbonne (1887) and the Hôtel de Ville (1891 to 1894).

97 *The Prodigal Son*, 1879. Sammlung Bührle, Zürich.
A remark of the artist made in the course of conversation, that he had particularly wanted to paint pigs and had thus been led to the theme of the Prodigal Son, may be taken as a typical artist's joke. Puvis de Chavannes' contemporaries suggested that the three pictures. *The dream, The Prodigal Son*, and *Le pauvre pecheur* (plate 166), should be made into a 'triptych of misfortune'.

166 *Le pauvre pecheur*, 1881. Musée du Luxembourg, Paris.
From the thematic point of view, the picture stands half way between the melancholy loneliness of the Romantics (C.D.Friedrich) and early expressionism (Munch). In its general mood, it comes very close to *Les illusions perdues* (1842) by Gleyre, one of the most famous Salon painters. In the nineties this picture was one of the starting points from which the Symbolists developed their 'synthetic' conception of form (it was copied by Maillol).

212 *L'hiver*, 1889–1893. Hôtel de Ville, Paris.

REDON, ODILON

b. 1840 in Bordeaux, d. 1916 in Paris. Influenced by the etchings of Bredin and by the botanist Clavaud who introduced him to the world of natural forms and to the works of Flaubert, Poe and Mallarmé. From 1870 onwards, in Paris; met Corot and Fantin-Latour. 1881 and 1882, one-man exhibitions which attracted the attention of Huysmans. Connected with the younger Symbolists (Mallarmé, Gide, Valéry, Jammes). Redon admired Moreau and Puvis de Chavannes.

113 *Birth of Venus*, 1910. Privately owned, Paris.

RENOIR, PIERRE-AUGUSTE

b. 1841 in Limoges, d. 1919 in Cagnes. Began his career as a porcelain-painter. 1862, pupil of Gleyre at the École des Beaux-Arts (meeting with Monet, Sisley and Bazille; worked with them in the forest of Fontainebleau). 1864, first exhibition in the Salon. 1872, under the influence of Monet adopted the Impressionist technique. 1881, travelled to Italy; came to terms with Ingres, Raphael and the Primitives. From 1906 onwards in Cagnes.

XIV *Le déjeuner*, 1879. Städelsches Kunstinstitut, Frankfurt am Main.
The seated female figure is Ellen André (cf. plate 188, Manet's *Chez le père Lathuille*, and plate 161 Degas *L'Absinthe*). The man is the son of an industrialist.

63 *Richard Wagner*, 1893. Musée de l' Opèra, Paris.

117 *Les grandes baigneuses*, 1885–1887. Philadelphia Museum of Art; Collection of Mrs. Carrol S. Tyson. Their gestures are thought to contain echoes of reliefs by Girardon at Versailles.

125 *L'esclave*, 1872. Collection of Prince Matsukata, Paris.
This picture was rejected by the Salon jury of 1872. In a sense it pays homage to Delacroix's *Women in Algeria* (note the servant in the right background). Cooper thought that he discerned in the heads of the three women the features of Lise (cf. plate 189).

180 *Le cabaret de la mère Anthony*, 1866.
Nationalmuseum, Stockholm.
From left to right; Nana, the daughter of the proprietor, the painter Lecœur, an unknown person, la mère Anthony, Sisley (with the paper *L'Evénement* to which Zola was a contributor); the caricature represents Murger, and may contain a playful allusion to the difference between the fictional and actual *vie de Bohème*.

189 *Lise*, 1867. Museum Folkwang, Essen.
Lise was an intimate friend of Renoir, who reproduced her features in more than a dozen of his paintings.

202 *Paysage*, c. 1873. Musée du Louvre, Paris.

204 *Le Moulin de la Galette*, 1876. Musée du Louvre, Paris.
A number of the artist's friends served as models for the group round the table and the dancing couples, among them the young painter and critic, Georges Rivière, who wrote as follows about the picture: 'This is a historical painting... never before had it occurred to anybody to reproduce such a commonplace scene on so large a canvas.'

205 *La balançoire*, 1876. Musée du Louvre, Paris.

RODIN, AUGUSTE

b. 1840 in Paris, d. 1918 in Meudon. With Barye at the age of seventeen. Worked for a decorator, and then for six years in the studio of Carrier-Belleuse. 1871–1877, in Belgium. 1875, journeyed to Italy; much impressed by Michelangelo. 1877, exhibited *The Iron Age*, which opened the way to fame for him. 1880, began work on the *Hell Gate*.

157 *Balzac*, 1897. (Photograph by Edward Steichen)

158 *Les bourgeois de Calais*, 1884–1886.

159 *Le Penseur de la 'Porte de l'Enfer' (The Thinker)*, 1879–1900.

ROMAKO, ANTON

b. 1832 in Atzgersdorf near Vienna, d. 1889 in Vienna (suicide). Studied in Vienna (Rahl), Munich (Kaulbach) and Venice. 1857 to 1876, in Rome; then in Vienna again.

77 *Tegetthoff during the Battle of Lissa*, c. 1880.
Österreichische Galerie, Vienna.
'The picture shows us the moment on the morning of 20th July 1866 when the Austrian flagship, *Erzherzog Ferdinand*

Max, is ramming the Italian ironclad *Re d'Italia*' (Novotny). In the centre of the bridge stands the Austrian admiral, and he is flanked by three officers.

ROSSETTI, DANTE GABRIEL

b. 1828 in London, d. 1882 in Birchington-on-Sea. Son of an Italian emigrant. Poet and painter. 1848, founded the Brotherhood of the Pre-Raphaelites. 1860, marriage with Elizabeth Siddal to whom he owed his ideal of feminine beauty (Beata Beatrix, 1863).

96 *Ecce Ancilla Domini (Annunciation)*,
The Tate Gallery London.

131 *Astarte Syriaca*, 1877. City Art Gallery, Manchester.
The best commentary on this picture is Rossetti's poem of the same title:

'Mystery: lo! betwixt the sun and moon,
Astarte of the Syrians: Venus Queen
Ere Aphrodite was. In silver sheen
Her twofold girdle glasps the infinite boon
Of bliss whereof the heaven and earth commune:
And from her neck's inclining flower-stem lean
Love-freighted lips and absolute eyes that wean
The pulse of hearts to the spheres' dominant tune.

Torch-bearing, her sweet ministers compel
All thrones of light beyond the sky and sea
The witnesses of Beauty's face to be:
That face, of Love's all-penetrative spell
Amulet, talisman, and oracle –
Between the sun and moon a mystery.

RUDE, FRANÇOIS

b. 1784 in Dijon, d. 1855 in Paris. Pupil of Devosge in Lyons, and of Cartellier in Paris. 1812, Rome Prize; did not go to Italy, however, but after the second restoration of the Bourbons went to Brussels. His chief work, the *Marseillaise*, on the Paris Arc de l'Étoile, was completed between 1832 and 1836.

12 *Napoleon waking to immortality*, 1845–1847.
Fixin, Côte d'Or.
Rude produced the monument for Noisot, a former officer of the Grand Army. It was set up on the latter's country estate at Fixin and surrounded by miniature fortifications.

RUNGE, PHILIPP OTTO

b. 1777 in Wolgast, d. 1810 in Hamburg. 1799–1801, at the Copenhagen Academy (J. Juel). Then till 1803 in Dresden where he met Tieck. 1803, settled in Hamburg. His work on the theory of colour brought him into contact with Goethe.

175 *The artist with his wife and brother*, 1804.
Formerly Kunsthalle, Hamburg. Burnt.
On the right, Runge with his wife; on the left, his brother Daniel (who, incidentally, financed him).

209 *The Morning* (first version), 1808. Kunsthalle, Hamburg.

RUSSELL, JOHN

b. 1745 in Guildford, d. 1806 in Yorkshire. Was chiefly prominent as a portrait-painter. His astronomical interests led him to invent a device for illustrating lunar phenomena.

10 *The Face of the Moon*, c. 1790.
City Museum and Art Gallery, Birmingham.
A study for, or possibly a reduced version of, a picture in Oxford. The theme was not new (as far back as 1634–1635 there are three engravings by Claude Mellan showing views of the moon). This study, however, is new in its general

mode of presentation. Its evocation of space, a correlative to the loneliness of the Romantics, reminds one of the cold solemnity of Boullée's *Newton cenotaph* (plates 8–9). It has that 'inherent power' (Urgewalt) of space that Stifter speaks of in the *Condor*.

SCHICK, GOTTLIEB

b. 1776 in Stuttgart, d. there 1812. Pupil of Hetsch. 1798 to 1802, studied under David in Paris. 1802–1811, in Rome; a friend of W. von Humboldt. 1811, returned to Stuttgart.

24 *Frau von Cotta*, 1802.
Württembergische Staatsgalerie, Stuttgart.
The first wife of the celebrated Stuttgart publisher.

SCHINKEL, KARL FRIEDRICH

b. 1781 in Neuruppin, d. 1841 in Berlin. From 1797 onwards, a pupil of Gilly at the Architectural Academy. 1803–1805, in Italy and France. 1839, Oberlandbaudirektor (a public office connected with building). Started out as a scene-painter and painter of dioramas. From 1816 onwards, actively employed as an architect, chiefly in Berlin (Neue Wache, Schauspielhaus, Altes Museum).

32 *Medieval town on a river*, 1815
Formerly Staatliche Museen Berlin, Nationalgalerie.
Like Schinkel's *View of Greece in its heyday* (Berlin Schinkel-Museum), a landscape showing a culture, or rather a synthesis of landscape and culture. In contrast to the 'manly' character of antique architecture, Schinkel felt the Gothic to be 'stimulating in an indefinable way, and for that reason female' (unbestimmt anregend, daher weiblich).

SCHNORR VON CAROLSFELD, JULIUS

b. 1794 in Leipzig, d. 1872 in Dresden. 1811, at the Vienna Academy (influenced by Olivier, and J.A.Koch). 1818–1827, in Rome; member of the circle of the Nazarenes. 1825, called to Munich (murals from the *Nibelungenlied* in the Residenz which were completed in 1867). 1827–1846, professor at Munich; then at Dresden, where he also directed the Gemäldegalerie.

95 *The Annunciation*, 1820. Formerly Staatliche Museen, Berlin, Nationalgalerie.

SEGANTINI, GIOVANNI

b. 1858 in Arco, d. 1899 in Pontresina. Studied in the Milan Brera. With regard to subject-matter, influenced by Millet. Formerly influenced by the 'divisionists'. 1888–1894, in Savognin (Graubünden); from 1894 onwards, in Maloja.

92 *Ave Maria* (second Version), 1886. Privately owned, Switzerland.
It was Segantini's conviction that 'art should be cult'. It should 'fill that empty space that has been left in us by religion'. Another illuminating remark of his is: 'Woman should be our goddess, and art our godhead.'

SEURAT, GEORGES-PIERRE

b. 1858 in Paris, d. there 1891. Studied with Lehmann, a pupil of Ingres, at the École des Beaux-Arts. Raphael, Holbein and Ingres became the guiding-stars in his art. 1884, with Redon and Signac, founded the Société des Indépendants. Initiator of the Neo-Impressionist movement.

43 *Port en Bessin*, 1888. The Minneapolis Institute of Arts.

190 *Un dimanche d'été à la Grande Jatte*, 1884–1886.
The Art Institute of Chicago, the Helen Birch Bartlett Memorial Collection.

Seurat visited the Seine islands for several months and made a number of studies there for his picture. This was painted in his studio. From the point of view of subject-matter, one might compare it with Courbet's *L'atelier* (plate 1–3). It contains all the ages of man and a cross-section of society. The composition is dominated by the 'fashionable pair of lovers'. The ape is a very ancient symbol denoting vanity and luxury.

198 *La Parade*, 1889. The Museum of Modern Art, New York; Stephen C. Clark Collection.

STIFTER, ADALBERT

b. 1805 in Oberplan, d. 1868 in Linz. 1824, studied at Vienna University; private tutor. 1840, publication of the *Condor* (Kondor). 1849–1865, Inspector of Elementary Schools in Linz, and Custodian of Monuments there. Stifter described himself in the forties as a 'landscape-painter'. He was self-taught, and was obviously influenced by Gauermann and Danhauser. In the fifties he had the idea of a cycle of symbolic landscapes.

35 *View of the Beatrixgasse at Vienna*, 1839.
Adalbert-Stifter-Gesellschaft, Vienna.

In his Wild Flowers (Feldblumen) Stifter described the view from his window: 'My room is so much higher than other buildings that I can indeed see a satisfying bit of heaven, but I can also see chimneys, several roofs, and a pair of suburban towers.'

TOULOUSE-LAUTREC, HENRI DE

b. 1864 in Albi, d. 1901 in Château de Malromé. Descended from one of the oldest noble French families. 1878–1879, two accidents; both his legs were crippled as a result. 1881–1884, in Paris; studied under Princeteau, Bonnat and Cormon. Met Degas and Van Gogh. 1889–1892, took part in the exhibitions of the Indépendants. 1893–1897, journeys to Spain, Portugal, Holland and England (where he met Wilde and Beardsley). 1899, physical breakdown, entered a sanatorium.

IX *May Belfort*, 1895. Frank K. Griesinger Collection, Gates Mills, Ohio.
May Belfort was a favourite cabaret singer of the artist's.

128 *Au salon de la rue des Moulins*, 1894. Musée Toulouse-Lautrec, Albi.
The same theme, namely that of the woman waiting for the man, is used by the Symbolist painters; cf. Moreau (*Les filles de Thestios*) and Hodler (*Young man admired by woman*).

129 *Maxime Dethomas (au bal de l'Opéra)*, 1896. National Gallery of Art, Washington D.C. Chester Dale Collection.
Dethomas was an etcher, and a friend of both Toulouse-Lautrec and Degas.

144 *Au Cirque Fernando*, c. 1888. The Art Institute of Chicago; Joseph Winterbotham Collection.

163 *Jane Avril sortant du Moulin Rouge*, 1892.
Wadsworth Atheneum Collection, Hartford.

195 '*Messaline*' *à l'Opéra de Bordeaux*, 1900. Sammlung Bührle, Zürich.
Toulouse-Lautrec painted six pictures of scenes from the opera, *Messaline*, by A. Silvestre and I. de Lara, which was produced in Bordeaux during the season 1900–1901. The degree to which he departed from the facts of this unimportant theatrical occasion, is shown by comparing this picture with Makart's *Charlotte Wolter as '*Messalina*'* (1876), a very definite representation of an actress in a stage part.

197 *Au Moulin Rouge*, c. 1892. The Art Institute of Chicago; the Helen Birch Bartlett Memorial Collection.

TURNER, JOSEPH MALLORD WILLIAM

b. 1775 in London, d. there 1851. Pupil of Thomas Malton and Girtin. 1796, exhibited his first oil-paintings. (From 1804 onwards he used a gallery in his house for exhibition purposes.) 1802, member of the Royal Academy. 1802, travelled on the continent to France and Switzerland; and in 1819 to Italy.

III *Rain, steam, and speed (The Great Western Railway)*.
National Gallery, London.
The nineteenth century ceased to represent the basic constituents of the world of natural phenomena in allegorical guise (in the way that Carstens did – who shows us time and space in the persons of Uranos and Kronos) and sought to depict them by means of the landscape. This ambition emerges plainly from the titles of their pictures. Turner is concerned with speed; Stifter paints a picture entitled *Movement* (1854), Chintreuil a huge landscape which he calls *Space* (Salon 1869).

22 *Snowstorm*, 1842. National Gallery, London.

29 *The opening of Valhalla*, 1843. The Tate Gallery, London.
Turner was not present at the event but created it out of his imagination.

VERNET, HORACE

b. 1789 in Paris, d. there 1863. Son and pupil of Carle Vernet. Father-in-law of Paul Delaroche. Was among the defenders of the barricade of Clichy in 1814; he perpetuated the event in his celebrated historical picture in 1820. 1826, Membre de l'Institut. 1829–1855, director of the French Academy in Rome. Numerous journeys.

135 *Mazeppa*, 1826. Kunsthalle, Bremen.
Studies for this picture are to be found in the Musée Calvet, Avignon. The inspiration for it came from Byron's *Mazeppa* (1819). The story was very popular among the French and English Romantics (Géricault, Delacroix, Boulanger, Chassériau, Th. Barker). In 1828 Victor Hugo made use of the figure of Mazeppa in *Les Orientales*. Later, he became the subject of a popular mimodrame in Paris. And a wellknown circus-rider, Miss Clara Mencken, appeared as Mazeppa in London; this forms a rather remarkable link with Toulouse-Lautrec's *Au Cirque Fernando*.

VUILLARD, EDOUARD

b. 1868 in Cuiseaux, d. 1940 in La Baule. 1886, studied at the Academy under Gérome. 1888, Académie Julian. 1889, co-founder of the 'Nabis'. 1890, shared a studio with Bonnard and Denis.

200 *Intérieur*, 1899. Sammlung Zumsteg, Zürich.

Index of Names

AHASUERUS (The Wandering Jew)
237, 238, 282, 283, 330, 351, 410
Alexis 232
Amiel 72
Anthony, St. 261
Astruc 227
Aurier 300

BACHELARD 34
Bachofen 36, 40, 319 et seq.
Badt 302
Ballanches 401
Barrault, Alexis 182
Barry, James 64, 149
Baudelaire 18, 22, 23, 94, 112, 181,
232, 254, 264, 329, 330, 350, 351
Berlioz 180
Bernard, Emile 401
Blake 35, 64, 76, 94, 251, 263, 264,
319, 331, 334, 335, 348, 361, 401,
404
Blechen 182, 295, 296
Böcklin 40, 129, 231, 238, 295, 332,
361
Böhme, Jakob 336
Bonaparte, Pauline 71, 348
Bonington 73
Bonnard 299
Bouilhet 225
Boulanger 240
Boullée 182
Brentano 238
Brown, F. M. 231
Bruckner, Anton 152
Brueghel 286
Bruyas 226
Büchner 363, 370
Burckhardt, Jacob 33, 40, 92, 135,
150, 252, 363, 402, 412
Burne-Jones 361
Byron 238, 240, 249, 250, 285

CANON, HANS 161
Canova 64, 71, 149
Carlyle 20, 91, 136, 194, 196, 231, 237
Carmen Sylva 238
Carpeaux 264
Carstens 78, 348
Carus 72, 273, 300
Castagnary 162, 363, 372
Celtes, Conrad 249
Cervantes 240
Cézanne 33, 152, 230, 231, 232, 249,
261, 282, 299, 300, 301, 302, 303,
304, 371, 372, 382, 383, 384, 387,
388

Champaigne 232
Champfleury 11, 12, 227, 350
Chardin 56
Chateaubriand 237, 238, 352
Chenavard 132, 133, 134, 135, 136,
152, 161, 162, 168, 199, 230, 250,
384
Cimabue 130
Cleopatra 38, 320, 351
Comte, Auguste 329, 367
Constable 72, 73, 293, 294
Constant 237
Copley 52, 64
Cormon 282
Cornelius 130, 150, 249, 252, 297,
319, 371
Corot 131, 296, 297, 303, 382
Courbet 11 et seq., 36, 40, 71, 129,
132, 134, 162, 163, 194, 195, 226,
232, 239, 282, 298, 303, 332, 334,
346, 350, 363, 384, 386, 406
Couture 250, 370, 371
Crane, Walter 195

DANTE 227, 231, 237, 249, 250, 252,
255, 263, 283, 331, 338
Daumier 21, 33, 40, 129, 130, 151,
163, 195, 199, 227, 228, 232, 240,
249, 252, 254, 281, 282, 283, 284,
287, 329, 332
David 50, 51, 52, 53, 54, 63, 71, 73,
76, 77, 112
Debussy 152
Degas 21, 199, 274, 276, 304, 332, 361
Delacroix 11, 33, 94, 95, 96, 109, 110,
130, 151, 152, 163, 166, 198, 200,
209, 212, 227, 230, 232, 237, 240,
249, 262, 263, 264, 275, 284, 285,
286, 294, 298, 329, 372, 381, 388,
404
Delaroche 230, 250
Delilah 320
Denis, Maurice 232
Diderot 95, 96, 129
Dido 134, 320
Don Juan 330, 351, 352, 410
Don Quixote 237, 240, 254, 256, 282,
351, 410
Doré 240, 249, 287
Dostoievski 255, 262, 284
Dürer 195, 230, 249
Dumesnil 19
Duval, Jeanne 22

ENFANTIN 183, 184, 193
Ensor 151, 281, 284, 295, 303

FANTIN-LATOUR 232
Fernow 78, 89, 237, 330, 404
Feuerbach 370, 371
Fichte 364, 368
Fiedler 23, 24, 302
Flaubert 24, 38, 152, 225, 237, 261,
273, 285, 295, 334, 348
Fourier 180, 181, 368
Fragonard 76
Freytag, Gustav 136
Friedrich, C. D. 33, 72, 73, 74, 75, 76,
77, 94, 112, 152, 237, 238, 239,
285, 294, 295, 302, 303, 319, 320,
403, 404, 412
Fuseli 61, 76, 94, 261, 264, 275, 348,
351, 371

GALERON 184
Galiani, Abbé 237
Gasquet 300, 383
Gaudí 184
Gauguin 92, 94, 152, 164, 239, 261,
281, 293, 298, 304, 334, 371, 372,
381, 382, 384, 387, 388, 401, 402
Gautier, Théophile 161, 227, 238,
250, 370
Géricault 33, 231, 240, 273, 274,
275, 281, 282, 283, 284, 285, 294,
298, 303
Gérome 132, 250
Gilly 149
Giotto 112, 130, 249
Görres 136, 251, 282, 320
Goethe 22, 40, 61, 74, 95, 115, 136,
228, 238, 261, 275, 347, 371, 412
Van Gogh 111, 152, 194, 195, 239,
287, 295, 304
Gogol 196
Goya 23, 33, 61, 71, 74, 76, 77, 112,
116, 151, 209, 210, 211, 212, 231,
256, 261, 263, 273, 281, 285, 286,
287, 303, 348, 350, 406
Gros 200, 209, 212
Guéroult 168
Gutzkow 209, 388

HAENDCKE 361
Hamlet 240, 262
Hegel 36, 90, 109, 165, 193, 200,
281, 297, 403, 411, 412
Heine 96, 110, 200, 352, 372, 381
Heinse 115, 276, 351, 371
Hemsterhuis François 364, 365
Herder 40, 64, 91, 115, 371
Hetzer, Theodor 55, 61
Hodler 348

435

Hölderlin 136, 251, 370
Hogarth 61
Hugo, Victor 167, 183, 238, 295
Hunt, Holman 361
Huysmans 24, 411

INGRES 17, 19, 62, 63, 71, 92, 93, 94,
    95, 109, 129, 152, 232, 238, 250,
    252, 256, 332, 346, 347, 348, 365,
    371, 372, 381, 384, 406

DR. JOHNSON 56
Joseph II of Austria 178
Journet, Jean 239
Julian, St. 255

KAULBACH 150
Keyzer, Nicaise de 130
Kierkegaard 237, 264, 273, 297, 319,
    351, 370, 410, 411
Kleist, Heinrich von 73
Klinger 251, 252, 351, 361

LAHARPES 225
Laurens, J.-P. 210
Lautréamont 237
Lavater 72, 94
Ledoux 178, 179, 180
Leibl 129, 332, 362
Le Nain 163
Löwith 63, 367
Ludwig II of Bavaria 182, 371

MACAIRE, ROBERT 281, 282, 283,
    284, 285
Makart 71, 130, 182, 195, 198, 230,
    370, 371
Manet 39, 164, 199, 210, 211, 227,
    228, 230, 262, 274, 293, 298, 334,
    350, 351, 381
Marées 23, 164, 231, 302, 371, 372,
    382, 386, 387
Martin, John 239, 295
Marx 33, 166, 195, 406, 411, 412
Maurice 231
Maximilian, Emperor of Mexico 210
Mayhew, Henry 136, 283
Mazeppa 237, 240, 261, 275, 410
Meinecke 63, 91
Meissonier 40, 129, 228
Menzel 52, 166, 195, 199, 211, 212,
    294, 296, 303, 304, 332, 361
Messalina 38, 348, 351
Michelangelo 227, 228, 237
Michelet 132, 134
Millet 151, 194, 195, 282, 298, 332,
    346, 372
Monet 152, 196, 297, 298, 299, 300,
    317, 332, 346, 381
Monfreid, Daniel de 387, 388
Montesquieu 91
Moore, George 274
Moreau 251, 334, 401
Morice 387, 388
Moritz, K. Ph. 22
Morris 180, 367, 368, 371, 382
Müller, Adam 320
Munch 251, 273, 281, 287, 295, 334,
    351, 361, 362, 401

NAPOLEON I 64, 71, 161, 200, 209,
    237, 250, 251, 255, 275
Napoleon, Prince 167, 182, 371
Nero, The Emperor 251, 262, 351, 370
Nietzsche 20, 24, 38, 39, 54, 90, 165,
    237, 238, 239, 252, 255, 261, 262,
    331, 352, 371, 387, 401, 403, 406
Novalis 23, 49, 152, 180, 232, 238,
    264, 288, 293, 300, 319, 336, 346,
    365, 366, 367, 412
Novotny 299

OEDIPUS 250, 348, 351
Olivier, Heinrich 230
Omphale 320, 329
Overbeck 130, 150, 230

PAGANINI 238
Papety, Dominique 387
Passavant 181
Paul, Jean 77
Paul I of Russia 178
Peladan 11, 17, 334
Pforr, Franz 230, 239
Phidias 92, 129, 230
Piloty 200, 209
Pissarro 298
Poe, E. A. 261, 295, 350,
Prometheus 237, 250, 251, 252, 253,
    254, 282, 286, 352, 410
Proudhon 11, 227
Pugin, A. W. 177
Puvis de Chavannes 195, 372, 382

QUINET 254, 283

RAPHAEL 39, 62, 92, 94, 112, 129,
    152, 230, 371
Ranke, Leopold von 91
Redon 346, 347
Rembrandt 17, 19, 115, 152
Renoir 129, 227, 231, 297, 298, 317,
    332, 334, 346, 371, 381, 384, 402
Rethel 283, 284
Richter 296
Riegl 115
Rilke 152, 249, 304
Rimbaud 237, 239, 255
Rivière 372
Robert, Hubert 295
Rodin 195, 238, 250, 251, 264, 286,
    331, 334, 351
Romako 211
Rops, Félicien 351, 371
Rosenkranz, Karl 200, 281, 282
Rossetti 249, 361
Rousseau 238, 320, 371, 372
Rubens 51
Rude 250, 284
Runge 72, 111, 114, 232, 293, 319,
    320, 334, 335, 336, 345, 347, 404
Ruskin 180, 367, 368, 405
Ruysdael 72

SADE, MARQUIS DE 264, 329
Saint-Beuve 225
Saint-Pierre 179, 180
Saint-Saëns 184

Saint-Simon 161, 368
Sardanapalus 227, 262, 264, 298, 410
Schadow 61, 115
Schelling 111, 112, 114, 237, 335,
    404
Schiefler 361
Schiller 22, 55, 411
Schinkel 150, 180, 181, 182, 365, 408
Schlegel, Friedrich 130, 232, 294,
    320, 330, 334, 368
Schlehmil 238
Schleiermacher 232, 320
Schopenhauer 40, 134, 151, 162, 225
Schwind, Moritz von 296
Segantini 152, 348
Semiramis 320
Semper, Gottfried 181, 381, 408
Seurat 164, 402
Silvestre, Théophile 161
Sisley 298
Soane 52, 295, 408
Spartacus 254
Spitzweg 296
Stendhal 64, 71, 200, 250, 283, 352,
    381
Stevens, Alfred 228
Stifter, Adalbert 210, 288, 294, 295,
    296, 317
Strindberg 273, 276, 387
Swinburne 336, 371

TAINE, HIPPOLYTE 225
Thoré-Bürger 132, 134
Thornhill 52
Tieck 232, 334
Tiepolo 56
Toulouse-Lautrec 21, 163, 199, 275,
    276, 283, 287, 334, 350, 351
Trübner 21
Turgenev 240
Turner 96, 131, 295

UHDE, FRITZ VON 252
Ugolino 263, 264, 282, 261

VENTURI 62
Vernet, Horace 238, 240
Vergil 227, 231, 331, 388
Vischer, Friedrich Theodor von 151,
    199, 405, 410
Voltaire 62, 63
Vuillard 299

WACKENRODER 152, 230
Wagner, Richard 92, 149, 168, 209,
    231, 238, 239, 283, 329, 330, 332,
    352
Wandering Jew, The see Ahasuerus
Wasmann 296
West 52, 64
Whistler 95
Winckelmann 91, 237
Wölfflin 386

ZOLA 24, 230, 231, 232, 293, 317, 329,
    348